THE EVERYDAY

366 Real Stories for Real people

Rebekah Trittipoe

Table of Contents

ACKNOWLEDGMENTS xxv

PREFACE xxvii
    December 31, 2019 xxvii

JANUARY 1 1
    Trails and traditions 1

JANUARY 2 2
    What now? 2

JANUARY 3 3
    Perfect parenting. not. 3

JANUARY 4 4
    Love, marriage, and babies 4

JANUARY 5 5
    The twilight zone 5

JANUARY 6 6
    Big, bad, belly flops 6

JANUARY 7 7
    Lost opportunity 7

JANUARY 8 8
    Integrity 8

JANUARY 9 9
    Waves of emotion 9

JANUARY 10 10
    When things do not go as planned....................................10

JANUARY 11 11
    Stinkbug conundrum 11

JANUARY 12 12
    Never say die 12

JANUARY 13 13
    It's complicated 13

JANUARY 14 14
    Scars 14

JANUARY 15 15
    Beauty for ashes 15

JANUARY 16 ....**16**
The commitment quandary 16

JANUARY 17 ....**17**
Warning signs 17

JANUARY 18 ....**18**
Under pressure 18

JANUARY 19 ....**19**
Lost lamby 19

JANUARY 20 ....**20**
It's hard, and that's okay 20

JANUARY 21 ....**21**
Quietness and confidence 21

JANUARY 22 ....**22**
Can the foundation be trusted? 22

JANUARY 23 ....**23**
Go ahead. laugh 23

JANUARY 24 ....**24**
Morning glory 24

JANUARY 25 ....**25**
Near misses 25

JANUARY 26 ....**26**
Tough trails to the top 26

JANUARY 27 ....**27**
Listen 27

JANUARY 28 ....**28**
Naked and afraid 28

JANUARY 29 ....**29**
Comparison 29

JANUARY 30 ....**30**
The masterpiece 30

JANUARY 31 ....**31**
Perfect the way you are 31

FEBRUARY 1 ....**32**
Rag-tag battles 32

FEBRUARY 2 ....**33**
Always the same 33

FEBRUARY 3 ....**34**
    Who is my coach? 34

FEBRUARY 4 ....**35**
    Be quick but don't hurry 35

FEBRUARY 5 ....**36**
    Prove your identity 36

FEBRUARY 6 ....**37**
    Bruised 37

JANUARY 7 ....**38**
    Best laid plans 38

FEBRUARY 8 ....**39**
    All i need is christ 39

FEBRUARY 9 ....**40**
    Takes one to know one 40

FEBRUARY 10 ....**41**
    Sucker! 41

FEBRUARY 11 ....**42**
    Me with you 42

FEBRUARY 12 ....**43**
    Broken legs and oily heads 43

FEBRUARY 13 ....**44**
    Not thinking straight 44

FEBRUARY 14 ....**45**
    Chocolate pie 45

FEBRUARY 15 ....**46**
    Headed south 46

FEBRUARY 16 ....**47**
    Old becomes new 47

FEBRUARY 17 ....**48**
    House and home 48

FEBRUARY 18 ....**49**
    Ugly bruises 49

FEBRUARY 19 ....**50**
    Birds of a feather 50

FEBRUARY 20 ....**51**
    Stop time, stop! 51

FEBRUARY 21 ....**52**
Take a bite out of bickering..52

FEBRUARY 22 ....**53**
Teach 'em young...53

FEBRUARY 23 ....**54**
No fear...54

FEBRUARY 24 ....**55**
When it hurts so bad 55

FEBRUARY 25 ....**56**
The purpose of pain 56

FEBRUARY 26 ....**57**
There. i said it...57

FEBRUARY 27 ....**58**
Who do you represent?...58

FEBRUARY 28 ....**59**
Birthdays...59

FEBRUARY 29 ....**60**
No hindrance because of difference 60

MARCH 1 ....**61**
To hide or not to hide 61

MARCH 2 ....**62**
Crowded ears..62

MARCH 3 ....**63**
When frustration calls 63

MARCH 4 ....**64**
My week-day sabbath 64

MARCH 5 ....**65**
Burn the ships 65

MARCH 6 ....**66**
Reassess 66

MARCH 7 ....**67**
Old becomes new 67

MARCH 8 ....**68**
Wherever 68

MARCH 9 ....**69**
Aromas 69

MARCH 10 ....**70**
    Go ahead. write a letter 70

MARCH 11 ....**71**
    The prodigal returns 71

MARCH 12 ....**72**
    Pandemic panic 72

MARCH 13 ....**73**
    Love, laughter, and life 73

MARCH 14 ....**74**
    Spring fling 74

MARCH 15 ....**75**
    Grace that is greater 75

MARCH 16 ....**76**
    The year of the virus 76

MARCH 17 ....**77**
    A wild hair project 77

MARCH 18 ....**78**
    It covers everything 78

MARCH 19 ....**79**
    Clean up your mess 79

MARCH 20 ....**80**
    I warned you! 80

MARCH 21 ....**81**
    Where do I run? 81

MARCH 22 ....**82**
    A strange kind of Sunday 82

MARCH 23 ....**83**
    Is there something wrong with me? 83

MARCH 24 ....**84**
    The territory 84

MARCH 25 ....**85**
    Lonely but never alone 85

MARCH 26 ....**86**
    Connections 86

MARCH 27 ....**87**
    Reshaped 87

MARCH 28..**88**
   Rocks are heavy and hard 88

MARCH 29..**89**
   Memorize at my age? 89

MARCH 30..**90**
   Quiet and peaceful 90

MARCH 31..**91**
   Rainy days and drips 91

APRIL 1..**92**
   Gullible granny 92

APRIL 2..**93**
   Makes no sense 93

APRIL 3..**94**
   Weeds...94

APRIL 4..**95**
   Weeds revisited 95

APRIL 5..**96**
   Guilt by association 96

APRIL 6..**97**
   In search of turkey sign 97

APRIL 7..**98**
   Privilege and responsibility 98

APRIL 8..**99**
   Step by step...99

APRIL 9..**100**
   Excuses 100

APRIL 10..**101**
   Powerless no more 101

APRIL 11..**102**
   Preparation 102

APRIL 12..**103**
   To seek or not to seek 103

APRIL 13..**104**
   Not a great start...104

APRIL 14..**105**
   Close call..105

APRIL 15..**106**
   The playbook 106

APRIL 16..**107**
   Family! 107

APRIL 17..**108**
   When is it time to stop pushing?..108

APRIL 18..**109**
   Messy Bessy 109

APRIL 19..**110**
   Cursed drywall 110

APRIL 20..**111**
   Confess 111

APRIL 21..**112**
   Goal or mission? 112

APRIL 22..**113**
   Self-control 113

APRIL 23..**114**
   Sit and think 114

APRIL 24..**115**
   A lesson quickly learned 115

APRIL 25..**116**
   Baby fruit trees..116

APRIL 26..**117**
   The next right thing 117

APRIL 27..**118**
   God cares about the little things 118

APRIL 28..**119**
   One by one 119

APRIL 29..**120**
   It's that time 120

APRIL 30..**121**
   Filling in the cracks 121

MAY 1...**122**
   Missional athletics..122

MAY 2...**123**
   Little is much 123

MAY 3..**124**
    VIRTUAL CHURCH...124

MAY 4..**125**
    THE WRONG CLEANING STRATEGY..125

MAY 5..**126**
    WHERE'S THE WATER?...126

MAY 6..**127**
    LIMITLESS GRACE..127

MAY 7..**128**
    A WALK DOWN MEMORY LANE..128

MAY 8..**129**
    IF. THEN. SINCE. THEREFORE...129

MAY 9..**130**
    TREE DOWN!...130

MAY 10..**131**
    A DAY FOR MOMS...131

MAY 11..**132**
    RUNNING DOWN (AND UP) MEMORY LANE..............................132

MAY 12..**133**
    OPEN WITH THE RIGHT APP...133

MAY 13..**134**
    BE VERY CAREFUL..134

MAY 14..**135**
    RAINBOW!..135

MAY 15..**136**
    GROUND MOVING...136

MAY 16..**137**
    ANCHORS..137

MAY 17..**138**
    GAG!..138

MAY 18..**139**
    SWEET FELLOWSHIP..139

MAY 19..**140**
    SLEEP, GLORIOUS SLEEP...140

MAY 20..**141**
    RAIN, RAIN GO AWAY..141

MAY 21 ....**142**
    On a mission 142

MAY 22 ....**143**
    Decisions, decisions 143

MAY 23 ....**144**
    Big, fat branches 144

MAY 24 ....**145**
    Sweet fellowship 145

MAY 25 ....**146**
    Snake! 146

MAY 26 ....**147**
    FPR 147

MAY 27 ....**148**
    Sing a song 148

MAY 28 ....**149**
    Unbelievable—but chosen still the same 149

MAY 29 ....**150**
    All things work together 150

MAY 30 ....**151**
    Why is it so had to stop? 151

MAY 31 ....**152**
    Forsaken and forgotten? 152

JUNE 1 ....**153**
    Protests 153

JUNE 2 ....**154**
    Stream of consciousness 154

JUNE 3 ....**155**
    Crooked 155

JUNE 4 ....**156**
    Watch your heart. don't follow it. 156

JUNE 5 ....**157**
    In but not of 157

JUNE 6 ....**158**
    Lazy slug 158

JUNE 7 ....**159**
    Only one thing remains 159

JUNE 8..**160**
    FACE TO FACE 160

JUNE 9..**161**
    FIRM FOUNDATIONS 161

JUNE 10..**162**
    TO FORGIVE OR NOT TO FORGIVE.....................162

JUNE 11..**163**
    WE ARE WHAT WE EAT...163

JUNE 12..**164**
    RETIREMENT DAY 164

JUNE 13..**165**
    DON'T LOSE IT...165

JUNE 14..**166**
    STAINS 166

JUNE 15..**167**
    LOST THINGS 167

JUNE 16..**168**
    THE RHYTHM OF THE HEART..............................168

JUNE 17..**169**
    LIVE INTENTIONALLY..169

JUNE 18..**170**
    AWARENESS 170

JUNE 19..**171**
    CRASH AND BURN 171

JUNE 20..**172**
    THUNDER AND LIGHTENING...............................172

JUNE 21..**173**
    GRANDCHILDREN 173

JUNE 22..**174**
    FAIR WARNING...174

JUNE 23..**175**
    A STINKY SITUATION..175

JUNE 24..**176**
    MAMA BIRD 176

JUNE 25..**177**
    TO PLAN OR NOT TO PLAN 177

JUNE 26..**178**
    Everlasting love..178

JUNE 27..**179**
    Forgetting...179

JUNE 28..**180**
    Peace and quiet..180

JUNE 29..**181**
    Baby birds...181

JUNE 30..**182**
    Mentoring..182

JULY 1...**183**
    Work with integrity...183

JULY 2...**184**
    Anniversary day..184

JULY 3...**185**
    Hot. hot. hot...185

JULY 4...**186**
    Freedom and friends...186

JULY 5...**187**
    Isn't that backwards?..187

JULY 6...**188**
    Unsolicited advice..188

JULY 7...**189**
    Family feuds..189

JULY 8...**190**
    Take the time to write.......................................190

JULY 9...**191**
    Is there a problem?..191

JULY 10...**192**
    Already?...192

JULY 11...**193**
    Clean up is contagious......................................193

JULY 12...**194**
    Around robin hood's barn.................................194

JULY 13...**195**
    Going with the flow...195

JULY 14 .... **196**
    KNOWING WHEN TO SHUT UP 196

JULY 15 .... **197**
    RUNNING INTO THE DARK 197

JULY 16 .... **198**
    ROLE MODEL 198

JULY 17 .... **199**
    THE LONE BLACKBERRY 199

JULY 18 .... **200**
    WARNING SIGNS 200

JULY 19 .... **201**
    CHOICES 201

JULY 20 .... **202**
    EMOTIONS 202

JULY 21 .... **203**
    MAKE LIKE A TREE 203

JULY 22 .... **204**
    SPLIT DECISIONS 204

JULY 23 .... **205**
    NEW SHOES 205

JULY 24 .... **206**
    FACE TO FACE 206

JULY 25 .... **207**
    UP FROM SLAVERY 207

JULY 26 .... **208**
    FRIENDS AND FELLOWSHIP 208

JULY 27 .... **209**
    EMBRACE THE MUD 209

JULY 28 .... **210**
    OVERCOME 210

JULY 29 .... **211**
    FINDING THE DOOR 211

JULY 30 .... **212**
    GOT GRIT? 212

AUGUST 1 .... **213**
    GRAND FUNK 213

AUGUST 2 ....**214**
    Changing weather 214

AUGUST 3 ....**215**
    The wee hours 215

AUGUST 4 ....**216**
    Clarity 216

AUGUST 5 ....**217**
    My pet rock 217

AUGUST 6 ....**218**
    The text 218

AUGUST 7 ....**219**
    Turn your eyes 219

AUGUST 8 ....**220**
    The stuff 220

AUGUST 9 ....**221**
    It didn't just happen 221

AUGUST 10 ....**222**
    Remember? 222

AUGUST 11 ....**223**
    The internment 223

AUGUST 12 ....**224**
    The common denominator 224

AUGUST 13 ....**225**
    You call this an anniversary? 225

AUGUST 14 ....**226**
    Suffering together 226

AUGUST 15 ....**227**
    Trash to treasure 227

AUGUST 16 ....**228**
    Loud and ugly sobs 228

AUGUST 17 ....**229**
    Smart watch sync 229

AUGUST 18 ....**230**
    A new role 230

AUGUST 19 ....**231**
    Get fit 231

AUGUST 20..**232**
    It takes time..232

AUGUST 21..**233**
    To monitor or not to monitor..................................233

AUGUST 22..**234**
    Before, behind, beside..234

AUGUST 23..**235**
    Why my foot slips..235

AUGUST 24..**236**
    Excuses...236

AUGUST 25..**237**
    Navigating the unknown..237

AUGUST 26..**238**
    Wise words...238

AUGUST 27..**239**
    Patience, please..239

AUGUST 28..**240**
    It's Friday..240

AUGUST 29..**241**
    Dwell or visit?..241

AUGUST 30..**242**
    Rattles in the woods...242

AUGUST 31..**243**
    Tell-tale numbers..243

SEPTEMBER 1...**244**
    Train 'em up...244

SEPTEMBER 2...**245**
    Decisions, decisions..245

SEPTEMBER 3...**246**
    Everyday...246

SEPTEMBER 4...**247**
    If you can hear me...247

SEPTEMBER 5...**248**
    To new heights..248

SEPTEMBER 6...**249**
    An honest count...249

SEPTEMBER 7..**250**
    Google it 250

SEPTEMBER 8..**251**
    Level ground 251

SEPTEMBER 9..**252**
    It's official 252

SEPTEMBER 10..**253**
    Don't waste your life 253

SEPTEMBER 11..**254**
    Failure 254

SEPTEMBER 12..**255**
    The molder 255

SEPTEMBER 13..**256**
    Integrity 256

SEPTEMBER 14..**257**
    Connections 257

SEPTEMBER 15..**258**
    Stop encouraging me? 258

SEPTEMBER 16..**259**
    Square peg. round hole 259

SEPTEMBER 17..**260**
    The bracelet 260

SEPTEMBER 18..**261**
    A changed heart 261

SEPTEMBER 19..**262**
    Clean the inside and out 262

SEPTEMBER 20..**263**
    As if? 263

SEPTEMBER 21..**264**
    Laugh out loud 264

SEPTEMBER 22..**265**
    Grand fails..265

SEPTEMBER 23..**266**
    Personal advertising 266

SEPTEMBER 24..**267**
    The ring..267

SEPTEMBER 25 ....**268**
   WHAT A PAIN 268

SEPTEMBER 26 ....**269**
   TREASURES IN THE JUNK 269

SEPTEMBER 27 ....**270**
   THE GRAND GIVE-AWAY 270

SEPTEMBER 28 ....**271**
   WHAT TO SAY 271

SEPTEMBER 29 ....**272**
   FADED PHOTOGRAPHS 272

SEPTEMBER 30 ....**273**
   RIGHTS AND RESPONSIBILITIES 273

OCTOBER 1 ....**274**
   THE VALUE OF A PICTURE 274

OCTOBER 2 ....**275**
   THE HIDDEN THINGS 275

OCTOBER 3 ....**276**
   NESTING 101 276

OCTOBER 4 ....**277**
   JUST SING 277

OCTOBER 5 ....**278**
   SWEET SMELL OF MANURE 278

OCTOBER 6 ....**279**
   CLARITY 279

OCTOBER 7 ....**280**
   EVEN THE STRONG LION 280

OCTOBER 8 ....**281**
   HIDDEN TREASURES 281

OCTOBER 9 ....**282**
   CHOOSING TO TRUST 282

OCTOBER 10 ....**283**
   RESOLVED 283

OCTOBER 11 ....**284**
   FAITHFULNESS 284

OCTOBER 12 ....**285**
   REAL LIFE IS GRAND. NOT. 285

OCTOBER 13 ....**286**
A plan? 286

OCTOBER 14 ....**287**
Heart search/job search 287

OCTOBER 15 ....**288**
Unbridled joy 288

OCTOBER 16 ....**289**
Just not feeling it 289

OCTOBER 17 ....**290**
Trapping an example 290

OCTOBER 18 ....**291**
Counting the years 291

OCTOBER 19 ....**292**
Sunny skies 292

OCTOBER 20 ....**293**
Does relaxing mean lazy? 293

OCTOBER 21 ....**294**
Stains be gone 294

OCTOBER 22 ....**295**
Straight paths 295

OCTOBER 23 ....**296**
Ready to focus 296

OCTOBER 24 ....**297**
Living scared 297

OCTOBER 25 ....**298**
A sunday afternoon nap 298

OCTOBER 26 ....**299**
The good samaritan? 299

OCTOBER 27 ....**300**
Digging in the dirt 300

OCTOBER 28 ....**301**
Keep chopping wood 301

OCTOBER 29 ....**302**
Bad teeth 302

OCTOBER 30 ....**303**
Gymnastics 101 303

OCTOBER 31..**304**
   Let the dead speak...304

NOVEMBER 1...**305**
   New hope rising...305

NOVEMBER 2...**306**
   A ray of hope..306

NOVEMBER 3...**307**
   Voting day...307

NOVEMBER 4...**308**
   Uncertainty...308

NOVEMBER 5...**309**
   Home is where the heart is..309

NOVEMBER 6...**310**
   More than expected...310

NOVEMBER 7...**311**
   Obscured view...311

NOVEMBER 8...**312**
   Choose today..312

NOVEMBER 9...**313**
   The perfect athlete...313

NOVEMBER 10...**314**
   Back to the future..314

NOVEMBER 11...**315**
   Fading spots..315

NOVEMBER 12...**316**
   Rain, rain, here to stay...316

NOVEMBER 13...**317**
   That bell—again...317

NOVEMBER 14...**318**
   A house full of stuff...318

NOVEMBER 15...**319**
   Peculiar people...319

NOVEMBER 16...**320**
   Losing focus..320

NOVEMBER 17...**321**
   Windy conditions...321

NOVEMBER 18 .... **322**
   Crazy 322

NOVEMBER 19 .... **323**
   Am i a quitter? 323

NOVEMBER 20 .... **324**
   Be kind. meet needs 324

NOVEMBER 21 .... **325**
   When the kids grow up 325

NOVEMBER 22 .... **326**
   It is well 326

NOVEMBER 23 .... **327**
   A jumbled mess of emotions 327

NOVEMBER 24 .... **328**
   In its time 328

NOVEMBER 25 .... **329**
   Light 'em up 329

NOVEMBER 26 .... **330**
   Thanksgiving 330

NOVEMBER 27 .... **331**
   The last testament 331

NOVEMBER 28 .... **332**
   Is it worth it? 332

NOVEMBER 29 .... **333**
   Faith, love, and hope 333

NOVEMBER 30 .... **334**
   Outside the camp 334

DECEMBER 1 .... **335**
   Walking blind 335

DECEMBER 2 .... **336**
   7, 10, or 14? 336

DECEMBER 3 .... **337**
   Just shut it 337

DECEMBER 4 .... **338**
   Moving on 338

DECEMBER 5 .... **339**
   The great tidy 339

DECEMBER 6 ....**340**
Car sheep 340

DECEMBER 7 ....**341**
Words are important 341

DECEMBER 8 ....**342**
Actively waiting 342

DECEMBER 9 ....**343**
A trip gone bad 343

DECEMBER 10 ....**344**
Please sign and return 344

DECEMBER 11 ....**345**
The mountains call 345

DECEMBER 12 ....**346**
I am jealous 346

DECEMBER 13 ....**347**
Get comfortable 347

DECEMBER 14 ....**348**
What to do? 348

DECEMBER 15 ....**349**
Just another day 349

DECEMBER 16 ....**350**
No snow. . . and other disappointments 350

DECEMBER 17 ....**351**
One cent 351

DECEMBER 18 ....**352**
Traveling mercy 352

DECEMBER 19 ....**353**
Crafty 353

DECEMBER 20 ....**354**
A bright contrast 354

DECEMBER 21 ....**355**
A tough day 355

DECEMBER 22 ....**356**
A messy route 356

DECEMBER 23 ....**357**
Solitude 357

DECEMBER 24 .... **358**
   Christmas eve 358

DECEMBER 25 .... **359**
   A day of thanks 359

DECEMBER 26 .... **360**
   Mixed messages 360

DECEMBER 27 .... **361**
   A make-over 361

DECEMBER 28 .... **362**
   No pain. no gain 362

DECEMBER 29 .... **363**
   A hiding place 363

DECEMBER 30 .... **364**
   Rejection 364

DECEMBER 31 .... **365**
   We made it! 365

POSTSCRIPT **367**
   In case you were wondering 367

ABOUT THE AUTHOR **369**

FINAL THOUGHTS **371**

ACKNOWLEDGMENTS

This work would have never come to fruition had it not been for the support and encouragement of my family. The personal nature of these stories demanded honest introspection and transparency. We went through rough times, many of those alluded to rather than dealt with directly early on in this project. It was only with the express permission of my family that I eventually revealed some of the ugly details. This was not an easy thing to do. However, it would have been dishonest to leave out the facts.

I wish no embarrassment to anyone. I simply hope and pray that all who read this work will clearly see the working of God in all situations, whether they be easy to talk about or not. Our God is all-powerful and fully capable of changing hearts and minds. We know this to be true because we saw it happen with our very own eyes. My deepest gratitude goes out to our youngest son, Seth, for allowing me to share some of his painful yet beautiful story of redemption.

January 3

Perfect parenting. Not.

Truth be told, I shudder when asked for parenting advise. I feel inadequate, hardly an example of what a good parent looks like. I sometimes wish for a do-over.

One of my runner friends, an original member of my high school runners turned adventuring "Shindiggler" group, is currently incubating a tiny human. I will be attending a celebration of said child tomorrow. I'm sure she will be offered lots of advice, most unsolicited, on the finer points of child rearing. The logistics of when to feed the kid and how to take care of diaper rash are some of the easier elements of childcare. What is not so easy is knowing how to guide his (or her) little pea-pick'n heart into righteous attitudes and behavior—even as a young child.

This Proverb is often tossed out the way one might mindlessly kick a can down the road on a carefree summer afternoon: *Train up a child in the way he should go; even when he is old he will not depart from it* (22:6). But how in the world do we do this? Is this an absolute guarantee that our children will eventually become spiritual giants?

Hum. Not sure on that one. But I do know that parents are called to obedience in teaching truth day and night (Deuteronomy 11:19), not exasperating our little (and big) darlings, and to instruct them in the Lord (Ephesians 6:4). Obedience to *act justly, love mercy, and walk humbly with your God* (Micah 6:8).

What we are not responsible for is actually "saving" their souls. Do we set the spiritual table? Yes. Do we call the children to the table to eat? Yes. But can we make them *taste and see that the Lord is good*? No. It is the Spirit of God alone that can give an individual- even our own children-the appetite to desire Him.

A college friend turned author once posed this question. If God, who is the only perfect Father, has less-than perfect children, how can we assume that we, as imperfect parents, will produce perfect God-loving children?

She has a point. I will never, ever be a perfect parent. But I do know this: Despite my shortcomings as a parent, God is still gracious and merciful. I need to trust my children to Him, THE perfect parent.

Today's Truth: See what kind of love the Father has given to us, that we should be called children of God. 1 John 3:1

January 4

Love, Marriage, and Babies

Funny how the craziest things pop into my head. Maybe I thought about this schoolyard quip because I wrote about parenting yesterday. Or maybe it is because I attended a baby shower today. Or could it be that chatting about an upcoming wedding stirred the memory? But whatever the cause, can you recall when you were in first grade and witnessed a budding romance between classmates. To egg them on, everyone joined in sing-songing, "Sarah and Jack, sitting in a tree, K-I-S-S-I-N-G. First comes love. Then comes marriage. Then comes baby in a baby carriage."

Catchy little poem, right? And so old-fashioned and traditional, too. But does traditional mean outdated and irrelevant? I don't think so.

Ever since Adam and Eve got thrown out of the garden, there has been a long history of sexual misconduct. In numerous Old and New Testament literature, we read of adultery, pre-marital sex, single sex interactions, and even twisted acts with animals. Of course, sex itself between a man and a woman was not the problem. It was a lack of both respect and unselfish commitment.

Marriage is always the God-given context for sexual intimacy. It demands a monogamous relationship that mimics the pure relationship that Christ has with his bride, the universal church. For that to happen, the man unselfishly gives of himself to please his wife. The wife serves her husband by meeting his needs. This love, marriage, intimacy sequence is only possible through selfless attitudes and the desire to fulfill the physical, emotional, and relational needs of the other.

Look around. Love, marriage, and baby-making potential may not be highly regarded these days, but it is worth pursuing.

Today's Truth: Husbands, love your wives, as Christ loved the church and gave himself up for her, that he might sanctify her, having cleansed her by the washing of water with the word, so that he might present the church to himself in splendor, without spot or wrinkle or any such thing, that she might be holy and without blemish. In the same way husbands should love their wives as their own bodies. He who loves his wife loves himself. For no one ever hated his own flesh, but nourishes and cherishes it, just as Christ does the church, because we are members of his body. "Therefore a man shall leave his father and mother and hold fast to his wife, and the two shall become one flesh." Ephesians 5:25-31

January 5

The twilight zone

It was about 5:45 p.m. and I was driving home from an event. The sun was sinking lower in the sky, creating an odd hue combining orange and gray. On one occasion, though I could not make it out, vague movement along the side of the road caught my attention. I slowed the car to identify a family of deer, barely visible in the dim light. I was straining to see, the visibility conditions tough. It was unnerving. I would have preferred it to be either full daylight or complete darkness. This inbetween stuff was hard to navigate.

Driving in the day is rarely a problem. Everything is clearly visible, colors distinct, objects discernable, and the roadway defined. Driving at night has it advantages as well. The headlights cut easily through the darkness, illuminating the road and surroundings. Animals daring to wander close by reveal themselves when their eyes reflect the headlights. But like tonight, that time between light and darkness is problematic. It is the twilight zone.

I got to thinking about other twilight zones. Consider our behavior patterns. Without doubt, we often know when something is 100% wrong: stealing, murder, malice, greed, immorality, gossip, lying, unkind words. In the light of day, we can be definitive about what is right and what is wrong. The problem I sometimes have is gaining the wisdom to discern what is not only right, but what is profitable and edifying.

The Apostle James wrote to fellow believers, asking them to view trials with joy, and as an opportunity to persevere in becoming mature and complete. I think he knew we would all find ourselves in situations where we had no idea what to do, or how to think and proceed. Hence, he goes on to say, *If any of you lacks wisdom, let him ask God, who gives generously to all without reproach, and it will be given him* (James 1:5).

Without doubt, we will end up in the twilight zone from time to time. That is an uncomfortable place to be. But I also know that I need to become comfortable with being uncomfortable, using the situation to redirect my attention to the Scripture for guidance and direction. There is no better place to turn when we can not see clearly.

Today's Truth: All Scripture is breathed out by God and profitable for teaching, for reproof, for correction, and for training in righteousness, that the man of God may be complete, equipped for every good work. 2 Timothy 3:16, 17

January 6

I work with a lot of D1 collegiate athletic teams, the diving team no exception. I fully enjoy being on the pool deck, awed by their incredible strength and flexibility. The athletes soar through the air on the trampoline, learning new movements before taking to the springboards and diving platforms. It is then I watch them twist and turn, somersaulting forwards, backwards, in reverse and inward directions. Diving is not for the faint of heart. Great mental skill must accompany the physical skill in order to conquer the fear in this dangerous sport.

One of the girls was asked to do an inward 2.5 off the three-meter board today, something she had never done before. However, Coach asked her to first throw an inward double just to be sure she was spinning fast enough. She stood poised at the end of the board, got the board moving, and proceeded to jump backwards before tucking inward toward the board. Around she went once. Then twice. Coach called out the signal for letting go of the tuck. Problem was, Emily hesitated. When she finally stretched out, she was horizontal rather than vertical. Sadly, it turned out to be a 2.25. She hit the water hard, belly first. We all gasped wondering if she was still alive. She was. Emily groaned and her face grimaced with pain. But she was not badly hurt because she led the racous laughter when we watched the playback on the monitor. I must admit, it was hilarious.

She was only a fraction of a second late. Had she immediately heeded the coach's call, the inward double would have been a success. Unfortunately, she paid the price for lack of express obedience.

Are there principles about obedience we can learn from this belly-flop? I think the answer is yes. 1) Obedience must be immediate and without hesitation and 2) It must be precise. Otherwise, there will be negative consequences.

God demands full and timely obedience. In Deuteronomy 12:28 he says *Be careful to obey all these words that I command you. . . . being careful to do according to all the law that Moses my servant commanded you. Do not turn from it to the right hand or to the left, that you may have good success wherever you go* (Joshua 1:7).

Obedience demands fully submitting to the one giving the command. Perhaps if we did that more often, we would belly-flop far less.

Today's Truth: All that the Lord has spoken we will do, and we will be obedient. Exodus 24:7

January 7

Lost opportunity

Though somewhat skeptical, I went to bed last night anticipating the first snow of the winter. The weather report on the late-night news told us snow would move into the area between 8 and 9 a.m. with accumulations of one to three inches. I went to bed wishing for a world turned white with snow.

Come morning when I finally paddled my way to the bathroom, the first few flakes of snow began to fall. "Hum. Maybe the forecast was right," I mused. But alas, within an hour the snow turned to rain, evidenced by the splish-splash in the fishpond outside the front door. Bummer. The window of opportunity to run in the snow had already closed. The thought of enduring cold rain was not appealing.

Honestly, this was not the first—nor will it be the last—time I failed to act promptly. I cannot begin to count the number of times I intended to do something but never quite got around to it: write an encouraging note, make a phone call, call my mother, read my Bible. The list goes on.

Curious about the idea of immediacy, a quick on-line search revealed an interesting perspective. Apparently, when Jesus wanted something done, it was normally a now or never kind of deal. With the diseased man in Matthew 8, Jesus gives the word, and this leper is immediately healed. And consider how Jesus not only demands immediacy from his disciples in Matthew 14, but also interacts with them promptly. *Immediately Jesus made the disciples get in the boat…Jesus immediately said to them…Immediately Jesus reached out his hand and caught him…* In fact, there are 34 times throughout the four Gospels where the actions of Jesus and those he interacted with were fast and furious.

I missed an opportunity to run among the flakes because I waited too long. Now I bear the consequences of procrastination; I did not get to enjoy a snowy run.

I wonder how many times my lack of immediacy has thwarted a blessing to myself or others. When I say, "I'll pray for you," why not pray right there and then? When I say, "Let me think about it," why not provide an immediate answer?

It is easy to procrastinate. It takes courage and intentionality to be like Jesus and act immediately.

Today's Truth: They said to him, "Lord, let our eyes be opened." And Jesus in pity touched their eyes, and immediately they recovered their sight and followed him. Matthew 20:33, 34

JANUARY 8

INTEGRITY

Today I had an interesting conversation with some coaches. After catching up on how their seasons were going, their frustrations with lack of commitment and integrity played naturally into the discussion. It was not as if these were isolated issues. Rather, the number of athletes who use and abuse the system seems to be on the rise.

For example, both coaches spoke of kids who had simply quit; walked away from all that was available to them athletically, academically, socially, and culturally. One spoke of a red-shirt athlete who accepted a full scholarship, only to discover she never intended to play after her red-shirt year. Her plan from the start was to take the money for a year before running off to the university where she *really* wanted to play. Now the norm rather than the exeption, lamented the coaches, are the many alumni who fail to have any sense of loyalty to their alma maters. It is a sad situation.

I am certain there are many athletes (and people in general) who are fully committed to conducting themselves with the highest level of integrity. However, there seems to be an upsurge in our culture to priortize selfish desires compared to staying true to what we promised.

Obviously, the Scriptures call us to live lives of integrity. Though there are many named individuals who were known for possessing integrity (David, Solomon, Job, Nehemiah, to name a few), perhaps the best-known entreaties for integrity are found in the Psalms and Proverbs. Among many pleas to guide his living, King David voices this to God: *May integrity and uprightness preserve me, for I wait for you* (Ps.25:21). Proverbs 11:2, 3 gives us further insight. *When pride comes, then comes disgrace, but with the humble is wisdom. The integrity of the upright guides them.*

It is all too easy to give our word and not follow through. It is also tempting to manipulate people or situations for our own good. How easy it is to cheat on a practice drill or test thinking it no big deal. But if we are to be men and women of integrity, then we need to be intentional about doing what is right – even in the small things.

Today's Truth: Whoever walks in integrity walks securely, but he who makes his ways crooked will be found out. Proverbs 10:9

January 9

Waves of Emotion

For the past week or so I have been sick. And tired. And riding tsunami-like waves of highs and lows. I have had just about all I can take.

I was thinking about this earlier in the day when I forced myself to run before work. It was a chilly 26 degrees, but the sun was out and skies clear. I wish I could say as much for my lungs and congested head. However, the jiggling created by running was probably good for me, if you consider hacking up mucus and blowing out snot rockets good. Still, there was something special about being in the forest alone, each foot strike creating a crackling sound as the ice crystals underfoot gave way to the impact.

I am looking forward to the day when it is not so hard to navigate life. A complex family situation has made life extremely complicated and challenging. For years we have begged God to intervene. On occasion we saw a glimmer of hope, only to be driven back to the throne with incessant prayer when the answer we desired seemed so far away, maybe even impossible. But now, though the logistics of the situation remain incredibly difficult, we are very encouraged with what appears to be a miraculous transformation of a repentant heart.

But why should I be experiencing such dramatic ups and downs? Why should there be as many bad days as good? Do I not believe that God can (and will) do the impossible even though I intellectually know he is all powerful? Is my faith simply too small?

God made us with the ability to experience a full range of emotions. I suspect he did that with intentionality, fully expecting us to feel them all at some point. Scripture is full of joy and despair, hopefulness and despondency, confidence and fear. David wrote *Weeping may tarry for the night, but joy comes with the morning* (Psalm 30:5).

God is Jeremiah's comforter in his deepest sorrow over the sinful nation for which he pleads (Jeremiah 8:18). But we know the Lord restores joy. He rescues and comforts, proclaims prophet Isaiah (Isaiah 51:11, 12). And when faced with despair, our first reaction should be to take those emotions and run to the Scriptures. It is only there we gain hope and perspective.

Today's Truth: Make me understand the way of your precepts, and I will meditate on your wondrous works. My soul melts away for sorrow; strengthen me according to your word! Psalm 119:27, 28

JANUARY 10

WHEN THINGS DO NOT GO AS PLANNED

I knew tackling my schedule could be challenging, but every one of my plans ran away faster than that stink'n Gingerbread Man.

In fact, two literal gingerbread men (and their humble house) showed up last night. When I picked up a clearance gingerbread house kit for a buck, I figured it would be a wonderful Thursday night activity with Addyson, our just-turned five-year old granddaughter. Sure enough, it turned out to be an architectural masterpiece, after which we played a matching game, drew a bubble bath for her and her mermaid toys, finally tucking her under a puffy bed quilt a bit later than normal. This morning I worked hard to wake her, carrying her to the couch to sleepily eat her breakfast. My time management skills were being challenged from the git-go.

The plan was to take her with me to the office until her mother could pick her up. It was a perfect plan until mom was unexpectedly delayed for five hours. Then, I had more folks pop into the office to chat than I normally do in a week. Addyson made those conversations interesting.

Later, we tromped across the expansive campus to basketball practice. It was then that Addy's mom came by to pick her up. By the time she was carried away, I was unable to get to diving practice, which had been on the original agenda. The only logical thing was to head home and pick-up Chinese for dinner. In retrospect, nothing bad happened today. But neither did anything happen as expected. That was frustrating.

I doubt there are any mind-blowing spiritual principles to apply to days like this. I did not have epic personal failures by losing my temper, yelling at people, or loathing any of my interactions. But I did need to remind myself that taking things as they come—you know, going with the flow—is not such a bad idea.

This kind of day teaches me to watch my attitude. To be kind. To be unselfish. To be patient. To love well. To regard other's needs more than my own. Simply put, to exhibit all the character traits that are expected of us because of who we are in Christ.

Today's Truth: But the fruit of the Spirit is love, joy, peace, patience, kindness, goodness, faithfulness, gentleness, self-control; against such things there is no law. Galatians 5:22, 23

January 11

Stinkbug Conundrum

When God cursed the earth, he could have done a pretty good job with stink bugs alone.

I never even heard of a brown marmorated stinkbug when I was growing up. And you know why? It is because they are not native to the United States. Those ugly and odiferous bugs did not hit our shores until September of 1998 when they were discovered in Allentown, PA. Apparently, they had hitched a ride in crates originating from either Japan or China, their native lands. But in these last two decades, the stinkbug has taken over the universe—or at least Bedford, Virginia.

With unseasonably warm temperatures, all the stinkbugs that had taken up residence in the nooks and crannies of our old farmhouse came out to play. This evening they were all over the kitchen light fixture, on windows, and around the doors. I went on a semi-rampage, coaxing them to jump into a glass full of water before tossing them out the door to die. I. Hate. Stinkbugs.

Think about their strategy for stinkbug success. When it begins to get cold, they find a way indoors. The tiniest crack can harbor a host of them. They seem content to hide, just biding their time. However, when a warm spell hits, they come out from hiding to torment all humans who share the same abode. Then, as soon as the weather turns frigid again, back into hiding they go. Though stinky, they are predictable.

We can be just as predictable. We get into a situation where conditions are not to our liking. Off we run to hide and wait it out. When we think it is safe, out we come to do our bidding, only to retreat when we suspect it will soon be uncomfortable once again.

What if we lived boldly regardless of the conditions? It is certainly harder than hiding, but this is what God calls us to do. When Joseph was sold into slavery and carried off to Egypt, enduring years in prison, he did not hide. When the disciples bounced around in a fishing boat in the middle of a storm, Jesus expected them to have faith. When first century Believers were tortured by Nero, they never ran. They counted it all joy.

Do not run and hide.

Today's Truth: preach the word; be ready in season and out of season; reprove, rebuke, and exhort, with complete patience and teaching. 2 Timothy 4:2

JANUARY 12

NEVER SAY DIE

Football is not my thing. I enjoy going to an occasional game, but cannot get too excited about the sport. Nevertheless, a game was on TV between the Houston Texans and the Kansas City Chiefs. At one point in the second quarter, the Chiefs were losing 24-0. It looked like it would not be much of a game.

Now, let's think about what they might have been saying on both sidelines. I suspect the Texans were feeling confident with such a widespread in the score. And what about the Chiefs? I'm thinking the tendency would be despondency with a dash of impending doom and embarrassment at such a loss. At least, that is how most teams getting a whooping would view their situation.

OK. So, what happened? Here's the good part. The Kansas City team reared up and started fighting back. They scored 41 unanswered points to make it 41 – 24. Incredible. Houston finally scored again to make it 41-31. That must have refocused and supercharged Kansas City. They went on to score a touchdown, extra point, and field goal to make it a memorable 51-31 win.

Personally, there is little better than a good come-from-behind story and today's example on the gridiron did not disappoint. The sporting world is rich with similar stories, many a coach drawing on such wins to inspire never-give-up attitudes.

A never-give-up attitude is a principle of biblical proportion. The New Testament equivalent is perseverance or endurance. In fact, we see the early church lauded for their perseverance with additional appeals to continue to stay the course even in the toughest hardships and suffering. In the ESV translation, the words endurance and perseverance are found sixteen times within the 27 books of the New Testament.

However, perseverance never stands alone. Character skills must be foundational in order to persevere, which leads to the development of other attributes. There is no doubt. Perseverance and endurance are necessary for our spiritual development.

Today's truth: Not only that, but we rejoice in our sufferings, knowing that suffering produces endurance, and endurance produces character, and character produces hope, Romans 5:3-5

January 13

It's complicated

It's complicated. What is? Well, just about everything.

There are certainly lots of complicated things in my life. When I look at my calendar trying to figure out how I can possibly serve all my athletic teams and coaches with a reasonable level of consistency, I get overwhelmed. Practice times overlap, competitions are on the same day, and someone is bound to feel neglected. Add to that responsibilities at home, granddaughter time, church and friends, and my running workouts, and there is little space left on the calendar. Time management is complicated.

At times, however, I suspect we make things more complicated than they need to be. Granted, many things are straightforeward. For instance, *sexual immorality and all impurity or covetousness must not even be named among you, as is proper among saints. Let there be no filthiness nor foolish talk nor crude joking, which are out of place,.. .*(Ephesian 5:3, 4). If we find ourselves dabbling, we simply need to stop. That is not complicated at all.

When I was teaching school and before any lesson was presented, I had my students stand and recite the answer to this question: "Class, what does the Lord require of us?" The response was three very simple directives that are anything but complicated. *To act justly and to love mercy, and to walk humbly with your God* (Micah 6:8 NIV).

These three standards can be used to evaluate every thought and action throughout our day. "Acting justly" has to do with behaviors that are good and right. "Loving mercy" will guide relationships and interactions with other people. And "walking humbly" has everything to do with an attitude that is contrite, unselfish, and serves others.

If we intentionally apply these three simple, straightforward directives as a measuring stick, I suspect our lives will become far less complicated than we make them out to be.

Today's Truth: He has told you, O man, what is good; and what does the Lord require of you but to do justice, and to love kindness, and to walk humbly with your God? Micah 6:8

JANUARY 14

SCARS

Do you have any scars? I have several surgical scars along with scars indicating too many unfortunate encounters with gravel back when I was a kid. But what about these scars and bruises? Are they merely ugly marks we wish to hide, or do they carry some significance?

The group "I am They" offers perspective on getting beat up, bruised, and scarred. Consider the first stanza and refrain.

Waking up to a new sunrise
Looking back from the other side
I can see now with open eyes
Darkest water and deepest pain
I wouldn't trade it for anything
'Cause my brokenness brought me to you
and these wounds are a story you'll use.
(Refrain) So I'm thankful for the scars
'Cause without them I wouldn't know your heart
And I know they'll always tell of who you are
So forever I am thankful for the scars.

To be physically bruised and scarred requires elements of pain and suffering. The scarring process is never pleasant. Even as the scars heal, the tissues yank and pull. Eventually, however, healing is complete, the wound closed. But that scar is a tell-tale sign of past injury, either by accident or our own doing. We tend to hide them. Cover them up. Who wants to see that kind of ugly?

But here's the truth. Only when we see the ugly can we appreciate the beautiful. "Matthew" struggled with alcohol. For a decade, his life was a series of self-inflicted wounds that cut deep. Chaos prevailed, friends and family left hurting. But even as the jailhouse doors closed behind him, the Spirit of God opened his eyes. The scarring caused by addiction is now a beautiful reminder of the healing in his heart.

Thanks be to Jesus Christ for the scars he endured so that we can endure our own.

Today's Truth: Then he said to Thomas, "Put your finger here, and see my hands; and put out your hand, and place it in my side. Do not disbelieve, but believe." Thomas answered him, "My Lord and my God!" John 20: 27, 28

January 15

Beauty for ashes

No judgment, please, but last night I hit the DVR to see what had been automatically recorded in the last few days. Selecting "America's Got Talent: The Champions," I settled in to kill some time, remote in hand to zip through the annoying commercials. One of the performers was a teenager, Luke Islam, with aspirations for Broadway. I was not familiar with the song he offered, but was drawn to one phrase: "Let beauty come out from ashes." It sounded so familiar.

In Isaiah 61, the prophet pens some amazing stuff. Israel has for centuries been in a steady cycle of obedience and disobedience. Blessing and cursing. Freedom and captivity. Now Isaiah providentially comes on the scene to encourage the rag-tag bunch. In the first verse he writes, *The Spirit of the Lord God is upon me, because the Lord has anointed me, to bring good news to the poor; he has sent me to bind up the brokenhearted, to proclaim liberty to the captives.*

Now before we get to what he says next, think back to yesterday's discussion about scars. God has an uncanny ability to take what is ugly and make something beautiful out of it. In fact, it is the contrast between our innate, sinful ugliness and God's beauty and righteousness that spotlights the necessity for God's grace and mercy in our lives.

Isaiah realized this truth. For the mourners, he offers joy. For those heavy-hearted, they are given the ability to praise. And for those decimated in spirit and soul, reduced to figurative ashes, they are made beautiful.

This is a story of contrasts that only God can provide. Scars testify of healing. Mourning turns to joy. Despondency give way to praise. And for those dirtied and trapped by sin, they are made beautiful by the grace of God. As Crystal Lewis penned in a song, "He gives beauty for ashes, Strength for fear. Gladness for mourning. Peace for despair…" Beauty for ashes is the redemptive trade agreement God generously and unconditionally offers to those that love Him.

Today's Truth: grant to those who mourn in Zion- to give them a beautiful headdress instead of ashes, the oil of gladness instead of mourning, the garment of praise instead of a faint spirit; that they may be called oaks of righteousness, the planting of the Lord, that he may be glorified. Isaiah 61:3

January 16

The commitment quandary

Commitment to a cause is, by definition, difficult. To truly commit takes a vast amount of fortitude, dedication, the ability to endure, and the capacity to do what needs to be done in the moment. The ability to commit is essential to our growth and maturity. But the demanding requirements keep most people from wholly giving of themselves athletically, professionally, avocationally, communally, or spititually.

However, there is an infinitesimally thin line between commitment and obsession, making it all too easy to slip into this landmine-fraught territory without even realizing it. This is when problems develop. Perspective is lost, and the honorable objective once set takes on idol-like status. The obsession skews our thinking, displaces values previously held, and sets off a series of actions and attitudes that can destroy.

On the opposite side of the spectrum, a thick line exists between involvement and commitment, making it difficult to take the big step required to shift upward. It is easy to be involved because involvement rarely demands sacrifice. Mere involvement does not mandate laser-focus. Great sacrifice is rarely required for involvement. If we want to move from involvement to commitment, we will need to submit to hard-work, discomfort, and maybe even a dose of pain and suffering. That becomes a weighty decision.

Tennis great Martina Navratilova once said "The difference between involvement and commitment is like ham and eggs. The chicken is involved; the pig is committed."

I read in the Gospels of first century Believers who were enslaved, beaten, and thrown into the depths of abysmal prisons. I hear modern-day stories of Christians who are being imprisoned and even martyred by haters of the Gospel in places such as China, Iran, Iraq, Pakistan, Eritrea, and India. Where should these past and present Believers be placed along this continuum? I assure you none were or are simply "involved." But neither should they be labeled as obsessed because all maintain(ed) perspective and single-minded focus about their security in Christ, kingdom advancement, and on the coming glory. Every single one, however, was or is fully committed to the cause.

Are we involved or committed? Committed or obsessed? Commit fully to the Worthy One.

Today's Truth: Commit your work to the Lord, and your plans will be established. Proverbs 16:3

January 17

Warning signs

I looked ahead and saw the road rise before me. Nope. It was not flat. It just seemed to be going in one direction. Up. I self-checked my body position. Shoulders a little back. Hips pulled forward. Shoulders, hips, and ankles all aligned. Stride length shortened as the incline increased. Be patient. Be steady. Keep your eyes forward. This was a day to build aerobic base. No need to be fast. Just need to keep going. Maintain effort. Keep breathing steady. Ah, made it!

Last summer, this run might have done me in. For a good long time, my running had been pitiful. I felt like I had a governor on my engine. No matter how hard I tried, I could not go more than a snail's pace. My breathing was very labored, legs and arms heavy as lead. Even on extended downhills, which should be easy with the gravity assist, I had to slow to a walk. Something was not right. I knew it. A screening test followed by a heart catheterization and subsequent stent placement confirmed my coronary artery disease.

Haven't we all heard stories about someone keeling over because they ignored the warning signs of a heart attack? Please do not think I am being judgmental. It is just so easy to get in the "this could never happen to me" mode.

We are all pretty good at rationalizing away our conditions. For me, I figured my failure to get fit was because I am getting older. Then again, when presented with clinical data, I had to face the reality of my disease and deal with it appropriately.

Jonathan, son of King Saul, warned his friend, David, to flee because His father was trying to kill him. He said, *be on your guard in the morning. Stay in a secret place and hide yourself* (1 Samuel 19:2). David heeded the warning and was spared.

The ancient prophet Nehemiah probably turned blue warning those Israelites to be obedient to God's laws and decrees. Guess what? *Yet they acted presumptuously and did not obey your commandments, but sinned against your rules* (Nehemiah 9:29). The result was not good. God allowed them to be conquered by neighboring nations.

Though two examples hardly comprise a doctoral dissertation on the subject, the imperative is clear. Heed warnings. Take action.

Today's Truth: But if you warn the righteous person not to sin, and he does not sin, he shall surely live, because he took warning, and you will have delivered your soul. Ezekiel 3:21

JANUARY 18

UNDER PRESSURE

Under normal circumstances, I would have been at the game tonight. As chaplain for the university's women's basketball team, I attend everything I possibly can. But a complicated schedule prevented me from being in the Vines Center. However, the real-time online stats provided an interesting picture of what was happening on the court.

By the end of the first quarter, we were down 20 to 9, shooting 26.7% to their 40%. Oops. Not a great way to start a game on your home court. During the second quarter, both teams shot poorly; 21% for us and 25% for them. It was bad by anyone's standards. By the time halftime rolled around, I am sure both teams were happy to take refuge in the locker rooms in search of the key to victory. The score was now 28 to 16, them.

When the referee's whistle launched the third quarter, we got hot, outscoring the opponent 22 to their 10. A shooting percentage of 43.8% certainly attributed to the score. Now the score was tied at 38. In the fourth quarter, I could only assume play was furious at both ends. As the buzzer sounded, the teams stood tied at the end of regulation at 55 apiece.

So now it was overtime. Our team lost in overtime earlier this week. What were they thinking when faced with another opportunity to play extended minutes? Would they rise to the occasion or fold? Become heroes or heels?

Until put under pressure, we never really know what we are made of. For sure, pressure can bring about tremendous benefit; increased focus, exponential growth, strength, and perseverance. But we also know that when "pressurized," the truth comes out. Consider the tennis player who trashes his racket, a coach who becomes so enraged that a flood of expletives erupts, or a team completely folds and is unable to perform the most basic plays. In many cases, succumbing to pressure will expose fear, lack of self-control, and actions and attitudes that are less than optimal.

Pressure can be good. Pressure can be bad. How will we let it affect us?

Today's Truth: But what comes out of the mouth proceeds from the heart, and this defiles a person. Matthew 15:18

Postscript: We out-shot the other team 9-5, winning 64 to 60 in that overtime period.

January 19

Lost lamby

She had her from birth. Rag-tagged and a little lumpy, but oddly adorable despite years of hard loving. Lamby belongs to Addyson, my five-year old granddaughter. She and Lamby go to bed together every night, snuggling under the covers. It is a perfect ending to her perfect days. So just imagine how difficult a Lamby-less evening could be to a sweet, sensitive little girl.

We were enjoying an overnight stay with relatives, Lamby in tow. Addyson and Lamby spent the night cuddling, rising to greet the morning healthy and happy. After some time playing with cousins, we left to travel home. Only problem was, Lamby did not make it into the car. That devastating fact did not make itself known until several hours later. We made calls back to Aunt Joy in a quest to find the stuffed animal. Despite looking high and low, Lamby was MIA.

I found Addy sitting at the dining room table, eyes moist and tears rolling down her cheeks. She looked at me with those sad, puppy-dog eyes. Addy spoke softly, her soul revealing the deepest pain. "Lamby was so special. I had her since I was a baby." Despite reassurances that Lamby could not run away and had to be *somewhere*, no amount of consoling soothed her hurting heart.

I tucked her into bed, privileged to hear her sweet prayers for her daddy. Then with tiny hands folded in prayer-like posture, the tears cascaded once again. "Why don't you pray that Lamby will be found?"

"Okay, Grandma. I will." Between sobs, she choked out the purest prayer. "Dear God, please keep Lamby safe. I love her and miss her so much. Please help her to be found. Amen."

As she prayed, I heard my phone beep from the other room. It was a simple text from Joy. "Lamby has been found." What?!? Could it be?

"Addyson, Aunt Joy found Lamby! She is safe and sound." Tears of joy replaced tears of sadness. It was a teachable moment of God's goodness, answered prayer, and His pursuit of those sheep who are lost, human and otherwise.

Today's Truth: "What man of you, having a hundred sheep, if he has lost one of them, does not leave the ninety-nine in the open country, and go after the one that is lost, until he finds it? Luke 15:3

January 20

It's hard, and that's okay

It was the start of the spring season. This NCAA Division 1 volleyball team was in the weight room at 6:00 a.m. this morning. Then it was a quick trip down the stairs at 7 and into the gym. The team was put through their paces, each drill conducted at a pace few could manage. It was evident these fine athletes had lost their peak conditioning they held eight weeks ago at the fall season's conclusion. This fact was not lost on the coach, who commented that the level of fatigue was common for this point in the season. It was their individual responsibility to earn it back.

I know what it is like to claw your way back after losing fitness to injury. When I first started ultrarunning in 1993, I became an unwilling expert in the crazy cycle of gaining fitness only to have it instantly unravel with an unexpected injury. In my first five years of endurance running, I suffered nine metatarsal stress fractures, a medial malleolus stress fracture, femoral neck stress fracture, and a variety of soft tissue injuries. My response was to crosstrain like crazy to retain that hard-earned fitness, spending hours on ellipticals or deep water running. Like a tadpole, I emerged from the pool weeks or months later, took to the roads clawing my way back, only to be hit by another injury. The train-injury-recovery cycle was a test of endurance in and of itself. It was hard. Really, really hard.

Any athlete understands that to rise to the highest level possible in their chosen sport, there will be gains and losses. Progress and setbacks. Disappointments and elation. As the modern proverb states, there can be "no gain without some pain." It is working to overcome the challenges that prompts growth.

Likewise, walking faith's road is not without difficulties. There are bumps and bruises to endure, potholes to fall into, and muddy mire that makes progress difficult. Think of John Bunyan's iconic Pilgrim in *Pilgrim's Progress*. The road to spiritual understanding, maturity and practical living was difficult for Pilgrim. And yet he continued to draw near to God, listened carefully for instruction, and kept on walking. He clearly understood that the perseverance required of him was a necessary part of the journey.

Today's Truth: And let steadfastness have its full effect, that you may be perfect and complete, lacking in nothing. James 1:4

January 21

Quietness and Confidence

Ryan Hall was—and still is—an incredible athlete. Among his many accolades, Hall is known for holding the American record in the half-marathon, is the only American to have run the full 26.2 miles in less than 2:05 and competed in both the Beijing and London Olympics. He is currently coaching a stable of elite athletes, including his wife who is making a bid for a spot on the USA 2020 Olympic marathon team.

I heard Ryan speak today. He carried to the platform what looked to be a hotel note pad, presumably scribbled with notes. However, if notes were written, he never really looked at them. No PowerPoint either. He just began to speak, having no problem holding the attention of the hearers. He apprised the audience of an inauspicious beginning to his running career. His rise to be America's best was meteoric at times, but also brought its share of ups and downs; periods of despair and depression that eventually morphed into brilliant performances. But more important than the facts and figures related to results was his approach to a faith-led life, marriage, and family structure.

Though he has had traditional coaches—and is now himself a coach for others—there was a time when God was his stated coach. This faith-based coaching, as he called it, was predicated on praying for wisdom and insight, being a student of the science, seeking opinions of others, but ultimately self-coaching while God directed his steps. Biblical principles allowed him to endure and suffer well, to stand again when knocked to the ground (Proverbs 24:16), and to eliminate any performance burden by running free with joy.

Applying biblical principle will inform every aspect of our lives. That might be athletic endeavors, interpersonal relationships, professional growth, community life, and such. Ryan and Sara Hall depended on that fact when they adopted four Ethiopian sisters, giving them a loving, caring home. They rely on that faith as they lead in their roles as husband, wife, parent, athlete, coach, and servant. They do not need attention and hoopla to live this way. Rather, they find their strength and confidence in those moments of quietness and calm.

Today's Truth: . . .in quietness and in confidence shall be your strength. . . (Isaiah 30:15 KJV)

JANUARY 22

CAN THE FOUNDATION BE TRUSTED?

The day got away from me, one unexpected thing after another demanding my attention. The window of opportunity to run a few miles turned into a slammed-shut door. Any fitness gains would need to be made from home after dinner. Since it is often difficult to get off the couch once the tasty food has settled in my tum-tum, I anticipated a lively self-argument whether I should start sweating.

But sweat I did. An old-time, people-powered, non-electric Nordic Track ski machine occupies space in our bedroom. I can "run" by maintaining a cross-country ski posture, altering the incline and resistance as I deem appropriate. This piece of equipment that can also double as a clothes depository is positioned smack-dab in front of an equally ancient TV. But at least it works.

I chose the show, "Building Alaska," as my workout distraction. The series chronicles three different families who decide to construct their homes in remote and nearly inaccessible parts of the state. Though each building is very different in style and materials, one thing is common to all: the need for a very strong foundation.

For as long as I have watched this series, there has never been a time where the owners were haphazard with the planning, preparation, and construction of their foundations. The success of their build rests upon—literally—the ability of the foundation to carry the load.

Remember the parable (and perhaps the kids' song) about the foolish man and the wise man who chose vastly different foundations for their houses? The foolish man built on sand. When the storms approached and the rain came down, so did the house. But the man who built his house on a rock was safe and secure inside his walls when the storm hit.

If we are not careful about the foundation upon which we build our lives, we are both foolish and doomed. But when we build on the Rock, the Lord Jesus Christ himself, we can and will stand firm.

Today's Truth: "Everyone then who hears these words of mine and does them will be like a wise man who built his house on the rock. And the rain fell, and the floods came, and the winds blew and beat on that house, but it did not fall, because it had been founded on the rock. Matthew 7:24-25

January 23

Go ahead. laugh.

When is the last time you laughed so hard it hurt? Or laughed in such a way that you had to cross your legs so as not to pee your pants? I am trying hard to think back to when I laughed this way, but sadly, nothing comes to mind. Sure, I laugh, but I might have to become more intentional about expressing that emotion more often.

The hypothalmus is about the size of an almond, located near the base of the brain. This tiny bit of tissue is incredibly important as a link between the endocrine and nervous systems. Of its many functions, it releases beta-endorphins, which then stimulates the release of nitric oxide, a potent vasodilator and anti-inflammatory.

This is all good news for the heart. Vasodilation of the coronary arteries means larger diameter arteries through which more than normal amounts of blood can flow. A happy heart is one that has all the blood flow it needs to deliver its precious load of oxygen to the heart tissue itself.

Conversely, when stress hormones such as cortisol and epinephrine are released, just the opposite happens. Arteries constrict, creating narrower vessels which limit blood flow. This makes the heart work harder by increasing heart rate and can create a sense of angst and panic.

Guess what can start the cascade of events that originate in the hypothalmus? If you said laughter and a happy countenance, you get bonus points! Laughter is good for us. This cheerfulness aids our immune system, protects us from harmful inflammation, and makes our heart smile with increased blood flow and slower heart rates that require less "work" than faster ones. A feeling of calm and well-being subsequently ensues.

We may find ourselves in extremely challenging situations. Consider the tennis player who is on the brink of a big loss. He is breathing hard, heart racing. The pressure he feels is crushing. He becomes tentative and ends up making unforced errors. Is there anything he can do? Yep. He needs to smile—literally—perhaps even let out a little giggle. He just might be able to get his physiology working for him rather than against him.

Today's Truth: A joyful heart is good medicine, but a crushed spirit dries up the bones. Proverbs 17:22

JANUARY 24

MORNING GLORY

I woke up 45 minutes before the alarm was set to sound. Ugh. The numbers on the clock told me it was 5:15 a.m. I tried to rest awhile longer, but eventually began preparing for the day's activities. These early morning sessions with the volleyball team has me burning the candle from both ends. However, getting a jump on the day certainly has its benefits.

Getting up early is not new to me. When I was in the medical field my days always started early. And during the hot summers, I often began my long training runs by five or six in the morning. Witnessing the first rays of light was wonderful. Better yet was to finish the run before most people got out of bed on those weekend mornings.

Even though my mind and body protest at the early hours, there is something special about O'dark 30. The world seems still, quiet and comforting. There is a prevailing calm. The darkness wraps me in a gentle caress. I have the day ahead in which to be productive. I can say, *This is the day the* LORD *has made; let us rejoice and be glad in it* (Psalm 118:24).

A few years ago, I stood at the start line of a 50-mile trail race, one I had run many times before. But on that day and in that darkness, my mind went to a song by Matt Redman. It became my song as I witnessed the sun come up and go back down again. I wonder what would happen if I began each new day with these sentiments in mind.

The sun comes up
It's a new day dawning
It's time to sing Your song again
Whatever may pass
And whatever lies before me
Let me be singing
When the evening comes
Refrain: Bless the Lord oh my soul
Oh my soul
Worship His Holy name
Sing like never before
Oh my soul
I'll worship Your Holy name

Today's Truth: From the rising of the sun to its setting, the name of the Lord is to be praised! Psalm 113:3

January 25

Near misses

The noise level in the natatorium had fallen from deafening to a dull roar in anticipation of the three-meter diving event. As the first diver climbed the sleek metal rungs of the ladder, the crowd turned the volume down yet another notch. The college divers needed to fully focus on their acrobatic somersaults and twists. Having a reasonable noise level would certainly help.

One by one they launched themselves into the air, the more talented divers piercing the water like a knife. It was impressive. I was taking in the competition from the pool deck as one of the divers from an opposing team stood atop the board. Her dive? A reverse one and a half in the pike position. She approached the end of the board, performed her hurdle, and took to the air. She went up and began to rotate back toward the board as she should. I gasped. As she spun backwards, she barely—and I mean barely—missed a collision with her launching pad. She was fine, but for those of us who saw just how close she was to disaster, our hearts skipped a few beats.

The diver's near miss made me think about all the near misses I have had. Some were obvious: like the time a car was speeding toward me in my lane. An abrupt swerve onto the shoulder of the road kept us from hitting head on. Or the time the pilot of a plane I was on pulled up at the very last second in pea-soup fog to keep from nose-diving us into the ground. However, I am curious about times when I was in danger but never knew it.

I believe in a sovereign God and am confident of his loving protection. Sometimes His agents are angels: *Behold, I send an angel before you to guard you on the way and to bring you to the place that I have prepared* (Exodus 23:20).

A pastor once said that our angels get out of the car once we exceed the speed limit. I do not know about the theological integrity of that idea, but I do trust God to assign the heavenly host roles of protection. I am grateful for that, whether I am aware of the what, when, where, and how or not.

Today's Truth: For he will command his angels concerning you to guard you in all your ways. On their hands they will bear you up, lest you strike your foot against a stone. Psalm 91:11-12

JANUARY 26

TOUGH TRAILS TO THE TOP

It was a chilly but relatively mild day for late January. A new friend of mine said she liked to hike. Well then, the only thing to do was to head for the hills. We met up at the base of the mountain, excited to be tromping northward on the Appalachian Trail.

After donning our light packs that carried a little water and a few snacks, we headed up the trail. And when I say up, I mean up—for nearly three miles. The first several minutes of zealousness for being outdoors induced heavy breathing on my part. I backed off the pace and settled in for the long climb ahead. Pam followed along, hiking hard.

I was chatting freely about this and that, thoroughly enjoying the time together. Within ten or fifteen minutes, however, Pam asked if we could take a break. "I think I'm going to throw up." Doubled over, it was obvious she was in a lot of pain. She stepped off the trail and began to gag and wretch. I was not sure what to do, but it did not strike me as a response to overdoing it. When she confessed she had eaten gas station chicken salad, we surmised a touch of food poisoning may be to blame. I thought maybe our hike would be short-lived. She was in a bad way. Nevertheless, once the active hurling subsided, she decided to soldier on. Afterall, she started with the goal of making it to the top. This unexpected set-back was not going to foil the plan.

Why is it that hard things often side-track us from forward progress? Why do we need to actively fight against the urge to quit and turn back? Why must we face the fear of what lies ahead? Because sometimes that is the only way to advance while growing stronger.

The phrase *be strong and courageous* followed by *do not be afraid, do not be discouraged* was an encouragement to the ancient Jewish leader, Moses. Moses passed it on to Joshua, and centuries later King David heard those words who then told his son Solomon, the wisest man ever to live. It was probably the first time ever that "whisper down the lane" maintained the integrity of the message.

When the trail to the top is tough, there is good reason to be strong and courageous; to not be afraid or discouraged. It was not just a message to the ancient. It is just as true today.

Today's Truth: Be on your guard; stand firm in the faith; be courageous; be strong. 1 Corinthians 16:13.

January 27

Listen

The women were going at it; serving, jumping, setting, transitioning, spiking, tipping, and diving all over the floor. Coach interrupted the frantic play at one point to ask the setter if she heard the hitter call for the ball. The answer was no. To the hitter went this advice. "Be loud and call for the ball. The setter needs to hear your voice to know where you are."

On another field of play not so familiar, Emperor penguins dot the Antarctica seascape. Once the females lay their eggs, each father carefully balances that egg on his feet, keeping the precious cargo tucked under his warm feathers for weeks at a time. The females head for the sea, sometimes 60 miles away. After gorging themselves for a month or two, they waddle their way back to the clan of 3000 father penguins, ready to provide much needed sustenance for the newly hatched babies who have remained safe under the father's protective covering.

But how do these penguins find their mates in the crowd where everyone looks dapper in their tuxedos? The male penguins form a line and march by the females, all the while sounding off their unique cries. Eventually, mommy and daddy penguin, along with the chick, reunite because they recognize the unique call. The process is extraordinary.

Coach Green, a women's basketball coach, challenges his players to "Stop, look, and listen." Why? Because he wants the teams' undivided attention. Listening intently is important. No less than 23 times does the writer of Proverbs instruct us to listen carefully. Listening is a mark of a wise person. The contrary, however, is total foolishness.

Sheep are not regarded as particularly astute animals. And yet, they do one thing well. They recognize their shepherd's voice. Jesus used this truth when pointing out our position as sheep and His as a shepherd. *I am the good shepherd; I know my sheep and my sheep know me... They too will listen to my voice, and there shall be one flock and one shepherd* (John 10:14, 16).

I need to be wise. I need to learn to be a better sheep. I need to shut up, talk less, and listen more.

Today's Truth: Listen to advice and accept discipline, and at the end you will be counted among the wise. Proverbs 19:20

JANUARY 28

NAKED AND AFRAID

Okay. No judgment please, but I have been curiously drawn to the TV show with buck naked people wandering around jungles, savannahs, and any other locale deemed God-forsaken and dangerous. One man and one woman must survive 21 days with only one survival item each. These go into a canvas bag that conveniently covers the most private bits of anatomy. Sometimes they make it. Sometimes they do not.

The producers recently added a twist. The challenge still involves nakedness, but there is no partner to help, no one to talk to. They are left alone to find food. Left alone to build shelter. Left alone to get fire. Left alone with no one to talk to or argue with. Being alone almost always proves to be simultaneously both a blessing and a curse.

I enjoy being alone though I have never had a multi-day, truly alone experience. Still, being alone is my way of recharging batteries and refocusing my priorities. However, lots of people hate being alone even for a single night. Instead, they make calls, find something to do, and head out.

The whole idea of being alone is interesting. Is it a good thing or bad? In the beginning, God stated that he did not make man for him to be alone. He gave him a woman. That was good.

On the other hand, aloneness is essential. Jacob was left alone to wrestle with the angel all night (Genesis 23). It was the only way to learn. Moses was to climb the mountain alone to fulfill his appointment to interact with God (Exodus 24). The woman in 1 Kings 3 bore a child and was alone three days later when he died. She had to mourn by herself to fully appreciate the miracle that would take place. In Matthew 14, Jesus went off by himself to pray. He needed that time alone, as did the disciples. Left alone in the storm-tossed boat, his followers needed the contrast of providential separation and their need of the Savior when he walked to them on the water.

There is purpose in being alone. And yet, while we might feel lonely, we are never wholly alone. Jesus said so.

Today's Truth: The one who sent me is with me; he has not left me alone, for I always do what pleases him. John 8:29

January 29

Comparison

I just looked up the entrants list for an upcoming 50K race and was dismayed at what I found. Selecting the female category and then the sub-category of 60–69-year-olds, I found not one or two names other than mine, but six total. That normally does not happen.

There are not a lot of female sexagenarians who race these kinds of distances. As a result, the pressure to outrun those in my age group is not that big of a deal. But now? In two and a half weeks, I will need to toe the line knowing I will be specifically compared to at least five other women. I already feel nervous and wimpy thinking that I might run poorly and get beat out by these other highly capable women. I do not like this performance-based comparison and the emotional baggage it bears.

Comparison is the kiss of death. For any tween girl not locked away in a convent, the pressure to look and dress a certain way is powerful. For the student bringing home a slate of "Cs" when a sibling's report contains nothing but "As," the comparison is suffocating. And when a "thick" athlete compares herself to a waif-like distance runner, she alters her eating, forcing her body into the perfect mold—at least as she sees it.

We all fall prey to this vixen of discontent. Try these: I am not gifted like her. I look old. Everyone on Facebook has perfect families. I am a spiritual lightweight. Just look at her flawlessly composed pics of coffee cup, open bible, and beautifully doodled journal.

Given, it is a human trait to compare. But should we? Is comparison valid? And if so, to whom or what standard shall the comparison be?

On a certain level, comparison for the purpose of defining where we are and where we want to be may be valid. "I run a 17:09 5K. I want to run 16:45 and qualify for that meet," for example. [I don't and never will, if you are wondering.] But when we start comparing ourselves to another, we run into difficulty. God made each of us with a specific purpose and has gifted us in unique ways. Should we strive for excellence? Yes. Should we be the best possible "me"? Of course. Should we try to be someone else? Nope.

Stop the insanity. Stop the comparison.

Today's Truth: For we are God's handiwork, created in Christ Jesus to do good works, which God prepared in advance for us to do. Ephesians 2:10

January 30

The Masterpiece

Grab a piece of paper, a pen, and find a friend to read you the instructions.

With a piece of paper in front of you and eyes closed (no cheating, please), try to draw what is read aloud.

1) Draw a rectangular house with a triangle roof in the middle of your paper. 2) Draw a tree to the left of the house 3) Draw a sun in the upper right corner of your paper 4) Draw a door in the middle of your house 5) Draw a dog under the tree 6) Draw a flower to the right of the door 7) Draw in two windows in the house 8) Draw a cat by the flower 9) Put a chimney on your roof with smoke coming out of it 10) Draw three stick figures holding hands to the right of the house.

Okay. You can now open your eyes. What does your artwork look like? My guess is that it is a bit of a mess. Why is that? Well, the simple answer is because you did it blind. It is hard to keep anything neat and clean if you 1) cannot see what you are doing and 2) don't even know what the picture is supposed to look like.

Sometimes our approach to life is made difficult by the blindfolds we wear. We do this and that and the other thing, but everything gets messy because we have no point of reference. So, try as we might, the pictures of our life are filled with people, places, and things that just don't mesh.

But what if our eyes were wide open? What if we realized what our God-given purpose looked like? Do you think the elements making up the whole would be recognizable? Do you think we would be more apt to be content in whatever that picture was intended to be?

Life is messy. Life is hard. But in a way, it needs to be. Perseverance is never actualized until we suffer. But I think it is possible to bring on unnecessary chaos simply because our eyes are shut tight to the truth.

Open your eyes. Let Jesus create a masterpiece.

Today's Truth: Therefore, since we are surrounded by such a great cloud of witnesses, let us throw off everything that hinders and the sin that so easily entangles. And let us run with perseverance the race marked out for us, fixing our eyes on Jesus, the pioneer and perfecter of faith. Hebrews 12:1, 2a

January 31

Perfect the Way You Are

Grandma went through the whole routine with her beloved granddaughter: make cookies, play dolls, bubble bath, jammies on, snacks, teeth brushed, and then off to bed. As she tucked the blond-headed waif-like sweetheart under the covers, the young girl suddenly fell contemplative. "I miss my Daddy," she whispered, hugging Mr. Bear tightly in her little arms.

"I know, Baby Girl. But Daddy is away getting better. He will be home in not too long," Grandma consoled.

With misty, wide-open eyes, the granddaughter offered but one comment before folding her tiny hands to offer a prayer of thanksgiving for her father. "But he doesn't need to get better. He's perfect just the way he is."

Perfect the way he is. Whoa. Despite her daddy's challenges with alcohol, she saw no imperfections. She had nothing but unconditional love for him.

This is a profound concept. When God looks at His children, we are positionally "perfect just the way we are." The shed blood of Jesus Christ makes us righteous. We have not merited the position. We bring absolutely nothing to the table. Rather, it is by grace alone through faith alone that brings reconciliation (Ephesians 2:8, 9).

But we err thinking we can continue in our sin. Paul said in Romans 6:1, *What shall we say then? Shall we continue in sin, that grace may abound?* Then he offers a logical treatise on what our mindset should be. *Therefore, do not let sin reign in your mortal body so that you obey its evil desires. Do not offer any part of yourself to sin as an instrument of wickedness, but rather offer yourselves to God as those who have been brought from death to life; and offer every part of yourself to him as an instrument of righteousness* (Vs 12, 13).

Though our sin is great, His grace is greater. His perfection makes us positionally perfect.

Today's Truth: What then? Are we to sin because we are not under law but under grace? By no means! . . . But thanks be to God, that you who were once slaves of sin have become obedient from the heart to the standard of teaching to which you were committed, and, having been set free from sin, have become slaves of righteousness. Romans 6:15-18

FEBRUARY 1

RAG-TAG BATTLES

With Addyson in tow, we made the trek across campus to the arena. Our women's basketball team was slated for a showdown with a top 25 program. We lost to them in the conference championship game last year and lost earlier this season on their home court. It was time for a do-over, but there was just one problem. Our bench had dwindled.

One of our starting point guards decided to quit right before Christmas. A tall, talented, red-shirted post player decided to transfer to another school just a few weeks ago. A senior starter is out for the season. A junior starting forward just tore the PCL in her knee. Two more players were out with the flu and stomach virus two days ago, and as it turned out, one of those players hurled five times during tonight's game. Another player lost her cookies watching the first one puke. During half-time a post player upchucked her lunch when she watched the sick guard have IV fluids run into her arm. Not exactly a promising line-up against a solid, high performing team.

If you are expecting a David and Goliath story, you will not get one. But we did have moments of brilliance even with a rag-tag team. We led the first quarter, were down by 1 at half, got outplayed in the 3rd by eight points, and could not pull it out in the 4th. The whole scenario reminds me of an ancient incident that was similar (except for the fact that those guys ended up winning.)

David had fled King Saul's wrath. Hiding out in a dank cave, news spread of the young warrior's new residence. And guess what? About 400 guys showed up to join forces, but this is how they were described: *And everyone who was in distress, and everyone who was in debt, and everyone who was bitter in soul, gathered to him. And he became commander over them* (1 Samuel 22:2-4).

I wonder if David was skeptical. Had I been put in that position, I would have called the nearest employment agency and hired up some highly trained mercenaries.

But that is not how God works. He uses those of us who are weak and worn, tired and torn. And when He does that, his purposes are completed. Just ask the Apostle Paul.

Today's Truth: For the sake of Christ, then, I am content with weaknesses, insults, hardships, persecutions, and calamities. For when I am weak, then I am strong. 2 Corinthians 12:10

February 2

Always the same

Today is special for several reasons. The simple fact that it is Sunday is reason enough to celebrate corporate worship. But it is also Super Bowl Sunday. Grocery stores are flooded with fans buying chips, salsa, and wings. But did you know that for the particularly well-informed, today, 02/02/2020, is the first palindromic date in this format to occur since 09/31/1390.

Okay. I admit it. I saw this fun fact on Facebook and needed to google the meaning of that impressive "p" word. Here is what I found a palindrome to be: "a word, number, phrase, or other sequence of characters which reads the same backward as forward." Consider madam, racecar, and 10801. All read the exact same whether it be left to right or right to left. Tattarrattat (a knock on the door) is the longest palindrome in the English language. Sentences can even be palindromic. Check this out: "Mr. Owl ate my metal worm."

So, what is the big deal? Besides it being a stimulating intellectual pursuit of debatable value, the idea that something can be the same forwards or backwards is sort of cool. Does that mean things can be the same right-side up or upside down? Is it possible for something to be true then and now? How about now and in the future? Are there things that simply do not change regardless of the who, what, where, when and why?

Though my questions are rhetorical, the answer is yes. Yes. Some things never change. The love of God. The faithfulness of God. The immutable character of God. The merciful and graciousness of God. The self-existent, self-sufficient infiniteness of God. God is always omnipresent, omniscient, and omnipotent. God is good, and wise, and just. God always hates sin because He is holy but provides redemption for the sinner. God is sovereign.

Children need to know what to expect from their parents. It provides consistency and confidence in the relationship. How much more valuable for the children of God to know what to expect of their Father?

Today's Truth: Jesus Christ is the same yesterday and today and forever. Hebrews 13:8

FEBRUARY 3

WHO IS MY COACH?

It was an awfully early Monday morning. But that did not stop the alarm from chirping before dawn. It was a new week, a new day, and we would all meet the newly appointed assistant coach. Anticipation was high.

Coaching on any level is tough, but college coaching is beastly. When the new head football coach arrived last year, not one of the previous coaches retained their jobs. Long-term stability is not a descriptive of college coaching. Every one of these coaches had to scatter to parts unknown to continue their careers, or they had to make the tough choice to shift gears onto a new career path. Either way, it is a brutal truth for the coach and family.

The flux in the life of a coach is tough. But what about the impact it has on the athlete? Consider the high school kid who was recruited by Coach A two years ago. Her life has been planned around being part of Coach A's program. But Coach A gets the axe. Coach B has other plans that do not include this player. The kid is left to wander the planet.

Or how about the athlete who played a couple years for Coach A. Coach B comes along and has a choice to make. Does he keep this player or fill the spot with one of the chosen few identified in his own recruiting process?

From the athlete's perspective, her academic pursuits, position and/or scholarship are all subject to the coach's decisions. Therefore, it is not a stretch to see that submitting oneself to this process can be incredibly taxing.

It is doubtful that the coaching conundrum will change anytime soon. But there is certainly ample opportunity for learning to submit to authority even when it has the potential to change. It is a chance to keep perspective. An opportunity to know what constitutes proper attitudes toward "masters," whether good or bad.

You do not have to be an athlete to understand the challenge of surrendering to authority. It takes a great deal of maturity to appreciate that while we cannot be responsible for the actions and attitudes of others, we are most certainly responsible for our own.

Today's Truth: Therefore, it is necessary to submit to the authorities, not only because of possible punishment but also as a matter of conscience. Romans 13:5

February 4

Be quick but don't hurry

In their desire to be loud, play aggressively, and pound the other team into the ground, the play was frantic. Sure, it was a practice session for this university volleyball team, but they were cultivating habits that would surely characterize them as a team.

"Okay. Hold there," instructed the head coach. "We need to be quick, but don't hurry."

This quote was one of his favorites from basketball legend, John Wooden, and it was exactly what the team needed. There was a lot of extraneous action that neither promoted nor facilitated optimal play. Rather, it looked helter-skelter with players screaming non-descriptive gobbledygook and reacting in poor timing to balls coming at them. What Coach really wanted them to do was take a deep breath, read the play, and then react quickly and with self-control. The hurriedness (crazy, unproductive actions) needed to go. Quick, accurate analysis and action needed to be developed.

What usually happens when we hurry? The quality of our work decreases. We make mistakes, often wasting time, money, and effort to yield only sub-optimal results. If we are hasty in decision-making, we fail to consider the ramifications of those decisions which are often not pleasurable. And what about the "open mouth, insert foot" haste mistake? Things fly out of our mouth that we wish could boomerang right back in. Words spoken in rage light a fire that is not easily extinguished.

Coach Wooden—and King David—were onto something. Hurrying haphazardly is not helpful, but being mindfully reactive is advantageous. David accentuated God's character by asking him to respond quickly. He wrote, *Hasten, O God, to save me; come quickly, Lord, to help me* (Psalm 70:1).

Perhaps we are talking about being prudent. Prudent people respond quickly to danger, but the foolish hurry along without thought (Proverbs 22:3). The prudent give thought to their ways before rushing along at break-neck speed (Proverbs 14:8). Prudence keeps us from letting our tongues get ahead of our brains (Proverbs 10:19).

Be prudent. Be quick. But do not hurry.

Today's Truth: Prudence is a fountain of life to the prudent, but folly brings punishment to fools. Proverbs 16:22

FEBRUARY 5

PROVE YOUR IDENTITY

It was ten years in the making. I could not put it off any longer. Having gathered all the documents I could possibly need, I inhaled deeply and took my place in line.

Visits to the DMV are like a woman's yearly trip to the mammography center: necessary but with a high potential for pain. It was time to renew my driver's license, and the new, fandangled Real ID type carried with it more requirements. I attempted to complete this task last month but was turned away. Though I had my current license, current passport, old passport with my maiden name, a bill with my address, my original social security card, and my birth certificate, I had nothing to prove that Rebekah Eleanor DeLancey was the same person as Rebekah Eleanor Trittipoe. I needed a current social security card and/or my marriage certificate showing the change of name. Alternately, a W2 that displayed my social security number would suffice.

Having no earthly idea where our nearly 43-year-old marriage certificate might be, I opted for the W2 option. Thirty minutes and $53.00 later, the task was accomplished.

Proving my identity was a complicated but necessary matter. But I wonder, is there also a need to prove our identity as true Believers? The answer is a resounding yes. We were known by God before being formed in the womb. By faith we believe and become a child of God. We were predestined to be adopted into God's family. We are made acceptable in God's eyes. Our old self is crucified with Christ. Our new self puts away sin. We are part of the body of Christ. We are given a specific role in that body. We are people who can declare the praises of Him who pulled us from darkness.

We are loved lavishly. We were chosen. We were given the faith to believe. We are heirs of God and no longer slaves. We know all things work together according to God's perfect plan. We are set free from sin. We are made righteous in and through the work of Christ. *His divine power has given us everything we need for a godly life through our knowledge of him who called us by his own glory and goodness* (2 Peter 1:3).

Let's prove who we really are by the way we live.

Today's Truth: In the same way, let your light shine before others, that they may see your good deeds and glorify your Father in heaven. Matthew 5:16

February 6

Bruised

Later today I have an appointment with my cardiologist. After failing a screening test for coronary disease, I ended up on the cardiac catheterization table on July 29, 2019. It was quite the experience. Having spent nearly 25-years as a cardiovascular perfusionist, I was well acquainted with cath labs and operating rooms. I contacted my favorite surgeon to make sure he was okay doing my case in the event surgery was necessary. He said yes, but there was no need to see him professionally. Rather, a stent in the left anterior descending coronary artery was sufficient to take care of the partially occluded vessel.

In the aftermath of that procedure, I was placed on a regimen of drugs. Given my strong family history of coronary disease and high cholesterol, I take a statin-type drug. But more importantly for the sake of stent patency, a low-dose aspirin and a platelet-inhibiting drug have also been prescribed. Because the platelets (that are necessary for clotting) are inhibited, I bleed and bruise easily. For how black, blue, and purple my arms and legs appear, I am surprised no one has called the police to report potential abuse.

I have been told I need to stay on these drugs for a lifetime. Obviously, it would not be optimal if that stent clotted off in such an important artery. The resulting heart attack—or worse—would not be good! But on the other hand, the obvious bruising on my legs make me question if this level of platelet inhibition is necessary.

Bruising always indicates injury, injury requires treatment, and treatment leads to healing. I think of the One who understood this the most. The prophet Isaiah wrote of the coming Savior, Jesus Christ, who would need to be bruised for our sake. He would need to personally endure the bleeding so that each of us could be treated and healed from our sinful status.

The cross was the venue for his substitutionary punishment. But his death and subsequent resurrection provided a way for our reconciliation to the Father.

Today's Truth: But he was pierced for our transgressions, he was crushed [bruised] for our iniquities; the punishment that brought us peace was on him, and by his wounds we are healed. Isaiah 53:5

JANUARY 7

BEST LAID PLANS

We had a visitor today at the early morning practice session. "Maggie" was a tall drink of water, as they say here in the south. At 6'1", she looked like the volleyball player she was. Maggie was at practice today because she is considering transferring to our program. It was a convoluted road that brought her here.

As a talented high school and club player, round one of the recruiting cycle began in her sophomore year. When she traveled to the most tropical, vacation-destination state in the Union, she fell in love with the program, gleefully signing on the dotted line. She was on a wide-open path for her college years, or so she thought.

Turns out the program lost all their funding, and with that, her scholarship was a thing of the past. Being in the spring of her senior year, a time when signed athletes are getting excited to begin their collegiate careers, Maggie was in flux. The recruiting season was basically done. Colleges and universities had, for the most part, completed their recruiting rosters. This left Maggie high and dry.

High and dry, that is, until a NCAA Division 1 school decided to build a volleyball program. Maggie signed a one-year scholarship contract, completed her first college semester, and looked forward to the upcoming fall season. But her world again turned upside down when she found out her contract would not be renewed. The school was attempting to recruit experienced college players for the first official D1 season. So, into the transfer portal she went, looking for a school to call home.

I doubt Maggie ever anticipated not one, not two, but three recruiting seasons. That was certainly not the way she planned it. She thought her future was all set the first time around. But that was not true. Rather, she is now experiencing God's sovereignty in a whole new way. Maggie can retrospectively see how providence brought her to this point. She is understanding how the circumstances are providing light for this journey. She is not quite sure how it will all turn out but is confident that God is the one in charge.

Today's Truth: In their hearts humans plan their course, but the Lord establishes their steps. Proverbs 16:9

February 8

All I Need Is Christ

It is a Saturday evening and Gary and I are doing what old people do—at least these old people: sitting on the couch, nodding off with the soft glow of the television in the background. It is laughable.

Nevertheless, we decided to watch a movie together, one we thought was Hallmark-like. What we got was not that. It turned out to be deeper with real-life conflict and temptation. At its conclusion, we felt a sense of heaviness.

Because we used Gary's computer to watch the movie, he started clicking through worship music videos at the end of the movie. He cued up various songs from the modern hymn writers, Sovereign Grace Music. We worshipped together, just him and me, without ear-deafening percussion. It was an opportunity to "Turn your eyes upon Jesus. Look full in His wonderful face. And the things of earth will become strangely dim in the light of his glory and grace."

Allow the first two stanzas of "All I need is Christ" speak for themselves.

Verse 1: I once was lost in darkest night
Yet thought I knew the way
The sin that promised joy and life
Had led me to the grave
I had no hope that You would own
A rebel to Your will
And if You had not loved me first
I would refuse You still
Verse 2: But as I ran my hell-bound race
Indifferent to the cost
You looked upon my helpless state
And led me to the cross
And I beheld God's love displayed
You suffered in my place
You bore the wrath reserved for me
Now all I know is grace
Chorus: Hallelujah! All I have is Christ
Hallelujah! Jesus is my life

Today's Truth: For even the Son of Man did not come to be served, but to serve, and to give his life as a ransom for many. Mark 10:45

FEBRUARY 9

My father was on his death bed in 1986 following high-risk cardiac surgery. As a perfusionist, I knew the gravity of the situation. After several rocky hours in post-surgical recovery, things went from bad to worse. A left ventricular assist device was inserted. But it was all for naught. Sometime the next day I was asked to access his condition and make the decision when to terminate support. It was heart-wrenching to turn off each machine and watch the last few beats of his heart fade and finally cease.

Little did I know the significance of that event in my own career. It seemed inevitable that I was the perfusionist tending the complicated devices when it was clear the patient would succumb. The surgeon and chaplain would hug me before inviting the family in to share those last moments. It was then my job to turn off one device and then another, the white noise lessening with each push of the off switch. I mourned with the family because I could truly say, "I know what you are going through."

We are in a family situation that few can understand. A few of our friends ask how things are going. But very few act. I do not believe for a second that it is lack of concern or disinterest. I suspect it is because they have no ability to empathize. They have never been in our situation. They do not know what it is like.

However, one elder has not only taken interest but has translated his interest into action. You know why? It is because he has challenges in his own family. Because he understands, his actions speak louder than words. We are forever indebted to his kindness and practical ministry to our family.

Let's not forget that the sum of our life experiences is for the purpose of pointing others to the Father. There is a reason why God providentially brings circumstances into our lives. Those hard things allow us to encourage, support, and empathize with what our brothers and sisters are going through.

God allowed me to be involved in my Dad's final days for a purpose: to minister to families who needed someone to say, "I understand." To whom can you say the same?

Today's Truth: Rejoice with those who rejoice; mourn with those who mourn. Romans 12:15

February 10

Sucker!

Neil has an office beside mine. Since arriving at the university, we have had plenty of opportunity to get to know each other. He is a professional counselor for our student athletes. I am a chaplain and character coach. Our work often complements each other's.

But we have something else in common. Neil is a runner. He has conquered seven marathons and enjoys racing frequently at any distance. But it was not until he arrived in Lynchburg that he began running trails. Of course, I take every opportunity to talk about ultrarunning and the "call of the wild."

Several months ago, I planted the idea of running Holiday Lake 50K for his first foray into the ultra world. The race is in six days. Earlier this morning he told me he signed up over the weekend. Got you, Sucker!

Neil is asking a lot of questions about strategies for this race. Having never run past the 26.1 mark, he does not know what to expect. What should he carry? What are the aid stations like? Should he have a drop bag? How should he adjust his pace for the single-track trail? Should he run or hike the hills? What things should he be thinking to mentally embrace the miles outside his current experience?

I understand his mixed emotions. As an experienced ultra-distance runner, there has never been a race where some of those same questions have not popped into my head. But the one thing I know to be true is this: learning to embrace the adventure, the unknown, the inevitable pain is paramount. We must accept what we encounter and adapt accordingly.

It takes faith to venture out. Noah never saw rain but built an ark. Abraham traveled to a place he had never been. Moses' parents hid him in a basket in an act of civil disobedience. The Israelites risked crossing a parted Red Sea despite their fear. Years later, their army did laps around Jericho to make the walls come tumblin' down. And throughout the centuries since, by faith Believers have endured torture and death because they dared to follow Christ into the unknown.

Be bold. Embrace the adventure. Accept the challenge. Walk (or run) by faith.

Today's Truth: For we walk by faith, not by sight. 2 Corinthians 5:7

FEBRUARY 11

ME WITH YOU

Brett Ledbetter wrote a book entitled "What Drives Winning." The author postulates that developing a great team depends wholly on developing both moral and performance character skills. His argument is compelling.

One of those performance character skills is being competitive. Many of us see competition as war; a battle to be won. Rivalries grow and produce "win at any cost" mentalities. It becomes us verses them, good verses evil, winner verses loser.

But there is competition between teammates. Pretend that there are three first basemen on the softball team. All three want to be the starting player, but only one can get the nod. Let's be honest. Might the other two hope their teammate commits a couple errors and goes 0 – 4 at the plate? My guess is yes. They might hope their teammate fails. Would it be good for the present benchsitters? Possibly. Would it be good for the team as a whole? No.

In its origin, the word compete means to "strive together," to achieve a level of play that we could not attain on our own. Competing cannot take place without a partner, whether it be a teammate or the team across the net. It should be a complementary relationship, not adversarial. I compete against what I was yesterday, but I do that by striving with you, not against you, to be the best I can be.

This concept is principled in Scripture. Remember when there was a conflict between the followers of Apollos and Paul? People took sides, creating an air of contempt that weakened the gospel team. In other words, they were competing against, not striving with, their fellow believers. The result? A divided, weaker house.

Paul addressed this situation by screaming "STOP IT!" The name of Christ was not going to be advanced with such attitudes. Those people needed to unite and hone each other as iron sharpens iron (Proverbs 27:17). Only then would their impact be the greatest.

Whether on the court, in the home, or in our churches, we are better together.

Today's Truth: I appeal to you, brothers and sisters, in the name of our Lord Jesus Christ, that all of you agree with one another in what you say and that there be no divisions among you, but that you be perfectly united in mind and thought. 1 Corinthians 1:10

February 12

Broken legs and oily heads

On the way home from work last night, I heard an interesting story about sheep. My ears perked up since I have so many images and assumptions about sheep from my Sunday School days.

My Grandma had a picture framed in her house. It depicted a shepherd with a baby lamb wrapped around his shoulders. Knowing Christ is depicted as the Good Shepherd, I assumed (until I knew better) that he was simply giving the little fella a ride. While Lamby got a ride, it was not free.

If a sheep refused to obey, the shepherd purposefully broke one of its legs. He then bound the leg and hoisted it to his shoulders. While this sounds cruel, it was for the sheep's own good. In the aftermath of healing, the sheep became very loyal and stayed by the shepherd's side.

You anoint my head with oil; my cup overflows (Psalm 23:5). This verse is so familiar, found in the chapter beginning with *The* Lord *is my shepherd*. I always thought the head anointing referred to the way a king was symbolically installed into royal office. I was wrong. The 23rd Psalm is about shepherds caring for sheep, not kings. A good shepherd knew to cover the heads of his sheep with oil. Why? Because the oil acted like insect repellant. If he failed to do this, insects such as flies, ticks, lice, and others would take up residence in the ear and nose canals. The insects then lay eggs which hatch. The new "hatchees" burrow themselves into the sheep's brain causing tremendous pain. The infected sheep was then driven to bang its head against rocks, breaking the skull and ultimately bringing on its own death. Not a pretty picture.

I am one of the Good Shepherd's lambs. Am I happy when he breaks one of my legs to get my attention? No. Am I pleased to become a greasy oil head? Probably not. Nonetheless, he does these things because he loves me and wants the best for me. All he wants in return is for me to stay close and follow Him .

Today's Truth: The Lord is my shepherd, I lack nothing. . . .. You anoint my head with oil; my cup overflows. Surely your goodness and love will follow me all the days of my life, and I will dwell in the house of the Lord forever. Psalm 23

FEBRUARY 13

NOT THINKING STRAIGHT

Have you ever had a moment when you looked around to see if anyone saw "it" happen? I did. Yesterday.

I was hurriedly walking across campus to my office, hands in coat pockets to fend off the chill that comes with drizzly days. To shortcut the walk, I left the sidewalk to step up onto the covered patio of the athletic center. Somehow, someway, I failed to navigate the eighteen-inch step up. I do not know what happened, but my ankle caught on the ledge and launched me headlong. Hands still stuck in my pockets, the first body part to hit the unforgiving concrete surface was my face. Yowzah! Did I just break my nose?

Scrambling to my feet once my head cleared, I looked around to see if anyone was sitting in the glass-walled room that marks that corner of the building. If they were, they would have seen me reaching to my face to access the damage. I worried that my nose would start bleeding and never stop. Turns out my nose and cheek were red and bleeding only slightly, but my scraped leg was saturating my tights with sticky blood. Dazed, I made a beeline for the bathroom. I looked rough and my face and head hurt—a lot. Two Tylenols and a heavy layer of makeup became top priority.

There is little doubt that the face plant gave me a concussion, one of the athletic trainers confirming that self-diagnosis. This morning, my face and head still ache, my vision is blurry, and I have trouble finding words when speaking. Even as I was dressing this morning, I kept forgetting what I was doing and what I should do next. Feeling this disjointed is not pleasant. I just want to go home and sleep it off.

I suspect we can fall victim to spiritual concussions as well. Take, for instance, what happens when we run into a brick wall of trouble. The concussion we suffer can make us take our eyes off the prize, to become discontent and despondent, even fearful. The non-concussed Believer keeps perspective and thinks biblically. Of course, thinking in clear biblical terms necessitates we know God by knowing his Word, which is the best dose of medicine for a jumbled brain.

Today's Truth: I have hidden your word in my heart that I might not sin against you. Psalm 119:11

February 14

Chocolate Pie

The way to a man's heart just might be chocolate pie. At least that is the way it works in our house.

I know this is Valentine's Day. There are expectations for couples to be incredibly romantic. But it's funny how "romantic" has an average price tag of $142. There are dinners at fancy restaurants, freshly cut flowers, and candy in red heart packages, not to mention jewelry that puts a major dent in the bank account.

But I have a confession to make. None of those things have ever been important to me—which is a good thing because Gary, the hubster of almost 43 years, is not like that either. I honestly cannot think of the last time Valentine's Day was anything but another day. However, do not fret, there are hardly any holidays that make our worlds stop spinning. For the most part, Valentine's Day comes and goes without much fanfare.

With all that said, Gary does love the chocolate pie that has become a standard in our family: a homemade crust, a layer of golden-tipped meringue followed by creamy dark chocolate ganache followed by a light and fluffy chocolate layer, all with a hint of cinnamon. The pie goes into the freezer and comes out ready to be eagerly consumed.

Tonight, I made that pie for Gary. It was not the conclusion to a special candlelit dinner. Nope. I made it after we ate pizza in front of the TV. I know this gift that comes in a glass pie plate is appreciated for the taste. But I suspect it is the effort it takes—which is substantial—that he appreciates more. It is how I can say "I love you" in a scrumpdilli-ish way.

"Love is a many splendid thing," but how it is shown is quite another. When Gary meets me at the car to help with groceries, that is love. When he checks the oil and replaces the front brakes on my car, that is love. When Gary rubs my feet, it is *real* love. (He hates feet.) And when he organizes the front bedroom that doubles as his hunting gear room, I know for sure his love is unbounded! I am a fortunate woman.

Today's Truth: Love is patient, love is kind. It does not envy, it does not boast, it is not proud. It does not dishonor others, it is not self-seeking, it is not easily angered, it keeps no record of wrongs. Love does not delight in evil but rejoices with the truth. It always protects, always trusts, always hopes, always perseveres. Love never fails. 1 Corinthians 13:4-8a

February 15

Headed South

It was as good an excuse as ever. Gary's two sisters were headed to Florida and it seemed like a good time to join them. Joy, the younger sister, and her husband own a house in Lakeland. They frequent it often since it is close to where her childhood bestie and family lives. Jackie, the oldest of the three sibs and recent widow, lives in California and decided to fly in. A week of doing a lot of nothing in the presence of family seemed like a really good idea.

With address locked and loaded in the GPS, we headed south, deciding to drive about half the total distance of 850 miles. Once on I-95, it was easy to navigate to our hotel somewhere in South Carolina. In fact, it was so easy there was not a single turn. All we had to do was stay the course on the long highway that runs the length of the east coast.

It is way easier to travel when you know where you are going. Pity the poor Israelites when their exodus from Egypt became a reality. Initially, all they had to do was head north. But alas, they ended up wandering around the giant sandbox like a herd of lost sheep simply because they chose not to obey. For forty years they disobeyed directives, complained, whined, and acted like a bunch of spoiled, discontented children. As a result, their path to the promised land was anything but straight. Would it not have been better to take the most direct path resulting from a commitment to obedience?

Lest you think I am copping a "holier than they" attitude, I am not. I would probably have deviated from following the cloud by day and flame by night long before most. So, no judgment from me. I just think we need to be honest about our tendencies to run amok.

To be certain, it does not always make sense when God diverts us from a straight road to a curvey one. Still, the expectation is to keep trusting, keep walking. But frankly, when we find ourselves on a twisty-turny path, it might be simply because we have refused to obey. That's just dumb.

Today's Truth: Show me your ways, Lord, teach me your paths. Guide me in your truth and teach me, for you are God my Savior, and my hope is in you all day long. Psalm 25:4, 5

FEBRUARY 16

OLD BECOMES NEW

The day started with continuing our drive south to join up with Gary's siblings. 530 more miles landed us in Lakeland at Joy and Skip's Florida home. Across the street from Florida Southern College, this 1925 bungalow is enchanting. From the intricate railing on the front porch to the light-filled sunroom, this house has charm unending. But the charm was not always so obvious.

When my sister-in-law and her husband bought this house, it did not look like it does now. The porch posts and pillars were rotten at the bottom, walls had to be removed, paint scraped, plumbing and electric redone, and a tiny closet morphd into a marbled-floor bathroom. At one point, most of the other floors came out as well so the joists below could be replaced. It was a hot mess.

The house is small but beautiful, though there is a list of projects yet to be completed. Well-appointed rooms with stylish furnishings adorn each room. Still, this previously run-down house did not become exquisitely comfortable without a lot of planning and work.

From the day Adam and Eve decided to eat that piece of forbidden fruit, everything has gone downhill. Entropy happens. Things disintegrate, machines wear out, crops fail, and we grow old and rickety. To temporarily reverse these declines, it takes intentionality and energy input to make positive changes.

The only exception to this rule is this: When we become believers in Christ, he makes us new. *Therefore, if any man be in Christ, he is a new creature, old things are passed away; behold, all things are become new* (2 Corinthians 5:17). He takes us from being dead in sin to having life breathed into us by His grace alone.

But by God's plan, we are expected to actively put off the "old man" and put on the new. That, my friend, takes effort. The "old" in this house had to be addressed to make it beautiful and acceptable for inhabiting. We too, have some work to do.

Today's Truth: You were taught, with regard to your former way of life, to put off your old self, which is being corrupted by its deceitful desires; to be made new in the attitude of your minds; and to put on the new self, created to be like God in true righteousness and holiness. Ephesian 4:22-24

FEBRUARY 17

HOUSE AND HOME

The automatic door parted as I approached, allowing me entrance into the vast store. I smiled thinking about Addyson and her predictable actions. When she approaches such doors, her stance is strong, one leg in front of the other, arms outstretched toward the doors, fingers wiggling. Somehow, her "magic" always works at the motion-sensored entrances. With great pleasure, she glides through the opening like the powerful princess she fancies herself to be. My entry into IKEA was much less eventful though my excitement was sky-high.

Gary's sisters, Jackie and Joy, were my companions through the isles marked by directional arrows on the floor. Entire rooms are set up to give the shopper ideas for home beautification. There are kitchens, dining rooms, offices, kids' rooms, tables and chairs, bathrooms, living rooms, lights and lamps, and an entire floor given to every sort of kitchenware, houseware, curtains and linens, gadgets, and organizational fare imaginable.

If I was starting over in creating a comfortable home, I just might earn a top shopper award at this store. Even though I am weary of "stuff" and am increasingly drawn toward minimalism, I like the aesthetic of many of the pieces. However, what constitutes a home? What do I really need? What are necessities? What has absolutely no value in the long run?

If you look at references to "home" in the Bible, it is always a place of protection, a center for raising children, a "homebase" to return to, and a venue to extend hospitality. Home is where the Gospel is shared, where husbands and wives encourage one another, and is a place to be busy in necessary activity. Nowhere is it said, directly or otherwise, that our homes need to be magazine-worthy.

I am not implying we should live in squalor. However, it is important to first evaluate if we are creating an appropriate environment from which we can base our service both inside the home and out. Once we can answer yes to that, then we can create style and comfort inside our walls that best equips us to whatever service God has called us.

Today's Truth: Then they can urge the younger women to love their husbands and children, to be self-controlled and pure, to be busy at home, to be kind, and to be subject to their husbands, so that no one will malign the word of God. Titus 2: 4, 5

February 18

Ugly bruises

If you looked at my foot this morning, you would have thought I was recovering from a horrible ankle fracture. Halfway up my calf, the skin is discolored with a gothic rainbow of deep purples. There is a huge knot on my shin, around which the skin is pulled taut, rendering it tender to the touch. The discoloration and swelling extends across the top of my foot, down to my toe tips, and flanks both sides of my ankle. It is so gross to anyone having to look at it!

I'm thinking the same thing. When my face had the unfortunate encounter with concrete six days ago, my right leg must have slammed into the edge of the patio. A small cut on my shin resulted, which kept bleeding for the next several days. But who would have imagined that my leg and ankle could become such a terrible-looking appendage! I do not have full range of motion, the ankle is still swollen and sore, which leaves me wondering when I will be back to normal.

Though the initial wound was small, the consequences were huge. It gets me thinking about how a small sin in our life can lead to devastating outcomes, leaving us wondering how we ended up in such a mess.

No one with addictive behaviors ever set out to become an addict. Many started out sipping away to fit in with the crowd. Perhaps they saw friends experimenting with various drugs, some of which they concluded were "harmless." As time went on, the occasional drink became a habit, the party scene grew, and behaviors never before considered became a way of life. Life decisions became clouded. In the increasingly rare moments of sobriety, a self-hatred develops, but without a way out, this self-loathing further propels the individual into despair and a continuation of bad behaviors and consequences.

It is always a good idea to guard our thoughts and actions as if our life depends on it—because it does. We should never assume that "it could never happen to me." Let's learn to be proactive in guarding our hearts, friends, and situations.

Today's Truth: One who has unreliable friends soon comes to ruin, but there is a friend who sticks closer than a brother. Proverbs 18:24

FEBRUARY 19

BIRDS OF A FEATHER

Vacation is a wonderful thing. It had been such a long time coming I almost forgot what it felt like to be off the clock, foot loose and fancy free. The last few days have been filled with browsing junk shops, chatting for hours, and leisurely sipping piping-hot coffee.

This afternoon we headed to Tampa to rent an electric boat. Trolling along we gazed at six million-dollar houses as we watched the sun set in the west, the glow creating a fiery, brilliant display. My brother-in-law, who was captaining the boat, turned us toward the high-rise buildings dotting the shores along the downtown area. The warm air and gentle breeze created the perfect night for taking in the sights. Ice cream treats after our boating adventure was a perfect way to end the evening.

Adding to the vacation ambience, a three-mile walkway around the lake is a mere block from the house. I spend late nights and early mornings on the lovely lakeside journey. I am not alone. Walkers and runners are out at all hours to enjoy the sights and sounds. With huge areas of waterlilies and trees rising through the water's surface, birds numbering in the hundreds perch on limbs or waddle along the grassy berm. Ducks, pelicans, herons, swans, ibises, and even the pretty-in-pink and white rosette spoonbills congregate together. They seem to enjoy just being birds. They sing and search for food in the daytime and rest together come darkness. They seem to have life-work balance under control.

There is something to be said for that. I tend to be driven. There is so much work and ministry to be done, the thought of having short workdays or time away from campus strikes me as unrealistic. Intellectually, I know I need to be intentional about creating margin. It is important for my own health and that of my family.

Rest is necessary. When we look at Jesus himself, he took time away from the crowds and even his closest disciples to spend time alone. It was his time to connect deeply with his Father and gain strength for the work that followed.

I am so thankful for this opportunity to rest and recharge.

Today's Truth: After six days Jesus took Peter, James and John with him and led them up a high mountain, where they were all alone. Mark 9:2

February 20

Stop time, stop!

My daily pill boxes do not lie. The morning, evening, and bedtime flip-top plastic strips are equipped to stash a week's-worth of medications. The pink, blue, and green boxes were filled with my medicinal supplies before Gary and I headed to Florida. Each day since then I have dutifully taken the meds on que. Saturday, Sunday, and Monday I did so without much thought. But now by Tuesday, the truth of fleeting time has made itself known. After today, a single day's worth of pills remains. Ugh. Then it will be time to head back to reality.

Am I the only one who thinks time flies like a falcon and sometimes slows to sloth-like speed? Either way, it can be incredibly frustrating. This simple vacation has whisked by. The break was a long time coming. But the wait itself can be a killer.

Our family has been in a holding pattern since early December. One of our own has been biding his time in forced confinement. While there appears to be a magnificent transformation of his heart and mind, the time until he returns to us crawls by. I cannot begin to fathom what it has been like for him.

At first, we told ourselves we just had to get through Christmas and New Year's. The next milestone was to make it to the end of January. Then we figured if we could get to Valentine's Day, February would not be so bad given the short 29 days. Now, we are within two weeks of his homecoming and my heart skips a beat wondering if I can make it that long. And yet, there is hope. The sun will surely come up and go down daily, striking off the days as they come.

Time and its intersection with human emotion is quite interesting. The writer of Ecclesiastes penned words that have stood the test of time. There is a time for everything, and if you do not like it, this too will pass.

Today's Truth: There is a time for everything, and a season for every activity under the heavens. Ecclesiastes 3:1

FEBRUARY 21

TAKE A BITE OUT OF BICKERING

Gary and I were both out of sorts this morning. Maybe it was because we got up at 4:00 a.m. Perhaps it was the knowledge we had a thirteen-hour drive ahead of us. Or it could have been the gloom of a rainy and cool morning. But whatever it was, I did not like it one little bit.

Six days of reprieve from the pressures of life and jobs was over. I came to grips with that fact sometime yesterday. I spent time separating dirty clothes from clean, gathering up snack foods for the trip, and organizing the trunk of the car. Try as I might, there was nothing I could do to postpone the inevitable.

The night was very short by the time the alarm sounded its mournful cry. I had hardly slept but rolled out of bed to ready myself. Suitcases were stowed in the trunk despite the raindrops. Off we went, first to the airport to drop off Gary's sister, turning the car northeast after that. We were both sleepy and conversation was sparse. A missed exit here and a confused GPS there prompted words that were neither kind nor patient. We both knew something had to change; namely, our attitudes.

Finally, after one ugly exchange I sat rigid in my seat, angry and frustrated. The silence that followed was necessary lest we say something we regretted. Finally, Gary broke that quiet. "Do you still love me?" He reached over and took my hand. Still peeved, I placed my hand over his.

"Maybe. I'm still trying to be mad at you," I replied, now trying to suppress a thin smile. I married a good man who is loving and kind and considerate. It was unlike him to be short. Then again, I had not been all that pleasant either. I probably got what I deserved.

We are still in the car traveling north, but the air has been cleared. There is now a calmness brought about by a willingness to admit failure and seek reconciliation. What a reminder to guard our hearts and our tongues, to rid ourselves of selfishness, and to put love into action.

Today's Truth: Love is patient, love is kind. It does not envy, it does not boast, it is not proud. It does not dishonor others, it is not self-seeking, it is not easily angered, it keeps no record of wrongs. Love does not delight in evil but rejoices with the truth. It always protects, always trusts, always hopes, always perseveres. 1 Corinthians 13: 4–7

FEBRUARY 22

TEACH 'EM YOUNG

Gary and I love spending time with our just-turned-five-in-December grandkid. I picked her up this morning and it has been non-stop since then. Our first stop was a university tennis match on a sun-kissed day. We took our places above the courts in the stadium seating. Before long, she could not control the urge to belt out songs from Disney's *Moana*. Though her performances were charming, heartfelt, and highly entertaining, we needed to review the guidelines for tennis match etiquette before heading over to the women's basketball game.

Although she knows all the women who play on our team, game time is filled with racing to the top of the arena before sliding down on each section of handrail. On one occasion I looked up and could not spot her at the top of the steep steps. I dashed up those same steps to find her chatting it up with a female security guard positioned at one of the exit doors. Though the conversation looked pleasant and engaging, another discussion about the importance of staying in sight at all times ensued.

Toward evening's end, the time came for a warm bath in the old-fashioned claw foot tub. Addy loves to dump out a variety of toys that include dolls, little ponies, mermaids, and measuring cups. Tonight, she took pleasure in filling up the cups and placing objects in them to see the water overflow. It was time for a simple lesson about displacement. She caught on rapidly, realizing that her fist placed in a full cup would displace the same amount of water as the volume of her fist. She took the time to eloquently inform her PopPop (Gary) of this important principle of physics before heading off to bed.

"Teachable moments" are everywhere. I wish I would have recognized more of them when my kids were little. But it is fun in my grandma role to teach a wide assortment of things ranging from math to reading to baking to character skills to biblical principle, and so much more. It is an awesome privilege as well as a responsibility.

Today's Truth: Fix these words of mine in your hearts and minds; tie them as symbols on your hands and bind them on your foreheads. Teach them to your children, talking about them when you sit at home and when you walk along the road, when you lie down and when you get up. Write them on the doorframes of your houses and on your gates, Deuteronomy 11:18-20

FEBRUARY 23

NO FEAR

The girl takes after her daddy. Their hashtag should be #nofear.

With some time to kill after church, Addyson and I decided to pop into the SeaQuest attraction at the mall. It contains many aquariums as the name implies, but there are plenty of terrestrial creatures to touch, hold, or just look at. To name a few, lizards, tortoises, birds, wallabies, a porcupine, dart frogs, snakes, hedgehogs, savannah cats, and even a lazy sloth have homes in the repurposed retail space. Of course, there are marine and fresh-water fish galore in huge tanks.

But did I mention snakes? I purchased year-long passes for Addyson and me before the place opened. On most of our visits, an employee has offered visitors an encounter with a snake. Addy never wanted to take advantage of that. But something was different today. My little five-year old plopped herself on the bench beside the snake keeper. She calmly waited for the reptile to be placed in her hand. Never flinching, she allowed the snake to move about, petting its sleek, cool skin and smiling for a picture or two. When she spent sufficient time with the reptile, she handed it back and went on her merry way.

I wonder what made the difference. She had always been adamant that playing with snakes was not on her bucket list. But today, she desired the encounter.

How do we conquer fear? Sometimes it is by gaining confidence through experience. Rehearsing with success produces the willingness and tools necessary to send fear packing. When we see others accomplish that which makes us fearful, we are encouraged in our own efforts. Perhaps we fear because we have been "burnt" before and have no desire to repeat the same. Or maybe we feel alone and susceptible, fear generated by solitude.

I am still not sure why Addyson held the snake. However, since fear is such a real emotion, we are wise to rely on these truths to battle fear: 1) we are never alone 2) the Lord strengthens and aids and 3) since the Lord has called us by name, we are His forever. In the light of these realities, fear has no chance.

Today's Truth: So do not fear, for I am with you; do not be dismayed, for I am your God. I will strengthen you and help you; I will uphold you with my righteous right hand. . . "Do not fear, for I have redeemed you; I have summoned you by name; you are mine." Isaiah 41:10 and 43:1b

FEBRUARY 24

WHEN IT HURTS SO BAD

Between early morning practices, a board of advisors' lunch meeting, and countless details to tend to after being away last week, my day has been busy. But perhaps the most important responsibility was to chat with several young ladies who are hurting deeply.

There has been somewhat of a divide on a team I work with here on campus. Individually, all the girls are lovely. Nevertheless, whenever you get a bunch of females together, taking sides seems to be the norm. Though the backstory is complex and not suited for this venue, three of the players have banded together for support. From my perspective, each of the girls have been ostracized for entirely different reasons, none of which have much merit. Hence, these three have joined hands in solidarity.

About a week ago, one of their teammates had a birthday resulting in a celebratory party. The only problem was this: the three outcasts were the only members of the team who did not get an invite. Those at the party did not hold back posting pictures of the affair on social media. Today I spoke separately with two of the three non-invitees. The hurt cut deeply. To be disregarded in such a public way was like plunging a knife into the depths of the belly. Both women feel unwanted and unaccepted.

Do we have biblical examples of how to handle situations like this? When Peter wrote to first century believers, many of whom were slaves, he told them to submit to all those in authority regardless of their demeanor. Why? Because *it is God's will that by doing good you should silence the ignorant talk of foolish people* (1 Peter 2:15).

In that same passage, he explains how Christ is the ultimate example. To *this you were called, because Christ suffered for you, leaving you an example, that you should follow in his steps… He committed no sin, and no deceit was found in his mouth." When they hurled their insults at him, he did not retaliate; when he suffered, he made no threats* (1 Peter 2:21-23).

The lesson for these girls—and for all of us? Control what you can control. Disregard what is out of your control. Live above reproach for the sake of the Gospel.

Today's Truth: Live such good lives among the pagans that, though they accuse you of doing wrong, they may see your good deeds and glorify God on the day he visits us. 1 Peter 2:12

FEBRUARY 25

THE PURPOSE OF PAIN

I am sitting at my desk writing this because I decided not to push the pain threshold. I am trying to decide if I am a wimp. Let me explain.

Remember when I wrote about the unfortunate encounter my face had with concrete nearly two weeks ago? What I did not describe very well was that somehow in the process, the bottom of my shin was injured, bleeding off and on for several days. There was a huge, hard bump at the site, which was not unexpected given the blood thinners I take. But what continued to amaze me was the progressive swelling and discoloration of my entire foot, right down to the tips of my toes. Once I've been sitting for a while, it is a painful task to walk. Flexing and extending my foot makes me yelp like a dog. Going down steps makes the area of on either side of the Achilles tendon protest. I have no recollection of what happened to cause the fall, and I am befuddled by all of this.

It is feeling a wee bit better than three days ago, but is it okay to run on it? Do I risk necessary healing if I run with pain? Or is it wise to put patience in the play and allow the symptoms of this mystery injury disappear? Tonight, I am choosing the latter—but I feel wimpy in doing so.

Pain can be very telling. Touch your fingers to a hot stove and see how fast your hand withdraws. Hence, the response to pain will limit the extent of the burn. Pity those born with a rare condition called congenital analgesia. These people have never—and will never—feel pain. Though this sounds great at first blush, they are in jeopardy for severely hurting themselves without realizing it. In fact, it is more common than not for the afflicted to die in childhood because injury or disease goes unrecognized.

Pain serves a purpose. It gets our attention and forces a reaction. We have three choices: 1) Identify the source of the pain and get rid of it, 2) Ignore the pain and continue in our misery, or 3) Accept the pain, using it to bring focus and serve its purpose.

Today's truth: He was despised and rejected by mankind, a man of suffering, and familiar with pain. Like one from whom people hide their faces he was despised, and we held him in low esteem. Surely he took up our pain and bore our suffering, yet we considered him punished by God, stricken by him, and afflicted. Isaiah 53:3, 4

February 26

There. I said it.

The coach asked the open-ended question. A few of the girls responded before there was a pregnant pause. Should I speak or should I keep silent? My legs began to shake as the catacholamines surged, the result of my emotionally fragile frame of mind. I did not want to weep in front of these people, but I knew it was inevitable if I opened my mouth. I waited just a moment more before listening to myself say, "We should remember that no one ever wishes they could become an alcoholic or drug addict. I should know because I have a son in jail right now. He thought it would never happen to him. But it did."

I failed miserably at choking back the tears and grief I felt. I had not felt this depth of emotion since the first few days when this saga began. But then again, this was the first time I had talked about it publicly. Continuing, I uttered, "Playing around with alcohol or drugs is like playing Russian Roulette. Do you really want to hold a loaded gun to your head and take the chance by squeezing that trigger?"

The girls looked at me in cold-stone silence. The evening before was a required session for all of athletics: staff, coaches, and athletes. For an hour and a half Chris Herren, former NBA player and recovering addict, spoke of his journey into alcohol and drugs. He never planned it that way. He did not intend to bring ruin to his own life and suffering to his family. But he did. The sirens' call of addiction could not be quieted for sixteen years despite near misses with death itself. If only he had said no.

I can intellectually attest that alcohol is not intrinsically evil. I cannot say all pharmacologic agents are bad. But I have personally seen the ugly side of both for the last dozen years. Had he only said "no," he would not be in a stark, cold cell. Had he only said "no," he would not have wrecked so many cars. Had he only said "no," he would have money in the bank. Had he only said "no," he would have been a more consistent father. Had he only said "no," he would have eliminated about 99.9% of the pain in his life and the lives of others. Had he only said "no," he would not have to deal with a tsunami of regret in the staggering wake of abysmal consequences.

Please, please, please. Just say no.

Today's Truth: Wine is a mocker and beer a brawler; whoever is led astray by them is not wise. Proverbs 20:1

FEBRUARY 27

WHO DO YOU REPRESENT?

The young women gathered around their coach before taking to the courts. The normal news was presented: time for tomorrow's practice, schedule for upcoming matches, team activities, and other such items. It was nothing out of the ordinary. But as the coach took in a deep breath, the observant could see a change in his demeanor. Coach was not angry, but he was very serious.

"Ladies, we need to make you aware of something. Some of you were late to the required meeting the other night. Furthermore, one of you got up and left early. We had a coaches' meeting this morning with administration and you as a team were talked about. The senior administrators saw you come in late and leave early. They were not happy. In fact, they said they were embarrassed by your actions, particularly given the seriousness of the speaker's message. Afterward, I got a personal phone call expressing administration's grave displeasure with our team."

The women stared down at their feet, aware of the predicament they had created. "You have to be aware that people are watching. We need to take care of the little things. We must understand our responsibility to represent well this school, the team, each other, and ourselves. We have to be considerate and mindful of how we do things."

Coach proceeded to tell them about an event scheduled for next week. "Figure out ahead of time where the room is. Calculate how long it will take to get there. And whatever you do, do NOT be late!"

As an observer to all of this, I have no doubt the women heard the message loud and clear. Some of them quietly apologized before being released to warm up. If I were a betting woman, I would risk big money that they will all be early for next Wednesday's affair.

Sometimes we need a reminder in practical applications of good living. We need to be kind. We need to be considerate. We need to be men and women of integrity. We need to live as if we are representing a royal kingdom—because we are. The Kingdom of God.

Today's truth: Remind the people to be subject to rulers and authorities, to be obedient, to be ready to do whatever is good, to slander no one, to be peaceable and considerate, and always to be gentle toward everyone. Titus 3:1, 2

February 28

BIRTHDAYS

It is my birthday, but I am not particularly excited about it. I do not mind a birthday, the mark of another year lived. I am simply not into all the hubbub that can accompany birthdays. My impulse is to ignore social media and the volumes of greetings that end up on my Facebook wall. I appreciate the sentiments, I really do. But honestly, the older I get, the more birthdays become relegated to just another day. It is hard to get excited about this chronologic milepost, except when it signals transition into a new and less-competitive age group when racing. This one, 63, does not fit that category.

There was a time, however, when certain birthdays were greatly celebrated. My parents provided full-fledged parties on key dates; the 12th and 16th birthdays. I clearly remember my 16th because boys were invited, including one guy I was crushing on. I saved every birthday card and constructed a scrapbook to help savor the landmark occasion. That was quite a day in 1973.

And then there was my 40th. Gary, with the help of our "cellar-dweller," Leona, pulled off a surprise party. It was quite shocking given Gary's history of ignoring special days. I very much appreciated the effort to make the day memorable, especially because I was dealing with yet another running injury that had me down in the dumps.

Earlier today we got news about our incarcerated son. When we found out he would not be released next week as we thought, the sky grew a little greyer. I wanted to crawl in a hole and pine away. But alas, the day could not be put on hold.

When I arrived at the tennis courts for the scheduled match, one of the women greeted me cheerfully. "Happy birthday, Rebekah!" Then another approached, and another, and another. Soon, the entire team offered hugs and best wishes. They presented me with a framed team poster, each girl having signed a greeting in their native tongue. (Yes, we have a lot of international players.) One of the athletes handed me an envelope with a personal letter to me. What a timely encouragement!

The outcropping of faith is found in everyday consideration and encouragement for one another. I am grateful for receiving such love on this very special day.

Today's Truth: By this everyone will know that you are my disciples, if you love one another. John 13:35

FEBRUARY 29

NO HINDRANCE BECAUSE OF DIFFERENCE

After several days of energy-sucking interactions with our grandchild, we were more than ready to relax with a little entertainment. "The Green Book" is a movie of unexpected friendship and comradery. In an era of rampant racism in the south, Dr. Don Shirley embarks on a concert tour. A world class and classically trained pianist, Shirley, an African American, hires a rough and tough, white-skinned man, Tony Lip, to be his driver and bodyguard. Since this true story occurs in 1962, it does not take a lot of imagination to understand that the further south they travel, the more discrimination they encounter.

Despite the difficulties, Tony and Don form a deep and lasting relationship. They are as different as night and day. Tony is Italian, a hardworking husband and father, and member of a loud, boisterous extended family. On the other hand, Dr. Shirley has no one to call kin save an estranged brother. Rich and well-known, he is well-educated and articulate, a stark contrast from his driver. Nevertheless, the two months on tour bond them together in a lasting friendship until both die in 2013 within months of each other.

I have not done the research to find out how much liberty was taken in the screen play. But whether or not all the details were presented accurately, the one thing that stood out was how differences do not have to be hindrances.

John, in his third epistle, gives cudos to the believers because of their ready relationships. He says, *Dear friend, you are faithful in what you are doing for the brothers and sisters, even though they are strangers to you* (3 John 1:5). The believers receiving this letter were commended for their kindness and acceptance of fellow believers, even though they did not know them previously.

It can be tough to venture out of our circle of friends. The unknown and unfamiliar can be very uncomfortable. Not everyone is like us, which can produce disquiet. It may not be an ethnic issue. It could be as simple as taste in music, traditions, or personal preferences. We should be careful to understand that we are united because of Christ, and that should show in our everyday lives.

Today's Truth: There is neither Jew nor Gentile, neither slave nor free, nor is there male and female, for you are all one in Christ Jesus. Galatians 3:28

March 1

To hide or not to hide

There are a lot of cars and motorcycles at our house. Soon after we moved onto this country property, Gary put up a big metal building. It was one of those rounded metal buildings resembling an airplane hanger. It worked well for keeping the farm equipment under cover and provided a place to work on vehicles. Then a few years ago he built an insulated garage in the middle of the building, installing a car lift to make his mechanical repairs easier. It served a purpose, but still left our everyday cars sit out in the weather.

Now the current plan is to build a garage to use for our daily drivers along with the excess motorcycles. There has been more than one discussion about where said garage will go. In fact, trees were toppled some months ago in preparation for this project. But now, the location for that building has changed. The structure will be on the backside of the house. It will not be in view when coming down the driveway.

I have mixed feelings about this plan. Trees that did not have to come down have already been been reduced to firewood. Additionally, the new location demands another large tree be brought down. But the good thing is this; the garage will be hidden from view. No one will really have to see it when approaching the house.

There are some things in life that should not be hidden. Remember the Sunday school song that went something like this? "This little light of mine, I'm gonna make it shine. This little light of mine, I'm gonna make it shine, let it shine, let it shine. . ." Written in 1920 by Harry Dixon Loes, it is based on the parable Jesus told in Matthew 5. Jesus had escaped the crowds, taking his disciples up on the mountainside for up close and personal teaching. He encouraged them to let their light shine to make a difference in the world.

The song continues, "Hide it under a bushel, no! I'm gonna let it shine. . ." Wise words then. Wise words now. Do not hide your light. Let it shine!

Today's Truth: You are the light of the world. A town built on a hill cannot be hidden. Neither do people light a lamp and put it under a bowl. Instead they put it on its stand, and it gives light to everyone in the house. In the same way, let your light shine before others, that they may see your good deeds and glorify your Father in heaven. Matthew 5:14–16

MARCH 2

CROWDED EARS

Volleyball practice was again before the break of dawn. The walk across the still-sleeping campus to the practice court was serene. Not too cold. Not too hot. Just brisk enough to encourage an invigorating pace along the walkways.

On the return trip and under a sunny sky, there were considerably more students and staff up and at 'em. Some seemed to be in a rush to make it to class on time. Others strolled along, in no great hurry to get anywhere quickly. Many were typical college age while others looked like they had been around for awhile. But the common denominator? With very few exceptions, crammed into ears were those tiny buds, some wired and connected to a phone directly, and others obviously Bluetooth. Everyone looked to be in their own little world. I can only assume they were listening to something.

Listening to what? That is a good question. But why? Why do we need to be plugged in all the time? What ever happened to good ol' fashioned quiet?

Few can argue the volume of noise we encounter each day. Whether it be conversations, extraneous sounds, social media messages, music, podcasts, videos, or movies, there is a barrage of distractions that crowd our days. Teams play pump up music during practices, the fitness center windows shake with pulsating beats, and even the solitary runner often keeps pace with whatever comes through his ear buds.

Please do not think I am passing judgment. But might we be better off embracing the quiet rather than drowning it out? When the prophet Isaiah wrote of the Lord's justice and righteousness, the by-product was quietness and confidence forever (Isaiah 32:17). He speaks of strength coming because of quietness and confidence (Isaiah 30:15). And David, the king and Psalmist, pens these wonderful words. *But I have calmed and quieted myself, I am like a weaned child with its mother; like a weaned child I am content* (Psalm 131:2).

Somehow, I doubt that neither Isaiah nor David would be plugged in if they lived in our society. Rather, I suspect they would be contentedly still and intently listening for God to speak. They would not risk missing out on what He said—and nor should we.

Today's Truth: Be still, and know that I am God; Psalm 46:10

March 3

When frustration calls

Oh boy. Have you ever been frustrated when it feels like you are being asked to do something "stupid" by someone in authority? That happened to me today. I guess that explains why my knee jerked so violently.

Let me explain the situation. The national support center for which I work rolled out a new website platform. Each territory was tasked with converting the old websites to this new platform. After figuring out the idiosyncrasies of the new technology, I spent hours converting the old to the new. The revitalized site looked great and met my needs.

A regional leader decided to create a list of non-negotiables for our websites. Unfortunately, those requirements were not included in the national rollout. When I got the specifics of what needed to be done, I was hot. I logged into the web editor to see if there was a simple solution. There was not. Multiple contacts with the tech guys answered my queries about the counter-intuitive technical process. After several hours, I think my local website will satisfy those in authority above me, but not before I emailed my direct boss to inform him of my aggravation. I do not recommend doing that!

I am not proud of my initial response. Did this request by the guy I am supposed to submit to deserve my growling and hissing, though he never personally heard those sounds of discontentment? No. Certainly not.

I know I'm not the only person who has gotten hot under the collar and then loosened it a bit to let the steam escape. Intellectually, I understood the reasoning behind the requests. However, the "thou shalts" of the directives seemed to be ill-timed, at best. It was only a couple hours of my life devoted to this particular "fix." I learned new skills in the process that should serve me well in the future. And that email? Well, I sent another one saying I had adjusted my attitude. Please forgive.

I doubt it is an accident that controlling our anger is an important character skill to possess.

Today's Truth: My dear brothers and sisters, take note of this: Everyone should be quick to listen, slow to speak and slow to become angry, because human anger does not produce the righteousness that God desires. James 1:19, 20

MARCH 4

MY WEEK-DAY SABBATH

After feeling exhausted for months, today was a breath of fresh air. Long hours with high expectations and the mental energy in dealing with our son's imprisonment left me feeling like a wrung-out dish rag. The logistics of being a worker bee by day, a housekeeper and cook by night, and a grandma tending to our little one on weekends have been a difficult juggle. I think that is why today was so special.

Our son had a court appearance this morning. The lawyers signed off on an agreement that will result in his jail time coming to an end one week from today. There are stipulations that come with the arrangement, but to know he will walk through the door and begin the process of getting his life in order has me nearly giddy.

My boss applauded my plans to take today off. Hence, warm temps and sunny skies drew me to the trails for a run. Though loss of fitness over the last couple of months was evident, I felt free as I ran through the forest without seeing a single soul. A stop for groceries along with a trip to a home improvement store filled the rest of the afternoon.

With a happy heart, I cleaned up around the house in preparation for a dinner guest. Pam, our son's soon-to-be bride was coming to share the evening with us. To leisurely sit, eat, laugh, and plan for the future was as delightful as a decadent brownie topped with ice cream and hot fudge, which we may or may not have had as well.

The few hours I spent in non-work-related activity recharged my depleted batteries. I tend to be on the go all the time. I am painfully aware I say "yes" to way too many things. My calendar is crowded trying to be all things to all people. My boss is making it his mission to help me be more discerning with my time. He wants me to be purposeful in taking much-needed "sabbaths"—and we are not just talking about the one day set aside for corporate worship.

God created in six days and then rested. He did not rest because He, the omnipotent Father, was physically tired. He rested to give us an example of a pattern for conducting our lives. The result when we "sabbath" well? Restoration and well-being. Sign me up.

Today's Truth: For in six days the Lord made the heavens and the earth, the sea, and all that is in them, but he rested on the seventh day. Therefore, the Lord blessed the Sabbath day and made it holy. Exodus 20:11

March 5

Burn the Ships

Imagine you are a captain of a sailing fleet, embarking on an expedition into unknown territory. You navigate across treacherous seas to finally make safe harbor, each man breathing a sigh of relief to feel safe and secure. Daily trips to shore serve the purpose of surveying the territory and identifying resources. But after each excursion, you and the men return to the ships.

The day comes to explore deeper inland. Your men are reluctant to embrace weeks spent in virgin territory. Possible battles with indigenous people, dangerous wildlife, and hostile terrain prompt protests. You fear an uprising. What do you do?

"Burn the ships, cut the ties. Send a flare into the night. . . So light a match, leave the past, burn the ships. And don't you look back."

Those words are from For King and Country's song, *Burn the Ships.* Though it was written for a family situation, it reminds me of the great exodus. What were the Israelites told repeatedly? I'll paraphrase: Don't look back. Trust God. Follow the cloud by day and the pillar of fire by night. Do not retreat!

When Lot and company vacated Sodom and Gomorrah, they were told specifically not to look back. Lot's wife failed to "burn the ship," choosing to gaze back to her previous place of belonging. She died in the process.

It is so easy to remain on the ship rather than burn it. The ship becomes a comfortable place that encourages passivity rather than action, pouting rather than new-found wonder and joy. But leaving the ship demands courage. Lots of it.

Just this morning, one of the volleyball players struggled in practice. She was converting to a new position and making mistakes. The frustration that had been mounting for weeks ran down her cheeks in the form of hot, salty tears. It was hard to console or encourage her. But this was an opportunity to ask her to burn the ships. Do not look back at what was. Forge ahead with courage and anticipate great things to come.

Have a ship to burn? Light the match and head to shore.

Today's Truth: As soon as they had brought them out, one of them said, "Flee for your lives! Don't look back, and don't stop anywhere in the plain!" Genesis 19: 17a

MARCH 6

REASSESS

In a recent meeting with my boss, he politely requested I look at the ministry plan written last summer in preparation for the upcoming school year. In our organization, these plans are a "write" of passage. In other words, if you do not write it out, there is no passing through the doors of continued ministry.

They say, whoever the proverbial "they" happens to be, that if you do not plan where you are going, you have zero chance of getting there. I suspect there is some truth to that idea. But when planning time comes rolling around each summer, my attitude turns south. The process has always seemed cumbersome to me, its helpfulness dubious. It has felt more like a paperwork chore rather than a useful tool, until recently.

Admittedly, there have been improvements to the planning process. When I pulled up what I wrote last year, it was a curious reminder of my intentions. Now at the half-way point through the fiscal year, I find myself giving grades of pass, fail, or needs improvement. It is a chance to reassess the validity of the initial plans, adjust if and when necessary, and get back on the road to accomplish the very best ideas.

Reassessment requires an analytical pause. Reassessment asks us to consider the facts and how those facts should impact our future behavior. The author of Psalm 119, perhaps Ezra the priest, asks the reader to consider how it was, how it is, and how it should be. He tells us, *I meditate on your precepts and consider your ways* (vs 15). The presupposition is that God's precepts and ways are the standard. Therefore, he is left with no choice but to consider his own ways and actions. Verse 59: *I have considered my ways* (the analysis) *and have turned my steps to your statutes* (the action).

For the Psalmist to be able to do this, he seriously pondered the precepts and ways of God. Then in response, he considered his own attitudes and actions, making the necessary alterations.

Assessments are only helpful when we recognize the standard, are honest in our considerations, and proactive in adjusting accordingly.

Today's Truth: and because I consider all your precepts right, I hate every wrong path. Psalm 119: 128

March 7

Old Becomes New

Call me weird, but I love to clean when a room is *really* dirty. I find great delight in creating order from a totally disorganized and chaotic garage or workspace. And I welcome the opportunity to take an ugly piece of furniture and turn it into a useful and stylish piece. I suppose my desire to see this metamorphosis is because I love the contrast between what was and what it can become.

I got in one of those moods this week. For a long time, I contemplated the look of the kitchen island. The more I looked, the more I thought it had too much stained wood. A few days ago, a trip to the local home improvement store resulted in me bringing home a new can of paint and a fresh brush. An hour and several coats of paint later, the sides and back of the island now sport a new look; deep navy. It makes that old, tired centerpiece of the kitchen look brand new.

But it did not stop there. Last night, after coming up empty at thrift stores, I found an old dresser, circa 1950s or 60s in an online marketplace. The goal was to place it in our large upstairs bathroom to provide additional storage. I had no interest in a new dresser. Too cookie-cutter. I wanted a drawered storage unit in need of a transformation.

This morning Gary and I went to fetch the dresser. It did not take too long to figure out a plan. Another quick trip to the store for more sandpaper was the first step. Soon after the sanding was completed, the dresser got spiffed up with paint left over from other projects. Even the sides of the drawers that are only seen when pulled out received a color boost. A beautiful liner was added to the base of each drawer for an unexpected bit of whimsy. The ugly and dated piece of furniture now has a novel look.

Old and ugly to fresh and new. That is exactly what God does for those He loves. He chooses our old dirty heart, takes the sander to it to expose and smooth out the imperfections, and then applies the transforming blood of the Savior. The result is an entirely new creation of the Father, priceless in value, and forever sealed with the Spirit.

Today's Truth: Therefore, if anyone is in Christ, the new creation has come: The old has gone, the new is here! 2 Corinthians 5:17

MARCH 8

WHEREVER

We had visitors this afternoon. Collin and Kendal have been married just under a year. Collin is a photographer, videographer, and web designer. Kendal is a neonatal intensive care nurse. But lest you think they live routine newlywed lives, think again.

From the get-go, they planned on traveling the country by taking short-term nursing assignments. They landed in CA, loving the assignment and the area. Then they traded a small apartment for an Airstream trailer, putting added meaning behind "travel nursing." They bought a truck to pull the trailer, sold the car, and headed to their second assignment. When the hospital canceled the contract, this young couple came up with a better idea.

Collin had a light-bulb moment of how to land photography assignments for outdoor retailers. Kendal fell in love with a health-related product and started developing that business. Now their home is where they park it, working remotely and visiting all the national parks they can find. Though they have great freedom, they live disciplined lives: rising at 5 a.m. to work out, putting in office hours before lunch, recreating at a gym or with a run, and then working in the afternoon as well. This summer they are headed to Alaska. It's a way of living that many desire, but few will ever realize.

As impressive as this wanderlust story may be, it was their attitudes that really impressed. Woven into the stories of adventure was the connecting thread of mission and purpose. Collin spoke often of their reliance on the Lord to make paths clear and providing for their needs. Kendal's passion for helping people get healthy and honor God with their entire being was evident. Both testified of God's protection when a tornado rushed by, pancaking a truck right next to them. They were left without a scratch despite the ferocity of the storm.

Cudos to this mid-20s couple. Their God-appointed mission does not require an address. They understand that less is more. They work hard but trust God. They are disciplined and focused. And they serve others by serving Jesus all day, every day, everywhere. What a life.

Today's Truth: Your decrees are the theme of my song wherever I lodge. Psalm 119:54

MARCH 9

AROMAS

Years ago, and in the stillness of cold winter mornings, I ran before heading to the hospital. Sometimes I took off down a tree-lined street, running toward downtown. It was nice to take in the huge historic houses and old, spired churches along the way. Nevertheless, the best part of this run was not the architecture. It was the sweet smell of bread.

Yes, bread. Just a block or two off Rivermont Avenue was a large commercial bakery. About a mile into the run, the aroma wafted its way to my nostrils. It reminded me of walking into our kitchen when Mother baked bread while we were at school. To this day, that smell is so memorable and delightful.

In contrast, there was another aroma, this one not so pleasant but just as memorable. I was racing through the Amazon jungle, contending with all the predictable trappings of a jungle; heat, humidity, swamps, snakes, ants, and a large predator or two. This was a self-sufficient race that required each competitor to carry all the food needed for the seven days of racing. Though I shall spare you the details of my culinary selections, let's just say I took more than one package of ramen noodles. The noodles tasted fine for a few days. But when sickness struck and the stench of the jungle overwhelmed, I could not bear to swallow a single bite more. In fact, it took years after the race before I could stomach the smell of ramen. The association with the jungle remained strong.

It is interesting that God is interested in aromas. There are multiple passages when God demanded various types of burnt offerings that possessed pleasing aromas. Why is that? Could it be that a pleasant aroma stirs a sense of joy, contentment, and well-being? Since we are created in the image of God, perhaps it is not far-fetched for us to appreciate fine aromas as well, for they remind us of God's goodness.

As wonderful the aroma of freshly baked bread can be, we must be reminded that our very lives are to be a sweet aroma that draws others to God. But woe to us if we live so poorly that we become a stench to those who surround us.

Today's Truth: But thanks be to God, who always leads us as captives in Christ's triumphal procession and uses us to spread the aroma of the knowledge of him everywhere. For we are to God the pleasing aroma of Christ among those who are being saved and those who are perishing. 2 Corinthians 2: 14-15

MARCH 10

GO AHEAD. WRITE A LETTER.

Oh, how I love getting real letters in the mail! Just yesterday, my heart skipped a beat when I reached into the mailbox and pulled out a letter from our son. It was all I could do to get back in the car and navigate down our long and rough driveway, letter still unopened. I carried that precious envelope into the house, placed my bag in the proper spot, and reached for a letter opener to carefully reveal the letter inside. Gary stopped what he was doing as I began to read aloud. My voice quivered as the words opened a floodgate of emotion. The penned words were answers to a thousand prayers.

Had those same words been texted or emailed, I doubt our responses would have felt so visceral. I could almost see him hunched over his paper, careful in combining words to accurately communicate his thoughts. I pondered not only the words but wondered what time of day it was when he wrote. Was he in his bunk? Did he find a private corner somewhere? But wherever and whenever he composed, filling two pages of ruled paper with his tiny handwriting took significant effort.

My mission today was to write personal notes to each one of my financial partners in ministry. Form letters spit from a copier just don't cut it. I hope that finding a little note card in the mailbox will make them feel special and appreciated.

I wonder if the Apostle Paul's hand ever got tired from writing. Think about it. How else was he supposed to instruct groups of believers or individuals? Blogging and printing services were not options. Traditionally, it is thought that Paul wrote thirteen books, four of which were scribed from prison and carried by individuals to various locales. To the Corinthians, Galatians, Colossians, Thessalonians, and to Philemon, he specifically makes sure the readers and listeners know he wrote the inspired words. "*I write to you with my own hand. . .*"

Can you imagine cramming into someone's modest home to hear those precious letters read aloud? The people had to be encouraged by such personal attention to their spiritual development. Encourage someone today. Make a difference. Show you care. Write a letter.

Today's Truth: I, Paul, write this greeting in my own hand, which is the distinguishing mark in all my letters. This is how I write. 2 Thessalonians 3:17

March 11

The Prodigal Returns

As the time approached, I felt the indescribable pull of my internal nesting syndrome. Both times, when the due date for our boys drew near, I set off in a flurry of activity; cleaning, organizing, arranging, then rearranging when a better idea hit in the middle of the night. Everything was perfect. I wanted to be ready for the blessed event of a child springing forth from my very own loins.

I found myself in nesting mode again this last week. No, I was not bringing home a baby, but my "baby" was coming home. Our son spent the last three months behind bars. He was paying the price for being under the influence and behind the wheel. It has been a tough go for all of us. By the grace of God, however, it appears that his heart has been transformed. The letters he wrote, conversations we had, and the way he thinks is now diametrically different from before he landed in jail. We are forever thankful. If this is what it took for God to get his attention, then it was well worth the price. Life may not be perfect from here on out, but it can be perfectly wonderful by His grace and mercy.

But today, today was the day we had anticipated for so long. His "get out of jail" card was March 11, and it could not come any sooner. Over the last week or two, I cleaned the house from top to bottom. I bought an old dresser for his bathroom and gave it new life. I repainted windowsills and mopped floors. I dusted everything in sight and even bleached the inside of the little refrigerator we keep upstairs. Today he is returning home where he can be loved, supported mentally and spiritually, and held accountable in his recovery process.

Our son is a repentant prodigal returning home and we, as his parents, are celebrating. For years we have anticipated this day. We rejoice!

Today's Truth: But the father said to his servants, "Quick! Bring the best robe and put it on him. Put a ring on his finger and sandals on his feet. Bring the fattened calf and kill it. Let's have a feast and celebrate. For this son of mine was dead and is alive again; he was lost and is found." So they began to celebrate. Luke 15: 22-24

MARCH 12

PANDEMIC PANIC

It is impossible to turn on the news without hearing the latest news on the Covid-19 virus. Several forms of this flu-like disease are sweeping through entire countries and are popping up in new locales daily. Here in the USA, schools are closing for weeks to come, state and local governments are forbidding public gatherings, workers are being told to stay home, and hospitals are preparing for the worst.

The sporting world has canceled NBA games, MLB spring training will not happen, and even March Madness with the NCAA basketball tournament will be conducted in empty arenas, if at all. Many colleges and universities have sent students home, converting classes to on-line, and have totally nixed spring sports. The impact financially, socially, and athletically is hard to calculate because it is so incredibly far-reaching.

The public is responding as if there is an impending health apocalypse, and according to some experts, there is. Hand-sanitizers are flying off the shelf. Surgical masks are nearly impossible to get. There is a limit on the number of antiseptic wipes one can purchase. There is full-speed ahead preparation driven by fear.

There is nothing wrong with solid preparation. If there was, God would not have given so many specific instructions about preparing food and sacrifices, for war or defense, and preparation to build and rebuild. But I wonder if we—no, make that if I—have a proactive desire to prepare my life to be a "living sacrifice," as encouraged in Romans 12:1. How do we do that? *Do not conform to the pattern of this world, but be transformed by the renewing of your mind. Then you will be able to test and approve what God's will is—his good, pleasing and perfect will* (vs. 2).

Seems to me that "not conforming" takes intentionality to change the way we think, which in turn will change the way we live. If we have that God-centered mindset, I believe we will make God smile with our attitudes and actions.

Prepare fully.

Today's Truth: And I'll say to myself, "You have plenty of grain laid up for many years. Take life easy; eat, drink and be merry."' "But God said to him, 'You fool! This very night your life will be demanded from you. Then who will get what you have prepared for yourself?' "This is how it will be with whoever stores up things for themselves but is not rich toward God." Luke 12:19-21

March 13

Love, laughter, and life

Last night I went to bed as happy as a gopher in a warm and cozy hole. The evening was one I had been waiting for for a very long time. I was surrounded by my husband, our children, their loves, and one precious grandchild. The feast we had was on par for a major holiday meal, maybe even better. The conversation was spiced with good-hearted banter and crazy stories from the past. Laughter was abundant and loud as we spent hours enjoying each other's company.

There was no suspicion of impairment for our son who was enjoying his second evening as a free man. We saw only his clear-eyed wit and charm. My heart's long-time desire to have my family gathered around the table had come to fruition. When I crawled between our well-worn sheets, my soul was satisfied.

I relate to the emotions the father of the biblical prodigal son experienced when his son returned from a season of dangerous living. My mother's heart has been through the ringer as I have watched my son struggle with his addiction for so long. Every time I heard a siren, I wondered if he was involved. I feared for his life. In times of sobriety, we saw glimpses of the boy we raised. But in general, his life was nothing less than chaotic.

Last night was a reminder of the transforming power of the Gospel. He is not the man who was arrested three months ago. He thinks differently. Acts differently. Talks differently. His desires are different. His perspective is different. He is different. He is no longer dead in *"trespasses and sin"* (Colossians 2:13).

Today, Seth and Pam were quietly married on the banks of the James River. They cemented their love and commitment to each other and to God. We could not be happier in celebrating this holy union between two souls who have been united in and because of Christ.

Today's Truth: And you hath he quickened, who were dead in trespasses and sins; Wherein in time past ye walked according to the course of this world, according to the prince of the power of the air, the spirit that now worketh in the children of disobedience: Among whom also we all had our conversation in times past in the lusts of our flesh, fulfilling the desires of the flesh and of the mind; and were by nature the children of wrath, even as others. But God, who is rich in mercy, for his great love wherewith he loved us, even when we were dead in sins, hath quickened us together with Christ, by grace ye are saved; Ephesians 2:1-5

MARCH 14

SPRING FLING

The combination of warm temps and just the right amount of rain has turned the bland brown of winter into a burgeoning pallet of rainbow colors. Shades of green are displayed in the grasses, the first leaves of perennial bulbs forcing their way through the surface, and, of course, weeds of every assortment. Tiny flowers of purple and blue fill portions of the yard and flower beds. The peach tree has produced delicate pink flowers, and the forsythia bush is lathered in bright yellow. The maple trees are showing off red buds.

It is spring. To see new growth come back year after year is truly wonderful. But there is a price to pay. My aching body tells me so.

I did not really mean to work so much today, but I wanted to be productive. With coffee in hand, I looked out the kitchen window and saw plenty to do. Weeds needed pulled, leaves in the flower beds had to be raked, a couple bushes needed a good pruning, and the ivy growing wild needed to be stopped in its tracks.

Seth volunteered to help, taking on the messy chore of weedwacking. I got busy wielding rake and loppers. Every time I thought I was at a stopping point, I looked up to see something else calling my name. There was nothing easy about the work. My arthritic hands ached and my lower back soon tired of bending over. At one point, I launched backwards, landing on my butt, the momentum gained from pulling hard on a stubborn vine until it finally gave way. I'm glad no one saw that.

Is it okay with you if I blame good 'ol Adam and Eve for this mess? Afterall, their sin ushered in all kinds of mayhem, including the cursed ground and toil required to work it (Genesis 3:17). But as hard as the labor is in making our landscapes acceptable, God still shows his faithfulness to us in creation. Bulbs know when to bloom, trees bud on que, and grass knows when to come back to life. So much beauty happens naturally without any help from us. God's got this. His power and creativity are seen in every aspect of creation, and every flower tells the story of his incredible love and care for us.

Today's Truth: Consider how the wildflowers grow. They do not labor or spin. Yet I tell you, not even Solomon in all his splendor was dressed like one of these. Luke 12:27

March 15

Grace That Is Greater

It's all about grace. That recurrent theme was evident in the music and teaching at church this morning. But the most impactful aspect of our gathering was the reminder of the wonderful work of grace in our own lives.

What is grace? Its origin comes from the Hebrew word meaning "to extend favor." We are told in Genesis 6, for example, that Noah found favor (or grace) in the sight of the Lord. Why? Well, the entirety of the earth's population – save Noah and his family—had become wicked in the sight of God. The penalty for such evil was to send a great flood to wipe out evil. But we find that Noah found favor with God. *Noah was a righteous man, blameless among the people of his time, and he walked faithfully with God* (Genesis 6:9). But was it of his own doing? No. Noah's ability to be righteous, blameless, and walk faithfully was because of God's grace alone. Grace is a curious but extraordinary gift that is hard to fully comprehend.

Seth, Pam, and my granddaughter sat next to us in church today. To say I am thankful for God's grace in their lives would be a gross understatement. We have come through a very long season of praying for grace to intercede. God has indeed been gracious to change the disposition of his heart and turn his eyes to Jesus. He and his wonderful little family are gifts that God in His faithfulness gave to us.

God's grace surely saves and sustains. His grace gives us what we need when we need it. As the refrain of the old hymn reminds us, He is the grace-giver when we are burdened, exhausted, and run out of resources. Praise God for that!

His love has no limits, His grace has no measure,
His power no boundary known unto men;
For out of His infinite riches in Jesus
He giveth, and giveth, and giveth again. (Author: Annie J Flint)

Today's Truth: But he said to me, "My grace is sufficient for you, for my power is made perfect in weakness." Therefore I will boast all the more gladly about my weaknesses, so that Christ's power may rest on me. 2 Corinthians 12:9

MARCH 16

THE YEAR OF THE VIRUS

With every passing day, and perhaps every hour, news of the Coronavirus continues to pummel us from every direction. The news outlets talk of little else. The buzz on the streets is loud and domineering. And the various opinions popping up on social media are, well, opinions. Some are based on what appears to be sound medical information, while others seem to be highly biased.

Schools are closing. At this point, meetings of more than 100 people (and in some places 50 people) are forbidden. Parents of school-age children are caught in the dilemma of what to do with their kids during the day. Businesses face shutdowns that promise huge financial set-backs, while employees wonder how long they can survive without a paycheck. Politicians weaponize the situation, making it even harder to discern what should be believed.

Just today, the ministry I work with conducted an online video conference outlining the steps the organization is taking to safeguard those we work with as well as ourselves. My world is doing back flips. Athletic seasons are over, though some coaches may continue with practices. It is unclear, however, if the athletes will be required to attend since campuses are shutting down. My bosses said I am not to attend any practices or serve teams or coaches in person for the foreseeable future.

The circumstances beg the question: how can I serve coaches and athletes without sharing the same address? Obviously, the status quo has suddenly gone obsolete.

I can be intentional about conveying these truths via texts and online meetings. I can use the time to plan. I can write notes and make phone calls. I can be purposeful in building relationships with individual coaches and athletes. I can be creative in finding ways to encourage and provide support for those who struggle. I can trust God that all things—even pandemics—will create opportunities for ministry that would not be available under normal circumstances.

God's ways are higher.

Today's Truth: As the heavens are higher than the earth, so are my ways higher than your ways and my thoughts than your thoughts. Isaiah 55:9

March 17

A wild hair project

When my curiosity got the best of me, I headed into my office housed in the campus Athletic Center. Though the school has decided to move most classes to an online format, many questions remain surrounding athletics considering the Covid-19 pandemic. I was hoping to get answers by being there in person. But the answers were not easy to come by. I headed home.

But I did not stay home. One look at my kitchen launched me on a mission to a large home improvement store. Having already painted three sides of my island a deep midnight blue, the wild hair that sometimes marks my impulsive activities led to a bold decision. I would paint the lower cabinets that same deep blue, and the solid oak uppers were slated to be slathered in an icy grey. It took about five minutes to pick the "right" shade. With paint in hand, I rushed home. Within a couple hours, the lowers morphed from stained oak to painted wood. The upper cabinets get the treatment tomorrow.

Though initially thrown by my organization's decision to have us work remotely, I am now excited to discover creative ways of interacting with coaches and athletes. But I am equally excited about a new schedule that should be much less hectic and way more flexible. My frustration of not having time to complete a myriad of home projects can now be appeased. By tomorrow, I anticipate a brand new-looking kitchen. Designing, painting, building, and creating makes my heart happy.

New things are cool, especially when God is the author of those changes. When the prophet Isaiah wrote in the 42nd chapter (and in the time of Israel's Babylonian exile), he reprimanded them for being figuratively blind and deaf to obeying God's commands and living accordingly. But along comes Chapter 43 and his opening words, *But now. . .* The tone of the chapter shifts to the coming blessings for God's redeemed simply *because I am the Lord your God.* The grace and mercy of God to *do a new thing* had to be encouraging, and it should be a reminder to us of His goodness, even in trying times.

Today's Truth: "Forget the former things; do not dwell on the past. See, I am doing a new thing! Now it springs up; do you not perceive it? I am making a way in the wilderness and streams in the wasteland." Isaiah 43:18-19

MARCH 18

IT COVERS EVERYTHING

The kitchen project I started yesterday continued throughout the day. The cabinet boxes, doors, and drawers got a good scrub and sanding. It is amazing how much grime amasses on the surfaces particularly close to the stove. At first glance it did not look that bad, but once I handled those greasy doors, the accumulated gunk could not be denied. But the mess was not relegated to the wood surfaces. Nope. Not so lucky. My painting prep necessarily included scouring down the tile backsplash and the utensils hanging from a rod above the stove.

The upper cabinets got all the attention today, but not without a paint change along the way. The "Icicle" white looked too stark. Hence, back to the store to get a quart of the color I was drawn to initially. The paint flowed smoothly as my brush re-visited the "Icicle" surfaces. This shade of light gray was a much better choice! The doors have now been painted on both sides, awaiting re-installation come morning.

It is amazing what a fresh coat of paint can do. All those years of cooking, grease splatters, and stale food smells have disappeared beneath the new color. The blemishes and years of wear and tear vanish. It all looks brand new.

I had the day to think about this concept of being covered over. James 5:19-20 speaks of the wisdom to pursue those who wander from the faith. Why? Because in doing so the person is saved and their *multitude of sins* are covered over. That is a big deal and sounds like true forgiveness to me.

1 Peter 4:8 presents a similar concept. *Above all, love each other deeply, because love covers over a multitude of sins.* But which comes first? Do we love first so we can engage without bias, or do we disregard ungodly attitudes and behaviors to free us to love? Somehow, I think it may be like a reversible chemical reaction that goes both ways. However, should we think ourselves to be the catalyst driving the reaction, we err. It is only the fact that our own sins have been covered by the blood of Jesus that we can even begin to let love cover another's sin.

Today's Truth: Just as David also speaks of the blessing of the one to whom God counts righteousness apart from works: "Blessed are those whose lawless deeds are forgiven, and whose sins are covered; blessed is the man against whom the Lord will not count his sin." Romans 4:6-8

March 19

Clean Up Your Mess

Hitting the floor with at least a modicum of excitement, the new day promised a certain level of fresh and new. I went to bed with all the cabinets and doors painted with two coats of color. I loved what I saw so far, but there were six upper cabinet doors that had to be hung. The full impact of the transformed kitchen was soon to be revealed.

With the help of my husband, it did not take long to install the new hinges and handles. I held the doors in place while he wielded the drill to start the tiny screws. It was a good partnership given the need for four hands to complete the task. With the last screw driven into the wood, I thanked him profusely before he wandered off to work on his own projects in the garage. Instinctively, I reached for my phone to document the new two-tone look. But I set the camera right back down as I realized the job was not yet complete.

For hours I picked up, cleaned up, and washed up every surface. Paint and the affiliated supplies went to the basement while tools belonging in the garage were gathered into a pile awaiting transport. Caulking around the window and backsplash proved to be as messy as ever. Finally, after much effort, I was able to take those tell-all pictures.

The initial impact of the painted kitchen was certainly noticeable as soon as the last brush stroke swept across the surface. Whether or not there was still a mess surrounding it did not diminish the fact that the space had been transformed. But to really appreciate the beauty that came from the conversion, the surroundings needed to be cleaned up. Only then could I marvel at the change without reservation.

Our Christian lives are not all that different. When God in his mercy saves us, we are changed; we become a new creation in Christ. But after that, we have some cleaning up to do. Why do you think Paul wrote constantly to the early church with directives to put off bad behavior, get rid of sexual impurities, clean up speech, do away with greed, abstain from losing control. . . and the list goes on?

Let's tidy up our mess by the power of Christ in us.

Today's Truth: As a prisoner for the Lord, then, I urge you to live a life worthy of the calling you have received. Ephesians 4:1

MARCH 20

I WARNED YOU!

The unseasonably warm weather warranted shorts and t-shirts on this first day of spring. With everyone hanging close to home due to Covid-19 and "social distancing," activity levels on the homefront are high. New siding on the house needs painting, the pool requires vacuuming, while Gary tackles tasks in the garage. Seth took charge of the painting while Addyson joined me for errands to fetch eggs, which proved futile in the shelf-ravaged grocery store.

After a quick lunch, Addyson took her bouncy self to the new trampoline. As a 5-year-old weighing in at 38 pounds, she could jump as hard as she wanted without putting the minutest strain on the frame. However, when her daddy and his wife joined in, the trampoline protested. "Stop! There is a 200-pound limit. The three of you are probably 350 pounds! You'll ruin it."

They laughed at me as if to say, "It's fine." Despite my previous concerns to curtail any and all flipping, Seth ramped up his bounce, setting himself up for a back flip. He is very athletic and capable. However, on a 15' diameter trampoline, his rotational momentum carried him toward the edge. He slammed into the protective netting and crashed to the surface, one leg managing to poke through the springs. At the same time, two of the poles holding the safety net bent and nearly snapped under his weight. The new trampoline's safety netting ripped. Seth avoided what could have been serious injury, but Addyson's favorite outdoor toy had been damaged. She began to cry.

I was mad! I wanted to scream, "I told you so! You nearly killed yourself and damaged your daughter's trampoline."

"I didn't mean to," lamented my grown son. I could tell he felt bad. Really bad.

Isn't that so typical? We know better but end up doing what we do not want to do, and do not do what we should do. Even the Apostle Paul had that problem. Perhaps we need to be more intentional about making stronger connections between what we know to be true and what we do or do not do.

Today's Truth: I do not understand what I do. For what I want to do I do not do, but what I hate I do. Romans 7:15

March 21

Where Do I Run?

After a very busy day of work around the house and interspersed with multiple trips to the home improvement store, Gary and I sat down to watch a newly-found series on Netflix. The producers of "Virgin River" do a brilliant job of intertwining the lives of intriguing characters.

Set in a tiny, backwoods Colorado hamlet, a nurse practitioner is recruited by the town's mayor, Hope. Hope is likely in her high 60's and is a cantankerous soul. Not to be a spoiler, but she is technically still married (though separated for 20 years) to the equally cantankerous doctor who is not convinced he needs help. Then there is Jack, the local bar and grill owner who is a marine vet with PTSD. And the nurse who came with the promise of a job complete with "quaint" cabin? She left a busy practice in Los Angeles to escape deep pain in her own life.

There are underlying storylines, but one thing is clear. The four main characters are all flawed in some way. Each has a history, dealing uniquely with the past and present. We see what drives Jack to drink too much by flashbacks to his nightmarish war experiences. The pain of infidelity and a bitter spirit is played out in Hope's relationship to Doc. The wall Doc puts up is from shame and guilt. And Mel, the nurse, is devasted from the birth of her stillborn daughter and death of her husband. Each is running hard, trying to find solace and meaning.

The Psalmist often used the analogy of running into the shadow of the Almighty. He pleads, *Keep me as the apple of your eye; hide me in the shadow of your wings* (17:8). *How priceless is your unfailing love, O God! People take refuge in the shadow of your wings* (36:7), he states. When pursued by the vengeful Saul, David knows where he goes for protection. *I will take refuge in the shadow of your wings until the disaster has passed* (57:1b).

Taking refuge in the shadow of his wings, however, is not a passive activity. We must move. We must go there if we are to experience the safety and security found in that protective environment. But the effort is so worth it. Taking refuge produces contentment despite difficulty and offers a song in the silence.

Today's Truth: Because you are my help, I sing in the shadow of your wings. Psalm 63:7

MARCH 22

A STRANGE KIND OF SUNDAY

There was no sense of urgency when we went to bed last night. A normal Saturday night concludes with necessary food preparations for the Sunday meal at church. Gary rehearses any readings or other duties he might have for the morning's service. I plan the timing of the day, including my coffee-making responsibilities for our church fellowship.

But none of that was necessary. The mandate from the state is that no more than ten people may meet in close proximity. No more than ten in a restaurant; hence the transition to carry out and drive through service. No more than ten in a gym at one time; makes it hard to get a group together for a workout. No more than ten in a meeting; hence the rise of virtual meetings. The world is rapidly changing.

With church services cancelled, it offers a glimpse on what it might be like in countries where Christianity is not tolerated. Meeting in a group of ten for an illegal church gathering in China risks imprisonment. Online bible teaching is now against the law in some Chinese provinces. Conversion to Christianity in Myanmar often results in persecution from the Buddhist monks, those practicing animism, or the government itself. On March 19, it was reported that a young woman in Morocco was divorced by her husband because she refused to renounce her faith in Christ. The courts denied any child support for that reason. A pastor and his family were assaulted by an angry mob led by monks in Sri Lanka on Feb 2 after leading a Christian worship service.

Purusing the *Voice of the Martyrs* website (**https://www.persecution.com/about/**) puts into perspective what believers around the world face daily. I presume our inability to meet as a church is a temporary inconvenience. But what if it became the new normal? Would we find ways for fellowship and accountability, or abandon meeting forever?

Sitting on my couch this morning listening to melodic, theologically sound music is worshipful and wonderful. But I miss my church family. Once the virus runs its course, perhaps we will have a greater appreciation for meeting together on Sunday mornings.

Today's Truth: Not forsaking the assembling of ourselves together, as the manner of some is; but exhorting one another: and so much the more, as ye see the day approaching. Hebrews 10:25

March 23

Is there something wrong with me?

A young tennis player asked to meet with me this morning. With careful regard to the six-foot mark for safe social distancing, we met face-to-face. Previous attempts to get together failed given team travel and complicated schedules. But with all university classes now being online, we were both more flexible.

"Jenny" is a quiet yet driven young athlete. She played her freshman year at another university before transferring here. Last year she was a "regular" student, choosing not to compete. But this year, the coaches honored her desire to return to collegiate tennis by offering a walk-on position. While the scholarship athletes have a "full-ride," Jenny is responsible for the cost of her education. She reaps the benefits of being a full-fledged team member, but pays tuition, room and board, and a myriad of other expenses.

Jenny is smart. She is cerebral and analytical. She is not one to holler and yell and exude excitement. Rather, she is reserved in demeanor, but intrinsically motivated to excel. She is a lioness. She is steady; never too high and never too low. She is coachable and willing. But she is also excluded or ignored by her teammates.

We spent time discussing why this might be. Could it be there is a wide gap in personalities? Is it possible the scholarship girls somehow disregard Jenny's importance on the team? Is it being socially unaware that sitting apart from Jenny or failing to invite her to an activity might be hurtful? As mature as Jenny appears to be, the emotions associated with not being wanted are certainly challenging. The wounds are deep.

So, what is our responsibility? We cannot make someone else change. But we can be aware of our own actions and attitudes. We can be above reproach and intentional with leaving our comfort zones to make deeper connections with others. We can be thankful that God purposely made us different. And at the end of the day with a clear conscience, we can leave the rest to God.

Today's Truth: Get rid of all bitterness, rage and anger, brawling and slander, along with every form of malice. Be kind and compassionate to one another, forgiving each other, just as in Christ God forgave you. Ephesians 4: 31, 32

March 24

The territory

Juno, our cat, has been around since 2008. She and her siblings came to the house as guests. Two stayed, and two were placed in other homes. Ra, Juno's brother, stuck around for several years until, we assume, he met his demise when he wandered off in a snowstorm. Since then, Juno has been queen of the castle.

Juno is very sweet. She is like a lap dog except for the fact she is a cat. Anytime I take a seat on the sofa, she deftly claims her spot. After kneading my belly with her front paws, making me feel kin to the Pillsbury Dough Boy, she wiggles onto my chest, her front legs on either side of my neck. Sometimes she licks me, which is simultaneously adorable and annoying.

Juno is an easy pet. Leave for a week and all she needs is a pile of food and a bowl of water. If she gets hungry, she goes on a hunting expedition. A litter box has never been part of the equation. There is a kitty door through which she can pass day or night. There has never been a problem with making a mess in the house—until the last couple months.

She seems to have developed an affinity for throw rugs. If we forget to pick up the bathmat when there is bad weather outside, she is likely to piddle. Good thing we can throw those rugs in the washer, although Gary has suggested we throw the cat in as well.

Animals have a way of marking territory with their pee. Come to think about it, people mark their territories as well: "Keep out. Private property." But if given the opportunity, most would love to expand their territory.

Jabez, the honorable son of Helah, had vision for what could be rather than what was. His prayer was for his territory to expand. He was convinced new opportunities awaited. He did not want the status quo. He was not afraid to venture out. He simply knew that God had a job for him that was far outside his current situation.

Perhaps we need to ask God to expand our territory, opening new avenues for caring, comforting, and kindness, especially in these uncertain days of a world-wide pandemic.

Today's Truth: "Oh, that you would bless me and enlarge my territory! Let your hand be with me, and keep me from harm so that I will be free from pain." And God granted his request. 1 Chronicles 4:10

MARCH 25

LONELY BUT NEVER ALONE

On this day 92 years ago, my mother was born in McKeesport, Pennsylvania. The oldest of six kids, the Wunderley family life was, well, wonderful. Times were tough through the depression years but love prevailed. Meals were simple, usually involving potatoes and other produce grown in the large garden. It was a tight family community, held together with love, honor, and integrity.

Mother is one of three siblings who are still alive. The three brothers have passed. The three sisters remain. Of the sisters, Mother is the only widow, my dad passing back in March of 1986. Since then, she has been through significant changes. From caring for my childhood home, to moving into an independent living apartment in a retirement community, to now spending her days in the assisted living unit of that same facility. It is a good place to live with excellent care. Meals are tasty, nurses and aides gifted and caring.

With the Covid-19 pandemic sweeping through the country, the facility has been under lockdown to protect their precious but vulnerable inhabitants. No visitors may enter, and no resident goes out except for emergencies. No longer are meals served in dining areas. Each resident is delivered a take-out box for breakfast, lunch, and dinner. There are no more hall movies, group puzzle sessions, or gatherings in the activity room. The already lonely residents are left to ponder away the long days and nights with very little human interaction.

Mother is terribly lonely. Anyone in her situation would be. But I am so glad she is never really alone. Nor are we. *The Spirit himself testifies with our spirit that we are God's children* (Romans 8:16).

During his ministry on earth, Jesus was often confronted by the Pharisees and other religious leaders. In one discussion there was question about who Jesus really was. He said, . . .*I am not alone. I stand with the Father, who sent me* (John 8:16b).

Is Mother lonely? Undoubtedly. Can any of us feel lonely and isolated? Indeed. Are we actually alone? Never.

Today's Truth: The one who sent me is with me; he has not left me alone, for I always do what pleases him. John 8:29

MARCH 26

CONNECTIONS

The world sure is changing. At least for the short-term, I am not going into my campus office every day. It was the norm for me to spend hours upon hours going to practices, meeting with coaches or athletes, and doing logistical planning that comes with sports-related ministry. But with Covid-19, those interactions are almost impossible. In our state of Virginia, the governor has made it a crime to meet privately or in public groups of ten or more. The penalty for such behavior is a misdemeanor on your police record. But in general, all face-to-face meetings are being discouraged. Hence, a change of work plans.

Good thing technology is so adaptive. Tomorrow I will be using video conferencing to meet a girl who needs internship hours. Later in the day there will be a huge video conference with many of my colleauges. Next Tuesday, women college coaches will meet me in a virtual room for encouragement, fellowship, prayer, and biblical truth. I will be inviting the members of the teams I work with to join me in similar fashion. Staying connected when everyone has dispersed to parts unknown is a privilege.

Staying connected—whether in person or in a virtual environment—is extremely important. God created us for relationship, and disregarding his intentions is never a good idea. Sure, there are times when solitude is desirable for renewal. Even Jesus needed alone time. But if you remember, Jesus also had a group of trusted followers by his side. Development of those relationships was critical to the individual. But consider the impact each disciple had on the early church and the furtherance of the Gospel. It would never have happened without the intimate relationship Christ had with those he loved.

There is truth for us in that first century example. Whether or not I am seated across a table or in front of a computer monitor, I have opportunity for connecting in meaningful ways with friends, family, colleagues, athletes, and coaches. And the chance to involve more people than ever before is very real given that being in the same place at the same time is not all that important.

Today's Truth: My goal is that they may be encouraged in heart and united in love, so that they may have the full riches of complete understanding, in order that they may know the mystery of God, namely, Christ, in whom are hidden all the treasures of wisdom and knowledge. Colossians 2:2, 3

March 27

Reshaped

One thing is for sure. I am tired. What started off as productive office work from the comfort of my dining room table has gotten a lot more physical.

UPS drivers have been protesting about the trees overhanging our long, rough driveway. To make them happy, it required taking down a huge cedar tree and dead locust that stood at the top of the hill, about a third of the way to the main road. Seth, having extensive experience working for an arborist, did most of the precision work. He cut off the lower branches, used rope and chains to secure the tree to the tractor, and made the necessary cuts to bring down the trees.

With Gary in the tractor, Seth instructed him to keep tension on the line. One tree and then the other fell safely away from the power lines. Then the real work began. The trees and all the branches needed to be dragged to the middle of the large field back down the hill toward the house. Load after load, tree limbs and trunks were put in piles, chained together, and then tractor-dragged to the appropriate spot for burning.

You know what was interesting when it was all said and done? Our very rough driveway looked so much better than before it was assaulted by loads of trees. High spots down the middle got flattened and ruts were filled in. We did not anticipate a smoother driveway when we cut down those trees, but that is exactly what happened.

If the driveway represents us, sometimes it takes a whole lot of pounding to get us looking decent. The process is rarely pleasant, but just like the driveway, if the process is not severe, the outcome would not be as favorable.

There are certainly many examples throughout Scripture making it clear that long-term suffering produces endurance and perseverance, both necessary for growth and maturity. But sometimes we need a drastic event rather than long, drawn out challenges. Like the blistering refiner's fire, it is possible to be radically and quickly changed.

Today's Truth: His third I will put into the fire; I will refine them like silver and test them like gold. They will call on my name and I will answer them; I will say, 'They are my people,' and they will say, 'The Lord *is our God.'" Zechariah 13:9*

MARCH 28

ROCKS ARE HEAVY AND HARD

If I was tired last night, double that for tonight.

About ten years ago I started digging a hole—a big one—in front of our door. We had just redone a very leaky and rotten sunroom, and the entrance was crying out for beautification. I love fishponds, having put in two at a previous house. Hence, I did the reasonable thing when I grabbed a shovel. To the right of the door was the largest and deepest part of the pond. To the left was a shallower side. A trough connected the two bodies of water, over which the covered porch decking was installed.

Having an endless supply of rocks on our property, the left side of the pond showcased a mountain of rocks. I created it to be a waterfall, but was never pleased with the look. Hence, I have tried various "spitters" perched on the rocks or in the water to provide more splish-splashes, a welcome sound on a warm summer night. However, I have wanted to rework that mound of rocks for quite some time. Today was the day.

The mountain was deconstructed, rocks strewn everywhere. I labored to mix 80 pounds of mortar. A new catch-basin to create a waterfall was incorporated into the design. Then, in puzzle-like fashion, each rock was positioned to create a well-balanced and stable mound, flatter on top than before. When I finally connected the pump and watched the water cascade into the pond, I was pleased.

The rocks were heavy and hard, something I knew intellectually, but experienced first-hand when I lifted each one multiple times. The largest of them had to serve as the foundation for the others. It was imperative to make sure I positioned them well, their places guaranteed by generous dollops of mortar. I am confident that should a thundering crowed of feral children play king of my mountain, the rocks will stand firm.

Without a firm foundation we may as well not build. Jesus Christ is the foundation of our faith. Without him, we cannot stand. The structures of our life will inevitably crumble.

Today's Truth: Therefore everyone who hears these words of mine and puts them into practice is like a wise man who built his house on the rock. The rain came down, the streams rose, and the winds blew and beat against that house; yet it did not fall, because it had its foundation on the rock. Matthew 7:24, 25

MARCH 29

MEMORIZE AT MY AGE?

My memory is embarrassingly poor. Especially names. I interact with people daily and come up blank with their name. I recognize them, can tell you what they do, but put a name to their face? Hardly ever. Or I look at a list of things or numbers and need to recreate it. Without a copy and paste function, I am doomed. Sometimes I think I should see a doctor since I am convinced there is pathology behind my weak-minded memory.

But then again, I can remember specific conversations I had on the trail with friends 25 years ago. Verbatim. At the exact spot. Sometimes even a scent of a flower can spawn a memory. So why the difference? Why can I recall some things and not others?

I opened Biblegateway.com this morning. On the home page was the "Verse of the Day." Today's verse came from 2 Corinthians 5:21: *God made him who had no sin to be sin for us, so that in him we might become the righteousness of God.*

As soon as I read the first three words, the rest of the verse raced through my brain. Wow. I had memorized that verse sometime in my youth (though likely in the King James Version). It was probably when I was involved in the Awana program at our church. Awana's focus on Scripture memorization had me learning a ton of verses. It is possible that the Timothy trophy I earned for memorizing 300 verses may still be packed away in the attic.

I read of prisoners of war that recall Scripture in their dank and lonely cells. I recall stories of people in ridiculously desperate situations that draw strength and solace from memorized Truth. And even as I write these daily stories, a relevant Scripture often comes to mind. I may not remember it in its entirety, but enough that I can find it.

Perhaps I need to be intentional with memorizing now, even in this decade of life. I have no doubt it will come in handy in guiding my every-day living.

Today's Truth: But as for you, continue in what you have learned and have become convinced of, because you know those from whom you learned it, and how from infancy you have known the Holy Scriptures, which are able to make you wise for salvation through faith in Christ Jesus. All Scripture is God-breathed and is useful for teaching, rebuking, correcting and training in righteousness, so that the servant of God may be thoroughly equipped for every good work. 2 Timothy 3:14-17

MARCH 30

QUIET AND PEACEFUL

At the beginning of this pandemic, I felt a strong pull to be tuned into the latest news about its spread and containment strategies. But now, after weeks of doomsday reporting, I seldom watch the broadcasts. I continue to be cautious as advised. I simply cannot watch it unfold on TV 24/7.

Even social media is becoming an issue for me. I suppose I fit the descriptive of Facebook users: the "older" generation. Yes, those of us 60 and above joined Facebook to stay in touch with family, friends, and connect with long-ago classmates. We never really moved on to Instagram, Twitter, or Snapchat. The younger set took care of that.

My Facebook participation has been decreasing over the last year for a variety of reasons. Seldom do I post anything personal save the antics of my granddaughter. I will post items of interest on the page related to sports ministry. But as I scroll down each screen, I see that while 50% of the posts are ego-centric, the other 50% are driven by political and social bias. Name calling, broad generalizations, and propagation of false information are rampant. It makes me gag, especially when someone who claims Christ seems to have checked civility at the Facebook doors.

Surely, there is reason to defend a position or a person. However, I cannot think of an instance when those words should not be coated by generous amounts of grace. We do more harm than good if we are mean, crude, and rude. But when it comes right down to it, maybe we need to severely limit our social media interactions to avoid getting stirred up by something perturbing.

Reading a passage in 1 Timothy has reminded me of an extremely important principle. We are to pray for those in authority. We are to lead quiet and peaceful lives. For in doing so, Jesus Christ is seen more clearly.

Today's truth: I urge, then, first of all, that petitions, prayers, intercession and thanksgiving be made for all people—for kings and all those in authority, that we may live peaceful and quiet lives in all godliness and holiness. This is good, and pleases God our Savior, who wants all people to be saved and to come to a knowledge of the truth. For there is one God and one mediator between God and mankind, the man Christ Jesus, who gave himself as a ransom for all people. 1 Timothy 2:1-6

MARCH 31

RAINY DAYS AND DRIPS

After being spoiled by warm, sunny weather, today is cold and rainy. In fact, it is so damp that our woodstove has been put to good use. The warmth emanating from the metal behemoth feels glorious.

Despite our coziness, Gary and I began to hear a very rhythmic "kerplunk" coming from the second floor of the house. After racing up the stairs, we witnessed the unfortunate scene of water dripping through the ceiling and onto the floor. That is never a good sign. Further inspection in the attic revealed what we suspected; a hard to identify roof leak. Honestly, we have known about the problem. Gary has been on the steep roof more than once applying thick, goopy tar in every nook and cranny. Nothing has solved the problem. Conceding temporary defeat, a plastic bin was placed to corral any leaks. Somehow, the bin had been pushed out of drip-catching position.

Of course, the leak is not a problem when it is not raining. But here's the rub: when it rains, it pours. The rain, a good thing in and of itself, simply reveals the underlying problem. The rain is not the problem. Our unsuccessful attempts to patch the roof is the problem. What we need is a new roof.

It is easy to glide along on a wish and a prayer when things are good. Our emotions are intact, we act like we are in control, and for anyone looking in from the outside, there are no visible "drips." However, when the rain starts falling, our deficiencies are quickly revealed. So starts our "leaking."

Honestly, it is our mouth that most often drips. A ref makes a bad call in a game. We explode in protest. Our spouse leaves his dirty clothes beside the hamper, not in it. Our offered quip is snide. A Facebook "friend" writes a post that angers us. We respond without grace.

Maybe we need a new roof in our mouths so that when it rains, nothing bad leaks out.

Today's Truth: A good man brings good things out of the good stored up in his heart, and an evil man brings evil things out of the evil stored up in his heart. For the mouth speaks what the heart is full of. Luke 6:45

APRIL 1

GULLIBLE GRANNY

I should have known better, but he sounded so sincere.

A group text came from the associate head women's tennis coach this morning. "Team. Please watch this video." Clicking the play arrow, I watched as he looked into the camera with sincerity oozing from his eyes. "As of today, I am resigning. Meredith has been offered a job at the hospital that will pay a lot of money. I am going to stay home to take care of the kids. This is the best thing for our family. But please let me know if I can do anything for you."

The video was a little over two minutes. At its completion, I fired off a sentiment equivalent to "I respect your decision. You will be missed." Within minutes, others responded in like manner.

But then Alex asked, "Is this an April Fool's joke?"

Uh-oh. I had not considered that possibility. But then again, he was so believable in that video. Other staff members had written "I understand" notes as well. If it were a joke, why would people in the know fall for the charade?

Moments ago, I got my answer. I was taken. I had become the gullible granny who bit it hook, line, and sinker. Coach must be feeling very pleased with himself. Perhaps he should switch his career to a pro poker player because he certainly outwitted us all.

It is easy to fall prey to foolishness. Proverbs offers descriptives: those who act poorly, disregard parents, have loose tongues and a quick temper, and those who lack wisdom, refusing to seek it. I think we get the idea.

The opposite of foolishness is the word "consider." It means to intentionally evaluate, to think carefully about, to regard. Approximately 130 verses use the word. The more telling directives are found in the Gospels. In Matthew 1, Joseph contemplates the angel's message and acts accordingly. Dr. Luke asks worried Believers to *consider the lilies of the field. . .* to put God's care for them in perspective. And Mark records that Jesus himself asks his followers to *Consider carefully what you hear* (Mark 4:24).

Christ calls us away from foolishness, and into careful, thoughtful consideration.

Today's Truth: O simple ones, learn prudence; O fools, learn sense. Proverbs 8:5

APRIL 2

MAKES NO SENSE

A few days ago, I was thinking about the use of social media. Not infrequently, posts from both the right and the left strike me as hateful and mean-spirited. Not only are alternate views attacked with a vengeance, but the people behind those posts are also bloodied in the process. I much prefer seeing pictures of friends' grandkids and playful kittens over anything debatable. Conflict is not my thing.

I did not want to "stir the pot" with anything controversial, though I admittedly have strong opinions about things related to faith and the natural out-living of those beliefs. To bring perspective, encourage others to take a gentle approach, and pray for those in authority, I made a Facebook post quoting from 1 Timothy 2:1-6. I made no other comment.

I urge, then, first of all, that petitions, prayers, intercession and thanksgiving be made for all people—for kings and all those in authority, that we may live peaceful and quiet lives in all godliness and holiness. This is good, and pleases God our Savior, who wants all people to be saved and to come to a knowledge of the truth. For there is one God and one mediator between God and mankind, the man Christ Jesus, who gave himself as a ransom for all people.

This evening I opened Facebook. The comments on the initial post had been affirming and pleasant, some thanking me for the reminder. But a new post popped up. I do not know the fella who commented, but here is what he said. "Actually, going by the current situation, god is about as useful as an ashtray on a motorbike. This planet is an insignificant speck in one of many universes."

I drew in a deep breath. Wow. As useful as an ashtray on a motorbike? An insignificant speck? How sad that someone is so far removed from the truth. It must be an awful feeling to have no hope, to feel so insignificant and without purpose. I simply replied, "I'm sorry you feel that way." Apart from the Spirit of God, nothing I say will change his mind. To him, anything spiritual is foolishness. It makes no sense.

I will ask God to give this man sight.

Today's Truth: For the word of the cross is folly to those who are perishing, but to us who are being saved it is the power of God. 1 Corinthians 1:18

APRIL 3

WEEDS

After hours of virtual meetings, a by-product of the Covid-19 social distancing mandates, I fled the screen that holds such power. With the sun shining and temps pleasant, I joined the rest of my family outside. After surveying the work possibilities, the bushes around the pool received their spring haircuts. Then it was on to pulling weeds, cutting grass, and tidying up. That was the easy part.

Seth and Pam (our son and daughter-in-law) have taken a strong interest in gardening. A large plot has been tilled, and their living room looks like it has been converted into a greenhouse. Earlier today they painted and labeled 25 stakes to make identifying the vast numbers of seedlings feasible. However, their ideas did not stop there. "Mom," Seth inquired. "What if we made that area along the house a raised bed? It would be a great place to plant all the herbs since it's so close to the kitchen."

Having no reason to be contrary, Seth set off on a mission to scoop up piles of rocks and tractor buckets of soil near the edge of the woods. I helped him lay out the landscape fiber for weed control before arranging what seemed like a bazillion stones. Filling the area with dirt, it was surprising how dark and rich the soil seemed to be. There was only one problem. Along with the worm-rich soil (and one small snake thrown in for good measure) came clumps of woodland grass and weeds.

We certainly did not want to contaminate the new bed with weeds. Hence, clump after clump got banged against the tractor's steel bucket to separate the dirt from the vegetation. Though tedious, it was necessary. The bed now stands ready to foster the tender sprouts.

Jesus understood how important good soil is for growth and transformation. He taught his disciples the parable of seeds falling on the path, in rocky places, among thorns, and in good soil.

Where do you think we should sow Gospel seeds?

Today's Truth: The sower sows the word. . . . But those that were sown on the good soil are the ones who hear the word and accept it and bear fruit, thirtyfold and sixtyfold and a hundredfold. Mark 4:14-20

April 4

Weeds Revisited

If I thought about weeds yesterday, I thought about them even more today. With the "stay at home" order in place, my desire to go anywhere but the grocery and home improvement stores was low. But that means only one thing: more work.

The first project was to clean out an area where old and discarded flowerpots called home. What a mess! Ivy from the other side of the fence had invaded the ignored space, entangling anything and everything in its verdant web. It took several hours to clear the space, fill two huge garbage bags with throw-aways, and clip off and pull out as many of the ivy runners as possible. My hands and back will never be the same.

I was glad to be done with that, but then looked over at the old brick sidewalk. I recall writing a story long ago about pesky grass and weeds that grow between bricks. I use present tense because those suckers are still there! Maybe not the same generation but relatives none the less. No matter how much herbicide I spray on the offending vegetation, unwanted green ends up growing back. Always. Without exception.

My thought back then was that I first needed to kill everything before meticulously, weed by weed, pulling them out by the roots. After that, the cracks needed to be filled in to decrease the possibility of weeds growing back.

It worked. My sidewalk looked beautiful for several weeks. Unfortunately, my neglect to do the proper maintenance meant that within a short period of time, I was right back where I started: an unkempt, weedy sidewalk.

This illustration is just as accurate now as it was then. If we do not kill sin at first sight, it will soon make an awful mess. We need to dig down deep, grabbing the root of the problem. Then, once we get rid of the offense, the gap must be filled with safe measures to prevent the sin from resurfacing.

Kill. Pull it out. Fill the void. Repeat as necessary.

Today's Truth: See to it that no one fails to obtain the grace of God; that no "root of bitterness" springs up and causes trouble, and by it many become defiled; Hebrews 12:15

APRIL 5

GUILT BY ASSOCIATION

Waiting for our virtual church service to convene, I began to read through John 12. Being Palm Sunday, my desire was to review the events of that first-century event. As a kid growing up in a Baptist church, I remember waving palm fronds to reenact Jesus' entrance into Jerusalem, shouting "Hosanna!" all the way down the middle isle. The memory is sweet, but after so many years, I wondered if the details had gone fuzzy.

The setting is the town of Bethany, six days before the Passover commemoration was to begin. A special meal has been prepared in the home of Mary, Martha, and Lazarus, siblings all. Remember, this is the same Lazarus that had died, but the Savior raised him from the dead in a most miraculous way.

As hard as it is for us to wrap our heads around that, it is not hard to imagine throngs of people interrupting this intimate dinner among friends. "Is this the Jesus that does miracles? Is he a man like us? I wonder if Lazarus looks wierd now that he is again alive. Let's go check it out!"

And go they did. So much so that the chief priests noticed the huge crowd. This much attention given to Jesus and Lazarus meant one thing: their power was threatened. John 12: 11 reports, *for on account of him* [Lazarus] *many of the Jews were going over to Jesus and believing in him* [Jesus]. They plotted to kill both Jesus AND Lazarus.

I am not sure I ever realized there was a plan to take out Lazarus. But why? Because he was associated with Jesus. I can only assume how grateful Lazarus was to be reunited with his sisters. But at what cost? His life was now in danger simply because Jesus gave him life.

Jesus does the same for us. Though we were dead, he extends to us new life in Christ. We should not be surprised when that miraculous work in our life draws the attention of nay-sayers, those who want nothing to do with Him who saves. Nevertheless, when we dare to follow Christ, we join the chorus of the people in the streets of Jerusalem on that first Palm Sunday, "Hosanna!"

Today's Truth: The next day the large crowd that had come to the feast heard that Jesus was coming to Jerusalem. So they took branches of palm trees and went out to meet him, crying out, "Hosanna! Blessed is he who comes in the name of the Lord, even the King of Israel!" John 12:12, 13

April 6

In search of turkey sign

Call us crazy, but Gary and I went to the woods. We hopped in the car and headed across the valley. Once on the picturesque Blue Ridge Parkway, he steered the car northward in search of his "spot." The goal was to scout for turkey sign as a precursor to the start of the upcoming season in six short days.

Here is the back story. Hunting turkeys is a favorite pastime for this husband of mine. For years he ventured into the national forest for a chance to call in a big 'ol turkey. He often took friends with him, parking in the dark, wee hours of the morning, bushwacking up the mountainside, and positioning himself to fool a gobbler in search of love. Many of his hunts were successful. An unproductive Elmer Fudd he was not.

Though it was not immediately clear which parking area he used to call home base, he figured it out based on his recall of how the climb began. So off we went; across the parkway, up a ridge line to the right, fighting our way through thick stands of mountain laurel, and eventually intersecting with ATV trails high on the mountain. The hike along the trails led us to a relatively flat area. We abandoned the easy trail and began to look for sign. "I'll head to the left and you walk to the right," Gary instructed. "You know what you're looking for, right?"

Good question. Turns out that turkeys scratch around in leaves in their quest for bugs or whatever it is they find tasty. "So, I'm looking for messy leaves?" Hum. This should be interesting in a forest with its leaf-covered floor.

It was not until we checked out another area of open hardwoods that I caught on. I began to recognize areas of dirt with leaves shoved to the side. "Is this it?" I queried Gary. As he affirmed each turkey scratch, I felt like I had added a vital life skill to my resume.

So, think about this. If wild turkeys routinely leave signs, how hard it should be to identify our presence as Christ-followers? It seems to me that we should be making a difference wherever we are. People should be able to say, "Look. A Christian has obviously been here. We can tell."

Today's Truth: By this all people will know that you are my disciples, if you have love for one another. John 13:35

April 7

Privilege and Responsibility

My granddaughter is a hoot. She turned five this past December. She is smart, witty, even if sometimes feral squirrel-like in her endless energy output. She has a vivid imagination, sings, and dances, loves to ride motorcycles with her daddy, goes through endless outfits each day, and astounds us with her vocabulary and analytical skills. (Remember. I am her Grandma. That allows me to have lofty opinions about my only grandchild.)

When she visited last week, we worked hard at creating a new planting bed. This raised bed is outlined with rocks confiscated from the woods on our farm. As I was placing a heavy, awkwardly shaped rock, it rolled back toward my shin. It scraped off a dime-sized piece of skin but immediately started to bleed. The surrounding skin swelled to marshmallow-like puffiness. This supercharged injury response is the result of the platelet-inhibitors I take because of my coronary artery stent. The bruises and bleeding that make me look like an assault victim have become commonplace.

When the blood reached my sock, it was time to tend to it. Addy went with me, leading the way to the cabinet where the Band-Aids are kept. She expertly picked the proper size, removing it from the wrapper before positioning it over the wound. "Well, Dr. Addyson. Thank you for fixing me up," I offered. "How much do I owe you?"

Without hesitation she looked straight into my eyes and responded. "Nothing. You do not owe me a thing. After all, you are my Grandma." I laughed out loud.

Being part of a family comes with perks. Spiritually, when God chose us, we became part of the royal family. We have unlimited access to the King, and to his Son and Spirit. We are given all spiritual blessings and abundant life. We are given a full supply of grace and mercy. But we must also assume the responsibilities of being royal. We are called to act appropriately: love well, be careful how we live, be patient, loyal, forgiving, and just. We are to love mercy and walk humbly.

Yes. Being related has its privilege, but it also comes with responsibility.

Today's Truth: But you are a chosen race, a royal priesthood, a holy nation, a people for his own possession, that you may proclaim the excellencies of him who called you out of darkness into his marvelous light. 1 Peter 2:9

April 8

Step by step

My run today came after being glued to my computer screen for hours. The ability to interface with coaches and athletes via technology is superb. Relationships are being built outside normal boundaries. Truly, my territory is being expanded.

Nevertheless, having reached my daily quota of Zoom calls, I flung open the front door to step into the fresh, country air. It was a t-shirt and shorts kind of day; sun shining, moderate temperature, and warm breeze blowing. I walked for a minute, basking in the reality of being able to run along country roads with nary a concern for my safety. When two puppies that live at the top of our lane relentlessly followed me down the road, I retreated to the owner's front door for help. With the dogs held at bay, my pace quickened to get out of sight sooner rather than later.

I currently have no satisfaction of being in peak physical condition. My training has slipped, my legs feel wimpy, my endurance suspect. Regardless, my inner self instructed my outer self to take one step at a time. Enjoy the moment. Do not rush. Look around. Take in the wide-open pastures, the grazing cows, the birds soaring overhead. Be content where you are. Continue to make forward progress.

I was pleased with how well OuterSelf took the advice of InnerSelf. The route I ran was not particularly easy, but heeding the instructions made it pleasant. It is not that my breathing didn't get labored. But when it did, I made the proper adjustments in stride length, pace, and most of all, attitude. I arrived home contented and satisfied.

I tend to feel disgruntled if I dwell on what I have not done that I wish I had; do weekly 20-mile runs in the mountains, average 70 miles per week, bomb through great speedwork. Though I have done all that before, that is not where I am now. My mission nowadays is to take one step at a time, enjoying the beauty in every stride.

Should we look ahead and plan? Have long-term goals? Adopt huge, bodacious undertakings? Sure. Nothing wrong with that. But when we forget to appreciate the place where our feet are currently planted, then perhaps we need to re-evaluate.

Today's Truth: Therefore do not be anxious about tomorrow, for tomorrow will be anxious for itself. Sufficient for the day is its own trouble. Matthew 6:34

APRIL 9

EXCUSES

I was planning on running this morning. With an empty house and a light work agenda, I figured I better head on down the road. Scheduled to be the granddaughter picker-upper this afternoon, the time that follows is spoken for. A morning run would be best.

But here it is, nearly 1:00 p.m.. Though dressed for running, I have not run. It is sunny, but the winds are fierce! Tree debris is flying all over the place. A second-floor window screen and flowerpot occupying the sill literally just got sucked out from the frame, dancing across the porch roof before crashing to the ground. If I ran out there now, I might get blown all the way to Oz.

Sounds like an excuse to me. Yes, the wind is brutal, but had I really wanted to run, the wind would not have stopped me. I am an expert excuse maker. Sometimes the excuses keep me from doing something I really should do. In other instances, the excuse gives me a way out from doing something I should not be doing.

There is probably no better excuse maker in the Bible than Moses. The children of Israel are being held captive in Egypt. They are poor and needy slaves. They need a leader, and God has chosen Moses. But here's the thing. He came up with all kinds of reasons why he could not possibly be the guy.

Moses was a shepherd, guiding his father-in law's sheep when he had his first up close and personal encounter with God. With sandals off and face covered to protect from the Lord's bright glory, he listened with rapt attention to God's plan to free the people. But when God basically said, "Tag. You're it," Moses protested greatly.

"Who am I?" he said. "What if Pharaoh doesn't listen to me? I am no good with words! I cannot do it by myself. Let me have a helper."

So many excuses. And yet, the Lord had a solution for each perceived deficiency. And guess what? God used an excuse-filled, lacking confidence kind of guy to rescue his people. I take solace in the fact that though I come up with excuses in accomplishing God-appointed tasks, God is bigger than that. When I am weak, He is strong.

Today' Truth: For the sake of Christ, then, I am content with weaknesses, insults, hardships, persecutions, and calamities. For when I am weak, then I am strong. 2 Corinthians 12:10

April 10

Powerless No More

At first blush, I am not sure I have a captivating story today. The morning began with a mentoring session with one of my athletes. I listened as she described a tough couple of weeks when she came face to face with her sin, selfishness, and the resulting brokenness and repentance. She spoke of her heart's renewal. Of restored relationships. Of clear thinking. Come to think of it, maybe I do have something to write about.

Later in the morning, I virtually met with another young woman. When I talked to her last week, she was feeling ostracized and could not understand why. Relationships with teammates were swirling down the toilet. She felt lonely and disenfranchised. Today she communicated with joy that a teammate came to her in the wee hours of the morning asking for forgiveness. Their relationship is healing. This too, is something to write about.

Ten minutes after saying good-bye, I hopped on a session with athletes from various colleges and universities. Being Good Friday, the group was not as large as it has been. Nevertheless, one after another, these student athletes clearly articulated the power of the Gospel in their lives—now. Not yesterday, a year ago, or a decade ago. They each declared what the Spirit of God is currently teaching them. These testimonies are note-worthy.

Could any of this have happened sans a tragedy of epic proportions over two millennia ago? No. Never. Jesus voluntarily offered himself as a sacrifice on that cruel cross. There was no other way for man to be reconciled to a holy Father. He had to take all past sins, current sins, and future sins to the grave. What a dark day as the Father turned his head away while his only son endured an excruciating death.

But He did not remain in the grave! It was Friday, but Sunday was on the way. Up from the grave he arose, making possible the testimony of every single Believer.

So yes, Christ working in the lives of those young people is something to write about!

Today's Truth: For while we were still weak, at the right time Christ died for the ungodly. For one will scarcely die for a righteous person—though perhaps for a good person one would dare even to die—but God shows his love for us in that while we were still sinners, Christ died for us. Romans 5:6-8

April 11

Preparation

Whoever invented the term "stream of consciousness" must have known how my brain works. Thoughts bounce around among the axons and dendrites like a ping-pong ball in a windstorm. Thoughts change so quickly I can hardly keep up. Stray reflections come at any time: sitting, standing, watching TV, eating meals, lying in bed, in my sleep, and of course, when I run. Today was no exception.

The run was a mere four miles. But my thoughts probably changed every 30 seconds, if that long. I am not sure I can describe everything that came to mind, but I recall contemplating shoes. On my feet was a brand-new pair. "How do they feel? Are they laced with the appropriate pattern? How's the cushioning, and do I like the zero drop? Color sure is nice. Cushion is OK. Love the width and slipper-like feel. . ." That analysis morphed into planning what I might say in a Facebook post with a nod to the running store who took my order and shipped the shoes to my door. My mind created the text of the post, which again shifted my thoughts to a post I read right before heading out the door. That started a new string of thoughts.

A physician friend was hired to go to New York City to assist in setting up a field hospital capable of caring for 900 patients. They worked hard and prepared for the worst.

An athlete must prepare well to perform well. A musician practices hour on end for the upcoming concert. A teacher creates lessons to inspire and motivate her students. Those students prepare for upcoming exams.

Preparation should never be underestimated, especially when the task at hand is brutally difficult. On the Eve of our Easter celebration, think about Jesus. Did he go to the cross flippantly? Absolutely not. As a child he prepared himself as a communicator and teacher in the synagogue. Inside his three-year ministry, he took responsibility to prepare his disciples to proclaim truth when he was gone. But more than anything, Jesus prepared his own heart for what was to come. Time alone with the Father was key in his preparation to bear the sins of the world.

How in the world do we think we can be prepared to do God's work without spending alone time with the Father?

Today's Truth: But he would withdraw to desolate places and pray. Luke 5:16

APRIL 12

TO SEEK OR NOT TO SEEK

It sure is fun to pretend. On this Easter morning when corporate worship was via Zoom, our family had a day to celebrate together. Seth and Pam joined us to watch Addyson look out to the front porch. She squealed with delight when she spotted a stuffed bunny with pink polka-dotted ears alongside baskets filled with treats. After investigating her newly found treasures, she begged for the candy-filled plastic eggs to be hidden.

While Seth and Pam ventured out to hide the eggs, Addy and I shared sofa snuggles. This sweet girl, however, occasionally left me to wander off to the windows to sneak a peek. "Look," she exclaimed. "I see an egg by the tree and another one on the motorcycle. Oh, there is one on the car. Daddy is not a very good hider, but I think the other ones will be harder to find."

When it was time, she roamed the front yard, the garden and pool areas to find her candy-filled eggs. Then it was off to the "enchanted forest." This trail that winds its way through a stand of cedars beckoned the wee one. She scampered from tree to tree, plucking eggs from nooks and crannies. She was in her element. Her body, soul, and spirit had but one focus: Find. The. Eggs.

We could all use a lesson in laser-focused seeking. Not in seeking treasure or reward, riches or fame, but in seeking that which is eternal and truly worthy. One of the reasons I love the Psalms so much is because I get a glimpse of what it is to seek after God. *O God,* David writes, *You are my God; earnestly I seek you; my soul thirsts for you; my flesh faints for you, as in a dry and weary land where there is no water* (Psalm 63:1).

Can't you hear the yearning in his words? I recall being so thirsty I was cotton-mouthed. There was not a morsel of moisture, not even spit, to make swallowing possible. It was awful. I so desperately desired water to appease my thirst, I would have given anything in return.

Have I ever sought fellowship with God in the same way; in the way that I would give anything to hear His voice? In times of desperation, perhaps. But do I seek Him daily? I may as well ask forgiveness now.

Today's Truth: You have said, "Seek my face." My heart says to you, "Your face, Lord, do I seek." Psalm 27:8

APRIL 13

NOT A GREAT START

I have had better starts to the day. While still nestled under the covers, Gary informed me the cat had peed on the tile floor in the bathroom. Ugh. This twelve-year old cat is so sweet, curling up for a nap in any open lap she can find. But as of late, she has been using the throw rugs in our house as a potty spot. Occasionally, like this morning, she piddles on the bare floor. Since she was a kitten, she has used a kitty door that allows her to come and go at will. But it was blustery and raining last night. Maybe she did not want to get wet.

A few minutes later he came back in. The news this time was that Juno had also deposited "tootsie rolls" on the living room rug close to his spot on the sofa. No pee. Just poo that is easy to pick up. The cat was in big doo-doo because of her poo-poo.

Turns out, Gary was in big doo-doo as well. He was so angry at "my" cat, that he left the puddle and the poo for me to clean up. It was not a hard job, but I could not fathom that he did not at least throw a towel on the pee to sop it up. He also had to go to great lengths to avoid having poop stuck to his shoes since it was right by his seat on the sofa. Seriously? He couldn't pick up the dried deposits himself? The cat was in my naughty book, but I put Gary there as well with my snide comments.

The cat may be losing her happy home if she continues doing this. I know this. We have discussed it before. It is upsetting because I am rather attached to that fluff ball. But Gary's refusal to deal with the cat's "offerings" other than complain about them seemed, well, selfish. I was angry at both the cat and my husband. I whipped the mop across the bathroom floor and scooped up the dried poop in the living room. Gary retreated to the garage in the wake of my silent (mostly) fury.

Regardless of the rightness or wrongness of Gary's lack of action, I must be responsible for my own actions. Now, there is an unsettledness between us. I know what I need to do, and it does not include the phrase, "You made me so mad." No. I chose to be perturbed. Gary is not responsible for my reaction. I am. I also know I need to apologize and ask forgiveness. Then we can figure out what to do with this crazy, neurotic feline.

Today's Truth: Therefore, confess your sins to one another and pray for one another, that you may be healed. The prayer of a righteous person has great power as it is working. James 5:16

April 14

Close call

I wrote yesterday of my angst with Gary for leaving me to clean up the bad kitty's pee and poo. I admitted to feeling angry about his unwillingness to take responsibility for the cat. I have since asked forgiveness for my choice to let it get to me. But I almost did not have the chance.

When he came in the door, he held his filthy hands in front of him, heading right for the sink. "Ah, I'm confused. Did you actually go to work, or have you been working in the garage?"

"I went to work," he stated mater-of-factly.

"But why are your hands so dirty?"

"Because I had an interesting trip home," he replied.

Interesting is not the word I would have choosen. Gary, a pillar in tough times, seemed a little shaken. "I was going about 70 mph down Route 460 when my back tired exploded. The sound was deafening. I had absolutely no control of the car, weaving back and forth until I ended up in the muddy median separating east and west bound traffic. The mud was up to one of the axels, but I was able to get it into 4WD and get it to where I could change the tire."

I stood there, dumbfounded. "How did the car not roll when you hit that ditch?"

"I don't know."

"Did you have on your seat belt?" I inquired. It is no secret he often goes without. I try not to nag him about it.

"No," he answered sheepishly.

I shivered at the thought of Gary bouncing around inside the Jeep had it rolled. It easily could have been his last ride.

We never know what a day will bring. I am so grateful my husband was not hurt. It could have been so much worse. What a reminder that we are never promised a next sunrise. Perhaps we should all be more intentional about making each day we are given count for something good.

Today's Truth: Do not boast about tomorrow, for you do not know what a day may bring. Proverbs 27:1

APRIL 15

THE PLAYBOOK

Football coaches are known for guarding the team's playbook with their life. A lot of effort and years of experience go into formulating the offensive and defensive plays the team practices and runs in game situations. Serious consequences result if any of this super-secret information gets leaked.

Of course, football is not the only one with a playbook. Basketball programs come to mind. When I attend collegiate basketball practices, the names of the plays sound like jibber-jabber to me since I do not really understand what is supposed to be happening. It is irritatingly confusing unless you understand the plays, executing them with precision.

Granted, there are some sports where a written playbook is not necessary. Swimming and diving come to mind. Perhaps even gymnastics. But there is no sport that is devoid of expectations of how things are to be done, even if on an individual basis. Those who excel in the sport are particularly adept at performing to meet or exceed the expectation.

I was on a Zoom call today with colleagues and college coaches. One of my friends was at the plate, so to speak, to offer biblical encouragement. His premise? Run the play. The Bible is our ultimate playbook.

We know that Scripture is powerful, God-breathed, and is useful for *teaching, for reproof, for correction, and for training in righteousness. . .* (2 Timothy 3:16). Why is that?. . .*that the man of God may be complete, equipped for every good work* (2 Timothy 3:17). Therefore, we can be confident that the Scriptures have a play we can run in any circumstance.

Does worry overwhelm us? Philippians 4:6-7 and 1 Peter 5:7 have something to say about that. Does fear do us in? Isaiah 41:10 along with Psalm 56:11 can be go-to verses. What about identity issues? Check out Galatians 2:20. What if we are feeling hopeless due to our circumstances? Find encouragement in Psalm 34:17, 20 and Philippians 4:11-13.

"The Playbook" can—and should—guide our actions and attitudes. But having the playbook and knowing the playbook are two completely different things. It takes intention, study, and skillful application to put that playbook to good use.

Today's Truth: so shall my word be that goes out from my mouth; it shall not return to me empty, but it shall accomplish that which I purpose, and shall succeed in the thing for which I sent it. Isaiah 55:11

April 16

Family!

I must admit to being cumquat-like this evening. Gary and I are relaxing on the sofa, watching a DVR'ed episode of "Survivor." The longest-standing reality show to ever be broadcast, this season's 20-person cast were all previous million-dollar winners. This time around, the prize is doubled. Not surprisingly, the war between winners is vicious.

Nevertheless, for the first time in the history of the show, the families of each cast member were flown in for a day-long and very unexpected visit. There was no competition to determine who got to spend time with the loved ones. There were no tearful good-byes after the briefest period of hugs and kisses. There was simply a day of pure bliss on the beach. Enemy lines were erased as kids struck up play with kids from other families. Even if for a day, contestants saw each other as real people; husbands, wives, sisters, fathers, and mothers. Laughter abounded and a time out was called in game play.

While watching the Survivor scenario play out, I was also listening to raucous laughter from the second-floor apartment in our home. Seth and Pam were up there, along with Addyson. I never figured out what was going on, but it included squealing, laughing, and joking. Sadness had no place between the walls. What I heard emanated out of pure love and joy.

The home, no matter how privileged or humble, should be a place of safety and security. Our homes should be a place where joy abounds, even in difficult times. Laughter should be music to the soul. There should be an abundance of grace when we offend another. Forgiveness should be offered promptly, particularly in the wake of confession. We must never take our family members for granted. Patience should persist, with loyalty and support assured. We should invite our family members to keep us accountable and return the favor to them.

Go ahead. Live, laugh and love. It is good for the soul. It is good for everyone.

Today's Truth: A joyful heart is good medicine, but a crushed spirit dries up the bones. Proverbs 17:22

APRIL 17

WHEN IS IT TIME TO STOP PUSHING?

Another virtual meeting just ended. Tension was palpable. Don't get me wrong. There was no yelling or screaming. Everyone was respectful. All spoke with pure motives. Still, the call started off in one direction and ended in another. The leader admitted he was discouraged, and clearly looked the part. Should we pursue a virtual college camp at the risk of Zoom burn-out?

On another front, I have been talking to many of our college athletes. Their lives have been turned upside down with seasons canceled and school closed. In the long haul, this down time is a Godsend. Our society—and particularly in sports— is push, push, push. Do. Do. Do. There is seldom time for deep-down rest. Many athletes are relieved, overjoyed even, at such a rare opportunity to take a break.

I have been thinking a lot about sabbath. We know it as a day of rest, patterned by the Father during creation. But this directive is expanded further in Israel's history. There was a Sabbath, also called Sabbatical, every seven years. There was to be no sowing nor reaping. The people hit the reset button and lived off what the land naturally provided. Their lands rested, and all lived more simply. God required the people to rest. He did not "need" them to continue working for his own work and will to be accomplished.

Even more significant was the Year of Jubilee. After seven cycles of Sabbath years (i.e., every 50 years) "normal" was radically reset. Slaves became free. Land and possessions reverted to original owners. The people once again lived simply, without laboring.

These reset marks were providentially ordained and necessary for the health of the land and well-being of the people. Why is it we feel compelled to be ever-working, ever reaching? Why is taking our foot off the gas-pedal so hard? Is God not big enough to do his bidding outside of our efforts? Let's not be lazy, but we need to trust God in our time of rest, reset, and renewal. His work will still be done, with or without us. That is guaranteed.

Today's Truth: but in the seventh year there shall be a Sabbath of solemn rest for the land, a Sabbath to the Lord. . . And you shall consecrate the fiftieth year, and proclaim liberty throughout the land to all its inhabitants. It shall be a jubilee for you, when each of you shall return to his property and each of you shall return to his clan. Leviticus 25:4, 10

April 18

Messy Bessy

Though it is nearly 10 p.m., moments ago was the first time I sat down all day. It was a DIY kind of day and I loved every minute of it.

Pam, Seth's wife, owns a 600 square foot cottage. It was built in the 1930's and consists of four rooms of equal size, a single bathroom added onto the back some years later. It has some charm but bigger issues. The ceilings are a mess, colors dark and dated, and floors need something drastic. The three of us finalized a game plan to get it "For Sale" worthy as we surveyed each room.

Then it was time to divide and conquer. The young couple headed to the home improvement store while I opened the first of many paint cans. Stir, roll, brush, clean, repeat. For the better part of ten hours, this transformed dingy to delightful. I became a Messy Bessy, paint splattered everywhere.

However, as busy as I was, Seth pulled the short straw. His job was to cover every inch of the ceilings with new dry wall. The flaking, heavily textured surface was beyond repair. The only option was to give it a face lift. Working overhead was not going to be fun.

Nevertheless, Seth worked smarter, not harder. For $25.00 he was able to rent a contraption that lifts the cumbersome drywall into place. If Pam and I had been required to hold the drywall above our heads until Seth had it screwed into the joists, it would have killed me. But had Seth tried to do the job by himself without the lift, it would have been impossible.

Being independent and capable are character skills worthy to be developed. However, I think we tend to put our egos front and center. We think we can do it all. We do not need any help. We seldom even think about asking for help. We refuse help. But that is not the way God designed us.

God designed us to be in community with one another. He wants us to care for our families, our neighbors, and our friends. We are to encourage, love, and contribute to the welfare of others. We are stronger together.

Today's Truth: God Almighty bless you and make you fruitful and multiply you, that you may become a company of peoples. Genesis 28:3

APRIL 19

CURSED DRYWALL

It was another morning to wake up naturally. No alarm needed. With a state-wide hunker down order remaining in place, church was on the couch via a Zoom call. With the 10:00 a.m. start, we enjoyed a leisurely breakfast. I had an idea I might need the energy later.

Like yesterday, there was a lot of work to be done at Pam's house. We made progress yesterday, but were under fire to finish off drywalling all the ceilings today. We did not want to pay another drywall lift fee. While I was the main painter yesterday, my job today was to tape and mud all the seams while Seth continued to work hanging the wretched panels. I presume you can deduce that neither of us has a passion for these jobs.

There was only once when Seth's frustration got the best of him. Without much fanfare, he simply walked out the back door and took refuge in the truck. Pam gave him some space before offering encouragement. Before too long, he came in, resumed the job, all the while singing along with the music blaring from the speakers.

By 7 p.m. we called it a day and headed home. As we warmed up left-overs for a late dinner, I asked them if they had thought of any spiritual lessons throughout the day. Seth quickly replied, "Yes. When God cursed the earth, he did it by inventing drywall."

We had a good laugh because it is clear no one in our household will ever aspire to do drywall professionally. Still, behind the humor, our responsibility to complete something we disdain is clear. Just because we do not like something is no reason to do a shoddy job. And just because a task is difficult, it does not give us the right to quit.

Think of the Apostle Paul. He had a very difficult assignment. He had to convince people he was no longer a Christian-killing machine, but a transformed, regenerate Believer. That caused some issues. Some chose to disregard his claims. Others, troubled that he had become a Christ-follower, repeatedly tried to kill him. He endured beatings, shipwrecks, and imprisonments. There was nothing easy or pleasant about those things. Still, Paul dealt with it because he knew that the cause of Christ trumped everything else.

Today's Truth: Whatever you do, work heartily, as for the Lord and not for men, knowing that from the Lord you will receive the inheritance as your reward. You are serving the Lord Christ. Colossians 3:23, 24

April 20

Confess

A colleague has used the TACOS prayer method for years. I have no idea if it was original with him, but it provides a purposeful approach to prayer. The alliteration is easy to remember.

The T stands for thanksgiving. Thanking God for who he is and what he has done is always a great way to begin a prayer. Reading the Scriptures back to God can also be key in the T part of your prayer time.

A is for adoration. Here we reflect on the character of God. We tell God why we love and adore Him, basing our prayers on what we know to be true.

Confession is what the C represents. We know that *If we confess our sins, he is faithful and just to forgive us our sins and to cleanse us from all unrighteousness"* (1 John 1:9). Just as a parent desires a child to confess a wrong-doing and ask forgiveness, so our Father asks of us the same courtesy.

O means we pray for others, and S asks us to pray for self.

I was part of our regional prayer Zoom call this morning with somewhere around 80 people on the call. The purpose was to pray through the five stages. In a group this size, I am not keen on opening my mouth. I take it in, my microphone muted with video on. But when our host announced we would separate into breakout rooms for confession, my heart skipped a few beats that even my medicines could not prevent.

"Confession? Why in the world would he chose THAT section? There is no way I am going to voice my blunders and inadequacies to a group of people I might not even know!" I immediately checked to confirm my microphone was muted and turned off my video. I disappeared, listening but remaining silent and wishing the time to be short.

I have been thinking all day about my decision to be a listener but not a doer. I doubt we need to pray out our deepest secrets with people we do not know, but confession is good for the soul. And besides that, God requires it.

I have no recourse but to confess today's sin right now.

Today's Truth: Therefore, confess your sins to one another and pray for one another, that you may be healed. The prayer of a righteous person has great power as it is working. James 5:16

April 21

Goal or mission?

I am privileged to interact with collegiate athletes daily. They challenge me to be better in so many ways: consistency, dedication, perspective, and being a genuine Christ-follower. My contact comes in various contexts, including individual mentoring and team studies.

I was asked to lead a series of virtual discussions with the women's basketball team. The content was to come from their reading of Joshua Medcalf's work titled "Chop Wood Carry Water." It is a quick and intriguing read. In this allegory, John, the main character, enters the process of becoming a samurai archer. Akira, the grand sensei, serves as John's guide and mentor in the ten-year progression of becoming great. There are many lessons learned along the way.

At one point, John talks with Akira about the upcoming apprentice tournament. John excitedly states his goal to win. Akira asks John to consider the possibility that "goals actually allow you to shirk your responsibility." Why? Because some goals, like winning a tournament or becoming a doctor, are not always in your complete control. Hence, if you fail, it gives you a way out.

Compare that to a mission. Mother Theresa's mission was "to serve the needs of the sick and the dying." See the difference? If you truly embrace a mission, there is NOTHING that will stop you from doing it.

We need more mission-minded people than goal-setting people. Knowing your mission uncomplicates life because it is the filter through which you analyze everything. If what we are doing does not contribute to the mission, we need to regroup. Being on mission gives us perspective for what is of value and importance—and what is not.

Paul was a man on a mission. His goal was not to start "X" number of churches nor create a large group of passionate followers. No. His mission was singular. It was to preach Christ only. Everything he did, every missionary trip he took, every imprisonment, every stoning and shipwreck, were all seen as steppingstones in fulfilling his mission.

What is my mission? What is yours?

Today's Truth: To me, though I am the very least of all the saints, this grace was given, to preach to the Gentiles the unsearchable riches of Christ, Ephesians 3:8

April 22

Self-control

If you have ever spent hours on the phone trying to resolve what should be a simple matter, you will relate to this story. We closed out an unfortunate history with a timeshare property last year. There were no sad tears to see it leave our humble property portfolio. What a blight to our finances whenever we received the ever-increasing owner dues each year, especially in the years when we were unable to vacation. We were ecstatic to be rid of those annual obligations.

However, we have been inundated with emails and phone calls trying to collect a debt they say we owe. When I became too frustrated to continue these conversations, Gary took over. In the last two series of conversations, he has gotten bounced around to at least ten people, spending a total of four to five hours on the phone. It seems like the organization's right hand has no interest in knowing what the left hand is doing. After today's extended discussion, in which Gary was close to super-human in maintaining his composure and patience, we are hopeful the situation is resolved.

Still, it begs the question: Why was I not able to handle the situation? Each time I tried to reason with the person on the other end of the phone my level of angst rose dramatically. My goal was to remain calm and logical, explaining in detail why she was wrong, and I was right. Something must have been lost in the translation. I was unable to get the representative to care about what I was telling her, let alone fix it.

Truth be told, I am disappointed in myself. Generally, I think I am good-natured, logical, and possess reasonably good communication skills. But why did this situation get under my skin? Why did my heart rate rise, my voice quiver, and my legs become antsy as I pled my case? So much for self-control. Wait. Make that Spirit-control—or lack thereof.

"Lord, help me be intentional in allowing your Spirit to control my own."

Today's Truth: Whoever is slow to anger is better than the mighty, and he who rules his spirit than he who takes a city. Proverbs 16:32

April 23

Sit and Think

On the dining room table, my office away from the office, sat several books in que for reading. With a fresh pot of coffee brewing and a love seat and blanket calling my name, I grabbed the books, my pen, and yellow highlighter. I was as snug as a bug in the proverbial rug, sipping away and soaking in each line. It was glorious.

I first re-read chapters from a book I was to discuss with the basketball women on a Zoom call. Once my memory was refreshed, I moved on to another book: "Get Out of Your Head" by Jennie Allen. The premise is that we must bring every thought—not just some—into captivity lest our thinking spiral out of the control. It is a spiritual war, insists the author, that we must learn to fight and win.

My mind reeled at the words I read. I related when Allen described an 18-month period of waking at 3 a.m., thoughts rampaging through her restless mind. Thoughts that made her question everything. Thoughts that went to worse-case scenarios. She prayed back God's own words by quoting from a Psalm memorized years prior; Psalm 139. She wanted badly to hold onto her faith, but the invasive seeds planted by the spiritual opposition wreaked havoc.

Jesus calls us to be thinking people. Looking through the early chapters of Matthew's gospel, Jesus asks the listeners to think; to evaluate what is said. In the middle and later chapters Jesus poses this question six times: "What do you think?" He was engaging them in conversation. He wanted them to process information and come to the correct conclusion.

Christianity is not a crutch. It is not for the weak-minded. Rather, it calls us to study to become *a worker who has no need to be ashamed, rightly handling the word of truth* (2 Timothy 2:15). It requires us to direct our thinking toward what is true, noble, right, pure, lovely, and admirable. That takes focused effort and intentionality. It takes the direction of the Holy Spirit in our lives.

Today's Truth: Finally, brothers, whatever is true, whatever is honorable, whatever is just, whatever is pure, whatever is lovely, whatever is commendable, if there is any excellence, if there is anything worthy of praise, think about these things. Philippians 4:8

April 24

A Lesson Quickly Learned

This morning I had a discussion with a college athlete. Admitting her propensity for allowing thoughts to run rampant, we planned our attack. We would work our way through Philippians in parallel with a book and video series by author Jennie Allen.

We need to *take captive every thought to make it obedient to Christ* (2 Corinthians 10:5). However, that is way harder than it sounds because we are in a spiritual battle with Satan and his demons. Hence, our minds become clogged with thoughts not consistent with the truth. The struggle is real, people. At least for me.

The first ten verses of Philippians 2 describe what controls the way Jesus thinks. It is humility. Nothing he said or did was anchored in selfishness. Though pulled at from every side, he remained steady and confident because he was other-centric; not ego-centric.

We learned today there are six things that battle for our thoughts: discontentment, noise, confusion, self-importance, complacency, cynicism, victimhood.

"Mallory, which on that list proves most problematic?" I asked. She responded honestly. Me? I reported that cynicism and victimhood were my biggest bugaboos.

Soon after, I had to deal with run-away thoughts. A colleague told me in an email a Zoom meeting was cancelled. I was texted by another friend. "Why are you not logged into Zoom?" I thought he was pulling my leg, but sure enough, the "there is no meeting today" was taking place at that very moment. Could it be the first guy lied? Could it be I was being excluded because I voiced a contrary opinion on last week's call? Feeling hurt, I immediately headed out the door to pound out some miles, mind whirling.

As it turns out, my feelings of being jilted were totally misplaced. I misunderstood the situation. I wasted precious time and energy because I was egocentric. It was a failed opportunity to bring those thoughts under the control of Christ.

Today's Truth: Do nothing from selfish ambition or conceit, but in humility count others more significant than yourselves. Let each of you look not only to his own interests, but also to the interests of others. Philippians 2:3, 4

APRIL 25

BABY FRUIT TREES

After being a lazy bum by stealing away extra minutes in bed, my productivity upon rising increased substantially. First came the kitchen cleanup and unloading the dishwasher. Then, our ancient 120+ year old wood floors soaked up the wax I rubbed on, knees protesting since this was an up close and personal kind of job. Between waxing and buffing, several loads of laundry began processing.

I headed out the door for a six-mile run, knowing time before the predicted rain was fleeting. Once home, jobs were quickly checked off the to-do list. The grass in the pool area got a haircut, items found a home in the cleaned out old shed, and weeds got yanked from the ground before mulch was spread.

But the peach tree just outside my front door needed attention. It is a supposed to be a dwarf tree with limited height and spread. Back in the fall, I gave it a serious trim, wondering at one point if I had been too aggressive. Granted, the tree has produced thousands, literally, of tiny peaches in the past, the boughs nearly breaking under the weight. Last year I pulled off many of the ping-pong ball size fruits, but none of the remaining ever matured enough to be edible.

Viewing it today, the tree apparently survived my trimming technique. The branches were thick with pea-size peaches. Out came my step stool to help me reach the highest branches. Though a tedious job, I plucked off 75% of the tiny orbs, hoping the remaining peaches will grow to normal size.

In the process, I noticed a couple dozen tiny trees growing in the mulch Inspecting the tender plants as I pulled them out, each had emerged from the seeds of fallen peaches.

I cannot help but wonder what might happen if we allow God to give us a good pruning. Will we become more fruitful? Will the process encourage those around us to produce fruit as well? Will a whole new generation of fruit-bearers rise up? I sure hope so. That is exactly the way God designed reproduction to be.

Today's Truth: Every branch in me that does not bear fruit he takes away, and every branch that does bear fruit he prunes, that it may bear more fruit. John 15:2

April 26

The next right thing

Our granddaughter knows all the songs. When she acts out the lyrics, she does so with remarkable accuracy and in dramatic fashion. This kid may be headed for the big stage.

What songs, you ask? Why, the score from Frozen 2 (and Frozen 1 and most of the other Disney movies.) Though I have seen Frozen, Frozen 2 was an unknown. So last night, Addy and I cuddled together to watch. She gave me hints about the plot and upcoming scenes before she abandoned me to run up the stairs to play with her Daddy and Pam. I had the screen to myself, Gary preferring his own distraction elsewhere.

In the whimsical show where two sisters discover truth and set free the enchanted forest, there is singing and dancing, sadness and remorse, wrongs righted, and evil reined in. Though I will not expound on the humanistic underpinnings of the movie, I will comment on the premise that no matter how hard it gets, no matter if hope seems lost, you must do the next right thing. Anna sings,

> *"Just do the next right thing,*
> *Take a step, step again, It is all that I can to do,*
> *The next right thing, I won't look too far ahead,*
> *It's too much for me to take, But break it down to this next breath,*
> *this next step. This next choice is one that I can make. . ."*

At first blush, it sounds like decent advice. But then the song concludes, "Then I'll make the choice to hear that voice and do the next right thing."

The voice? Therein lays the problem. "The voice" comes from within. The people of Israel were thrown into ruin when *every man did that which was right in his own eyes.* They listened to their own voice and paid the price. On the other hand, blessing came when men like David and his son, Asa, *did what was good and right in the eyes of the* Lord *his God.*

Should we be doing the next right thing? Absolutely. Should we be relying on our own wisdom? Absolutely not. When we become Christians, our "voice" is the very Spirit of God. Listen carefully, and then do the next right thing.

Today's Truth: Whoever is of God hears the words of God. The reason why you do not hear them is that you are not of God. John 8:47

April 27

God Cares About the Little Things

Have you ever met someone who could lose his head if it were not attached? Yep. That's my youngest son, who shall remain nameless less he be incriminated. He is good at losing things. Talented, in fact. And the more expensive or important, the higher the probability of it going MIA.

Let's see. In the past he has had to apply for a new driver's license because it went missing from his wallet. Then there have been a couple phones that disappeared, although one device ended up under the track of a skidsteer before it was found. And if I recall correctly, more than once a search for his GoPro camera went into full swing.

Guess what? His trend of losing track of possessions continued these last few days. That stealthy little GoPro I mentioned? Before leaving for an overnight camping trip with Pam and Addyson, he mentioned he was not sure where it was. He did not seem too concerned as he thought it was at Pam's house. Earlier today, Pam asked if I could stop by this house to see if I could find it. However, in the same text, she also asked me to look in the car for Seth's phone. Within the last few hours, his phone disappeared into thin air.

"What?!?! Again?" I thought to myself. I stopped by the house and looked behind the boards leaning against the wall, in the kitchen, on the windowsills, and in between sofa cushions. I looked everywhere but to no avail. When I texted back the bad news, both Pam and Seth responded. Seth's phone was found somewhere in the yard. It must have fallen out of his pocket when he and Addy were tooling around on the motorcycle.

I offered a prayer of thanksgiving for the found phone right before I pleaded for help in finding the GoPro. Seth's financial situation could not handle buying a new one, but his photography work requires it. In fact, I prayed multiple times for that little black piece of technology.

When I got home, Pam and Seth reported they found it. It was hiding in a bag with other random items brought from the house. Was it "magic" that the GoPro was found after I prayed? No. I do not call it magic. I call it the work of a compassionate God who hears and answers our prayers.

Today's Truth: casting all your anxieties on him, because he cares for you. 1 Peter 5:7

April 28

One by One

In recent days, much of my workday revolves around Zoom calls with coaches and athletes. One of my favorite calls includes women college coaches who gather at 10 a.m. every Tuesday morning. Usually, ten colleges and universities are represented. The group is becoming tight knit as the women lean into each other for support.

The group is growing organically. I have no interest in building a mega huddle that allows members to "hide." I value the intimacy of coaches who feel free to talk about concerns and strategies. Still, I am thrilled when someone new joins us.

One of our coaches is in a high profile D1 basketball program. Prior to this position, she was an assistant at the university where I serve. Being a very personable coach, she has maintained relationship with one of our former players. This player is now part of the coaching staff at an ACC school. Coach Erin texted Coach Sheana about today's call. Sure enough, Sheana popped up on my screen. I like this kind of growth.

As I skirted along country roads on my daily run, I thought about growth and how effective it can be on a one-to-one basis. Think about this. In the first century, Jesus started out with twelve guys. Counting out Judas, that group was responsible for continuing ministry. Though it is difficult, if not impossible, to verify these numbers, I found an estimate* that the global Christian population in 150 AD, approximately 120 years after Jesus's earthy ministry ended, was 40,000. However, just 50 years later, that number is estimated to have jumped to 218,000, and 1.17 million by 250 AD.

How did that happen? It happened because one person told another person, and that person told someone else. The good news of Jesus, the Gospel, spread like wildfire because people were obedient to evangelize.

That encourages me. I can feel very small and insignificant, but amazing things happen when we proclaim the power of the Gospel.

Today's Truth: For I am not ashamed of the gospel, for it is the power of God for salvation to everyone who believes, to the Jew first and also to the Greek. Romans 1:16

*https://www.thegospelcoalition.org/blogs/evangelical-history/how-many-christians-were-there-in-200-a-d/

APRIL 29

IT'S THAT TIME

I could hardly wait for the time to set aside my computer, open the door, and head for the open road. Though the sun hid behind the clouds, the warm temperatures and brisk breeze made for a lovely spring day. I was looking forward to "me" time when I could be alone in my thoughts with no rush to get back. Work was in my rear-view mirror.

I concentrated on taking in every little detail along the way: the newly sprouted neon green vines along the driveway, the treetops bending in the wind, an orange-colored wildflower standing alone in a mass of yellow blooms, the way a bird floated on the wings of the wind, and a lone squirrel scampering across the road and up a tree. I was content to make joyful, but pedestrian progress.

This being an out-and-back run, I touched the "End of road" sign, turned, and retraced my steps. I narrowly avoided being bit by a yippy, teeth-baring dog before turning right, 1.8 miles remaining of the 6-mile run. I passed a large pasture and pond, cows blissfully grazing. Then it was up a hill while watching the tall grass on the right dance freely in the breeze. As I passed an old schoolhouse long ago abandoned, I noticed multiple clumps of bearded iris in full bloom. Shades of purple and blue colored the pristine flowers. I nodded to them as if to say, "I see your beauty" before turning my focus to the upcoming hill.

For as long as we have lived in the area, those irises push their way through the soil every spring. And every year, seeing their beauty suggests the old song, "What a wonderful world," popularized by Louis Armstrong in 1967.

I never want to forget—even amidst pain and suffering and disruption of life due to the virus—what a wonderful world God has gifted to us season after season.

Today's Truth: for behold, the winter is past; the rain is over and gone. The flowers appear on the earth, the time of singing has come, and the voice of the turtledove is heard in our land. The fig tree ripens its figs, and the vines are in blossom; they give forth fragrance. Arise, my love, my beautiful one, and come away. O my dove, in the clefts of the rock. Song of Solomon 2:11-13

April 30

Filling in the Cracks

Even though it is tiring, I love manual labor. That is, I love most kinds of manual labor. The exception is, without a doubt, sanding down drywall mud.

Ecstatic that I had no scheduled Zoom calls today, I was pumped to grab some groceries before heading off to work at Pam's house. Getting this little house on the market is a priority, and it simply will not get done by itself. While Pam was at work for a few hours, Seth got started on the nasty job of sanding down the ceiling we installed last week. When I walked in to join him, he looked Casper-like; white from head to toe, covered in dust. The air was almost as thick with the fine particles clouding the air.

I joined him with the second sanding pole, but immediately knew I would not last long. I could not seem to find the correct angle for optimal sanding. Nevertheless, I completed one room before doubling back to re-mud the seams that needed additional attention. I was still working overhead, but it was far more satisfying.

When Seth left to pick up his daughter, I remained to clean up, organize, and move on to more painting in the kitchen. Curiously, as I moved between the four rooms, I noticed an interesting phenomenon. Three of the rooms have the original 90-year-old wooden floors. They are by no means perfect. However, since we are going for a country cottage look, we will be painting those floors white. Sweeping up the mounds of dust, I noticed that the little cracks between the narrow floorboards readily welcomed the dust. It was quite advantageous. The floors looked less beaten and worn with the dust filling in the cracks. I began to use my foot to force the dust where I wanted it. In the end, the paint should seal in the dust and the floor should look less rugged.

Who knew that choke-provoking dust could come in so handy? I wonder if some of the things we consider insignificant can serve a greater purpose than imagined. The "please and thank you's" of good manners. Simple kindnesses such as opening a door or allowing someone to go ahead in the check-out line. Completing chores with a smile. Being kind and considerate.

Go ahead. Fill some cracks and see how much better things look.

Today's Truth: And let us not grow weary of doing good, for in due season we will reap, if we do not give up. Galatians 6:9

MAY 1

MISSIONAL ATHLETICS

Thanks to the words of a colleague, I have a lot to think about. The context was a Zoom call with 45 college athletes, a few coaches, and an assortment of collegiate FCA (Fellowship of Christian Athletes) staffers. Nick, the speaker for the day, laid the foundation for understanding athletics as a pathway to fulfill Jesus's last commandment.

There are two realities for every believer: to first be personally transformed by the Gospel, and to subsequently take that faith and multiply it in the public sector. Jesus promised the transforming power of the Holy Spirit that should be used to witness in four different regions: Jerusalem, Judea, Samaria, and the "ends of the earth." Roughly speaking, the disciples were to be bold ambassadors at home, in surrounding areas, in enemy territory, and to the far reaches of the world.

Nick suggested that a believing athlete or coach is handed the same set of expectations. A soccer player from Virginia may never get to Jerusalem, but her Jerusalem is the very team on which she plays. There she can be a witness by loving her teammates and living out the instructions given in Philippians 2.

A field hockey team's Judea could be the administrators, and officials. A believing athlete or coach becomes an ambassador when attitudes and actions are filled with grace.

But what about our "enemies," the Samarian equivalent? It is unfortunate we view opponents as needing to be killed or crushed. Play should be optimal, but our actions and attitudes should bring out the best in us and the other team.

Then, what about the "ends of the earth"? What could that represent for the athlete who wants to be Christ's ambassador? Consider the bus drivers, custodians, grounds keepers, often "invisible" to all but the most observant. A team can have a huge impact by mindfully caring for and serving these folks.

The take way from today's lesson? There are plenty of ways to represent Christ in the athletic arena.

Today's Truth: But you will receive power when the Holy Spirit has come upon you, and you will be my witnesses in Jerusalem and in all Judea and Samaria, and to the end of the earth. Acts 1:8

MAY 2

LITTLE IS MUCH

Today was another project day at Pam's house. The pint-size house is begging for a hefty dose of TLC. Since she and Seth want to build on our acreage, that house is no longer needed. Hence, a serious rehab effort is necessary to get it ready for a favorable sale.

So far, the crumbling ceilings are covered over with drywall, all the walls and trim are the recipients of fresh paint, a dingy refrigerator got a facelift, and the front porch and railings are turning a different color. But remember those floors I wrote about last week? The ones we were going to paint for a country cabin look? Well, that plan got detoured when we discovered water damage and a few "mushy" boards.

Game Plan B is budget friendly. Before today, I had only read about this option in DIY magazines. The idea is simple. Buy inexpensive half-inch plywood, cut it into strips, nail it down, stain, seal, and presto-chango, a new floor.

Fourteen sheets with five cuts each meant 70 rips to create the eight-inch-wide boards. Each one was then sanded on the edges and lightly on the top. Into the house they went to be nailed down after being cut into appropriate lengths. Of course, staining and sealing comes next, but first we need to finish the remaining room and a half.

So far, the floors look remarkable. I can hardly wait until they are stained and sealed. What we did—and are still doing—is taking humble bits of wood and turning them into a floor that resembles one ten times the cost.

God has a habit of taking the small and insignificant and multiplying it over and over. He did that with his chosen, Israel. He took that rag-tag bunch of problem children who had trouble obeying, making them into a great and mighty nation.

We may feel like we are of little value, but we need to be content and allow God to do his thing.

Today's Truth: The least one shall become a clan and the smallest one a mighty nation; I am the Lord; in its time I will hasten it. Isaiah 60:22

MAY 3

VIRTUAL CHURCH

In these days and weeks of "stay at home" orders, church groups are prohibited from meeting. It is a bizarre to not go to church for weeks on end. I assure you, from the time I was a mere babe, I spent more Sundays (and Wednesdays) inside the walls of a church than not. It was what we did as a family.

Gary and I continued that habit in college, and once we became a family, our kids joined us. Our church attendance was not entirely out of habit, although a habit is not necessarily a bad thing. We understood that Believers need fellowship, accountability, and to be under the teaching and authority of a local church.

We attend a small fellowship that meets in a school gymnasium. Every week we set up chairs, distribute song sheets, and drink a lot of coffee before the service begins. (I happen to be the official coffee maker, valuing this opportunity to serve.) There are lots of families, packs of children taking advantage of wide-open spaces to run and play before and after the service. Our format involves Scripture reading, congregational singing, and teaching. Following every service, save on certain holidays, we share a common meal, each family contributing food. We consider our fellowship as family and an essential part of our gathering.

Seeing the other families on a computer screen does not feel the same. There are no hugs, no catching up, no mutual coffee guzzling. And it is difficult to concentrate as our elders teach while looking awkwardly into their cameras.

Despite that, I must admit that I am beginning to understand why so many have abandoned churchgoing. There is no dress code for "doing church" these days. No make-up either, though I normally manage to brush my hair into a tidy ponytail. We have no travel time, and often launch into activities as soon as the final amen is proclaimed.

As different as our Sundays have come to be, I know deep inside that fellowship is more important than sleeping in late. We were created for community. Though Sunday routines will need to be re-established, I look forward to the future when we congregate together.

Today's Truth: And let us consider how to stir up one another to love and good works, not neglecting to meet together, as is the habit of some, but encouraging one another, and all the more as you see the Day drawing near. Hebrews 10:24, 25

MAY 4

THE WRONG CLEANING STRATEGY

We are up against a deadline to get my daughter-in-law's house ready for the market. Of course, we have no idea how the pandemic might affect real estate, but spring is a great time to sell. Plus, it is conceivable that the houses at the lower end of affordable may be more appealing to those who desperately need reasonably priced housing.

With that in mind, I prioritized getting the porch, railing, and shutters painted today, sandwiched between Zoom meetings. I was more than delighted to wield a paintbrush outside. The weather was picture perfect with sunny skies, pleasant temperatures, and a delightful breeze. What more could I ask?

However, I first made a stop at the home improvement store to pick up a gallon of paint thinner. It was curious that Pam asked me yesterday how to clean a sticky paint brush. We always use water-based paint and I have seen her clean many brushes with hot soapy water. But then again, I recall poking my head out the door as she was starting the porch floor. I noted a strong odor. Could it be she accidentally purchased an oil-based porch paint?

I plopped the brush into a pool of paint thinner and got the result I wanted. Despite the instructions on the improperly labeled can, this was indeed oil-based. No amount of soaking in soapy, hot water would clean that sucker. The terrible mess left on Pam's hands and between the bristles yesterday certainly proved that point!

Between this experience and thoughts of bringing every thought captive to Christ, my brain was ripe to ponder how we clean away guilt. If we are not careful, gut-wrenching guilt can be buried deep inside, depression or mental quandaries resulting. Other times, substance abuse is an attempt to make the bad feelings go away. Submarined relationships may also occur if we do not take the proper steps to clean away the ugly, messy guilt.

I am reminded that though the consequences of my sin may not disappear, the associated guilt is already dealt with by a gracious and merciful God.

Today's Truth: I acknowledged my sin to you, and I did not cover my iniquity; said, "I will confess my transgressions to the Lord," and you forgave the iniquity [guilt] of my sin. Psalm 32:5

May 5

Where's the Water?

Since we moved to our old country farmhouse more than fifteen years ago, we never had to deal with the septic system. Two weeks ago, however, it came to a head. Toilets bubbled up when laundry was washed. Sinks drained slowly. And the outlet of the drain field stayed saturated, with or without rain. Gary made the call to the pooper-scoopers.

The job was completed successfully, but the obvious problem with the distribution box and drain field remains. In a stroke of coincidence, we got notice from the county that our permit to build a detached garage on the other side of the house was contingent on a septic inspection by the state health department. Hence, an appointment was set.

I will not bore you with details, but there is no problem placing the garage where we want it to be. And there was never any question from Inspector Man about the actual status of our system. He was simply there to make certain this property had a septic, something that is apparently missing from many old farms outside city limits. What was fascinating, however, was his ability to locate the drain lines by "divining" with a landscape flag he found lying on the ground. With the wire held loosely in his hand, it rotated 90 degrees each time he crossed the path of a drainage line. "How does that work?" Gary inquired.

"I have no idea. An old guy taught me how to do it."

Just today, a well driller came to give a quote for a well up in the stand of cedars. With the possibility of building a cabin among the trees, Seth needed the estimate. Wouldn't you know it? This guy used two "witching sticks" instead of one, but according to him, every time the sticks spontaneously crossed, water was underground.

No water diviner is right 100% of the time. But there is a 100% need for water. The Samaritan woman met Jesus at the well as she was drawing up water in the middle of the day. Jesus knew her need not only for liquid water, but for living water that would quench her spiritual thirst forever. She drank deeply, as should we, and was satisfied.

Today's Truth: Jesus said to her, "Everyone who drinks of this water will be thirsty again, but whoever drinks of the water that I will give him will never be thirsty again. The water that I will give him will become in him a spring of water welling up to eternal life." John 4:13, 14

MAY 6

LIMITLESS GRACE

Today I was able to spend over an hour each with three of the athletes I mentor. Though our discussions began by catching up on progress with finals, projects, and life in general, each session was incredibly powerful.

With Kathleen, we enjoyed watching a gifted apologist answer perplexing questions. In the context of suffering, he told the story of Annie Johnson Flint. Bedridden for decades with rheumatoid arthritis, cancer, boils, bedsores, and failing eyesight, she wrote hymns, including, "He Giveth More Grace." Because Kathleen was not familiar with the hymn, I found an online rendition. How much more meaningful the words, knowing the author's personal experience of extended, excruciating suffering.

1) He giveth more grace when the burdens grow greater,
He sendeth more strength when the labors increase;
To added affliction He addeth His mercy,
To multiplied trials His multiplied peace.
Refrain: His love has no limit, His grace has no measure,
His pow'r has no boundary known unto men;
For out of His infinite riches in Jesus,
He giveth, and giveth, and giveth again.
2) When we have exhausted our store of endurance,
When our strength has failed ere the day is half done;
When we reach the end of our hoarded resources,
Our Father's full giving is only begun.

I could tell Kathleen was impacted with Flint's ability to maintain perspective. We contemplated if it was even possible to fully understand grace until we suffered. Though we do not all suffer physically, we certainly suffer spiritually. If we did not, there would be no need for grace in the first place. But sometimes, I think we appreciate grace more fully "When we reach the end of our hoarded resources" and realize "Our Father's full giving is only begun."

Today's Truth: For if, because of one man's trespass, death reigned through that one man, much more will those who receive the abundance of grace and the free gift of righteousness reign in life through the one man Jesus Christ. Romans 5:17

MAY 7

A WALK DOWN MEMORY LANE

A teacher wanted to engage with her students in a novel way, introducing them to new people and avocations, in this case, ultrarunning. She asked me for some photos and videos from middle school and high school. I laughed out loud at her request. At 27-years-old, she did not realize that video was hard to come by in the early 1970s. Back then, a Super 8 movie camera would probably be the weapon of choice. It was a far cry from today's omnipresent digital phone cameras.

Once I stopped laughing, I tried to oblige her request for photos. It was not hard to find photos from my ultrarunning career, although the further back I went, my only choice was to take pictures of printed ones. But when it came to finding photos from the earliest days, there was only one possibility. I made my way to the upstairs library and searched for two specific scrap books.

As I leafed through the now-yellowed pages filled with newspaper articles, I smiled. So many memories of days gone by. Moments of glory along with disappointments. Field hockey. Gymnastics. Softball. Track. Scholastic awards. School activities and offices. It was all there. My Dad meticulously cut out every single newspaper article that contained my picture or my name. Page after page, my four years of varsity sports were fully documented, thanks to a hometown newspaper that prioritized high school athletics.

It took a lot of time for Dad to do this. But oh, how I love that he did. To see little notes written in the margins, and notice circles around my name warms my heart. He could have been uninterested. But he wasn't. I cherish those scrap books. But more so, I cherish the memories of my father.

Dad died young of heart disease. Age 62. That is a year younger than my current age. He witnessed my wedding but never met his grandchildren. Though it has been since March of 1986, I miss him. He was a wonderful father. He worked hard, taught us to never quit, cherished my mother, and loved the Lord with all his heart. I am eternally grateful for his love and acts of kindness to preserve my high school memories.

Today's Truth: Honor your father and your mother, so that you may live long in the land the Lord your God is giving you. Exodus 20:12

May 8

If. Then. Since. Therefore.

Think back to a time when your mother said something like this: "If you clean your room, then you can go out to play." We use these expressions all the time. If this, then that. Because of these facts, it follows that... If A=B and B=C, then A=C. It's good 'ol fashioned logic.

I recently became interested in the logic contained in the Bible. Now, do not get too excited about the figures I use because I know they will vary according to the version you read. But the general idea is this. "Therefore" is used about 785 times, "since" is written nearly 300 times, and the combination of "if/thens" in the same verse occur about 200 times. Of course, these terms are implied many more times even when the word(s) are not used verbatim.

In the Old Testament, the preponderance of "if/thens" are used in the context of making expectations abundantly clear. For example, Deuteronomy 7:12 says, *If you pay attention to these laws and are careful to follow them, then the Lord your God will keep his covenant of love with you, as he swore to your ancestors.* Many of these statements are in a positive connotation. Obviously, others reveal negative consequences.

Jesus often used "if/thens" as an example of what to do, communicate expectations, and encourage people to think. Paul, the Apostle, followed suit. He would have made a great lawyer. His writings offer foundational truth before expertly leading the reader to what the next course of action or attitude needs to be.

While faith may not seem logical to the unbelieving observer, if we truly understood foundational truth about our position in Christ, I suspect we would live very differently.

Today's Truth: His divine power has granted to us all things that pertain to life and godliness, through the knowledge of him who called us to his own glory and excellence... For this very reason, make every effort to supplement your faith with virtue, and virtue with knowledge, and knowledge with self-control, and self-control with steadfastness, and steadfastness with godliness, and godliness with brotherly affection, and brotherly affection with love. For if these qualities are yours and are increasing, [THEN] they keep you from being ineffective or unfruitful in the knowledge of our Lord Jesus Christ. 2 Peter 1:3, 5–8

MAY 9

TREE DOWN!

After putting in another full day of mudding drywall, sanding, and painting at my daughter-in-law's home, I made one stop on the way home, hoping to score boneless chicken breasts and toilet paper. Sadly, I was unsuccessful. I guess this pandemic continues its grip on food and personal hygiene.

Down but not out, I redirected my focus on the drive home. Hum? What to make for supper since it was already 6:30 p.m.? By the time I turned down our bumpy gravel driveway, I concluded dinner would be simple: English muffin pizzas and a few warmed-up veggies. But even that would have to wait. The humongous tree outside the pool fence was quite different compared to this morning. Most of it no longer towered over the pool.

Gary, Seth, and I talked about the need for the tree to come down. Yes. It was a very cool tree, although no one had ever been able to identify it. Multiple, thick branches spread out near the bottom, making it an easy tree to climb. However, over fifteen years, its reach had extended beyond anything we could have imagined. It provided plenty of shade for a corner of the pool area, but in doing so, this dirty tree wreaked havoc in pool maintenance. In both spring and early fall, it was impossible to keep the water clean and free of tree debris.

Most of the tree was now on the ground. Gary was in the tractor, heavy ropes and chains keeping tension on one of four remaining branches. Seth was precariously perched in what was left of the tree, chain saw in hand. He skillfully cut away chunks of the branch until a sharp crack resounded as the wood splintered and gave way. Now, only three branches remain.

It will be strange to have a shadeless corner of the pool area, but I know I can create shade, a trellis already in place. Bigger was not better regarding this tree. It only served to make a huge mess.

I wonder if anyone feels the same way when I am around? Do I end up just making a mess? Do I create a situation that constantly needs tended and tidied up? If I am not careful, I can be like that toublesome tree, wreaking havoc simply by opening my mouth.

Today's Truth: There is one whose rash words are like sword thrusts, but the tongue of the wise brings healing. Proverbs 12:18

MAY 10

A DAY FOR MOMS

It frosted last night. What's with that?!? Mother's Day weekend is supposed to be wonderfully warm and sunny. But that is not what we got. Nevertheless, the sun is shining, and we have attended our Zoom church. That leaves the day ahead for whatever strikes the fancy.

I have not seen my mother for months. She is in an assisted living facility in Pennsylvania, sequestered off from the world because of Covid-19. I suppose her faulty short-term memory is a blessing. She told me that she has not been to the dining room with the other residents for "four or five days." It has been more like six or seven weeks. I'm just glad I remember what a wonderful mother she was and continues to be.

Yesterday I found a message from one of my "Shindigglers." (These are six young ladies, all of whom I coached in their high school years, and all of whom turned into ultrarunners.) She informed our pack of people that she was pregnant with her first child! Her little Shindigglet will join three others born to "my girls," who refer to me as TrailMama. I love it.

Then of course, I think of my own mothering to our boys, Caleb and Seth. Now 32 and 28 years old, memories of their growing up years remain fresh. After all, young men do not need their mothers simply to make them lunches to carry to school, or make sure they change into play clothes rather than rip holes in their school uniform pants. There was (and remains to be) a whole lot more to that story.

Still, I am left to wonder if I did a good job as a mom. To be honest, I sometimes have my doubts. For many of their formative years, I was in a demanding, high-pressure medical profession. Plus, there was a period where my ultrarunning training took way too much importance, sucking the life out of the remaining hours in the day. For this, I have regret and hope my children can forgive me.

Though I am acutely aware of my deficiencies as a matriarchal figure, I am very thankful for the privilege to look to my own mother as an example.

Today's Truth: May your father and mother rejoice; may she who gave you birth be joyful! Let your father and mother be glad; let her who bore you rejoice. Proverbs 23:25

MAY 11

RUNNING DOWN (AND UP) MEMORY LANE

I arrived back at my car at 1:23 a.m. A long-time friend, ultrarunner, and all-around crazy dude turned 50 years old. As in years past, Neal organizes a celebratory run, always at night, and invites us old-timers to join in. When he turned 30, it was a 30-mile run. Now at 50, it was to be a 50K run on the Blue Ridge Parkway, a roadway that is anything but flat.

At 50, there were only two of the eight participants that were younger. Hence, it was not surprising that of the eight celebrants, four were on bicycles. It was a happy crew starting out as daylight faded. We laughed and joked, bikers and runners jockeying for position to engage in the most interesting conversations. With food and water previously stashed ten miles into the adventure, two of the cyclists and two of the runners did an about face, enjoying the predominantly downhill journey back to the cars. That meant that Birthday Boy, me, and friends "D-Ho" and "Muffy" continued in quest of an adventure.

It was cold and blustery at the higher elevations. Continuing down the parkway for several miles, Neal decided we would run half his age in miles rather than the 50 kilometers. Since neither of us had been doing long runs in training, I was happy for the news. We turned around and began the steep trek back to the stashed snacks. My lower back was protesting by then, so I opted out of the half mile detour to the radar tower. Instead, I continued solo down the parkway, thinking they would catch up.

They never did. I had ten miles in the dark by myself. Except on a few occasions when I heard movement in the woods beside me, I ran without a light, my eyes adjusting to see the double lines down the middle of the road. I let my mind drift back to when my Shindigglers and I ran this same stretch, singing hymns into the night. I thought of the time I ran this road in the dead of winter, ice and snow making conditions treacherous. I prayed as I ran. I sang a little. I was startled by how the moon seemed to rise suddenly, its reflected light brightening the road. After 25 miles, I arrived back at the car, thankful I could still cover the distance after all these years.

Today's Truth: but they who wait for the Lord shall renew their strength; they shall mount up with wings like eagles; they shall run and not be weary; Isaiah 40:31

May 12

Open with the Right App

I just received an email from a big wig in the organization I work for. Beginning on Thursday this week, we are required to attend sessions two hours in length for the next four weeks. Additionally, there is a one-hour follow-up to each training session that will occur in the context of a virtual small group. We have been instructed to download and read the material associated with these educational efforts.

It is not a bad thing we are receiving training. What is not so great is that there is no app on my computer that is able to open the material. I cannot tell what kind of file it is, nor will any of the suggested apps work to unravel the secrets that lie within. What's a girl to do?

I emailed the guy back with a screen shot of the unfortunate situation. It said, "This file does not have an app associated with it for performing this action. Please install an app, or if one is already installed, create an association in the Default Apps Settings page." Until I have a way of deciphering the message, it will do me no good.

I cannot help but think about how necessary the Spirit of God is in making Scripture understandable. The Spirit is like the necessary app to open the files of truth and have them make sense. We should not be surprised that to an unbeliever, there is nothing about faith or Scripture that is logical.

Paul knew this: *For the word of the cross is folly to those who are perishing, but to us who are being saved it is the power of God* (1 Cor. 1:18). *The foolish not only deny the power of God but deny God himself. The natural person does not accept the things of the Spirit of God, for they are folly to him, and he is not able to understand them because they are spiritually discerned* (1 Cor. 2:14).

Thank God for the Holy Spirit who gives us the ability to understand spiritual things, including the confidence we gain in knowing we are His.

Today's Truth: The Spirit himself bears witness with our spirit that we are children of God, Romans 8:16.

May 13

Be very careful

My emotions ranged from terrified to very impressed to simply thankful that no one died.

The tree outside the pool fence has always been a mystery. One arborist thought it was a type of elm tree, but it has never been positively identified. It has become a behemoth in the backyard, towering over the pool and making maintenance excruciatingly painful. It had to go.

"The Evil Tree," dubbed as such by granddaughter Addyson, had but three huge branches remaining. These were the ones that towered over the pool fence, the built-in furniture, and the pool itself. It was going to take a Herculean effort to get those massive limbs on the ground without demolishing something.

Taking a break from a Zoom call, I walked outside to view the process. The pool area was littered with branches. That was fine. But one glance upward made my heart skip a beat. Our extension ladder was rachet strapped to a limb 22 feet above the ground. Seth was standing on the top rung, one foot on the ladder, the other leg thrown over the branch itself. He and his Dad theorized what would happen when an even bigger limb next to it was cut. They surmised the top would sweep downward and hit the ladder before hitting the ground. Hence, they confirmed the ladder was secured to the limb against which it was leaning, as Seth began hand-sawing. He held on with one hand and sawed with the other. It was tense. Soon, the limb cracked, beginning its downward journey. As predicted, it slammed into the ladder but did not displace it. Seth climbed safely to the ground, and I could finally breathe.

Their success came because they were smart, creative, analytical, and practical. There was nothing haphazard about the process. Everything was calculated.

As Believers, we are called to be intentional and careful in our attitudes and actions. There should be nothing haphazard as we represent Jesus Christ. So, be careful.

Today's Truth: Look carefully then how you walk, not as unwise but as wise, making the best use of the time, because the days are evil. Therefore, do not be foolish, but understand what the will of the Lord is. Ephesians 5:15-17

May 14

Rainbow!

I was sitting on my bed, computer on lap and watching a video for work. I could hear the low rumble of thunder along with the pitter-patter of rain. Gary was in the living room, while Seth and Pam were playing school with Addyson at her request. The house was quiet and peaceful in the aftermath of a nice family dinner.

Suddenly, the quiet was replaced with a thundering herd coming down the stairs, continuing across the living room, through the kitchen and out the front door. Addyson was ecstatic. "Come on! Come on! There's a double rainbow!!! I've heard about them but didn't know they were real." As she stood under the porch roof, her squeals of delight drew me off my bed to join her outside. Pam joined us, as did Gary. Seth fired up the drone and sent it high into the sky to capture a bird's eye view of the colorful arches reaching from horizon to horizon. It was spectacular.

"Grandma, why did God make this rainbow?" the inquisitive little girl inquired.

"Well, do you remember the first time God made a rainbow? I asked.

"Yes. He made a rainbow to promise the people he would never again flood the world."

"You are absolutely right, Sweet Pea. I think rainbows form so we can remember the kindness and faithfulness of our God. He is a good Father who loves us very much." Addyson nodded and shook her head in agreement.

With that, the spry five-year old did a special little dance in front of the drone as it hovered before landing. The family retreated upstairs to their apartment, Gary took his place on the sofa, and I resumed the online training. The house is again quiet, and my heart is happy.

We do not see rainbows every day, and seeing a full double rainbow is much rarer. I am forever grateful, however, that a little girl's excitement can serve as a reminder for her grandmother: a reminder that God is faithful.

Today's Truth: When the bow is in the clouds, I will see it and remember the everlasting covenant between God and every living creature of all flesh that is on the earth. Genesis 9:16

MAY 15

GROUND MOVING

The unexpected opportunity to operate a mini excavator transported Seth to a very happy place. A friend of ours who rented the equipment thought he could do his job in one day. He could not. He needed two days. But if he rented it for three days, he would pay the same as for a week. Knowing our propensity for heavy construction projects around the farm, he asked if we would go in on it, giving us four full days of fun. Yes. Thank you very much!

There is an old road on our farm that descends into a gully before climbing again to the back pastures and food plots. A stream that seldom dries up even in summer runs through that gully, the road atop a too-small culvert. During hard rains, the pipe is not capable of handling the gushing water, causing the stream to overflow the banks and eat away at the primitive road's surface. The excavator was exactly what we needed to dig out the failing bridge, place a larger pipe, and redirect the stream itself.

Seth is a talented equipment operator. He did not need to be asked twice to take his place in the controller's seat. For the last eight hours, he has worked steadily to dig, scoop, flatten, and fill. I just returned from down the hill to check on the progress. It sure looks different than before! The pipe has been positioned and the stream banks sculpted to handle rushing waters. Chunks of concrete were placed to direct the water into the new pipe. The road over the pipe is wider and more stable than before.

On this beautiful and sunny day, it would be tempting to assume that the previous bridge was adequate. The now small, placid stream hardly seems capable of causing damage warranting such a huge fix. However, Gary assures me that a hard rain changes that docile trickle into an angry, raging torrent, destroying everything in its path.

Did you know that Job likened unsolicited advice of friends to the destruction brought on by raging waters? We, too, may need to consider if our words are capable of ruin. If so, we might want to reconfigure the stream of syllables that flow so easily out of our mouths.

Today's Truth: "But the mountain falls and crumbles away, and the rock is removed from its place; the waters wear away the stones; the torrents wash away the soil of the earth; so you destroy the hope of man. You prevail forever against him, and he passes; you change his countenance, and send him away." Job 14: 18-20

May 16

Anchors

With temps in the 80s and a fair dose of humidity, it sure seemed like we transitioned from spring to summer in a flash. My thoughts drifted back to a lazy day at the lake. One of my favorites was to float the day away, anchored to a corner of the dock. That way, if I happened to doze off, I did not end up in the path of an oncoming speed boat. The anchor line gave me freedom to bob safely.

As I was working today at Pam's house, the main objective was to create shelving in the bedroom closets. This included adding a rod for hanging clothes, an important but missing element. After hours of measuring and cutting, the shelves were completed. All that remained was installing the wooden dowels. To make the task simpler, I made a quick run to the home improvement store and purchased self-tapping anchors rated for holding 75 pounds. I figured on a quick five-minute job.

I'll cut to the chase. It was not a five-minute job. As much as I hate to admit it, the job remains unfinished. The self-tapping anchor refused to penetrate the drywall. I even tried creating a pilot hole with a screw. It should not be this hard! My frustration level got so high I walked away from the job, leaving it for another day when I have a different kind of anchor—and a better attitude.

There is no doubt that an anchor is necessary to support the weight of the rod and clothes. And ask any sailor, a boat without an appropriate anchor is doomed. It simply cannot maintain its position without being tethered to an immovable object.

Our faith is anchored in Christ Jesus. As the old hymn states:

We have an anchor that keeps the soul
Steadfast and sure while the billows roll,
Fastened to the Rock which cannot move,
Grounded firm and deep in the Savior's love.

Today's Truth: We have this as a sure and steadfast anchor of the soul, a hope that enters into the inner place behind the curtain, where Jesus has gone as a forerunner on our behalf, having become a high priest forever after the order of Melchizedek. Hebrews 6:19, 20

MAY 17

GAG!

Last night was a glorious evening for a run.

I had put in long hours on construction projects earlier today. Once I got home, it was a pleasant surprise that take-out Japanese was waiting for me. Relieved I did not have to cook, I heartily consumed the delicious meal before relaxing for an hour or two before setting off for a run. The air was warm with a pleasant breeze. Though it was still light when I left, I donned my reflective vest, clipping on a small but bright light to increase my visibility. I was planning on about four miles.

I took a right turn onto a gravel road, and before I knew it, found myself on a familiar but longer country road loop. By the time I completed it, it would come in at nearly nine miles. I hoped Gary would not worry when I failed to show up at the house after what he thought was a short run. Still, I felt good, content to run in solitude and silence.

With about three miles to go, my dinner became unsettled in my stomach. I burped loud and often, hoping to relieve the pressure. It was uncomfortable but doable to continue running. But suddenly, a bug flew into my open mouth and set off a gag reflex. What resulted was not pretty. I hurled all over the road, continuing to gag when I felt the insect still squirming at the back of my throat. Secretions increased which upped the gagging. It was awful. I walked a steep hill, hoping to calm myself and discharge that nasty insect. After spewing out spit, thick mucus, and finally the intruder, I started to feel better. My pace picked up. I arrived home hot and sweaty, but none the worse for wear.

The incident remineded me of running the 100-yard conference finals back in high school. It was at 75 yards that an insect flew in my mouth. I had the same response. Gag! Fortunately, I was able to hold on for the win. Still, it was a revolting situation.

Gagging is a terrible feeling. The result is gross. And yet, I cannot help but think that we make God gag when we are lukewarm in our faith and living. He would rather us be hot or cold—but lukewarm is the worst!

I certainly do not want to gag God with my namby-pamby actions and attitudes.

Today's Truth: "I know your works: you are neither cold nor hot. Would that you were either cold or hot! So, because you are lukewarm, and neither hot nor cold, I will spit you out of my mouth." Revelations 3:16

May 18

Sweet fellowship

Some weeks ago, I wondered if months of virtual church would make going back to church difficult. With the convenience of being on the couch, in your pajamas, and sipping coffee, it may become a hard-to-break habit. But with state rules loosening a bit, we saw for ourselves what would happen.

Yesterday was Sunday and our church was "open" for the first time in months. Abiding by set standards of seating family groups apart from other families, abandoning our normal coffee bar, and foregoing our shared meal, by the time our service started nearly every family was present. Some offered hugs, a habit hard to break. But there was an abundance of interaction and catching up. The singing, something that was clearly absent from our virtual church, was heartfelt. After the service, people lingered, hungry for the face-to-face encounters deemed so precious.

One of our close friends from church invited us for dinner tonight. It has been even longer since we enjoyed fellowship in another's home. For the second day in a row, we dressed casually but in "real" clothes for an evening out. I made double chocolate mint chip cookies to share. We arrived at 6:30 p.m. to sit around the table with Josh, Meghan, and their three kids. We were still talking, laughing, and solving most of the world's problems when 9:45 rolled around.

Yes, virtual relationships can be worthwhile, but nothing compares to sitting across a table and talking for hours. And there is not much better than being in a group with fellow believers on a Sunday morning, singing together and being instructed from the Scriptures. If there is an upside to weeks of stay-at-home orders, it is the realization that we need each other. We were created for meaningful relationship—and we should never take that for granted.

Today's Truth: not neglecting to meet together, as is the habit of some, but encouraging one another, and all the more as you see the Day drawing near. Hebrews 10:25

MAY 19

SLEEP, GLORIOUS SLEEP

I feel somewhat refreshed this morning. I slept more than normal last night despite waking up three times.

Nowadays, I approach bedtime with trepidation. It used to be that I could fall asleep mid-sentence, an aggravating fact to my dear husband when he was trying to carry on a conversation. But something has changed. Now, no matter how tired I feel, I am hard pressed to fall into slumber. I often lay in bed for at least an hour, legs restless and mind racing. I sometimes rise to take a couple night-time Tylenols, the melatonin taken earlier not seeming to have had any *zzz*-producing effect. Other times, I draw a hot bath, spending time reading in our old claw-foot tub. Once dried off, I head to the couch and snuggle under a puffy black blanket, praying the tick-tock of the mantle clock will lull me into much needed sleep.

It is not uncommon for me to grab a mere three or four hours of sleep per night, and sometimes less. Even on a good night, I wake at least three or four times. I look at the clock, drink water from my bedside cup, and sometimes head to the bathroom. Then comes the struggle to get back to sleep. I'm not sure what wakes me up, although the night sweats are certainly a contributing factor. Trying to cool off, the covers get thrown aside as I turn my back to the fan blowing on my side of the bed.

All the coaches I work with tout a common theme: the importance of sleep. I totally agree. But I wish I knew the secret of slumber. The only good thing about the solitude of the wee hours is the time to pray, to seek God, and to quote back Scripture memorized as a child. If I were a good sleeper, I would miss out on those encounters with the Father.

Wise 'ol Solomon wrote often about the peril of too much sleep. Certainly, that is not a problem for me! On the other hand, I know that God promises to give strength needed for each day, despite the amount of sleep I get. That fact is something to appreciate in the middle of the night.

Today's Truth: I lay down and slept; I woke again, for the Lord sustained me. Psalm 3:5

May 20

Rain, rain go away

Oh, boy. My fishpond outside my front door tells the story. It is full and overflowing. The fountain that normally bubbles up ten inches above the water now barely breaks the surface. I hope the fish do not float away and end up stranded in the front yard once the rain stops. Make that IF the rain stops.

The pool is similarly full. The water is a mere three inches from overflowing the coping and spilling onto the concrete surround. The top steps of the ladders, which are normally out of the water, are submerged. If mermaids lived in those waters (which would please Addyson to no end), they would be frolicking right about now.

This weather, cold, windy, and incessantly wet for days, is predicted to last several more days. A few days out from Memorial Day weekend, I woke this morning to a house that was 62 degrees, outside temperatures in the 40s. My motivation to do much of anything is low. Exceptionally low. I even took a nap—in the bed and under the covers—after completing my "have to" checklist. That seldom happens.

It is possible that news of a cancelled mission trip, the loss of an expensive non-refundable airline ticket, and decreases in ministry funding contributed to the bleakness. I suppose my feelings are normal, since I am seeing similar sentiments posted by reasonable people on social media streams. Sure, we all experience ups and downs in our daily lives. But it leaves me to wonder if we as Believers should have a built-in perspective to save us from being fickle and easily influenced by circumstances—even the weather.

Back in the 70's a song by *The Carpenters*, touted the phrase, "rainy days and Mondays always get me down." I get it. We are human and prone to let emotions rule. Still, if Paul can say "whatever" regarding his deplorable imprisonment when writing to the Philippians, then maybe I should make more of an effort to stay strong and steady despite the world around me.

Today's Truth: Only let your manner of life be worthy of the gospel of Christ, so that whether I come and see you or am absent, I may hear of you that you are standing firm in one spirit, with one mind striving side by side for the faith of the gospel, and not frightened in anything by your opponents. This is a clear sign to them of their destruction, but of your salvation, and that from God. Philippians 1:27, 28

May 21

On a mission

Yesterday I wrote wanting the rain to go away. While it is true that I am craving sunny skies and summer-like temperatures, I made peace with today's continued wet drops.

With canceled Zoom calls this morning, I had time to answer a few emails before making a fresh pot of coffee and curling up with a book. Tucked under my blanket on the sofa, I was encouraged by the words on the page. It was a lovely reprieve from the standard fare of virtual meetings. Besides, if I could have a morning without being forced to notice how old and plain I look in a Zoom window, all the better!

Alas, come noon, I was again part of a Zoom bible study with a bunch of college athletes. A colleague presented the pattern of redemptive/restorative-driven mission throughout Scripture. From Genesis to Revelation, this missional God of ours seeks to redeem and restore, using those who are willing in His story. It is interesting that both Moses and Jonah, for example, were told God's mission, and then promptly tried to run away. Isaiah, on the other hand, heard the Lord ask *Whom shall I send? And who will go for us?* and promptly responded, *Here am I. Send me!* (Isaiah 6:8).

God used all three men to fulfill His plan. But what a difference we see. Moses and Jonah were both told the plan before being recruited. Moses felt inadequate and Jonah's escape plan involved a boat ride and transfer to a big 'ol fish. God obviously used these men despite their reluctance, which is consolation for when I am hesitant. However, Isaiah volunteered to be part of the God story *before* he was told the mission.

The difference is this: Moses and Jonah failed to see God—and love God deeply enough—to believe they could be pivotal in God's doings. However, Isaiah saw and loved a missional God so much that trusting him enough to say "yes" before the assignment was clear came naturally.

Trying to complete a mission without loving and appreciating the God behind the mission will only lead to frustration. We must learn to love and trust our missional God before we can successfully undertake any assignment wholly and unequivocally.

Today's Truth: And I heard the voice of the Lord saying, "Whom shall I send, and who will go for us?" Then I said, "Here I am! Send me." Isaiah 6:8

May 22

Decisions, decisions

I am almost to the point that I do not want to watch the news. Social media (Facebook, since old people like me tend to gravitate toward this venue) is just as bad. The spin on Covid-19-related news, myths, and opinions is getting old. One expert says this. Another says that. Both have credentials that seem legit, yet the conclusions they come to are completely different. It is hard to discern what is true science and what reflects political bias.

Then you have folks on social media, screaming at the top of their lungs about how stupid and idiotic anyone is who opposes their own views. Rare is the person capable of having a reasonable discussion with an open mind to entertain and assess opposing ideas. Rather, those from the left—and the right—dig in their heels to commence a terrible war of words. It is uncomfortable to read. I try hard to keep my eyes from landing anywhere near those posts.

The impact of the virus in our area has not been dire. Yes, thus far, there have been 75 cases in our immediate area, some have been hospitalized, all but one recovered. Percentage-wise, the chance of acquiring the virus is slim. As a family, we have taken normal precautions: handwashing and sanitizing surfaces. We have obeyed state mandates concerning social gatherings and adjusted to on-line work and church situations. Admittedly, I have gone grocery shopping and frequented home improvement stores when necessary.

Here's the dilemma. The state is beginning to open. We even got to go to church last Sunday. However, our governor, who is radically liberal and socially "progressive," warned everyone in an announcement today that as of this coming Tuesday, it will be mandatory to wear a face mask in public. I'm not sure how I feel about that, especially given the conflicting data on their effectiveness.

What will I do? Do I wear a mask? Do I take my chances of a fine or arrest by not wearing one? It is a very difficult decision to make. And yet, I think I am likely bound by what Paul wrote to the Romans long ago.

I will obey out of respect for authority.

Today's Truth: Let every person be subject to the governing authorities. For there is no authority except from God, and those that exist have been instituted by God. Therefore whoever resists the authorities resists what God has appointed, and those who resist will incur judgment. Romans 13:1, 2

MAY 23

BIG, FAT BRANCHES

A behemoth of a playhouse rose from the ground today. No. Actually, except for a few support columns, the playhouse is perched six feet above the ground. Addyson is more than excited.

It all began when the humongous, out of control tree right outside the pool fence was cut down. It took a lot of skillful planning and execution to get that tree on the ground. Huge branches overhung the fence and the pool itself. Nevertheless, Gary and Seth used unique but ingenious methods to reduce the tree to a very large stump.

Said stump is no ordinary stump. The base of the trunk is about three feet in diameter. However, two or three feet up from the ground, the trunk divides into seven thick side branches. Before they were cut away, each grew up to 25 feet in length. It was massive.

Seth had the bright idea to cut each of the side branches to a uniform height. Once he did that, you could see the remaining trunk begging for a platform to be built upon it. The platform of Addyson's soon-to-be playhouse is an impressive four-foot by sixteen-foot, hovering six feet above the ground. It has eight-foot-tall walls, half the area under roof (complete with electricity), and the remainder a deck. It will soon have windows with curtains and flower boxes. It should be spectacular.

When I was out surveying the progress, I noticed something interesting. This tree, drastically cut away, was still showing signs of life. There on one of the stumps, a green shoot with leaves has already emerged. Perhaps its life is not quite through.

My mind immediately went to the passage in John 15 that begins with *I am the vine and you are the branches.* It is a beautiful picture of Believers who are grafted into the tree of life. Apart from the vigorous vine (who is Christ), there is no life. Branches cut away are dead and will never show signs of life.

But just like our tree, life is still evident because the stubs of the branches that remain are producing leaves. Staying attached to the trunk is the only way life is possible.

Today's Truth: I am the vine; you are the branches. Whoever abides in me and I in him, he it is that bears much fruit, for apart from me you can do nothing. If anyone does not abide in me he is thrown away like a branch and withers; and the branches are gathered, thrown into the fire, and burned. John 15:5, 6

MAY 24

SWEET FELLOWSHIP

It was the second time in as many weeks that we met as a church family. Gone was the copious amount of guzzled coffee normal for our fellowship before the service begins. Absent also was the family-style lunch we share following worship. But what was intact was the friendly chatter. Kids played together, facilitated by meeting in a gymnasium. Seating by family groups on folding chairs set up with space between did not prevent catching up with neighbors. The congregational singing was fervent and sweet, the teaching from Scripture sound. We sat in the same row with Seth, Pam, and Addyson. I left with a smile on my face and joy in my heart.

Once home on this beautiful Sunday, I hurried around the house in preparation for friends coming for dinner. It had been a long time since we felt comfortable inviting non-family to visit. We did not want to put anyone in the awkward situation of turning down an invite because of safety concerns. But our friends jumped at the chance to get out of their house and drive out to ours. Since I told Addy yesterday that Chloe, a seven-year-old, and her family were all coming for a visit, she has had trouble controlling her excitement.

Sure enough, as soon as they parked in front of the house, Addy was in the pool, urging Chloe and brother Riley to follow. Then the discovery of a tiny orange newt set into motion playing with and caring for the creature. They even researched what a newt eats, providing a worm and several grubs to offer their newest animal friend. All the while, we adults carried on relaxed conversation before dinner, after dinner, and around the smoldering firepit. This perfect evening was the perfect ending to a perfect day.

Perhaps a positive outcome of "social distancing" is the realization of just how important fellowship is with our brothers and sisters. I am going to bed with a much greater appreciation for sharing hospitality and practical acts of kindness with friends and family.

Today's Truth: And they devoted themselves to the apostles' teaching and the fellowship, to the breaking of bread and the prayers. Acts 2:42

MAY 25

SNAKE!

Springtime is snake time—especially when you live in the country.

A few years ago, I was as surprised as anyone. All I did was open the snack cabinet door, Addyson by my side. We were looking for something tasty, but as we stared into the crowded storage space, a forked tongue twitched back at us. There he was. A 14-inch pencil-thin snake had wrangled itself into our house. How does that happen?

A few weeks passed when I noticed something move on the floor. Shoot! Another snake, this one in the living room about four feet from where I was sitting. With gloved hand, Seth escorted the serpent outside, although I am not exactly sure what the final disposition of the reptile happened to be. What I do remember is going to bed quite sure there was an entire colony of snakes in the crawl space under the kitchen.

About two weeks ago Seth and I encountered two five-foot black snakes as we were cleaning out a shed. He picked up a box containing an old paint sprayer. Something inside a hole in the corner of the box moved. "Put it down! Snake!" He did. Promptly. Upon further inspection, not one but two five-foot black snakes slithered from the box. Since they keep down the rodent population, we allowed them to live on in the forest.

I had yet another snake experience today. I was doing outside work at Pam's house when I discovered a slender snake underneath discarded construction material. It was skinny and a little over a foot in length. Its skin pattern was interesting. It looked as if a black and white design had been stenciled on its back, a yellow stripe running the length of its spine and two more stripes on either side of its body. Inside its triangular head, a bright red tongue flicked at me. It was kinda cute. I tried to transport it to the woods on a shovel and a rake, but the thing squirmed away. I saw it four more times before it eventually maneuvered under the house.

After texting a picture of it to Seth, he messaged back and asked me to kill it. It was poisonous. Unfortunately, I did not see the message until I was on my way home. It reminds me that all too often we fail to recognize danger when it stares us in the face. A call to vigilance and great discernment is certainly appropriate.

Today's Truth: But I am afraid that as the serpent deceived Eve by his cunning, your thoughts will be led astray from a sincere and pure devotion to Christ. 2 Corinthians 11:3

May 26

FPR

It was one of those runs that reminded me of past jaunts down the road. As it turned out, returning home was much more pleasant than leaving home.

Sometime long ago, I created for myself the activity of FPRs: Flower-pick'n runs. The need for such a thing arose when my run was so labored, so egregious, so pitiful, that a distraction was needed. In this case, it was picking wildflowers along country roads. Obviously, the strategy allowed me to slow down and stop to do the picking. I was always grateful for the chance to take a breather and refocus on something other than a run that felt way too hard.

It was only after hours more of construction labor on Pam's house that I finally arrived home, hungry for food and exercise. Since food before exercise produces unfortunate consequences, I chose to forgo the food, heading down the road instead. I felt old and sluggish, a rather common feeling for me. Nevertheless, I moseyed along, trying to find a rhythm, quieting my foot-strike, and running with the greatest efficiency possible. Despite my intentionality, I felt stiff and awkward.

The evening was, however, most pleasant. A little overcast with a gentle breeze, the perfect temperature made the effort palatable. Still, I wished for the days when I felt strong and agile, gliding along like a graceful deer. And then I noticed them; wild daisies growing in large clumps along the roadway. My mind flashed back to prior FPRs. Yes, I decided. I would stop fussing over how slow I was. Picking daisies was exactly what I needed.

Armed with a huge bouquet, I am certain the infrequent cars passing by wondered why I was carrying them as I ran. I smiled thinking about their reactions. And then suddenly, I noticed I no longer felt bogged down. I felt released to appreciate the moment. Free to take in the smell of freshly cut hay, able to run with fluidity.

Sometimes, it is a small thing—like the beautiful little flowers in a ditch—that is just what we need to change our perspective.

Today's Truth: Consider the lilies, how they grow: they neither toil nor spin, yet I tell you, even Solomon in all his glory was not arrayed like one of these. Luke 12:27

MAY 27

SING A SONG

With coffee in one hand and protein bar in the other, I booted my laptop in preparation for the day. Gary was gone to work, and Seth and Pam headed out. The house was quiet and mine to enjoy. What bliss.

Though the predicted rain had not yet started, it was overcast, still, and on the cool side. I suppose that is why my ears tuned into the birdsongs outside the windows. I am no expert—or even a novice—at identifying the songs. Nonetheless, it was obvious there was an ongoing conversation. One bird rang out its song. Within a few seconds, another bird answered with a slightly different tune. This continued back and forth for five minutes. I do not speak bird and have absolutely no idea what was said. But it must have been meaningful for both parties to continue communicating.

This ornithological exchange reminded me of antiphonal singing. Two choirs (or individuals) sing phrases back and forth to each other. In most cases, the singing of the alternating groups is a mirror image of the other. Sometimes the choirs occupy the same stage. In formal churches, the antiphonal choir may respond from their perch in a balcony. Either way, it is a beautiful interchange of both melody and words.

One of our former elders occasionally asked members of the congregation to physically turn toward the middle isle and sing directly to those on the other side. Though at first it felt weird, I came to appreciate singing directly to other believers and to God.

We are instructed to speak to one another in "psalms and hymns and spiritual songs." Music is meant to be sung directly to another. I get the idea that singing is simple, full of truth, melodic, allowing for complementary harmonies. What a contrast to the approach of many churches to create a "show," complete with lighting effects and music so loud, one cannot hear their own voice, let alone the singing of their neighbor.

I choose singing as ministry and encouragement to my brothers and sisters, and as a pleasing offering to God.

Today's Truth: but be filled with the Spirit, addressing one another in psalms and hymns and spiritual songs, singing and making melody to the Lord with your heart, giving thanks always and for everything to God the Father in the name of our Lord Jesus Christ, Ephesians 5:18b-20

May 28

Unbelievable—But Chosen Still the Same

I want to study the book of Romans. With sixteen chapters in the book, the plan is to concentrate on a single chapter for the next sixteen days. But instead of reading the chapters silently, I clicked the audible icon, listening carefully to the narrator read chapter one aloud. After listening the first time, I listened a second and third time, eyes closed, to shut out any distraction around me.

There is a lot in the introductory paragraphs written to the Roman believers. But what struck me from the onset was this simple phrase from the first verse: *Paul, a servant of Christ Jesus, called to be an apostle and set apart for the gospel of God.* Called and set apart? Seriously? Did God forget who Paul was and what he did? What was God thinking?

If you recall, Paul, formally known as Saul, was a Jew by birth. He was born in Tarsus, which is in present-day Turkey. He was very well-educated, studying under a guy named Gamaliel. Very prestigious, indeed. In Acts, he writes that he was extremely zealous in his religion, which also meant he was totally against any and all who believed in this man, Jesus. He made a habit of throwing men and women in squalid prisons, even standing by to gleefully watch as Stephen was stoned to death for his faith. How in the world could a guy like this be called and set apart for service to the Savior?

I suppose the answer can be found on the dusty road to Damascus. Jesus appeared in a bright light, blinding Saul. After asking, "Who are you?" Saul immediately recognized his need to obey the Master. He followed instructions, was led into the city, met by Ananias, his sight restored. His life would never be the same. The 180-degree turn, possible only by saving faith, led Saul—now Paul—down a very different road. A road of service and changed hearts, relentless ministry, selflessness—but also brutal beatings, shipwrecks, and frequent imprisonments.

I have been called by grace through faith. But me being set apart? Therein lies the conflict. What makes me apt to serve? Am I doing what I am called to do? Though I may have questions, if God called and set apart Paul with his crazy background, then maybe God can also call me.

Today's Truth: Paul, a servant of Christ Jesus, called to be an apostle, set apart for the gospel of God, Romans 1:1

MAY 29

ALL THINGS WORK TOGETHER

It was about fifteen years ago when I met Jordan. He was a young single guy who already had more life experiences at that age of than most people in a lifetime. Jordan was one of several self-described hobos that started coming to church. They were train-hoppers. Born and raised in Wyoming, Jordan and his older brother were accustomed to living a wild, outdoor life. When the elder brother became a professional hobo riding the rails for seven years, he eventually asked Jordan to join him.

And join him, he did. Though I had known some stories about that time, I heard more when I listened to Jordan being interviewed by Joe Rogan on his popular podcast. But why was he being interviewed? It was because beyond train-hopping, Jordan has lived in a treehouse made of found materials, bought a one-way ticket to Russia, learned the language, and ended up living with and learning from the Evenki reindeer herders in northern Siberia. A teepee was home, even in -50-degree weather. He herded the reindeer, built fences, and trapped for fur. Near death experiences were not uncommon for himself and others.

After a year, he returned to the States before returning to again serve the Evenki. More adventures ensued. It is no wonder the producers of the show "Alone" came calling. Left in the northwest territories of Canada, ten contestants selected ten survival items each before being dropped off in ten separate areas. The goal was to survive longer than the other nine. The winner claims a $500,000 award.

It is almost unfair that Jordan was on the show. He won, although some of the other contestants did a fine job. But truth be known, Jordan had enough food supply and mental stamina that he could have lasted several more months.

His life story reminds me of how God weaves the events of our life into a beautiful tapestry for His own glory. Nothing happens by accident, but all is ordained by the Father. We may not always understand the events of our lives. However, we can rest assured that in the big overall plan, each has been purposefully placed.

Today's Truth: And we know that for those who love God all things work together for good, for those who are called according to his purpose. Romans 8:28

May 30

Why is it so had to stop?

The fact that my laptop is on my lap is a miracle. I have been trying to have it nest there for the last several hours.

It is Saturday. With no race to train for, my morning was open for the bazillion projects waiting for my attention. By 8 a.m., I was up in the treehouse, paint brush in hand. Painting the studs before the siding is screwed on will be a much easier job than the reverse.

The next move was to vacuum the pool after mowing the grass in the pool enclosure. Chemicals were added, and for just a moment, I decided to sit under the umbrella and chill with a glass of iced tea. The plan was also to listen to Romans 3, my select chapter of the day. But as I was sitting there, I noticed a few toys needing picked up. Then I saw weeds that needed pulled and towels thrown over the fence to dry. I doubt I heard a single word being played aloud.

Lunch time came and went, but I was busy catching fish and transferring them to a large tub. My pond has developed a slow leak. I was waiting for a nice warm day to drain the pond, find the leak, and add another liner. This took hours with all the rock removal and cleaning, bailing the water, making the trip to buy necessary supplies, along with several attempts to scrub off the head-to toe slime that accumulated on my body. It was exhausting. Several times I sat down in the old rocking chair pond-side to rest. But if I sat for two minutes, that was long. The fern needed watering. Discarded pond sludge needed cleaned from the sidewalk. Oh, and my car needed vacuumed since the dry vac was sitting by the pond. I may as well wash the car. And since the hose is out, the garden could stand a good dousing.

See my problem? I have a terrible problem sitting still. It is only with the utmost determination that I write now. Looking around, so many things have been left undone. I suppose it is good to work hard and long, but somehow, I tend to mis-prioritize. I have yet to spend quality time today with the Father. As soon as I finish this entry, perhaps I should take care of that.

Today's Truth: For God alone, O my soul, wait in silence, for my hope is from him. Psalm 62:5

MAY 31

FORSAKEN AND FORGOTTEN?

Seth and Pam just returned home after looking at property on Smith Mountain Lake. It was expensive and not what they hoped it to be. However, driving back roads, they came upon a twenty-acre parcel with rolling hills and pastureland. As they began to walk the property, they noticed a decrepit old house hidden away among weeds and overgrown bushes. Their curiosity aroused, they bush-whacked through the briars to find the front door. They expected to find rooms filled with nothing but cobwebs. Not so.

It was as if a family had just walked out of the humble farmhouse one day in the 1940's. Trunks overflowed with clothes decades old. A picture of a World War II warrior hung beside his Army jacket with the name "Murphy" printed on the badge. A vintage record player resided on a table, and in the kitchen was a beautiful wood-burning cook stove, complete with a large pot sitting atop the beast of an appliance. Also found was a Kelvinator refrigerator standing guard. It was as though the world stood still inside those wooded walls for the last 80 years.

It makes me wonder. What happened to that family? Were there no relatives to preserve things of sentimental and monetary value? Tell me how no one cared enough to preserve the family legacy and heritage. I cannot wrap my arms around that.

I think back to the widowed Ruth and her mother-in-law, Naomi. Both were living in Moab in the middle of a famine when their husbands died. Although Ruth, a Moabite woman was not obligated, she willingly returned to the homeland of Naomi, Bethlehem in Judea. Boaz, a close relative of Naomi's deceased husband lived there as well.

In a series of events, Ruth gleans in the harvested barley fields to provide for the two women. When Boaz realizes who the young women is, he graciously pursues his option to buy back Naomi's land, and in doing so, take Ruth as his bride. Boaz became the kinsman-redeemer. When Ruth bore him a son, Obed, he ensured the lineage of Jesus himself, for Obed was the father of Jesse, who was the father of David, who in turn was in the Savior's direct line.

What a heritage that will never be forgotten or abandoned.

Today's Truth: Then the women said to Naomi, "Blessed be the Lord, who has not left you this day without a redeemer, and may his name be renowned in Israel!" Ruth 4:14

June 1

PROTESTS

It has been a hard couple of days. Following the death of George Floyd at the hands of a Minneapolis police officer, the country has exploded into violent protests, mayhem, and anarchy. It is disconcerting, to say the least.

Washington DC, Los Angeles, New York City, and Minneapolis are but a few of the cities in revolt. Some might question whether the police officer and the three other officers looking on were at fault. A knee to the neck remained until Mr. Floyd turned lifeless, despite pleas of not being able to breath. It was all caught on video and disturbing to watch. Because the victim was a black man, the rallying cry became the injustice to not only this man, but to all whose skin color is a darker shade.

I am not black. I never will be black. I cannot say I understand what people of color have been subjected to in the past or in the future. I have heard from friends who have experienced an increased suspicion because of their skin color. I have listened to stories of prejudice and disrespect. I have no reason to question any of this, empathizing if they have been mistreated or maligned. I can also understand how an over-reach of power can ignite a fire.

Peaceful protests to bring awareness of injustice are the right of the people. No problem there. However, the criminal actions of many can in no way be justified. Some have taken advantage of the situation, injuring police officers and even killing a federal security guard. Police stations have been burnt to the ground, store windows breached, and businesses ransacked, entire inventories stolen. Curfews in cities are being ignored, violence and hate promoted in the name of justice. It is sickening.

I am not writing to refute or debate racism. I write only to point out the obvious. Sinful man is desperately wicked. Sinful man justifies his actions to satisfy his own desires. Violence and hate never "fix" violence and hate. The only thing to replace violence and hate is a changed disposition of the heart by the power and control of the Holy Spirit.

Oh, that God would be merciful. I pray that many across this nation will have changed hearts, for this is the only way to right injustice.

Today's Truth: The heart is deceitful above all things, and desperately sick; who can understand it? Jeremiah 17:9

June 2

Stream of Consciousness

So, if you want a glimpse into how my wacko mind works, try to follow along.

I took off down the road to ensure my daily run would happen before our dinner guests arrived. It was hot, sunny, and humid. Still, the first half felt reasonable. The second part? Not so much. Every step was work.

Back at the house, the cool waters of the pool beckoned. Ah. So refreshing. I climbed aboard one of the rafts, drawing in a deep breath as I laid across the surface warmed by the sun. That is when my thoughts started bobbing in concert with the raft. I abruptly and unexpectedly recalled the days of my childhood marked by simple family vacations in Cape May and Ocean City, NJ.

My father loved the ocean, though his non-swimmer status prevented him from venturing beyond where he could stand. He sometimes treated us, however, by renting canvas rafts from a beach vendor. The sturdy rafts with a rope around the perimeter could support two people laying across the top. Though I had not thought about this for decades, I now remember with such clarity my dad and I sharing the raft, facing the oncoming waves. Bellies on the raft, feet dragging behind, arms flailing to paddle, we positioned ourselves to float up and over the swells. That feeling of rising and falling was delightful. I laughed with glee as we shared these moments for hours, only occasionally misreading a wave to get pummeled by the breaking water. But in those instances, Dad held me tight, protecting me. He was able to recognize danger and save me from mishap.

My father could not stop the waves, but because he understood the power of the water, he was my salvation against the tide. How much more our heavenly Father? God controls the waves. He makes them rise up as well as calm down. They reflect his majesty and power. His faithfulness is greater than the rhythmic, relentless crashing of waves onto the shore. Governing even the boundaries of the sea, God governs our coming and going. Praise be to God.

Today's Truth: O Lord *God of hosts, who is mighty as you are, O* Lord, *with your faithfulness all around you? You rule the raging of the sea; when its waves rise, you still them. Psalm 89: 8, 9*

June 3

Crooked

The truth is, I am orthopedically impaired—especially when it comes to feet. In 1997, the bunions on both feet presented problems. Of course, my feet looked ridiculous with my big toes positioned at awkward angles. My second toes were much longer than the big toes. This put undue pressure on the second metatarsals. Add in the extra bone out on the little toes, and you end up with a big mess.

With painful blistering from impossible to fit shoes and nine metatarsal fractures in five years, I ended up on the operating table. Seven incisions, six screws, and two wires sticking out of the tips of my toes later, my feet were truly a mangled mess. The pain was incredible, though I was only able to take four days off from work. I counted down the 60 days that would mark my doctor's approval to begin running again. Those first runs were incredibly painful, leaving me to wonder if I would ever be able to run with wild abandon.

Now, 23 years later, I think I might need a do-over on my left foot. My big toe has again taken a turn for the worse—literally. It lays on top of my second toe, forcing the bunion to be exaggerated. I can still run on it, a silicone spacer providing some relief. But ugly? Yes! I am self-conscious about how deformed my foot looks, especially when a relative stranger asks, "How in the world can you even walk?"

I had to laugh, however, when I slipped into new sandals. The right foot presented no problem. However, my left big toe is so crooked I physically had to pull my toe over to allow it to fit in the assigned spot. That should not be.

"Crooked" is never used in Scripture in a positive sense. Proverbs speaks of crooked speech, crooked paths, crooked integrity, and crooked hearts. Isaiah, the prophet, references the coming of the Christ: *Prepare the way of the Lord, make his paths straight. . .and the crooked shall become straight,* Paul writes to the Philippians reminding them to stand out from the *crooked and perverse* generation by being bright lights in a dark world.

My toe might be crooked, but I do not want my life to follow suit.

Today's Truth: Do all things without grumbling or disputing, that you may be blameless and innocent, children of God without blemish in the midst of a crooked and twisted generation, among whom you shine as lights in the world, holding fast to the word of life, so that in the day of Christ I may be proud that I did not run in vain or labor in vain. Philippians 2:14-16

JUNE 4

WATCH YOUR HEART. DON'T FOLLOW IT.

It was a privilege to be on a Zoom call with 146 college athletes, nine college coaches, and at least twenty fellow FCA staffers. The purpose? To come together in studying the Scriptures, making application to our lives.

The message tonight came from Deuteronomy 6. The crux of the matter is the heart. In fact, the heart is mentioned 44 times throughout Deuteronomy, indicating that it must be pivotal. But why? We associate the heart as the seat of our emotions. We view the heart as our essence, our core. But what must we understand about this analogous pairing of a life-sustaining organ with who we are, how we think, and how we act?

To quote a book title, "You are what you love." That is a true statement. If you say you love being an athlete, then you best be consistently training. If you say you love your family, then you make them a priority. The problem is that there is often a gap between what we say we love and what we do.

Culture tells us to "follow our heart." Whoa. That is dangerous. Our heart is a "desire factory," setting the course to obtain those things of questionable, if any, value. But we know from what Jeremiah wrote that the heart cannot be trusted for it is *desperately wicked*. The natural orientation of our heart, therefore, will take us in a direction we should not go.

There is a story of two ships colliding, and in doing so, over forty lives were lost. How do two ships in a big ocean find each other? Turns out the compass on one ship was off by a mere two degrees. That does not seem very significant, does it? But the consequences were devastating.

We must guard our hearts. We dare not follow them blindly lest we veer off course—even a little bit. Our hearts must be oriented to true north by intentionally loving God with our whole heart, soul, mind, and strength.

Today's Truth: You shall love the LORD *your God with all your heart and with all your soul and with all your might. And these words that I command you today shall be on your heart. Deuteronomy 6:5, 6*

June 5

In but not of

Our granddaughter, Addyson, thinks she is a mermaid—or at least wishes and pretends to be. Weeks ago, when the pool temperature barely hit 60 degrees, she insisted on swimming. Now that the temp has risen to 78 degrees, it is a comparative bathtub. She spends nearly every waking minute in the pool, giving lessons on how to dive like a mermaid, fetching toys from the bottom, and performing handstands and underwater acrobatics.

Those of us who are older enjoy floating more than swimming. Hence, there are two blow up camping mattresses in the pool. Then today, we blew up a ginormous inflatable swan to join the fleet. We have a standard pool float with cup holder and have recently added a float for babies. If everything is in the water at the same time, you might be hard pressed to find any clear sailing.

Addyson, at five years old, knows she must have an adult watch her when she is in the pool. We have tried to impress upon her why this is an important safety rule without giving her nightmares about accidental drowning. She is an obedient child whose norm is to do exactly as asked. But. . .

She had come in from swimming, changed clothes, and went back outside to play. Working in the kitchen, I had a clear view of the pool. What I saw was a fully dressed little girl floating around high and dry on one of the air mattresses. I flew out the back door to inform her of the rule infraction. "But Grandma, I'm not actually in the pool. I'm floating on it." I tried not to laugh.

Trying to look stern, I corrected her erroneous thinking. I think she now fully understands what was wrong with her logic, and I suspect we will not have repeated disobedience. However, before we get too judgmental, consider the truth that we are to be in the world but not of it. The concept comes from 1 John 2. Paraphrased: Live in the world but do not love the things of the world. If you love the world, the love of the Father is not in you.

We cannot afford to mess around. We either love God or the world. We cannot do both.

Today's Truth: Do not love the world or the things in the world. If anyone loves the world, the love of the Father is not in him. For all that is in the world—the desires of the flesh and the desires of the eyes and pride of life—is not from the Father but is from the world. 1 John 2: 15, 16

JUNE 6

LAZY SLUG

Had it not been for a better-than-expected twilight run, I might have considered the day a waste.

When I woke up and realized it was Saturday, try as I might, I could not land on a plan for the day. It was another day to feel bad about not getting in a long run in the mountains. Over the last five- or six-months motivation to train has plummeted, possibly related to the statin I take that causes joint and muscle weakness. That be as it may, this morning was also void of motivation to do anything. It is not like there was nothing to do. Chores galore awaited. But I wasn't feeling it.

What I felt was exhausted and "off." Slug-like. I could not put my finger on it, but my energy level was nearly non-existent. After coffee, I mustered up enough strength to mow the grass by the pool and start a load of laundry. Then I ventured off to the re-opened Goodwill store to convince myself I felt better. It did not help. A stop on the way home to pick up three heavy bags of garden soil about did me in. I was done with a capital D.

When I got home, I floated on a raft before heading inside to wiggle my way into a favorite corner of the sofa. Seth had mentioned how he wanted to put in another large, raised planting bed, intending to border it with rock from the property. When I drifted off to la-la napland, it was merely an idea. Not so much when I woke up.

Within a span of a few hours, Seth completed constructing a 20' x 3' raised bed. When I looked out the window, he was covered in dirt from head to toe. Though he used the mechanical power of the tractor to move the tons—literally— of rock and soil, it was good 'ol fashioned manual labor to position all the rocks, fill with soil, and begin planting. He was anything but lazy today. He saw a task to be done and conquered it.

I could not be prouder of this kid. He is exhibiting a very admirable character skill: hard work. He understands the value in labor and the satisfaction in the result.

Today's Truth: Go to the ant, O sluggard; consider her ways, and be wise. Proverbs 6:6

June 7

Only One Thing Remains

The world is a curious place. So much to see. So much to hear. So much to contemplate.

We just returned home from a casual dinner at a friend's home. But there was no opportunity to talk about our kids, grandkids, or coming retirement. Those conversations never happened because our collection of friends gathered there were forty-some years younger than us.

Our hosts were Rebecca and Jamie. Rebecca is one of the original Shindigglers, and is married to Jamie, a young pastor of a country church. They are expecting their first child. Then there was Caroline, sister of Rebecca and fellow Shindiggler. She is married to Caleb and both are in medical school. Abby, who is also a Shindiggler and a critical care nurse, is married to Jordan. They brought along their baby boy. Yet another Shindiggler and critical care nurse, Kendal, and her husband Collin rounded out the group. It seems like yesterday when I was their high school coach, leading them to the mountains whenever possible. Things sure have changed!

All these girls (and significant others) are real-live adults. They are professionals, own homes, some are moms, and all are happily married. How in the world did this happen? We toured Rebecca and Jamie's home, scouted the bedroom that will soon be a nursery, marveled at the newly refurbished kitchen, and checked out the garden and buzzing beehives. I was flattered that these four young couples thought to invite us oldies.

I suppose I should not be shocked at young people growing up. But on the way home, Gary commented about the kids we both taught in the early years of our lives together. Could it be that our students are now in their 60's? Yes. It is strange but true.

These are small examples of how life changes quickly. But the way society thinks and functions seems to be changing at record pace. What used to be known as right is now deemed wrong. What was taboo is now acceptable. Sin is glorified.

The comforting thing is this: one thing never changes. Our sovereign Father is the same yesterday, today, and forever.

Today's Truth: Before the mountains were brought forth, or ever you had formed the earth and the world, from everlasting to everlasting you are God. Psalm 90:2

June 8

Face to Face

For the first time in weeks, I directed my car down the country road, along the highway, and onto the college campus where my office is located. Instead of one or two cars in the parking lot, today there were many. "Hum. Something must be changing," I reasoned.

As I walked into the athletic center, I first saw one of the volleyball players who I have been mentoring online. Wow. Standing beside her, I felt so little. She has legs that don't stop, and is a tall drink of water, to quote a Southern-ism. Immediately after that, I ran into two of the tennis gals coming out of the weight room. We hugged and spent a few minutes catching up. Ascending the steps, my path took me past the copy machine. There, two tennis players were busy printing off needed documents. More happy greetings and hugs were exchanged.

I have been "seeing" all these girls in a virtual environment for months. But wow, what a difference a face-to-face encounter makes. Even though there were no sit-down, serious conversations, just being in front of these women made all the difference in the world. I cannot wait until face-to-face is the norm and virtual the exception.

I grew up in a church that valued the singing of hymns. Because of this familiarity, I thought of the 1898 hymn entitled "Face to Face." It is but one of 1500 hymns penned by Carrie Ellis Breck. In the first stanza, she asks "Face to face—what will it be when with rapture I behold him, Jesus Christ who died for me?" Whoa! When she puts it that way, what will we say, what will we do, when we stand in front of the one who saved us?

In the second verse, Breck writes, "Only faintly now I see him, with the darkened veil between, but a blessed day is coming when His glory will be seen." I wonder if this came from 1 Corinthians when it speaks of "seeing through a glass darkly"?

"Banished grief and pain," are spoken of in verse three. Verse four acknowledges the sure bliss when we see our Redeemer face to face. Then the melodic chorus chimes in with this thought: "Face to face in all His glory, I shall see him by and by."

I will take face to face any day!

Today's Truth: For now we see in a mirror dimly, but then face to face. Now I know in part; then I shall know fully, even as I have been fully known. 1 Corinthians 13: 12

JUNE 9

FIRM FOUNDATIONS

We have waited for weeks and weeks and weeks. Plans to build a detached garage started months ago. After copious amounts of research about what kind of structure to build and who to hire, Gary finally settled on a reputable fellow. Start to finish was expected to be six to eight weeks.

It started out well. Earth moving equipment descended on our property. Our side yard was scraped off to become the new driveway. Load after load of fill dirt was hauled in to create a large pad for the garage. Once there was sufficient dirt in place, a compactor was brought in to pound away, compressing the soil. The foundation was next on the agenda.

But then the rains came. Lots of rain. With soggy soil, it was impossible to pour the foundation. And then Covid-19 came, slowing down everything, even the steel manufacturing for the building. Now, of course, the builder is behind in all his projects, at no fault of his own.

It was our great pleasure to see two of his workers come today. With the aid of a transit, they set boards for the perimeter of the foundation, making sure everything was square and level. The forms look solid and capable of holding in the rock and concrete. However, they also drilled in 24" long corkscrew anchors every ten feet around the perimeter. Each has a metal loop at the top that sticks out of the ground eight inches through which re-bar will pass. Though we were not familiar with this type of foundation, we are told that the screws keep the entire concrete pad from shifting.

It is vitally important for this new garage to be supported by a strong, properly constructed foundation. However, the foundation we set to support the building of our biblical world view is immensely more important. We cannot begin to interact with culture without understanding Scripture and its relevancy to every aspect of our lives. Like the difficulty we would have if the builders skipped steps in the garage foundation, we are certain to be swayed by errant thinking if we do not arm ourselves with the truth of Scripture. Otherwise, the only thing we can offer is baseless opinion, hardly capable of supporting strong, consistent living.

Today's Truth: And he gave the apostles, the prophets, the evangelists, the shepherds and teachers, to equip the saints for the work of ministry, for building up the body of Christ, until we all attain to the unity of the faith and of the knowledge of the Son of God, to mature manhood to the measure of the stature of the fullness of Christ, so that we may no longer be children, tossed to and fro by the waves and carried about by every wind of doctrine, by human cunning, by craftiness in deceitful schemes. Ephesians 4:11–14

June 10

TO FORGIVE OR NOT TO FORGIVE

We are two weeks out from the death of George Floyd at the hands of a police officer. There have been many nights of protests and violent rioting, leading to the looting and destruction of many businesses. Multitudes are calling for defunding and abolition of police departments. Discussions related to race often focus on accusations of unfairness, inequity, discrimination, prejudice, and reparations for the sins of past generations. Without doubt, these are complex issues.

I am not attempting to dissect any of the social issues. But it does give me opportunity to think about the intricacies and implications of forgiveness. Many of our brothers and sisters with deeper melanin-laden skin compared to me as a Caucasian, point back to the suffering of enslaved people. There is a call for financial reparations as a payback of what many believe they are owed. Additionally, if I am properly interpreting the message, there is a large group calling for social measures to "even the score."

I am taking a deep plunge into contemplating these issues. The idea of forgiveness originates from God and is exemplified by the sacrificial offering of Jesus in atonement for our sins. In the New Testament alone, there are nearly 70 references to forgive/forgiveness. It must be important.

Are we expected to forgive? Yes. Jesus said we must forgive sins as the Father has forgiven us. How many times must we forgive? 77 times. When are we to forgive? When praying. Who are we to forgive? Anyone who has sinned against us. Why forgive? If we forgive, we will be forgiven.

Generations ago, atrocities were committed against those who were enslaved. Are descendants responsible for those sins today? Is there still injustice according to God's standard of justice? Certainly. Though each person is an image-bearer of God, *All have sinned and fallen short of the kingdom of God (Romans 3:23)*. Imperfect people will never create a perfect society. But dare we sin because we expect another to forgive. In no way! Is lack of forgiveness a sin? Indeed.

I wonder what would happen if every individual took responsibility to offer forgiveness, no matter how hard that may be?

Today's Truth: bearing with one another and, if one has a complaint against another, forgiving each other; as the Lord has forgiven you, so you also must forgive. Colossians 3:13

June 11

We Are What We Eat

Rasta is a dog, a beagle to be precise. A nice dog, but a dog none the less. Rasta is the fur child of Pam, my daughter-in-law, both of whom live with us. I never grew up with dogs. When I was growing up, we were a cat family. A dog was never a consideration while I was living at home, although my dad did get a dog after all of us kids were gone. And, in our nearly 43 years of married life, any pet we have owned meowed rather than barked. Thankfully, this transition to a dog in the house has been easier than expected.

Easier than expected, that is, until today. After returning from my morning slog in oppressive heat and humidity, I found a large puddle on my kitchen rug. Upon further investigation, the rug in front of the front door was covered with a nasty pile of puke. When I walked into the bedroom where the printer resides, a large mass of poo greeted me. What was going on?

I informed Pam of my discoveries. Rasta was lethargic and Pam was worried. She carried the sad-eyed dog up the stairs to the apartment, where she reported the pup slept for hours. When Pam had to leave for work, the dog was transferred to my care. Over the next several hours, she threw up various shades of green and yellow fluid three or four times. Finally, her last vomiting episode produced a disgusting puddle filled with what looked like seaweed. Ah, now it was clear. The dog must have eaten massive quantities of grass and weeds to the point of making herself sick. She is now recovering quietly on the sofa.

I guess we could make several life applications, the first of which is simple. Do not eat grass if your body cannot process grass. It will make you sicker than a dog—pun intended. The other application is more conceptual. We can make ourselves spiritually sick when we carelessly partake of things that are not good for us: friends who do not edify, behaviors and attitudes that are unkind, certain media and music, selfishness, slander, and gossip. The list goes on. The only way to get better is to get rid of this stuff, even if the ridding process is unpleasant. Though the wrenching hurts, spiritual health returns only after we get rid of the bad and take in what is good.

Today's Truth: Let all bitterness and wrath and anger and clamor and slander be put away from you, along with all malice. Be kind to one another, tenderhearted, forgiving one another, as God in Christ forgave you. Ephesians 4:31-32

JUNE 12

RETIREMENT DAY

Today is the day. When Gary returns home from work, he will be officially retired. Whoa. How did that happen? How did he get to the age of 66 and pull the plug on the daily go-to-work grind? It seems odd. Only old people retire. Is he old? Am I old since I am not far behind? Yikes.

This idea of retirement means different things to different people. For some, the free time is a ticket to travel and adventure. Of course, only those whose retirements are well-funded are privileged to take that approach. For others, most days are marked by a leisurely wake-up time, followed by drinking volumes of coffee out on the front porch as a gentle breeze blows across a well-manicured lawn. At least that is what the TV commercials portray. But I have a sneak'n suspicion that retirement in our household will look very different.

Gary liked his job as a school facilities manager. Being the hard-working "McGyver" that he is, he proved himself an asset to the staff. He was a practical manager, could fix anything, and worked well with people. But in preparation for this day, he got a head start by upping his game in the E-Bay world. His plan is to buy and sell cars, motorcycles, and find buyers for the hundreds, if not thousands, of accumulated parts and manuals laying around the garage. He has proven successful in this ramp-up period.

Gary has been a hard-working husband over the years, always making sure that our family's needs are met. He can work from dawn to dusk, although we laugh at his ability to do some serious head bobbing when he takes a break nestled in his corner of the sofa. I suspect, however, that though an alarm clock will no longer dictate his day, he will make wise use of his time, even at his own discretion.

Work is honorable. Work is a necessary part of the human experience. Even God modeled the fact that 6/7 th of His time was spent in productive activity. Whether someone else is paying us or we are left on our own, we really should be thankful for the opportunity to labor, for by laboring, we appreciate the practical spoils of our work and the deserved rest when the job is complete.

Today's Truth: Whoever works his land will have plenty of bread, but he who follows worthless pursuits will have plenty of poverty. Proverbs 28:19

June 13

Don't lose it

The weather was as predicted: 70s, sunny, and a nice breeze to rustle my still unkempt bed-head hair. It would have been a glorious day to be in the mountains running along verdant trail. But after several weeks of becoming prematurely winded and feeling an odd flutter in my chest, I am hesitant to go to the mountains alone. Besides, the side effects of the statin I take has produced joint pain and extreme muscle weakness. The dosage is being reduced, but all of this is completely off-topic for today. I mention it only because it explains why I took on a project rather than running.

The treehouse has not had much attention as of late, still standing in a state of incompleteness. Incompleteness bothers me. When I do something, I do it fast and keep going until the very end. But this project has been primarily Seth's doing. Unfortunately, he has been distracted by more pressing issues, such as completing Pam's house rehab. Hence, I figured I could conquer a few more steps needed for completion of the treehouse.

The task was to add framing for the windows and then cut away the siding to reveal the empty space. Of course, windows need shutters, so that was next on the agenda. I made the trip across the field to the garage to gather some of the specialty tools the job required. As hard as I looked, the Kreg™ jig and all the parts to the kit had gone missing. Grrr. Someone apparently took the entire bin where I kept all the bits and pieces in one place and never put it back. I'm sure it will turn up someday, somewhere, but for now, I am left feeling aggravated. When I made a run to the store to get other hardware, I considered buying another kit. Nope. At $100 give or take, it was too expensive.

In a twisted series of thought, I contemplated the similarities between this scenario and—wait for it—reputations. Fine reputations are built over time and with great care. However, just like the carelessness that made my tools go missing, careless behavior can destroy in an instant that which had great value at one time. It can be near to impossible to rebuild that reputation unless great care is taken to re-focus on right thinking and behavior. And yes, it will cost a great deal to get back in good standing. It sure is easier to never get careless and sloppy in the first place.

Today's Truth: A good name is to be chosen rather than great riches, and favor is better than silver or gold. Proverbs 22:1

June 14

STAINS

The simple task of going to the store to select just the right pink paint for Addyson's treehouse did not end in the way I anticipated.

Wanting to keep the momentum going on the treehouse work, I happily choked down a quick salad after church before heading outside. There was new window trim to paint and horizontal supports to add between the studs. All went along swimmingly as I cut boards to length, drove in screws, and wielded the paint-laden brush. With time to spare, I zipped off to the home improvement store to choose that perfect pink paint I mentioned at the get-go. Even with way too many pink paint chips to choose from, it took less than two minutes to pick the shade. "One gallon, exterior, water-based paint, satin finish, please" I requested of the young employee. He got busy mixing the paint and gave the can a good shake. After that, he removed the lid, put a dot of the paint on the top of the can, replaced the lid and give it a couple whacks with a rubber mallet. I headed home, anxious to slather the paint on the walls.

With less than a mile to go, I turned the car sharply to the left and started up the hill close to home. Simultaneously, I heard a ker-thunk. Glancing backwards, I saw beautiful pink paint oozing all over the floor. Oh no! Still driving, I reached behind me to right the can. Unfortunately, now my hand was covered in pink, as was the gear shifter when I needed to down shift. What a mess!

Once home, I drove directly to the outdoor hose and began the process. Much of the paint was on the carpeted floor mat. With my already-painted hand, I scraped off as much paint as possible back into the can. Then I tried to scoop up the paint on the floor carpet itself. Oh, and that shifter needed scrubbed down as well.

Even with a powerful stream of water on the floor mat and the tedious job of blotting up the paint on the carpet, there will always be a pink tinge and a few splatters to remind me of this unfortunate event. But this is not the way God operates. When he cleans up our mess, Christ's shed blood washes us spic and span. We are made righteous and acceptable to God by His grace and mercy. Gone are the old stains. We are made spotless. Praise God.

Today's Truth: Come now, let us reason together, says the Lord: though your sins are like scarlet, they shall be as white as snow; though they are red like crimson, they shall become like wool. Isaiah 1:18

June 15

Lost things

The four of us, Gary, Seth, Pam, and myself, have been looking for a stupid ring of keys since Saturday night. That is two days of relentless searching. Ugh.

With Seth and Pam riding motorcycles all day, they took Gary's jeep and trailer, leaving their car here. The check engine light had been coming on, indicating some sort of problem. While they were gone, Gary took it down the road to assess the issue. Then it was into the garage to code out the computer. He unhooked the battery, resetting the indicator light. He then drove the car out of the garage and to its parking spot.

When the "kids" came home, they asked for the keys. While three of us saw them on the kitchen counter earlier in the day, they were no longer there. Gary retraced his steps, Pam and Seth began digging through everything they owned. No keys. But unfortunately, the lost keys were for two different cars, one of which had a sunroof that happened to be open. Doubly unfortunate. It began to rain. No, pour. A heavy camping mattress was placed over the gaping hole to keep it from becoming a swimming pool on wheels.

Today is the third day of searching for those blasted keys. We even checked the oddest of places; refrigerators and freezers. Pam's house keys, which need to be given to the new renters, also share the same ring. The only thing I knew to do was pray all day for those keys to be found!

Though Gary was certain he left them on the counter, I followed him to the garage to look there. Coming up empty, we walked past the parked Corvette. Gary glanced inside. There they were sitting on the console! Thank you, Lord! He suddenly remembered putting his car away after dealing with Pam's. He obviously had them in his hand but failed to grab them after driving his car to the garage.

God is in the habit of valuing the lost. Jesus used parables to tell of lost sheep, lost coins, and lost sons. The simple act of seeking indicates a level of commitment to find that which is lost. I am so thankful God chose to seek, find—and save—this lost soul of mine.

Today's Truth: For the Son of Man came to seek and to save the lost. Luke 19:10

JUNE 16

THE RHYTHM OF THE HEART

Tonight, I go to bed with a new companion. This companion has the capacity to track every beat of my heart and make sense of it. Or let's hope it does.

For several weeks, something has not felt right. I have had increasing muscle weakness—especially my quads—and the top of my knees hurt so bad I must use my hands to stand up or sit down. If I kneel to tie my shoe or go to the floor for some other reason, getting up again is a fiasco. I look like a decrepit 90-year-old lady. (No offense to 90-year-old ladies.) My energy is low, and I get short of breath when I do physical labor. Sometimes, I feel my heart get out of sync from a steady, easy beat. At least I think that is what's happening.

When I had a physical last week, my primary care practicioner recommended a heart monitor for two weeks. Since I have lost confidence because of how bad I feel, I have been hesitant to go on solo long runs in the mountains, something I miss terribly. So, I agreed. Today I went to the cardiology office. They taped the device to my chest, and assuming I can get it to stay on despite the sweat, I should have some answers in a couple of weeks.

I am told to press the button on the device if I feel anything goofy, recording the date, time, and circumstances on a phone app. In a way, I am scared, and maybe even embarrassed to push the button. What if it is all my imagination? What if everything proves to be perfectly normal? Then it makes me look like a hypochondriac, or at the very least, a little girl crying wolf.

Apparently, when I send in the device after two weeks, it can analyze every one of my heart beats. That is a lot of beating! It should be able to detect anomalies even if I cannot feel them. That is spectacular technology to make sense out of my heart.

Even more so, as a Believer, I have a heart analyzer as well. It is the Holy Spirit. He knows my every thought and intent of my heart. He discerns my motives and attitudes. He convicts to correct. He chides to bring me to repentance. He is 100% accurate in his assessment.

Today's Truth: The Spirit himself bears witness with our spirit that we are children of God, and if children, then heirs—heirs of God and fellow heirs with Christ, provided we suffer with him in order that we may also be glorified with him. Romans 8:16, 17

JUNE 17

LIVE INTENTIONALLY

It was good to see all of them. Their bright and shining faces looked back at me from the depths of my glossy computer screen. I had been invited by the tennis coaches to join in a discussion over an assigned book reading: "Keep Chopping Wood" by Kevin Deshazo. It is a simple read, barely over 50 pages in length. But it is a story with a purpose. A story that teaches principle. A story that if grasped in meaning, can change thinking, and thus behavior.

The long and short of it is this. A high school athlete learns the hard way that one chops wood not for this season, but to have fuel to burn next year. Understanding the principle leads to focusing on the present so you can be prepared for the future. It is accepting the idea that "Greatness is boring. Be brilliant in the basics." Belief drives behavior. A team is built on trust. We must learn to live intentionally, not accidentally.

Accidental living. It is so easy to live that way. Go with the flow. Be spontaneous. Who needs plans? Que sera, sera. What will be, will be. Certainly, there are times when this approach can be applauded. But then again, it normally does not lead to an efficient, forward-progress approach.

So, what does intentional living look like? For the tennis player, it might be hitting hundreds of forehands down the line and cross court, followed by backhand shots. Thousands of balls need to be played at the net, and just as many serves served. Purposeful repetition is key to build that firm foundation of fundamentals. There is nothing electrifying about day in - day out practice, but it is necessary in preparing for stellar competitive play.

Of course, these principles apply to every aspect of our lives. We need to practice kindness and compassion. Generosity and hospitality should be frequently rehearsed. Living in community, even when solitude is preferred, can be an act of personal discipline. And spiritually? Whoa. The sky is the limit! But really, if we daily practice loving our God with all our heart, soul, mind, and strength, that belief will drive our behavior. It will become a litmus test for everything we do.

Now, that is living intentionally.

Today's Truth: You shall love the LORD *your God with all your heart and with all your soul and with all your might. Deuteronomy 6:5*

JUNE 18

AWARENESS

I loved being at my desk in the office today. My real office, that is. Not the dining room table or love seat over by Addy's dollhouse that became the Covid-19 substitute workspaces. However, after four or five hours of hard thinking, it was time to get outside. Constant rain over the last three days had stopped, making the thought of a run through the woods even more appealing.

I normally do not take my phone when I am running locally. But now that I am wearing a heart monitor for the next two weeks, I strapped on a stretchy belt where my cell phone could ride along. I needed to have it for app access, allowing me to give details of any heart flip-flops. I was hoping there would be none.

My mind raced along as I started out, though I would hardly call the speed of my feet race worthy. It was so pedestrian. Still, everything felt normal given that on the best of days, it takes me forever to get in the groove. Now, as I set course on the mountain trails, I found myself second guessing everything. "Should I be breathing this hard? Am I really feeling something abnormal? Give it a minute and see if I feel different. Ah, should I punch the button on the monitor to indicate an event. I don't know. Let it ride. Oh, I do not feel too bad now. I am simply old and out of shape, Well, no. Maybe I should have pushed the button just in case but now it's too late." My left brain argued with my right brain the entire time. Assessing this heart situation was more complicated than I thought.

It is a good thing that no matter if I push the button or not, the device, assuming it functions properly, will record and analyze every single beat. Amazing, huh? What that means is this: Even if I am unaware of an abnormality, the algorithm should be able to detect it. Conversely, if I mis-identify an event, there will be evidence that everything was A-OK.

Two thoughts come to mind. I wonder what would happen if I was as attentive to monitor my spiritual heart and longings as I am the physical heart? And secondly, there is one extremely accurate analyzer of my heart; God himself in the person of his Spirit. I just need to be signed up for the service.

Today's Truth: Search me, O God, and know my heart! Try me and know my thoughts. And see if there be any grievous way in me, and lead me in the way everlasting. Psalm 139:23, 24

JUNE 19

CRASH AND BURN

Like a couple of old folks, Gary and I spent the evening watching a movie. The house was quiet, Seth, Pam and Addyson having left to drive up on the Blue Ridge Parkway in search of a beautiful sunset. It was pleasant to stop and relax, immersed in a heart-warming movie.

In time, we heard a car door close and paused the movie to wait for the front door to open. The first one in was Rasta Dog, a cute if somewhat pudgy beagle who always knows when I start cooking dinner. Then came Pam carrying Addy. Seth appeared in the dooray looking like the wind had been taken out of his sails. Oh dear. What could the matter be?

And so started the sad story. He was flying his drone out from a spectacular overlook. Seth is a gifted pilot despite unfortunate accidents with two previous and expensive drones. This refurbished drone was purchased with the intent of using it to create promotional footage for small business in the area. With plenty of time left on the battery, he turned the drone to return to his position. When it was 300 feet away and 250 feet off the ground, two of the four propellers stopped rotating. That is never good. He instantly lost all control. The only thing to do was watch it plummet to the mountainside below. Soon there was silence. Seth marked the crash position in his mind, clamoring down the rough terrain, crawling through thick rhododendron until he came upon the mangled mess. It was shattered, wires sticking out, arms broken off, and propellers splintered. Thankfully, the Go-Pro camera was intact. Still, standing in the kitchen and sadly shaking his head he muttered, "I'm done. No more drones."

I feel for Seth. My heart aches at the disappointment and disruption of plans. The crash represents a lot of money, time, and effort. It's not like his life is over because of the damaged-beyond-repair drone, but it's a hard pill to swallow, nonetheless.

There have certainly been times in my own life when I felt like everything around me had crashed and burned. I felt caught in a vacuum, devoid of hope and filled with anguish. Like ancient King David, I stared at the ceiling many nights just crying out to God for relief. True to form and in His own timing, God has always been faithful to bring restoration and peace.

Today's Truth: But I will sing of your strength; I will sing aloud of your steadfast love in the morning. For you have been to me a fortress and a refuge in the day of my distress. Psalm 59:16

JUNE 20

THUNDER AND LIGHTENING

On this first day of summer, I woke not at all refreshed. It was another sleep-deprived night, hitting the bed, two different sofas and a love seat in search of the magic spot. I contemplated driving to the mountains and getting in a long run. However, I felt so puny and, to be honest, a little nervous about going by myself under these circumstances. Nevertheless, if I wanted to be busy, there was plenty to do around the farm.

If I was going to make progress on the treehouse, time had to be spent rounding up all the tools that had mysteriously walked away. That accomplished, I measured, sawed, fit, and screwed in the remaining odd-shaped pieces of siding. Then it was on to caulking all the seams and around the windows before touching up with trim paint. I considered myself fortunate to not have fallen off the ladder while precariously balancing, holding pieces in place, and wielding the impact driver, caulking gun, and paint brush.

Soon, it was close to 6 p.m. Distant rumbles echoed across the sky. Gary reported that a storm band was coming in from the north. Undaunted because it was sunny in the present, I decided to run. The initial climb to the top of the driveway was slow but calculated. By the time I reached the road, my feet broke into a run.

As I rounded the big curve, I began to pay more attention to the ominous clouds in front of me. Thunder became more frequent, and bolts of lightning pierced the sky. In another mile, I was in the thick of it, sheets of rain pounding down. A particularly loud boom and massive lightning strike made me jump completely off the ground. I instinctively prayed I would not turn into a smoldering puddle of protoplasm.

Eventually, I ran out from under the storm, although a few good thunder and lightning duos made me push the pace. In doing so, I took opportunity to offer praise to the One who controls that powerful thunder and awesome electric bolts cutting through the atmosphere. My prayers for other matters where uttered with a little more power and faith, having been reminded that the God who sends the storm has no problem taking care of my simple requests.

Today's Truth: The crash of your thunder was in the whirlwind; your lightnings lighted up the world; the earth trembled and shook. Psalm 17:18

June 21

Grandchildren

We celebrated Father's Day today. It was wonderful. Addy remembered the moment she woke up. She scampered down the steps, making her way to the prepared gift bags for her Daddy and "Work PopPop."

She dutifully delivered the appropriate bag to her grandfather before carrying the other bag to her father. She had carefully addressed the cards yesterday in preparation, astutely noticing that spelling "Daddy" was simply "Addy" with an extra D. I heard Seth exclaim thanks for the gifts. When Pam came down a little while later, she reported he shed tears when reading the cards.

Seth has become a wonderful father, partly because he had a great example in watching Gary. There's little doubt, however, that his progressive transformation into a Godly father for Addyson has been a long time coming. Seth went through very difficult years but is now clear-headed and focused. God has changed the disposition of his heart. We had a glimpse of that in church this morning.

It was with great pleasure that we arranged our five chairs in a row, socially distant from other families. As our pastor began his sermon, Addyson climbed up in her daddy's lap. Her eyelids grew heavy. Before long, that little blond head fell back against Seth's shoulder. She remained that way through the final amen, content to be nestled in her father's arms. I am pretty sure I saw my son wipe away a tear or two as he contemplated the pastor's admonitions for fathers, simultaneously holding his precious little girl. My own heart swelled at the sight of a father's love for his child.

Gary and I are certainly blessed to be grandparents to Addyson. We have the pleasure of being with her often. Her charm and wit highlight her personality. Addy's sense of humor makes us laugh out loud, her sophisticated questions sometimes perplexing us. We delight as she conquers newly acquired skills, like diving to the deepest end of the pool. But our greatest joy is when we witness her tender heart and spiritually-minded ponderings. We are forever thankful for the grandchild Seth graced us with five years ago.

Today's Truth: Grandchildren are the crown of the aged, and the glory of children is their fathers. Proverbs 17:6

JUNE 22

FAIR WARNING

It was nice change to be in my campus office. I worked without interruption save a medical appointment in the middle of the day. When I had enough, I informed those at home that I was going to the woods before heading home. A run was just what the doctor ordered, I hoped.

Had I run in the full sunshine, I doubt I would have lasted too long. But be-bopping along forest trails was a welcome relief. A stiff breeze contributed to the pleasant feeling of being alone with my thoughts. The meandering and sometimes rocky, rooty trail required careful attention to footing. But when the single track intersected with a gravel forest road that was predominantly downhill, I opened it up. This is not to imply I was fast. Just faster than I had been on the trail.

I skimmed along the road, taking in my surroundings. I felt better than anticipated. I was thankful for that. My mind wandered as my feet manufactured the steady crunch of gravel underfoot. A young deer stood eating browse not far from the road. For the briefest second, I pulled up, turned to face the animal, and began a one-sided conversation. "Well, hello, little girl. You're a pretty one."

Not waiting for a response that would never come, I continued running the lengthy downhill road. It was then I saw another runner, a woman, the first human sighting so far. With a green running skirt and black shirt, she was standing still when I first spotted her fifty yards down the road. When she heard me coming, she began an easy saunter. I caught up to her in no time, exchanging a quick greeting before sliding past. But what was that noise I heard?

The noise was a bell. With every step it jingled and clanged. I knew carrying bear bells was expedient in big bear country. But here on campus trails? That seemed a little over the top. Given, there are occasional bear sightings. I saw a mama and two cubs a couple years ago. But what were the chances a bear would be scared off today? Slim to none. I used considerable strength not to tease. "Looks like your bear bell is working. I've seen nary a one." I put distance between her and me. The bell was driving me crazy.

There is wisdom in sounding an alarm, in giving fair warning. Warriors of old blasted trumpets to signal war. Voices shouted to commence the fight. Take heed when warned. Better safe than sorry.

Today's Truth: Blow a trumpet in Zion; sound an alarm on my holy mountain! Let all the inhabitants of the land tremble, for the day of the Lord is coming; it is near, Joel 2:1

June 23

A stinky situation

Truth be told, it is nearing midnight. Gary and I had gone to bed and began talking about a pressing project for the week. It was only then I realized I had not yet written for the day. "Oh dear," I lamented to Gary. "How in the world am I going to make spiritual sense from of a pile of poo?"

Allow me to clarify. There seems to be an issue with our septic system. Despite having the tank pumped out a month ago, the leach field is not draining properly. To have it redone professionally would cost $8000. Hum. That's not gonna happen. Hence, Gary and Seth decided to rent a mini-excavator for a week. So far, they have located the distribution box by digging deep trenches. When the trenches filled with sewage water, more trenches had to be dug to drain off that fluid. What awaits in the next few days is to remove the cover off the box, pinpoint the existing drainage lines, dig more trenches following those drain lines, and then redo everything with the proper combination of pipe and gravel. In the meantime, the yard looks as if giant alien groundhogs moved in and took over.

So where can I possibly take this story to turn it into a spiritual lesson? My first thought is to allude to a dog returning to its own vomit as seen in Proverbs 26:11. How gross. But, nah. That is a different type of excrement. But I guess the biblical equivalent to this topic is dung. Are you aware that cities like Jerusalem had "Dung Gates?" It was the gate through which refuse, including human waste, was removed from inside the city walls and burned some distance from the city. It was a sustainable and safe way of reducing the waste to relatively inert ash.

There are nine different words in the Hebrew Old Testament that refer to dung. The connotation is that these are things which are defiled, worthless, unclean, degraded, and not worthy of sacrifice. The Apostle Paul uses the term "rubbish." Discussing all the benefits he had as a circumcised, educated Jew, he gladly gave up that "rubbish." Paul traded the inherent stench of religiosity for imputed righteousness through faith in Christ.

Today's Truth: For his sake I have suffered the loss of all things and count them as rubbish, in order that I may gain Christ and be found in him, not having a righteousness of my own that comes from the law, but that which comes through faith in Christ, the righteousness from God that depends on faith. Colossians 3: 8, 9

JUNE 24

MAMA BIRD

Not wanting to repeat writing in the wee hours like last night, I took up residence in a favorite spot, computer in my lap. Our front porch is small. Though a mere six feet wide, it is a protected space with a roof overhead. The floor is decking material that spans a small channel of water connecting fishponds on either side. With a fountain bubbling up on one side and a waterfall on the other, the babbling sounds are soothing and pleasant. Large flowerpots and hanging ferns adorn this approach to the front door. Positioned in the corner and to the left of the door is an old metal rocking chair. It was on my parents' front porch chair for years. To have my own front porch to sit, think, and write is quite wonderful.

It did not take long to boot the laptop. But I took opportunity to look around and take in my surroundings. Suddenly, a swift movement took place overhead. I looked up. Ah, yes. A mama bird had constructed a perfectly formed nest on top of the light pendant. Its mossy exterior looked like it could have been manufactured and sold in a high-end craft store. But this was the real thing. For weeks we have seen Mama come and go, preparing her nest for the coming family.

When I took my place on the chair, Mama took her cue to leave. However, she did not go far. I watched as she flew to a nearby perch, chirping and waiting. Several times she flitted off to another vantage point. I suppose she wanted to make sure her babies were safe. Not wanting Mama to be upset, I moved to a spot by the pool.

I find the parenting skills of birds fascinating. Their nests are works of art, assembled from discarded bits and pieces of nature. How did they figure out how to make a nest that not only protects the eggs and hatched birdies, but are so architecturally sound they can withstand the strongest of storms? Who showed that mother bird how to care for her newborns? How does she know to feed her young ones worms and insects rather than grass and weeds? Only an immensely creative God could come up with such a plan for our winged friends.

Today's Truth: indeed, there the night bird settles and finds for herself a resting place. There the owl nests and lays and hatches and gathers her young in her shadow; indeed, there the hawks are gathered, each one with her mate. Isaiah 34: 14b, 15

June 25

To Plan or Not to Plan

To plan or not to plan. That seems to be the question.

My morning has been filled with writing emails to various camp and outdoor recreation facilities. The purpose is to find out if any of these places are available to host pre-season team retreats. These retreats have proven beneficial to team unification in the past.

Here is the problem. Even with some states entertaining more relaxed rules related to Covid-19, the college sports world awaits big decisions from the NCAA. Twenty-three football players at Clemson just tested positive. That sent planning into a tailspin with worry about the safety of allowing any fall sports to take place. Specifically, they should be deciding today if and when fall sports other than football will—or even are allowed—to report for training.

I face a conundrum. Even if I can find a facility to host us (which looks doubtful at this point), should I plan the content of the teaching? How do I figure out what activities are possible? Does my offer to host the teams out on our farm meet with compliance standards? I feel like I am twiddling my thumbs doing nothing useful in this waiting period.

Uncertainty is never pleasant. I think back to standing on the start lines of 50 and 100-mile races. I never feel 100% certain of what will happen. No matter the amount and quality of training, the unexpected can attack at any point along the trail. Because of that, the only recourse is to take it one step at a time. Always be thinking. Always be analyzing. Should I be running or hiking? Is the pace too fast? Too slow? Do I need to eat and drink? I feel a hotspot developing on my heel. Take care of it now before it gets worse.

You get the idea. When uncertainty challenges us, we cannot panic. We must simply put one foot in front of the other, doing what we can in the moment. We do our best to control what we can control and release what we cannot. Uncertainty is a test. A test to see if we really believe that God is Sovereign in all things. A test to see if we trust Him as much as we say we do.

Today's Truth: Many are the plans in the mind of a man, but it is the purpose of the Lord that will stand. Proverbs 19:21

JUNE 26

EVERLASTING LOVE

After coming in from a run earlier this evening, a single piece of warmed up pizza served as supper. I was in no mood to cook. Gary was out on the mower and had helped himself to some of the leftovers a little earlier. Seth, Pam, and Addyson were gone camping, and I was tired from more work on the tree house. Hence, the pizza was as good as it was gonna get.

I consumed that slice of Italian pie in front of the TV. There were but a few channels pulled in by the antenna to choose from, having gotten rid of our satellite television subscription. A glance at the clock told me it was 9:00 p.m. The show "20/20" was just coming on. I put the clicker down and settled in.

I watched as a very strange story evolved over the next two hours. The saga began in 1978 when two babies were switched in a small Florida hospital. The switch was not discovered until one child, at ten years old, required extensive heart surgery to survive. Despite best efforts, she did not. However, blood typing revealed she could not possibly be the biologic daughter of the parents. That started a complicated cascade of events.

To say there was tragedy beyond belief in this Mays-Twigg case is a grave understatement. Where do I being? Besides the actual switch, which many believe was not an accident but a crime, there was the unimaginable childhood of Mrs. Twigg. The death of her baby girl thirteen years prior to the day as the child who died in surgery. The death of Mrs. Mays when the child she brought home from the hospital (who was actually a Twigg) was two years old. Protracted court proceedings to gain visitation rights for the Twiggs. Court proceedings by the child in question, Kimberly Mays, to "divorce" her biologic parents. Accusations of abuse by Mr. Mays on Kimberly. And so much more. If none of this makes sense, that's ok. It is a convoluted story.

The expose' wondered aloud about what constitutes a family? Is it who you grow up with or is it all a matter of genetics? Families love—or at least should—but that love is often complicated, as in this story. The only Father who loves His children perfectly is the one who is heavenly. Praise Him that no matter what the circumstances, His love is unconditional for his children from the very beginning. There is never a question to whom we belong.

Today's Truth: The Lord appeared to him from far away. I have loved you with an everlasting love; therefore I have continued my faithfulness to you. Jeremiah 31:3

JUNE 27

FORGETTING

I just got off the phone with my dear mother. She is a 92-year-old, wonderful woman.

Though she never worked outside the home, she was non-stop busy raising four kids, being the music director at church for decades, and visiting shut-ins like clockwork. She headed up the cancer support group, making tens of calls every month to check on those afflicted. During these conversations, she took copious notes, relying on her nursing education from long ago. In fact, though she never practiced as a registered nurse, she earned continuing education credits to maintain her Pennsylvania license until she was in mid-80s. When my dad died in 1986, she picked up his speaking opportunities on biblical creationism, as well as serving mission hospitals and participating in archeologic digs around the world. And to top it off, she even wrote a book with stories from her life. She was—and still is some kind of wonderful!

Unfortunately, her batteries are finally running down. She lives in an assisted living facility and receives great care. However, she often tells me she is tired, weak, and ready to head home. I think she is a little disappointed when she wakes every morning. Her memory is failing, and she becomes easily confused. "Is your birthday the 28th?" she inquired tonight.

"Yes Mother. February 28.

"What month is it now?" she asked inquisitively?

"June. It's June 27."

"Oh my. I get so confused. It is like we are in solitary confinement. We cannot leave our rooms, there are no visitors, and all our meals are brought to the room. It is terribly lonely. It's been like this for about three weeks."

I did not have the heart to tell her it has been like that for three months. But here's the thing. Though she forgets days, and months and conversations that happened five minutes ago, she never fails to remember her creator and savior. Her faith sustains and keeps her going.

Today's Truth: Bless the LORD, *O my soul, and all that is within me, bless his holy name! Bless the* LORD, *O my soul, and forget not all his benefits, who forgives all your iniquity, who heals all your diseases, who redeems your life from the pit, who crowns you with steadfast love and mercy, who satisfies you with good so that your youth is renewed like the eagle's. Psalm 103: 1-5*

JUNE 28

PEACE AND QUIET

My vantage point this evening is lovely. The tree house I have been working on is approaching the final stages of construction. Under cloudy and cooler skies compared to the last several days, it was a pleasure to construct the railings. With a six-foot drop should you take the plunge, the safety precaution is necessary. Now with supper cleaned up and everyone dispersed to their spots, I sit in a plush brown chair that has found a new home in this hide-a-way haven.

The project today was a combination of ingenuity and necessity. Ingenuity because every time I woke up last night, I was thinking about what I wanted the railings to look like. Necessity, because I was using found supplies: left over plastic lattice and a bunch of cheapo 1x3 lumber. The 4x4 posts were repurposed from another project. The only unfortunate event happened when drilling a hole in the top of the posts to house a solar light. My arthritic wrist took a beating when the drill bit got stuck. The base of the drill spun around and hit me square on my head. It was not until I went in the house and saw my white hair turned red that I realized my scalp was bleeding. Still, it was not a mortal injury.

When Addy saw the finished railings, she became excited about her treehouse. She began to gather supplies to dress it up. She grabbed a planted flowerpot and picked the corner of the deck where it should reside. Then off she went to grab a citronella lantern along with her pink Mini Mouse camp chair. She busied herself cleaning up the tools in the tiny but lofted cabin before plopping into her chair and announcing, "Ah, this is nice. I'm just gonna relax up here on the deck."

I know what she means. Sitting here on the deck overlooking the pool, I listen to an evening chorus of bird song. The air is cool, and a gentle breeze carries with it the scents of the surrounding forest. As the light fades and the solar lights begin to flicker, I am content to be in this moment. I have no desire to fill my mind with the latest demonstration of anarchy or the proliferation of virtue signaling at every turn. No. All I want right now is to be in the presence of the Father. To understand more fully his faithfulness, to embrace his will, and to be empowered by the Spirit to live from this moment on in the likeness of Christ.

Today's Truth: And I will ask the Father, and he will give you another Helper, to be with you forever, even the Spirit of truth, whom the world cannot receive, because it neither sees him nor knows him. You know him, for he dwells with you and will be in you. John 14: 16, 17

JUNE 29

BABY BIRDS

I heard Pam and Addyson come down the steps this morning as I was getting ready for the day. I smiled at their chatter and heard the front door open. Soon, the lyric of "Happy birthday" reached my listening ear. Addyson's tone was crystal clear and on pitch, something that does not always happen when she sings with vigor. This time, however, it was as sweet as a siren's song. She came back inside and rushed to me. "Grandma, Grandma!" she excitedly called. "The baby birds hatched. I sang Happy Birthday to them. They are so cute!"

Ah. That explains it. Some weeks ago, we found remnants of a light bulb on the decking. We could not understand how that came to be until we looked up. There atop the porch chandelier was a beautifully sculpted, moss-covered nest. Daily we watched as the nest grew taller and wider, the work of an expert architect. MamaBird came and went often, bringing back building materials at every opportunity. We dared not investigate the nest lest we disturb her incubating eggs and discourage Mama's maternal instincts. But today the wait was over. Four little heads poked over the brim, tiny peeps and open mouths awaiting their mother's return.

I cannot tell you how many times I have read Scripture urging us not to fret, not to worry. Surely, if God takes care of the birds, he can take care of us. But reading further in Matthew, we get this idea: *Foxes have holes and birds have nests, but Jesus has nowhere to sleep.*

Surely, Jesus had a place to call home in the early days with his family. And even when his vocation was carpentry, he likely had a place to reside after a good day's work. But everything changed when he entered ministry. His days were spent traveling on foot. He stayed in homes where he was invited. There was no income or guaranteed government assistance. He was *despised and rejected by men.* He was falsely accused yet remained silent. And ultimately, he bore the unspeakable torture of crucifixion.

The ministry life of the very Son of God was no picnic. It was not fun nor was it frivolous. It was simply work driven by love and a sense of responsibility to do the Father's will. The trappings of "normal" life proved to be of no importance in the long run.

Today's Truth: And Jesus said to him, "Foxes have holes, and birds of the air have nests, but the Son of Man has nowhere to lay his head." Matthew 8:20

JUNE 30

MENTORING

I just returned from lunch with Raise, a 25-year-old, wise beyond her years. Tall and slender with long, wispy chestnut-colored hair, she was dressed in jeans and a gauzy bohemian-style top. It reminded me of the shirts I wore back in the 70's. We ordered food before finding our way to the outdoor seating, claiming a table in the protective shade.

I met Raise when she was in high school. She was a runner on the cross-country team as well as the indoor and outdoor track teams. She was a brilliant student and committed athlete. As a coach, I could always count on her for doing the workouts as instructed. She was the kind of teammate you wish everyone would be; kind, loving, supportive, and encouraging. If she ever had a bad attitude, I never saw it.

Raise went on to college, feeling strongly that God was calling her to international missions. Having interned in Hungary, she became convinced that she should return there to be the hands and feet of Jesus. And return she did. God faithfully provided 100% of her necessary support in less than a year. Her email updates are engaging and filled with news of language school updates and relationships being built.

With the advent of Covid-19, the mission board brought her back home for the time being. She is thankful for the time to help care for her ALS-afflicted father. But now, she is anxious to return to her life in Hungary in the coming months once immigration stipulations are lifted.

As I prayed with her, my voice faltered, and I could feel tears begin to form. I make no claim at all for her spiritual maturity and focus. And yet, I am so grateful to see God's faithfulness in her life. However, my hope is that our interaction in the past made a positive impact in her life. Perhaps it was the physical discipline in training that transferred to the discipline of spiritual training? Could it be that her experience as a part of a team positively affected the meshing with teammates in Hungary?

I cannot adamantly answer those questions one way or the other, but I am thankful that we have a biblical model of older women mentoring younger women. It encourages me in the daily interactions I have with young women athletes.

"Use me, Father, in some small way."

Today's Truth: Older women likewise are to be reverent in behavior, not slanderers or slaves to much wine. They are to teach what is good, and so train the young women to love their husbands and children, to be self-controlled, pure, working at home, kind, and submissive to their own husbands, that the word of God may not be reviled. Titus 2:3-5

July 1

Work with Integrity

I was hot, sweaty and in need of a shower. Though I was running by 8 a.m., the heat was oppressive. But then again, I felt sluggish, struggling to find anything even close to a rhythm. Nevertheless, I slogged my way through the miles, arriving at work one hot mess.

I dropped my bag in the office before heading to the locker room, a perk of working in the university's athletic center. Rounding the corner, I noticed the "Closed for cleaning" rod spanning the distance between the door frames. Normally, the custodians prop the door open when cleaning, but not today. Not yesterday either, for that matter.

I went through the same routine yesterday. When I got to the locker room door, it was blocked. I hesitated, but decided it was imperative that I shower before working in my office. I was smelling rank! Hence, I ducked under the tension rod bearing the sign, pushed upon the door, and entered. I saw the janitor's cart parked in the middle of the room. But where was the housekeeper? Ah, there she was. Around the corner, leaning against the sinks with nose buried in her phone. It took a second for her to notice me. She hurriedly stuffed her phone into the back pocket of her jeans.

When I ducked and entered again today, I found this same young lady sitting on the sink, phone in hand. She jumped off the sink when she noticed me, simultaneously uttering, "It's OK if you want to shower." Her embarrassment was obvious at twice being caught not working when she was supposed to be scrubbing away.

As I showered, I wondered if I should say anything to her. By the time I rinsed out the conditioner, I decided I would present a challenge in hopes she would catch on. "Thanks for your service. Be sure to be a woman of integrity today," I offered with a smile. She smiled back and thanked me.

I have no idea if she connected the dots or not. But I hope so. It was obvious to me she was using the "Closed for cleaning" option as a time to hide. But would harsh or condemning words have been effective? Probably not, especially since I am not her boss. The challenge to work with integrity was certainly a kinder, gentler challenge appropriate for all of us.

Today's Truth: A soft answer turns away wrath, but a harsh word stirs up anger.
Proverbs 15:1

JULY 2

ANNIVERSARY DAY

43-years ago today Gary and I got married. Whoa. 43 sounds like a big number, and I guess it is. To put it in perspective, we got hitched about 25 years before the young women I work with were even born! That does not seem right.

Last night as we were getting ready for bed, I asked Gary if he realized our anniversary was upon us. A puzzled look turned into a smile as he responded, "Well, I guess it is. I would have remembered when I saw the date pop up tomorrow." We both chuckled.

This morning the hubster asked where I wanted to go for dinner. To be honest, going out to spend money on a meal that soon will pass—if you get my drift—is not my thing. I'm being dead serious. Besides, we ate at a restaurant last night with his sister and we will be gone next weekend for a wedding. That will be more opportunity to eat out. So, thanks but no thank you.

I know Gary asked me out to dinner to be kind. But I am certain he was relieved that I did not want to go. "Well, how about we go get ice cream once it cools off a little?"

"Perfect!" A simple date is fine with me.

I am uninspired about days that most consider significant. We celebrate holidays, but it really is just another day. Birthdays? Same thing. We acknowledge the day but have a hard time getting too excited about it—especially as we get older. And, I already told you about the anniversary attitude.

Don't get me wrong. I celebrate that Gary is MY husband and not someone else's. I fell hard for him. He was a college senior. I was in the first quarter of my college career. Once we went out, the Monday before Thanksgiving break in 1975, we decided within a week that we would marry. He was the night in shining armor. Or rather, he looked like "The Fonz" from the sitcom "Happy Days." He began teaching, I hurried my graduation, and we said "I do" on July 2, 1977.

I sure am glad God ordained marriage between a man and a woman. And I sure am glad that he providentially ordained that man to be Gary Lewis Trittipoe.

Today's Truth: Therefore a man shall leave his father and his mother and hold fast to his wife, and they shall become one flesh. Genesis 2:24

July 3

Hot. hot. hot

It wasn't like it was O'Dark 30, but at least I was running by 7:30 a.m. With a forecast of temps in the 90s, I knew if I did not run in the morning, the likelihood to do so later would be kin to jumping into a raging fire. At first blush, it did not seem too bad making my way up the driveway and through the trees. Neither did the country road that led out to the divided highway. But the couple of miles slogging along the shoulder got a little tougher. I was in the full reach of the sun. By the time I turned onto the narrow two-lane that lead home, I was toasty. The heat combined with hips, knees, and quads that felt sub-par reduced me to walking a few hills. No one who saw me on the road would ever think I could run fleet footed.

Once back in home territory, the gentle movement of the pool water drew me in clothes and all. It was cool and refreshing. The misery of the run moved to the rear of the bus. Dripping wet, I watered a few plants before using the hose to take an outdoor shower. "This isn't so bad after all. I should be able to get a lot of yard work done today."

Wrong. As soon as I changed into dry clothes, it felt like a blast furnace when I made my second outdoor appearance of the day. Deciding to forego—or at least postpone—any manual labor, errands came next. I busied myself with indoor chores upon returning, still planning on tackling the pesky weeding. But every time I opened the door, I concluded that outdoor work was not feasible for this old lady. Pool time was again the only logical course of action.

A few well-placed texts beckoned two adults and five kids to come splash. It was a free for all with rowdy play, cannonballs, and splashing. The temperature had not changed, but my attitude did. I could do nothing about the heat except find a way to deal with it. Accepting the circumstances, I enjoyed a few hours in the water with friends. The heat was no bother at all.

Just as I felt that there was no escape from the heat when I was running, we may feel as if our circumstances are more than we can handle. But God has made a provision for escape. We can endure.

Today's Truth: No temptation has overtaken you that is not common to man. God is faithful, and he will not let you be tempted beyond your ability, but with the temptation he will also provide the way of escape, that you may be able to endure it. 1 Corinthians 10:13

JULY 4

FREEDOM AND FRIENDS

For some reason, it seems odd to have July 4th on a Saturday. For that matter, any holiday tied to a weekend does not seem quite right. Not sure about you, but I feel like I am gipped out of a workday reprieve, even though the Friday before or Monday after normally serves as the "off" day. But hey, today is Saturday. Today is July 4th. It is what it is.

What it was at the start was anything but a holiday. A sleepless night and a general lack of well-being dominated my morning. I had zero motivation to do anything. I felt lightheaded anytime I got up and moved around. Nevertheless, wanting to do something productive, I tried pulling weeds. But in the stifling heat, it did not last long. I took a nap instead. Then I tried floating in the pool and reading a book. It was even too hot for that. I came back inside after an hour and took another nap. So much for a memorable 4th. Instead of feeling summertime free and spontaneous, I felt beholden to the energy-limiting state of my body.

Under the circumstances, I was somewhat relieved to know that none of the families I had invited for a cookout and swim could come. But in the meantime, we were invited to the home of dear friends. Ken, a cardiovascular surgeon, and I worked together for years. I became good friends with Liz, his wife. For the four of us to catch up over a meal and unrushed conversation was just what the doctor ordered, no pun intended.

After dinner, the guys tooled around the property on the four-wheeler while Liz and I hit the huge garden to pick beans, zucchini, and chase Little Bunny Foo Foo right out of the fenced area. As dusk morphed into darkness, a fireworks display, though launched several miles away, lit up the sky in exploding arrays of brilliance. It was a prelude to the plethora of fireworks we viewed on the 25-minute drive home.

In God's providence, I was born in the USA. For that I am thankful and am proud to be an American.

Today's Truth: For you were called to freedom, brothers. Only do not use your freedom as an opportunity for the flesh, but through love serve one another. For the whole law is fulfilled in one word: "You shall love your neighbor as yourself." Galatians 5:13, 14

July 5

Isn't that Backwards?

Listening to the birds chirp from my personal buoyant island, I basked in the pleasure of a lazy Sunday afternoon. Eyes closed, I laid back on the pear-shaped float, drinking in the warmth of the sun's rays. In reality, the warmth of the sun was downright scorching. The only saving grace was the relative coolness of the water.

In the quietness, my mind went to the lesson presented at church. It was from Genesis 20. Here's the gist. Abraham and Sarah are in Gerar with King Abimelech presiding. Sarah was gorgeous. Apparently, when a king saw something—or someone—he wanted, he simply sent his goons to go fetch. He wanted Sarah. He got Sarah.

But we need the back story. Abraham and Sarah decided that if it they were caught together by King Abi, they would say they were brother and sister. That way, they figured, the king would not have Abraham meet an untimely demise. So, that is exactly what they did.

However, Abimelech, a king not given to the faith of Abraham and Sarah, received a dream sent by God. In it, God revealed He had kept Abimelech from consummating the marriage to Sarah. Along with that came the instruction to return the woman to Abraham. Can you imagine the impact that had on the poor guy who took a wife and had no idea she was already married? But he did the right thing because he had integrity.

On the other hand, Abraham, who was supposed to be the righteous one, is the one who fabricated the partial truth about Sarah being his sister. (Sarah was a half-sister whom he married.) Abraham finally admitted that the plan was concocted because he figured the king to be pagan and vengeful. Therefore, he convinced himself that he had to take things into his own hands. In hindsight, this was an obvious miscalculation of God's providence.

It is unfortunate that sometimes the heathens in our lives act better than we who claim Christ.

Today's Truth: Then God said to him in the dream, "Yes, I know that you have done this in the integrity of your heart, and it was I who kept you from sinning against me." Genesis 20: 6

July 6

Unsolicited Advice

Gary and I plan to attend the wedding of my friend. It was nice to select a gift from her online registry. Still, that seems a bit impersonal. I decided to share some unsolicited "WOW" with the bride-to-be.

War of Words: This war can be best avoided if we lay our egos aside and shut up. Listen first. Evaluate. Then respond—maybe. But maybe not. Quiet may be better. Just be warned not to bury what you really wish you could say. Consider how the hubster will process your words—AND fill in the spaces between the syllables. Do not keep telling him what he already knows.

World of Wonder: Do not get in a rut. Men see that as boring. Boring was not on their "top 10 attributes I want in a wife" list. Make it your goal to make him wonder what's for dinner (and not because he anticipates an unrecognizable burnt offering). Wonder when you will make his favorite dessert. Wonder when you will reach over and rub his back without asking you to. Wonder when he will find the next love note in his underwear drawer. Wonder about what you will wear to bed. Wonder about how your crazy love for him will reveal itself IN bed. Create a world of anticipatory wonder.

Worn out Welcome: You are excited to get married and play house all you want. You can cook and clean together. Share a bathroom. Oh joy. But hate to tell ya, the newness and fun will wear off, and the mundane will come knocking. Try not to let "normal" make your man feel like he has worn out his welcome. Men respond well to personal attention. Give it to him—a lot. Make him know he is always more than welcome in your home and in your life.

Wimp or Weasel: Actually, this would be more grammatically correct if it were Wimp nor Weasel because we should be neither. Be strong and confident rather than weak, worried, and noodle-like. Mean what you say and say what you mean (but very carefully and cautiously, of course, as already discussed above.) Do not be wishy-washy. Do not be conniving and colluding.

Warrior of Wholeheartedness: With your whole heart, you must commit to love and cherish. To forgive. To be unselfish. To be kind and loving. To be dependable. To work hard. To honor. To submit. To grow and mature. To pursue excellence. To be righteous. . .and not just a little. This is a 100% all the time thing. You must pursue wholeheartedness just as a warrior pursues victory. So, take heed; a warrior who fails to pursue victory is never happy with the ending.

Today's Truth: Therefore a man shall leave his father and his mother and hold fast to his wife, and they shall become one flesh. Genesis 2:24

JULY 7

FAMILY FEUDS

Supper has been made, eaten, and the kitchen cleaned up. Afterward, I pulled out my old and decrepit food processor to shred up garden-fresh zucchini to make bread. I was hankering for the treat that was more dessert-like than bread, considering I throw in a hefty dose of dark chocolate chips. That qualifies as health food, right? Anyway, after the two loaves went into the oven, I sat down on the couch to catch my breath and find something on TV to bide my time. I clicked off the news and stumbled upon the show, "Family Feud." I stopped to watch. Do not judge.

"Family Feud" is as old as the hills. I remember watching it when I was in college. If you have been living on another planet for the last four decades and missed it, the audience is surveyed for answers to random situations, leaving the teams to guess at the answers. For example, "Name something you find in a jungle." Whichever of the initial sparring partners from each team gives the answer with the highest survey results, that team is rewarded the chance to continue to match audience survey answers. It is fun to guess along with the feuding families.

The show that originated in 1976 is a laugh. Real family feuds are not. The Hatfields and McCoys of West Virginia and Kentucky fame come to mind. The families warred for years over a prized pig. A pig, mind you. In all, thirteen people died in the middle of this ridiculous battle.

To this day, there are many descendants of both families. In fact, in 1979 the Hatfields and McCoys battled it out for a week on the very show titled as a nod to their conflict. Nothing sinister was birthed from the gameshow appearance, thank goodness. But what a waste of time to hold a grudge so long and so hard that the surnames are held in infamy.

People are human. They will be wicked and selfish. Churches divide over the color of carpet. Parents and grown children refuse to speak to one another. Brothers and sisters decline to share a holiday meal under the same roof, all the result of unforgiveness and humility. Simply tragic.

Mend fences. Make it right. Fight the feud and win.

Today's Truth: Judge not, and you will not be judged; condemn not, and you will not be condemned; forgive, and you will be forgiven; Luke 6:37

JULY 8

TAKE THE TIME TO WRITE

I hit the trails early this morning. I wanted to give myself every advantage possible. The weather forecast last night speculated it would be "cooler" this morning. That sounded good to me. The older I get, the worse I tolerate heat and humidity.

It may have been cooler than normal, but I was drenched in short order. Still, I muddled my way along gravel roads and wooded trail, picking a route where I was unlikely to see anyone. I suppose ego prompts the avoidance of being seen. I am embarrassed with how slow I run and how many walk breaks I need. I much prefer to keep my performance a personal matter.

Wouldn't you know it? With a half mile remaining, Noel and a teammate intersected with me. Noel is a talented runner whom I coached in middle school and high school. Now a rising college senior, she sets records in cross country and on the oval. "Oh, hey Noel!" I was surprised by this chance meeting.

"Coach T, how are you?" she inquired without breaking stride. My answer was monosyllabic. "Fine." They were on a mission, running hard. There was no sense trying to start up a conversation. I kept pace with them for about three nanoseconds before they began to widen the distance.

When I got back to the office, I texted Noel. "It was good to see you this morning. Looks like you were working hard. Would love to catch up."

The response back was timely but began with an apology. "Whoa. When I opened this up my response to your last message was still there unsent. So sorry! The day you sent that, I was very discouraged, and God really used that to encourage me. Thank you so much!"

I looked at what I had written back in April. "Just came back from running and the Lord brought you to mind. Grace and peace to you along with health, fitness, and encouragement. Yours truly, Coach T."

Who could have guessed that a simple text then and a chance encounter today could be used by God? I suppose we should never forget that even the smallest gesture can be providentially used in ways never anticipated.

Words prompted by the Spirit have power.

Today's Truth: And when they had read it, they rejoiced because of its encouragement. Acts 15:31

July 9

Is there a problem?

Remember how I wrote about the heart monitor I wore for several weeks? My cardiologist called me last night to discuss the results. The long and the short of it is this: abnormalities were detected but those arrythmias probably will not kill me. So, questions remain. Why do I feel so bad? Why can I hardly run? Why do I get lightheaded and short of breath? In an odd way, I wish a specific problem would have been discovered that explains my symptoms. That way, treatment could be planned.

On the other hand, everything is related to everything else. There is a better than average possibility that one of the drugs I take to reduce lipid levels is causing issues. Muscle weakness, joint pain, lethargy, and sleeplessness are all side effects. Each one of these symptoms has reared its ugly head in significant ways. Could it be those things are causing my misery?

Today's run was atrocious. My self-talk was something like this: "Don't worry. My heart is fine. I will not keel over. It is all in my head. I can push through the suffering if I really want to." But despite the positivity, I walked about half of this trail "run," mainly on the uphill portions. I tried forcing myself to continue when I wanted to stop, but it was like the clutch had slipped, resulting in no forward motion.

I now have a dilemma. Do I obsess over symptoms that could indicate a heart problem? After all, I do have known coronary disease and already have a stent. Or alternatively, should I assume I am being a hypochondriac, simply conjuring up symptoms inside my brain? The heart monitor failed to reveal anything grossly significant, and the drug side effects can explain away at least some of what I feel. But honestly, I cannot figure out the balance between prudence and foolishness.

Tomorrow morning, I will be running again, trying to be smooth, efficient, and trying hard to enjoy the journey. However, I do not think my conflicted situation is confined to running. There are many situations that make decision-making difficult. Perhaps that's why wise 'ol King Solomon spoke so much about prudence and foolishness. Foolishness seems to happen naturally. Prudence, on the other hand, takes intentionality in controlling the way we think, which in turn dictates how we act. I will need to pray hard for an extra dose of prudence to know how to proceed with my running.

Today's Truth: O simple ones, learn prudence; O fools, learn sense. Proverbs 5:8

JULY 10

ALREADY?

Yesterday I wrote about discerning between "symptoms" that needed to be disregarded and those that needed to be taken seriously. What I did not mention was a discussion with my primary care provider. She suggested I stop taking the statin for a week before changing over to another. That way, my body gets to reset, which theoretically makes it easier to evaluate my response to the changes.

I skipped my bedtime dose last night, feeling somewhat like a little kid trying to get away with evilness. I wondered if my cardiologist would flip at the plan. But then again, feeling the way I have been feeling is untenable in the long term. I went to bed hopeful.

I rose early, donned my running clothes that were laid out, and drove to the trailhead. I began with a downhill trail to ease into the run. It struck me as odd that I felt little to no strain as I ran. The effort was appropriate. Even as I merged onto other trails that went up instead of down, I was able to make reasonable progress. Was this a reverse placebo effect? Did I simply presume that not taking the medicine for one night would instantaneously eradicate my symptoms?

I prayed very specifically last night that I would have clarity with regards to medications and safety in running. Whether or not I can contribute feeling good this morning as a sign from God is unclear. However, it makes me contemplate this whole idea of God's timing.

Elijah found himself in a contest with the prophets of Baal. Whose God could consume the sacrifices on the alters? Elijah upped the ante by flooding his alter and surrounding trenches with water—three times, no less! But when he beseeched God to do his thing, he did not have to wait long. The fire came down and consumed the sacrifice, the stone alter, and even the water in the trench.

On the other hand, the Israelites wandered around in the wilderness for forty years. I am certain there were prayers for the sandbox experience to come to an end sooner rather than later, but that was not what God had in mind. They had to wait it out. It must have been frustrating.

Whether God answers quickly, waits until later, or remains silent, I know He hears.

Today's Truth: "Answer me, O Lord, *answer me, that this people may know that you, O* Lord, *are God, and that you have turned their hearts back." Then the fire of the* Lord *fell and consumed the burnt offering and the wood and the stones and the dust, and licked up the water that was in the trench. 1 Kings 18:37, 38*

July 11

Clean up is contagious

If I had walked in our guest room one more time looking the way it did, I might have spontaneously combusted. That cheery yellow "Grandparent room" used to be delightful. With my mother's christening dress, my dad's framed diplomas from college and dental school, a wide-angle picture of my father-in-law's squadron, and some of my mother-in-law's favorite mementos, the space between the walls oozed a sweet sentimentality. But that has hardly been the case as of late.

Now that Gary is retired, he is in full-on E-Bay mode. Finding hundreds of things to sell, mountains of cardboard boxes and packaging materials covered the floor and crept up onto the bed like an oozing form of fungus. As if that was not enough, Seth is following suit, some of his sellable stuff occupying space as well. I could stand the chaos no longer.

Fur started flying as I began unloading the room so I could make sense of it. Large shelves that had been in Seth's room got worked into the plan after I reinforced the broken wooden shelves. These shelves now hold the shipping materials, computer, and printer. Then it was off to the store to purchase another set of shelves to conveniently hold items currently up for sale. I repurposed a desk to serve as the packaging station. Now that I am done with the organization and prettied up the space with a few pieces of art, it stands ready to once again host guests.

I guess my busyness inspired Pam. She went to work tearing apart Addyson's room. Toys and clothes to donate were set aside, shelves reorganized, and everything in sight was tidied. If I am not mistaken, the process is still ongoing. The content of that kid's room seems to double every seven days.

I often hear Pam run the vacuum and empty trash. She is a neat person. But would she have gone on a cleaning/purging spree had I not confronted the guest room? No. (She said as much so I know this to be true.) The moral of the story? Our actions influence others. And we need to understand that others also influence us. Hang around with good people, and we tend to do likewise. Hang with those who aren't so good? Well, be careful. It is all too easy to get sucked into mayhem. The example we set or follow, whether good or bad, is a big responsibility.

Today's Truth: Brothers, join in imitating me, and keep your eyes on those who walk according to the example you have in us. Philippians 3:17

JULY 12

AROUND ROBIN HOOD'S BARN

Gary and I have not been away from home by ourselves for quite a while. When we were invited to the wedding of one of the young tennis coaches I work with, we decided a road trip was in order. Besides, it was a chance to take the 1994 Corvette out for an extended spin. Charlotte, NC was the destination. To drive straightway would take about three and a half hours. But how long did it take us today from start to hotel check-in? About six.

Yep. Six hours. We wanted to take the scenic route, staying off major highways as much as possible. With the convertible roof tucked away, the breeze was chilly as we started out. We watched the beautiful countryside come and go as we rolled along within the speed limits. We were in no hurry. We did not follow the cyborg-like GPS voice. Rather, I occasionally pulled out handwritten instructions that Gary had scribbled out before we left home. Who has a paper map anymore?

We eventually pulled into the hotel parking lot, glad we had taken the road less traveld, though our bum-bums were delighted to get out of the capsule-like seats. After a nap and a couple hours of relaxation, we made it to the wedding to see the young couple commit themselves to one another. Tomorrow we will take the direct route home.

Sometimes we need to stay the course and other times, take the long way around. I think about first century Samaria. The Samaritans were not well-regarded. Most people did what we did on the way to North Carolina. They sacrificed time and energy to go around Samaria rather than risk encountering those considered to be ethnically less worthy than themselves. Jesus, on the other hand, made it a point to go straight through. In fact, he providentially encountered a woman at a well.

It is a familiar story. Jesus asks the woman to draw water from the well, which leads to his challenge about lifestyle and the need for "living water." She believes, goes back into town to share her new-found testimony, many others come to Christ, and Jesus stays to carry on ministry for several days.

We need to be like Jesus, having the wisdom to know why, when, and where to go.

Today's Truth: Many Samaritans from that town believed in him because of the woman's testimony, "He told me all that I ever did." So when the Samaritans came to him, they asked him to stay with them, and he stayed there two days. And many more believed because of his word. John 4:39-41

July 13

Going with the Flow

Gary and I woke up this morning in Charlotte, NC. Last night we attended the wedding of a former college tennis player, enjoying the intimacy of the event and the opportunity to change up our routine. Though we took the scenic route on the ride yesterday, we had no desire to repeat those long miles. Instead, we hit the freeway and started the journey north.

I-85 is a massive interstate, most often sporting five lanes in each direction. In some areas, the speed limit was 60, in others, 65, with the top posted speed set at 70 mph. But no matter what section of road we travelled, the traffic was flying. What was the hurry?

Gary and I have different perspectives on what to do in situations like this. Personally, I do not view posted speed limits as suggestions. Whether or not I like the posted number, someone with authority and the law behind them picked it. That number should inform the speed at which I drive.

Gary does not share my opinion. His view is that a dangerous situation is created if you drive at a rate much slower than the flow of traffic. Hence, if the traffic is driving 75 in a 65, that's cool. Besides, how could a cop pick out a single car if the entire field of cars is traveling at the same, if not higher than posted speeds?

Why then, did every car around us, including ours, slow down at the sight of two-unmarked Camaros sitting in the median? Everyone must have known they were disobeying the rules if the reaction was to slow the rate of travel suddenly and significantly.

I trust Gary and the way he drives but feel uncomfortable following suit. I feel guilty even if I am momentarily two miles per hour over the limit when trying to get around a slower vehicle. I figure I never have to fear getting a speeding ticket if I do not speed.

So, is the speed at which we drive a matter of personal preference or social responsibility? I understand that slow moving cars can create a hazard, but I also know that we are to be submissive to those in authority. Does that include those who make up speed limits? Hum. That's something to think about.

Today's Truth: Have confidence in your leaders and submit to their authority, because they keep watch over you as those who must give an account. Hebrews 13:17a

JULY 14

KNOWING WHEN TO SHUT UP

There was no incident to frame the topic of the day. I suppose I started this contemplation because I was asked to write a story for another purpose. It all centered around Hannah.

Somewhere prior to 1070 BC, Hannah was a wife of Elkanah, a Jewish man. However, Hannah was was not his *only* wife. Peninnah was the other bride who could pop out children like gumballs from a vending machine. From the Scriptures we know that Peninnah tormented Hannah over her inability to have children. Like rubbing salt into the wound, Peninnah was given a portion of meat equal to the number of her children on the annual trips to the temple. Hannah received but one for herself. She had no children.

Hannah was heart broken. She desired children more than life itself. But though Peninnah was the source of ridicule, Hannah showed remarkable control by not lashing back at the wretched other woman. Rather, her frustration was directed not at God, but to God. *She was deeply distressed and prayed to the* LORD *and wept bitterly* (1 Sam 1:10).

I wonder if I could have remained silent under such duress. Even when Priest Eli saw her praying and wrongly accused her of being drunk, she showed respect for his office in her response. In the end, Eli took up for Hannah, praying that God would not only grant one son, Samuel, but many children. And He did. Hannah was no longer sad.

I think there is a lesson to be learned from Hannah's response—and lack thereof. She apparently had great wisdom to know when to shut up and be silent, and when to cry out to the only one who could make a difference. Lashing out at competitors or referees, for example, is seldom wise or effective. It does nothing but aggravate the party on the receiving end. But self-imposed silence, speaking only to God about the situation? Therein lies the power to change us from the inside out.

Today's Truth: Then Eli answered, "Go in peace, and the God of Israel grant your petition that you have made to him." And she said, "Let your servant find favor in your eyes." Then the woman went her way and ate, and her face was no longer sad. 1 Samuel 1:17, 18

July 15

Running into the Dark

It is a little after midnight and I cannot fall asleep, not that this is an odd occurrence. I am simply surprised that after running seventeen-ish miles in the mountains, I am not capable of producing any *zzzz*'s.

I feel better compared to a month ago. The statin I had been taking was eliminated from my nightly routine for the last week. My muscles and joints are less fatigued, and I have been able to sleep a little better (tonight not withstanding). I was anxious to test myself in the mountains, and last evening was the time to do it.

The temperature when I left at 5:10 p.m. was about 92 degrees F. However, it did not feel that oppressive with lowered humidity. I was running by 5:37 p.m., having parked at the base of a mountain. Either way I went was up. That meant only one thing: sweat and hard work. I trudged along until I reached the highest point of my run, some eight or nine miles later. I made sure to take in the songs of birds readying themselves for bed, the rustling of squirrels, and the rushing waters of the streams as they coursed lithely over boulders within their banks.

It was right at 8 p.m. when I made the transition from overgrown trail to the macadamed surface of the Blue Ridge Parkway. I estimated another eight or nine miles of downhill, the last three and a half on gravel road. I had the Parkway to myself and was as happy as could be. But I was losing daylight and knew I had forgotten to add a running light to my pack. With dusk heavy upon me as I turned onto the gravel road, I wondered how well my eyes could adapt in the waning light.

Running with much more freedom than anticipated, my pupils dilated to adjust to the impending darkness. It was only until I had 400 yards to go that I pulled out my phone and clicked on the flashlight app. I arrived back at the car without incident.

My humble phone light made it so I could navigate in the dark. Is my own life light shining brightly enough to cut through the darkness around me? It does not take many lumens to make a difference.

Light it up!

Today's Truth: In the same way, let your light shine before others, so that they may see your good works and give glory to your Father who is in heaven. Matthew 5:16

JULY 16

ROLE MODEL

Everyone wants a great role model and Deborah just might be your woman.

Deborah is not exactly a contemporary personality. You must travel back to 1216 BC to see her show up in history. But wow. Show up she did. Deborah was a multi-talented gal. She was an honorable judge, a prophetess, a fierce warrior, and brilliant strategist, demonstrating her creative side by incorporating singer-songwriting into her illustrious career. Can you say WonderWoman?

Think of the context in which she lived. It was a male dominated society. In fact, even in Scripture, there are very few occasions where a woman is acknowledged as something other than a wife or mother. That is not to imply that those roles are less than admirable, but there are few biblically historic women who are described by stand-alone appointments.

Take a stroll through Judges 4 and 5. In her role as judge, her office was beneath a palm tree in Ephraim. When a dispute or argument arose, the people of Israel knew to ask wise Deborah for a ruling. But she also had the responsibility as commander-in-chief. Barak, her right-hand man, was her subordinate. When Sisera, the general of neighboring King Jabin, needed to be crushed, Barak was asked to go fight with his 10,000 soldiers. His response? *If you will go with me, I will go, but if you will not go with me, I will not go.* And what did she say? *I will surely go with you* (Judges 4:8, 9).

The encroaching army with its 900 chariots was soundly defeated. But think about the courage Deborah demonstrated. She was surrounded by raging testosterone on every side. And yet, she was confident enough in her God-appointed role to devise and implement a plan for battle, becoming an active participant in the foray. In the aftermath, she and Barak were able to work together to compose and sing a song about the events and the faithfulness of God.

Whatever we do in life, we can be as equally courageous and confident as Deborah when we fulfill the roles God assigns to us. Be a good listener. Make sound judgments. Plan well. Take action. Lead by example. Be a team player. Be creative. Honor God with your whole being.

Today's Truth: Barak said to her, "If you will go with me, I will go, but if you will not go with me, I will not go." And she said, "I will surely go with you." Judges 4: 8, 9a

July 17

The lone blackberry

If I did not run early, I knew running later would have a slim chance of happening. The heat index is supposed to be near 100 degrees today. At 7:45 a.m. it was well on its way.

When I run, I think. Sometimes I think too much. Like today. I wrote last week about my dilemma of appreciating the fact I have coronary disease and not being stupid or taking unnecessary risks. I was quite pleased a few days ago when, as a test, I completed a mountain run of about seventeen miles. Other than being turtle-like on the climbs, I felt I ran well the rest of the time. Or at least, I never felt like I was going to die. Today I did not have a great start but was intentional about being positive, enjoying the moment, and not trying to assess fitness in the oppressive conditions.

As I ran, I prayed that I would have discernment to know when to push and when to back off. At all costs, I want to avoid becoming neurotic over a relatively minor heart problem that has been treated. As I neared the top of a gravel road climbing up the backside of a mountain, I realized I felt decent. Great! I resolved to continue to push to the gate that stood guard at the road's end. "I got this!"

And then guess what happened? With the gate in sight, my peripheral vision caught sight of a lone, ripe blackberry dangling from a branch. My desire to reach the gate without walking disappeared into thin air. I HAD to have that blackberry! I stopped, pulled it off, and savored the sweetness. I looked for other ripe berries but found none. I'm not sure it was worth abandoning the attainable goal of running to the gate for a tiny bite of fruit.

Following the blackberry pause, I ran again, now having a mere half mile to go. "Okay. Run to the car. This hill isn't too bad. You can do it." More resolve. But oops. This time it was blueberries. The tiniest blueberries ever. I stopped, picked one and popped it in my mouth. It might have been tiny, but it sure was sweet. I enjoyed several handfuls. I made it back to the car dripping with sweat but amazed at how easily I became distracted.

It takes focus and resolve to stay the course.

Today's Truth: looking to Jesus, the founder and perfecter of our faith, who for the joy that was set before him endured the cross, despising the shame, and is seated at the right hand of the throne of God. Hebrews 12:2

JULY 18

WARNING SIGNS

"Oh, no," Gary moaned in a tone I instantly recognized. This was not good.

We were on the way home from a wedding and about to pull onto a divided four-lane highway. It was not far from the house, maybe three miles, tops. But to get there we had to make a right turn, hang a U-turn at the next median cut-through, go up a hill, make a right turn off the highway, then navigate the hilly 1.8 miles to our front door. That sounds simple enough unless you are running out of gas—again.

Yep. Gary's "Oh, no" meant that for the second time in as many weeks, he had let the gas in the Corvette hit gone. That is G.O.N.E. Gone. The car sputtered and spit as we both knew what was coming. The "reserve" indicator was first to light up. Then it was the "Check engine light." He did what he could, letting it roll down hills and coaxing it up the next hill by jerking the steering wheel side to side, hoping to give the few remaining droplets of gas a chance to make it to the engine. Finally, as we nearly crested a hill, the engine quit. It was a poor place to stop, our position blind to cars flying up and over the hill from the opposite direction.

I refrained from being snarky, but it was hard. A call to Seth at home, a mere 0.6 miles away, went out. He arrived on a dirt bike. Gary climbed aboard behind Seth, went back to the house, bringing a gas can back in another car. With a gallon in the tank, Gary puttered home. I followed, miffed. Does he not pay attention to that gauge right in front of his face?

My mom and dad had this "thing." When the gas gauge hit half a tank, they headed to the gas station. Always. A full tank is a safe tank. My men tease me when I stop for gas with the gauge barely in the southern hemisphere. But alongside the road and looking them both in the eyes, I could not resist. "Don't either one of you EVER give me a hard time for getting gas early!" Seth laughed. Gary said nothing.

A gauge tells us important information so we can take appropriate action. The Bible is our gauge. There are warning signs at every turn. Do this. Do not do that. Be careful. Live wisely. Take to heart. Pay attention. But the crux of the matter? We need to look at the gauge for it to be of any value.

Today's Truth: so that those who have believed in God may be careful to devote themselves to good works. These things are excellent and profitable for people. Titus 3:8b

July 19

Choices

We all have choices to make. Lots of them. And on this horrendously hot Sunday with the heat index at 106 degrees F, each member of the family made different choices.

Let's begin with Gary. He hates the heat. His choice was not unexpected. He took his place on the couch with his laptop. His head bobbed intermittently as the doze devils took control of his eyelids.

What about me? I choose to prepare food for our family dinner. It was Seth's birthday earlier this week, but this was the best time to celebrate. After preparing what I could ahead of time, I donned my bathing suit, adding another layer of sunscreen to my face, and headed outdoors. Dancing across the scorching brick sidewalk, I hurled myself into the 86-degree water. My choice at that point was to stay submerged expect for my head and hands, holding a magazine just above the water's surface. I stayed there for hours. Pam chose to join me for a good part of the time.

But then there was Seth and two of his dirt bike racing friends. It is hard to comprehend their choice. Each put on layers of protective equipment, including helmets, boots, Kevlar pants, long sleeves, and chest protectors. They mounted their mechanical steeds and chased each other over hill and dale—for three hours. When they finally stripped to take a dip, I breathed a sigh of relief on their behalf. Their choice to persist despite the furnace-like conditions was risky.

As I did a little research on a biblical perspective of choosing, I found 75 references. But as I read down the list, I was startled that the huge preponderance of them said, "the Lord chooses" or "God chooses." I know God is sovereign and controls all things, but to see this list emphasizes who is in charge. And yet, His choices do not eliminate our responsibility to choose responsibly, for Joshua says, *choose this day whom you will serve* (Joshua 24:15).

The intersection of God's choosing and our choices will forever be a mystery. And yet, we can be confident that God's choices are perfect, while ours are not.

Today's Truth: You did not choose me, but I chose you and appointed you that you should go and bear fruit and that your fruit should abide, so that whatever you ask the Father in my name, he may give it to you. John 15:16

JULY 20

EMOTIONS

I have been sitting in my office putting together a group discussion for college coaches. We are working our way through a course called "3-Dimensional Coaching." The gist is that a coach needs to reach her players on three levels (or dimensions): skill set, mind set, and heart set.

Skill set includes those first dimensional physical elements such as strength, power, quickness, speed, cardiovascular, quickness, repetition, technique, and tactics. The second dimension contains the psychological elements: motivation, emotions, team cohesion, confidence, and goal setting. The elements of identity, character, significance, self-worth, values, and purpose all comprise the third dimension.

In our discussion tomorrow we will be addressing the idea of emotions. The way I see it, emotions can be the good, the bad, and the ugly. Emotions can positively impact outcome when they are appropriate and controlled. But on the other hand, emotions running amok will produce nothing good. In fact, that is where the ugly comes in. A kid gets taken out of the game and sulks on the bench. A gymnast becomes so nervous, she underrotates a back tuck on beam and crashes hard. A basketball player is submarined on the way to the basket. He takes a swing at the defender and is immediately ejected from the game.

Isn't it interesting that the familiar verse, *the joy of the LORD is your strength*, ties together all three dimensions? Strength is a first-dimension element, while the emotion of joy is second- dimensional. And what about third dimension? Well, the Lord is the object of the joy, therefore the heart, or third dimension, is involved.

Joy is such an important emotion. It is so much more than being happy. The word is used over 200 times in the bible. I assume that means it is an important concept. When we work, live, and play with joy, it is delightful, even if challenging on a physical level. But think of the converse. Working, living, and playing in the absence of joy is horrible. It is a drain. It feels so hard. It is unpleasant and egregious.

Joy is so much better. Find joy.

Today's Truth: And do not be grieved, for the joy of the LORD *is your strength. Nehemiah 8:10b*

July 21

Make like a tree

It was only 8:00 a.m. The mercury thermometer read 86 degrees. The humidity was likely equal. Parking in the shade at the trail head, I let out a big sigh before opening the door. I knew what was coming. It would be just short of a masochistic massacre.

Though I had mentally planned my route, I took a few turns not originally intended. The thought of traversing an oft-taken trail was repugnant. If I was going to suffer in the heat—and that was guaranteed—I wanted something out of the way. I had no intention of encountering other runners. I needed to give myself grace to run when I could and walk when the fun meter plummeted—without any witnesses.

My choice of trail accomplished the purpose. I was in forward motion for an hour. It was not pretty, but it provided the desired solitude. I left a trail of sweat droplets on gravel roads, single track, along lake shores, in earshot of day camp kids oblivious to the heat, and parallel to a gently cascading stream. The portion of trail meandering its way back up the mountain was rooty, the unfortunate result of rains and occasional swollen stream waters sweeping away the protective dirt.

I passed one large tree, massive roots exposed. I stopped to take a better look. A stream was on one side of the trail. On the other was a natural ditch that channeled heavy rains. The tree's gigantic branches extended out in every direction. Masses of leaves created a canopy. A squirrel chattered playfully high above the ground. But it was those roots. Though exposed, I could follow the direction each took before tunneling underground once again. It was curious that each one seemed headed for the water. No wonder it remained strong, tall, and unmovable.

A question comes to mind much like the chicken and the egg. Which came first? The water or the tree? Without the water, the tree could not exist. Without the tree, there would be no need for the water to carve out channels around the tree.

Am I like a tree firmly rooted? Have I planted myself in the right place? Am I protected by seeking out life-saving water? New life goal: Make like a tree.

Today's Truth: He is like a tree planted by water, that sends out its roots by the stream, and does not fear when heat comes, for its leaves remain green, and is not anxious in the year of drought, for it does not cease to bear fruit. Jeremiah 17:8

JULY 22

SPLIT DECISIONS

If you guess I will again reference running, you are correct. I am pretty sure that if I did not run, I would be incapable of thinking. Running solo is when I figure out solutions to problems, contemplate great mysteries, or sometimes let my brain exercise itself by running wild. Today was such a day.

Trying to avoid the heat—again—I was conflicted as I drove myself to the trail head. Where should I run? How much should I run? Do I need an easy day? Whatever it was, I was far from being the poster child for "Excitement Mounts, Inc." The night had been short, and I already felt wiped out. Nevertheless, as anyone trying to be disciplined would do, I dutifully pulled into a parking spot, turned off the ignition and opened the door to explore my limits.

I ran east to an area called Five Points. Choosing a trail I helped create long ago, I flowed with it, descending into a lush creek bottom. Before too long, Horton's Loop, the trail I was on, took a sharp turn to the right. I continued straight. The only thing that changed was the name: Split Decision.

A sign informed me that Split Decision was 1.8 miles long. "Hum. Did a past group of runners go in two different directions when they got to this point?" I mused as I ran along. "Is that how Split Decision got the name?"

I never reached a conclusion on the origin of the name, but I determined I did not like it. (The trail, that is. The name was fine.) Portions of the trail have eroded over the years, leaving it a rocky, rooty, ankle-busting mess. I turned into a scaredy-cat, tip-toeing my way to kinder, gentler trails.

I wonder if there are examples in the Bible of split decisions. Ah, yes. Caleb and Joshua and the other ten spies. Remember? The dozen men had been selected to spy out the land God promised them. Over forty days they conducted a reconnaissance mission, after which they reported back to Moses. Caleb and Joshua were all about taking over Canaan. The others? "No way, those giants will squash us like bugs!"

How could two groups come to such diverse conclusions? Perspective. It is all about perspective. When we see our situation as God sees it, we have the courage to make those difficult decisions that separate us from the crowd.

Today's Truth: But Caleb quieted the people before Moses and said, "Let us go up at once and occupy it, for we are well able to overcome it." Then the men who had gone up with him said, "We are not able to go up against the people, for they are stronger than we are." Numbers 13: 30, 31

July 23

New shoes

I took one look at the shoes I normally wear. It was obvious they were destined for relegation to yard work, if even that. It was not as if the treads on the trail shoes were worn down. The problem was the padding in the heel. It was generous enough. However, little by little, the fabric has worn thin. What remains are gaping holes. It looks like a mouse got to gnawing and carried away all the plushness. Despite trying to patch the divots in the padding, my heels felt the inadequacy of that fix.

I grabbed a box sitting by the shoe shelves. Inside was a brand-new pair of shoes. So clean and fresh I could not resist sniffing that new shoe scent. Discarding the cardboard forms inside each shoe and removing the tags, I sat down and slipped them on. Ah. So much better. The sticky rubber that is so good for traction squeaked as I made my way across the wood floors and out the door. The drive to the trail was filled with anticipation, the new kicks laced up and ready to go.

My feet were happy as I put in the necessary miles. Not once did I think about my heels because they were cradled in comfortable, intact padding. Arriving back at the car, however, I looked down at my feet. The shoes no longer looked new. They were dirty and wet, mud stuck between the treads. My travels had taken me on dirt paths, through stands of wet weeds, and demanded a good share of puddle-hopping. A thorough hosing off might reveal their original glory once again.

Sometimes I feel like a new shoe, but that never lasts very long. Most times, I feel more like an old, worn out shoe. I get soiled, sometimes filthy. Life does that. But I know that by God's grace alone, He made me a new creation in Christ. The old goes away and new is ushered in. That is the truth.

But that old sin nature complicates things. We mess up and what others see is a filthy, smelly, muddy shoe. Perhaps if we allowed the Holy Spirit to be a spiritual hose, others would see Christ's beauty rather than our failings.

Today's Truth: Therefore, if anyone is in Christ, he is a new creation. The old has passed away; behold, the new has come. 2 Corinthians 5:17

July 24

My 92-year-old mother tells me she is living in solitary confinement. And she is. She lives in an assisted living facility in Pennsylvania, a seven-hour drive from here. With the Covid lockdowns, she has had no visitors since March. Until recently, she has eaten all her meals in her room, not even permitted to sit with other residents in their private dining room. "This week has been the loneliest of my life. I've had no visitors," she told me. Good thing her short-term memory keeps her from realizing she has had no visitors for five months.

The facility created a means for families to talk with their loved ones via Facetime or Google Chat. I planned to chat at 2 p.m. today. On their end, they take a large iPad into my mother and call our phone, in this case, Gary's. We can speak for as long as we wish.

The phone connection was made and there she was. Lilac-colored top, white cardigan, a string of beads, silver white hair brushed neatly back. She was sitting in her flowered armchair, head tilted to the side and resting on her propped-up hand. She looked tired and worn. I dared not say a word about how depressed she looked lest she begin a downward spiral of continuous "I'm so weary" commiserations.

Trying to be cheerful and informative, I walked with the phone to show her around the house, garden, and even took her into the treehouse with me. I pointed out that the four leafless-sticks I had dug up from my childhood home when she moved out ten years ago had morphed into beautiful flowering Rose of Sharon bushes. When I went back inside, Addyson joined me, singing a tune or two for her great-grandmother. Then Addy answered some math questions to show off her arithmetic skills. Mother brightened as she interacted with Addy.

There is something about seeing another's face that is not possible with a mere phone conversation. Not that phone conversations are bad. It's just that they are not complete.

Prayer is like a phone conversation. Wonderfully connected but without the benefit of seeing the Savior's face. But it will not be this way forever. As the hymn writer penned, "Face to face with Christ, my Savior, Face to face what will it be? When with rapture I behold Him, Jesus Christ Who died for me?"

Today's Truth: For now we see in a mirror dimly, but then face to face. Now I know in part; then I shall know fully, even as I have been fully known. 1 Corinthians 12:13

July 25

Up from Slavery

Domestic duties occupied my day from sun-up until darkness outran dusk. I raged war on the seemingly immortal ants campaigning in the kitchen cupboards, which led to a major cleaning effort. The abundance of chores kept me occupied with plenty of time to think.

As I worked, I listened to thought-provoking podcasts, contemplated ministry, and planned out my training goals. When I joined Seth in hauling dirt and maneuvering hundreds of rocks into place for yet another raised garden, I ended up on all fours, pushing dirt around like a dog. That deterred my run. I suppose any of today's activities could be the basis for today's writing. But no. Instead, I am contemplating a book I finished at 2 a.m. when sleep alluded me.

"Up from Slavery" is the short autobiography of Booker T. Washington. Birthed sometime in the spring of 1856, he was born into slavery. On the plantation, a mere ten miles from where we call home, he lived in a log cabin with his mother, two siblings, and a half-sister. He never knew his father though he was reported to be a white man. The masters of his plantation were not particularly cruel, but the living conditions were horrendous. The responsibilities placed on the boy stole from him a proper childhood.

Then emancipation happened. Booker was nine years old. Suddenly, former slaves had to figure out how to manage free life. It was harder than they thought. Through an incredible string of purposeful and brave decisions, Booker eventually became an educated young man through study at Hampton Institute. He saw value in both the formal and practical education of black men and women. His legacy in founding Tuskegee Institute is impressive. By 1901, there were 1400 students from many states, Puerto Rico, Jamaica, Cuba, Africa, and other countries. Another 457 students studied at night. They learned from books, but all became proficient in a specific trade as well. The students themselves built the campus buildings, furniture, carts, and wagons. They became prepared for life.

Against all odds and with incredible tenacity, Booker T. Washington never let the odds stacked against him win. His faith, perseverance, and biblical anthropologic viewpoint directed his every action and way of thinking. He accomplished what was nearly impossible.

Today's Truth: No, in all these things we are more than conquerors through him who loved us. Romans 8:37

JULY 26

FRIENDS AND FELLOWSHIP

It started off as a normal day: sunny, hot, and very humid. But it was Sunday, and that meant a break from the normal work routine. In all honesty, I was not feeling very refreshed. It had been another sleepless night. I tried to be productive reading and writing until 2:30 a.m. When I finally took my place on the sofa, slumber did not visit until 4 a.m. I woke at 6 a.m. Not a great way to start the day.

Nevertheless, I managed to get dressed for church in a casual and bright outfit, figuring I could fake alertness if not feel it. It was good to chat with other church members before the service began. When it was time to take our seats that were socially distanced from other families, I was encouraged by the quality of the singing. Of course, the two guest musicians oozing with talent helped matters considerably. With the Scripture readings, music, and message completed, it was time to check that our intended lunch guests had directions to our house.

In the meantime, I asked another family to come swimming after lunch. They have two daughters and a son that Addy enjoys playing with. After that, a single dad approached and intimated that he would love to bring his son over for a dip, "Of course! You are more than welcome." When Renee, otherwise known as Nene P Packer, mentioned she heard there was a party going on, I extended the invite to her as well. She had been Addy's nanny and Addy loved her! "Sure. The more the merrier. Come and join in!"

We had a wonderful meal with our guests. When the others arrived, we had eleven extra people splashing in the pool. It was chaos with kids diving, jumping, cannonballing, catching footballs, and playing keep away with the two dads who energetically joined in the mayhem.

We are fortunate to have true-blue friends who love and care for us. They are people we can count on in good times and bad. They listen when we share our deepest concerns but will join in belly laughter in lighter moments. A life without trustworthy friends would be no life at all.

Today's Truth: Oil and perfume make the heart glad, and the sweetness of a friend comes from his earnest counsel. Proverbs 27:9

July 27

Embrace the Mud

I parked in the nearly empty lot and began my run, embracing the crunching gravel underneath my feet. As I made a turn down a wide trail, I looked up to see Makena, one of my Shindigglers. We enjoyed the next few moments catching up on life's happenings. In the process, we committed to a long night run. Soon.

I continued alone, feeling free and light in spirit. Down the mountain, across a connecting trail, and back up a long climb to the top. But then, there it was in all its glory. THE mudpit. Memories flooded my mind as ferociously as the sweat escaped my pores.

Without much rain, the state of the mudpit was not very impressive compared to what it was in the best of years. In my tenure of coaching high school cross country, it had become a tradition to designate one day of the season as Mud Run Day. We strategically watched the weather report. When it was apparent that heavy rains and warm temps were in the mix, the team was notified of THE day. "Be sure to bring towels and maybe even a tarp. Your parents will not allow you in the car otherwise. Guaranteed." The mood was electric, even giddy.

On the appointed day, we started out from the school, not in the least worried about the immediate climb up the mountain. After all, it was MUD DAY! Laughter abounded as anticipation grew the closer we got to the quagmire. It was ideal when the pit was at least a foot deep with muddy water. We ran and frolicked. We conducted wheelbarrow races through the muck. Then the sticky, icky mud started flying. Handfuls of the oozing brown sludge ended up mashed onto heads and stuffed down shirts. The muddier, the better. It was a badge of belonging. For most.

Every year, there were one or two runners who despised this annual outing. They thought it a worthless, juvenile, senseless activity that contributed nothing to their fitness. I always pitied them for not taking part, for it was in those crazy times that solidarity was strengthened, and team unity tightly knit.

Embrace the mess. It has purpose.

Today's Truth: Behold, how good and pleasant it is when brothers dwell in unity! Psalm 133:1

JULY 28

OVERCOME

Ever have one of those days when things just seem to be "off"? I'm there. I hate it.

It was a non-energetic start to the morning. Nevertheless, and with coffee cup in hand, I was out the door and driving to the trails by half-past seven. Once parked, a mile on the hardtop road to the trail head was uncomfortable. My legs felt weak, and my joints ached. I hoped the run would get better.

It did not. It did not really get a lot worse either, but stellar it was not. I felt old and decrepit. But I finished the run, got to the office, showered, and took my place at my desk. My legs ached so much I had a hard time concentrating on the Zoom call with coaches. Afterwards, there was no focus on two major writing projects. I gave up.

"Maybe going out to pick up lunch might help," I thought to myself. After choosing a meal that would easily serve me well for two lunches, I drove up the mountain near campus and parked in the shade. I wanted to nibble and then steal away a quick nap. Fail. As tired as I was, sleep would not come. I gave up—again— and drove to a dollar store to pick up notecards. Then it was back to the office.

Was I re-energized back at my desk? Nope. I forced myself to complete another chapter before deciding to bag it and head home. Maybe it was bad biorhythms. Maybe my achy quads. Maybe it was the incessant tic-toc of my office clock that dulled my senses.

I suppose what I feel is not unique. We all struggle with consistency. Some days are productive. Some not. But what should be our response, especially when we are having difficulty willing ourselves to overcome?

There is a common saying among ultrarunning: Keep making forward progress. Forward progress means to take just one step, and then another, and another until you reach your goal. The process can be frustrating because it seems impossibly slow. But if we are faithful to the task, we will see it to completion regardless of the emotions that come with it.

Keep the faith. Overcome.

Today's Truth: For everyone who has been born of God overcomes the world. And this is the victory that has overcome the world—our faith. 1 John 5:4

July 29

Finding the door

Yep. This story begins with another reference to running. It started out okay but ended up as a slogfest on tricky, technical, spider-web strewn trail. To tell you the truth, it was in no way pleasant. In fact, it was brutal. I was dripping wet with sweat, nauseous, and dizzy. I needed both fluid and calories. But the circumstances served a purpose.

I cannot be sure when the idea popped into my head. I have been praying for wisdom about the future of my work and play. Deep into two writing projects (this book included), I began to ask God for another book-worthy idea. It needed to be something with broad appeal, had the potential to inspire and motivate, and open doors for speaking and working with coaches and athletes. I think this morning's difficulty out on the trail provided the starting point for the book.

In the last years of my cross-country coaching career, my parting words to the runners waiting at the start line were "Find the door!" You see, we all know that at some point in our journey we will hit the proverbial wall. Endurance athletes describe the wall as impenetrable. Breathing is labored, arms and legs flail, the pain is overwhelming, and in many cases, the wall offers an excuse to back off into a more comfortable zone. In some cases, the athlete quits all together.

In every wall there is a door. Think about that. The 13,170 miles-long Great Wall of China had hundreds of doors. Even the highest security prison has at least one door, albeit heavily guarded. Farmers build walls that extend across acres and acres, but even there, a door or gate is added to make passage into and out of the fields possible. The problem is in finding the door.

For the athlete, there are but two choices when she hits the wall. Will she back off and quit, or will she use the last ounce of energy to find the door, kicking it open to see what is on the other side? The fact is, having the courage to pass through the door can lead to unprecedented performance; performance that the athlete once thought impossible. But that revelation is only for the bravest of souls, only possible by enduring the associated pain of hitting the wall in quest of the door.

When life becomes unbearable, search for the door and allow God to reveal what is on the other side.

Today's Truth: For nothing will be impossible with God. Luke 1:37

JULY 30

GOT GRIT?

The sweat poured from my body like water cascading off a cliff. My mind was busy talking to my body. "This is a mental decision. Make it to that next tree. Come on now. Good biomechanics. Keep your feet under you. This too shall pass. Keep running even if it is slow. Do. Not. Walk. You will not die. Get to the gate. Get to the gate. Show some grit!"

I got to the gate and I did not walk. It was hard work. But the whole time I ran toward the top of the mountain, I had much to contemplate. Last night I began reading the book entitled "*Grit: The Power of Passion and Perseverance*" by Angela Duckworth. Although I am only a third of the way through, I am hooked. Duckworth is a PhD psychologist who has long been intrigued about why "talent" is not necessarily a prerequisite of success. Many talented people quit when the going gets tough, while those not as innately blessed achieve great things. Through her research she contends that outstanding achievement is an intermingling of passion and perseverance. Duckworth calls that combination grit.

Is grit learned or inherited? Is it in our DNA, destining us for great things? Does the environment influence the amount of grit we display? If we lack grit, can grit be grown?

I grew up in a houseful of gritty people. "DeLanceys never quit." That was the motto. Feeling sick? Get up and start moving. Never give up. Strive. You can always do better. Push. Drive. Conquer. Then conquer some more.

I thought about those things this morning as I struggled to make it to the gate. My grittiness in that moment was simply a decision. I would not walk no matter how bad it felt. And I suspect that when it comes right down to it, grit—or lack thereof—is always a decision. If grit has become a habit, then perhaps it is an unconscious decision, but a decision, nonetheless. The converse is also true. Not exhibiting grit is also a decision.

Our Christian walk should be filled with grit, that wonderful blend of passion and perseverance. God never promised an easy life, but he promised an abundant life. Our Christian grit is a decision. As described in the old hymn, "I have decided to follow Jesus. . .no turning back. No turning back."

Today's Truth: For I decided to know nothing among you except Jesus Christ and him crucified. 1 Corinthians 2:2

AUGUST 1

GRAND FUNK

I was in a funk all day. A grand funk. Last night I contemplated getting up and heading to the mountains before the sun had a chance to rise. I even charged my GPS watch for the occasion. But did I get up when I woke at 5 a.m.? Nope. How about 6? No way. In fact, I did not hit the floor until nearly 8 a.m. So much for running long.

Before the first cup of coffee, I stepped outside to deal with pool chemicals and remove the frogs—dead and alive—from the skimmer. By this time, I realized how lousy I felt. I gave it a half-hearted try with a trip to good 'ol Tractor Supply to search out a needed element for a lighting project. Coming up blank, I returned home, ate lunch, and headed to the pool to float, nap, and read. Thunder clouds and torrential rain put an end to that.

Our bed with freshly washed sheets was my next stop. I flipped channels, nothing really interesting me. A book was by my side, but neither did I feel like reading. For the life of me, I could not figure out what to do.

I will not bore with you with other details of my uninspired, do-nothing day. (I did end up crawling in the dirt to yank weeds.) I felt guilty for not being more productive. I felt fat and lazy from not running a step. And as much as I tried, I could think of nothing to write about—until now.

For any children of the 70's, I assume the title of this piece got your attention. Realizing I was in a funk, I thought back to the band, "Grand Funk Railroad," that made its debut in mid-1969. Of course, I used Google for a refresher course on their most popular songs. In the process, I learned that though the band took a few breaks along the way, they reunited again in 2017 and get this, were amid their 2020 tour when Covid hit. That is a 51-year history! Imagine. 51 years through thick and thin. Good times and bad. But the three original guys? They are still making music after all these years. That is quite a legacy.

How many couples make it 50 years? How many pastors stay the course? How many churches are as solid now as when they started a half century ago? How many believers still have a passion for the Gospel and their faith through the decades? Steadfastness should be embraced and celebrated.

Today's Truth: Therefore, my beloved brothers, be steadfast, immovable, always abounding in the work of the Lord, knowing that in the Lord your labor is not in vain. 1 Corinthians 15:58

AUGUST 2

CHANGING WEATHER

The weather cannot seem to make up its mind. Even the weather apps are having a hard time keeping up. Last time I checked, today brought only a negligible chance of showers. Granted, it was still supposed to be hot and very humid, and the predictors were not wrong about that. But as they say, the proof is in the pudding, or in this case, those clouds.

When we left for church it was cloudy. Occasionally, the sun popped out as if to say, "Here I am!" Then in a toddler's game of hide and seek, off it would go, dark clouds menacing. Rain showered down for a slim minute before the sun's rays played another inning of the game. Fickle defined both sun and clouds.

I feel just as fickle and that does not sit well with me. I have so much to think about these days. It is like I am still trying to figure out what to do with my life at age 63. So many things interest me. There is some uncertainty with my job and how long it will be available. There are directions and decisions being made that require submission, and I am not entirely comfortable with some of that. Then there is a pull to go back into the medical field. But then again, getting involved with a new business that Seth and Gary are planning has appeal. And just being able to restore, refurbish, and reinvent discarded furniture and items sounds like great fun. Add to that the new book idea screaming to be written.

What's a gal to do? One minute I feel content where I am at. But just like the peek-a-boo games played by the bright sun and dark clouds, the winds shift, and plans change. It is hard to keep up. It is difficult to tell which direction is the right one for me. For me, it is tough to separate ego and emotion with more informed decisions.

I want to honor the Lord with my life. I do not want to run from a challenge nor miss an opportunity to serve. I do not think I have ever prayed with such intensity about the future and my place in it. Honestly, handwriting on the wall would be very much appreciated. But for now, I suspect the angst I feel is part of the process. There is no recourse but to seek and pray until the answer comes.

Today's Truth: The heart of man plans his way, but the Lord establishes his steps. Proverbs 16:9

August 3

The wee hours

The house is quiet at 3:18 a.m. Outside, faint rumbles of thunder roll as lightening sporadically brightens the dark sky with jagged spears of light. I look outside to see if it is raining. It is not. But from my vantage point, my heart quickens to see a bear has come to visit, taking a seat by the sidewalk. But alas, a closer look informs my better senses that the black shape I view is simply the garden cart left there after weeding. "Perhaps it is the lack of sleep that fools my eyes," I think as I paddle bare footed back to the sofa and the comforter spread there.

Sleep does not come easily though I wish it to. Some nights I fall asleep only to wake within an hour or two, restless and unable to fall back into the embrace of slumber. Other times, like tonight, I lay quietly in bed, jealously listening to my husband find his rest. When it becomes clear to me that I will not sleep, like a ninja I make my way to what has become my reading spot. There, a book and reading glasses await. The paragraphs roll by until I wistfully believe to be tired. I shift to the couch, arrange the blanket, and anticipate eventual sleep lulled into existence by the soothing, rhythmic tic-toc of the clock.

I tell myself to let go. Relax. But soon, no matter how tightly or long I hold my eyes shut, I am as awake as ever. I try the guest bed, but in time find the stillness of the air sans fan to be oppressive. An hour passes. Gary's snores from the other room have silenced and I am hopeful. But the hope is in vain as my fingers now alight on the keyboard. Oh, how I wish I could sleep.

I used to look forward to bed and nearly instantaneous sleep. Now, bedtime is dreaded, not knowing if the night will be a source of respite and recovery. But in an odd sense, there are times that in the stillness, I put aside my angst for the weariness I am sure to feel come morning. The solitude directs my thinking. I share my innermost thoughts and fears with the Father. I ask for clarity and guidance. I plan and pray. I am embraced by the creator of the universe. And that is enough for this moment.

Today's Truth: I bless the Lord who gives me counsel; in the night also my heart instructs me. Psalm 16:7

AUGUST 4

CLARITY

By the time I hit the trails, it was nearly noon. But after inches of rain yesterday, the bright skies beckoned. I had been in my office, busy with video calls and correspondence. My restless legs thumped and bumped. It was impossible to sit still in my chair, as comfortable as it was. My mind swirled, perhaps chasing down those legs of mine. I had to get out.

The only thing I had decided about the run was that it needed to start out downhill. Going down right off the bat gives me at least a fighting chance to ease into a runnable rhythm. I followed my nose along a creek, through very overgrown trails, and splish-splashed through water-crossings. Though getting caught a few times on briars and needing to swipe at the spider webs on the infrequently used trail, it should have been no surprise it was aptly named "Idiot's Run."

Eventually, the trail wound around to escape the creek bottom. That meant one thing: up. But today I did not mind. The humidity was much lower than the last week or two, the air clear. Admittedly, I cannot remember the last time I ran this trail in a counter-clockwise direction. Hence, I did not realize that it bordered an area that had been clear-cut a few months ago. With the most wonderful, refreshing breeze blowing back the wisps of hair that escaped my ponytail, the view was breathtaking. With no compulsion to rush, I perched on a rock to take it all in. I had never, ever seen the trail and surrounding area from this perspective. I liked—no, loved—what I saw.

My speed and endurance did not suddenly morph into world class performance. Still, I surprised myself with a willingness to go with the flow. Take in the view. Appreciate the stiff, warm breeze in my face. Enjoy the moment. My mind cleared, new ideas entering swiftly. Alone in the woods, I voiced those ideas out loud, hoping to inscribe them in my overused memory banks. By the time I got back to the car, I was dirty and dog-tired, but oh, so happy.

A change of pace and place is a good thing. Take the proverbial road less traveled. Do not rush. Look around. Listen intently to the natural surround sound. Take one step at a time. Slow down and smell the roses (or eat wild blueberries, if you prefer.)

Life is good.

Today's Truth: For you shall go out in joy and be led forth in peace; the mountains and the hills before you shall break forth into singing, and all the trees of the field shall clap their hands. Isaiah 55:12

August 5

My pet rock

The beep sounded. An email had flown into my inbox, its author an owner of a publishing house. We had been conversing about the book you now hold in your hands.

Pretend you're God. You create something really, really hard. It's also heavy. At least it is for Adam. You place it next to the path on which Adam walks each morning when he is strolling the Garden. Adam finds this object and calls it "rock." Adam shows it to Eve. She goes, "Eh, big deal. What's if for?"
"No idea. I just found it."
"Okay, smart guy, but what do you do with it?"
"Told you, I'm not sure. But it looks really cool, right?"
"Not to me. To me it looks like a rock."
Adam takes his rock and shows it to the animals who seem interested but being animals don't really offer any great suggestions. Well, Adam's dog does. He pees on "rock."
Days, weeks, years later "rock" has become a tool for banging with, a wheel for ox carts used by people with compressed discs along their spine, a flat spot for grinding grain.
That's what you have: a rock. Now you have to figure out what your rock can become. To do that you need to look at the people around you and see how your rock might be a solution to some issue they have. For Cain, rock was a weapon. For Gideon rock was a threshing floor thingy. For Abraham, rock was a sacrifice altar.
Show your rock to others. Ask them what it can be used for. Perhaps then you'll begin to get an idea of how it can become a tool.

OK, then. Let me think about this. My work in progress is a rock. What do I do with that? Do I, like a sculptor, faithfully pound that rock until it is shaped into something useful? Do I use my rock as a paperweight or door stop? Do I cast my rock upon the waters? Oh, wait. Wrong directive. Solomon said cast your bread—not rocks—on the waters. Rocks sink. That would not be good. Regardless, what do I do with this rock of mine?

"Devotionals avoid the use of I, me, and my," he explained. "And by the way, there are so many out there, it's hard to stand out in the crowd."

Hum. "I really never intended this to be a devotional per se," I think to myself.

He added, "Memoirs" don't sell either." Well, I do write about my daily experiences, but does that count as a memoir? His comments are true, but not encouraging.

My intent in writing is that readers learn to evaluate their everyday normal to identify truth in the ordinary. "God, please use this rock in any way you see fit. But please, don't hit me over the head with it."

Today's Truth: There is none holy like the **Lord***: for there is none besides you; there is no rock like our God. 1 Samuel 2:2*

AUGUST 6

THE TEXT

The text was waiting for me on my phone when I got finished with another slog through the woods. "Grandma is going to the ER. She's vomiting dark stuff. Possibly a GI bleed." An hour later: "Still vomiting. They're doing blood work now."

Oh dear. My wonderful, sweet mother is in trouble. At 92, she struggles. Two years ago, she had to move from independent living to an assisted care section of the retirement home. She is weary and worn. This once vibrant, energy-filled woman who could work circles around everyone can barely manage to use her walker to make it to the bathroom. She is a cancer survivor and had a coronary stent placed when she was about my age. She had a pacemaker inserted some time ago, and reportedly has a leaky mitral valve. "There's nothing they can do for me," she mourns. I get the feeling she is disappointed when she awakes in the morning. She is ready to go home.

Times like this make me introspective and sad. There is so much to emulate in my mother, clearly a role model on so many levels. But now she is tired, so very tired. She has been alone for a long time, my dad dying in 1986. For years after that she traveled the world to aid missionaries and teach children. She drove thousands of miles to speak to various audiences. She wrote a book that has encouraged many. She directed church choirs forever. But now, we are separated by miles, me in my office and she in a hospital bed.

My mother taught me to pray by example. An index card for each day of the week, those cards guided our breakfast prayers before heading off to school. As one card got filled with names, she stapled another to it. When God answered a prayer, she made note of the date. Some of the people on those cards have been prayed for steadily for over sixty years. Should mother pass, I plan on cherishing those cards.

I do not know what will happen with Mother in the following hours and days. But I am grateful that God holds her future securely in His hands. I pray that He encourages her and makes His presence known in this very moment.

Today's Truth: The Lord sustains him on his sickbed; Psalm 41:3a

August 7

Turn Your Eyes

Yesterday I got THE text. Today I got THE call. Mother was gone. Her physical struggle ended. She went home to see her Savior. And I was not there. Gary and I were stuck in traffic on I-81.

Mother was not alone. My niece and nephew had been vigilant ever since Mother was taken to the hospital yesterday morning. They stayed by her side, talking to her, watching her sleep, and wandering if this was going to be THE time mother was 100% right about something being 100% wrong.

There was something wrong. She had developed a GI bleed, vomiting up a black, grainy substance. She also aspirated some of that, compromising her lungs. Should we let them intubate her to allow a scope procedure with hopes of identifying the source of bleeding, that they may or may not be able to fix? It was unlikely she would ever be extubated should that happen. Or do we try to make her as comfortable as possible and let nature take its course? We decided on the latter knowing she signed a DNR (Do Not Resuscitate) order and wanted nothing to prolong her life.

As we drove, a constant barrage of updates and information distribution occurred. Brooke texted me and my three brothers, and I passed along those messages to my kids. The data given to me hinted of an impending cardiovascular collapse. When asked if she was in pain, she moved her head slightly to the right and left as if to say "no." That was a relief. My brothers, in the meantime, were making decisions on how and when to close the mileage gap that separated them from her.

My phone rang. It was Brooke. "I am so sorry. We were playing hymns for her all morning. I had just finished singing 'The Old Rugged Cross' when her breathing slowed. But as I sang 'Turn your eyes upon Jesus,' she drew in one last breath. And then she was gone."

Last night she told my nephew it was time to fly away. And fly away she did, right into the arms of Jesus. Tonight, she sings praises. She reunites with my dad, my grandparents, three brothers, and so many others.

My heart aches and tears cascade. But as she often prayed, I pray for her. "May the angels go before, behind and beside you."

Today's Truth: When the perishable puts on the imperishable, and the mortal puts on immortality, then shall come to pass the saying that is written: "Death is swallowed up in victory." "O death, where is your victory? O death, where is your sting?" 1 Corinthians 15:54, 55

AUGUST 8

THE STUFF

With August 6 came the text that told us of mom's admission to the hospital. August 7 brought the call of Mother's final breath this side of eternity. And today, August 8, offered the reminder that what is left behind in the form of "stuff" is of little to no value.

It was a surreal day. Gary and I, along with my brother John and niece Brooke met with the funeral director. We laughed as we recalled happy, even raucous times when we were all together as a family. But tsunamis of tears and grief flattened us when we least expected it. It was odd to be allowed into her room where she spent her last years. I almost expected her to come out of the bathroom and brighten up when she realized she had visitors. But alas, her chair was empty, just as she left it. All her personal belongings sat on shelves, hung in closets, or were tucked away in her lone dresser drawers. Where to begin?

We started in on a plan, piling donatable items onto the sofa. Then we stuffed large garbage bags with magazines, old notebooks, and mounds of greeting cards and letters from those she held special—which was just about everyone. Each of us selected pictures, wall art, hand-made quilts and other mementos that held extra special meaning, making sure to create piles for my siblings who had yet to arrive. But when it was all said and done, the stuff was just stuff. That stuff would not go with her in the casket. That stuff would fail to make the trip to eternity.

What mattered was the legacy Mother left: her unrelenting, disciplined prayers, the countless folks she introduced to the Gospel, her service to church and those in need, her love for choral music, the travel to the uttermost parts of the world in service to the King, and her passionate love and care for her family, friends, and anyone she met. She never held back. Even the social media posts from others give testimony to the difference she made in the lives of so many.

Saying good-bye to Mother makes me realize I am an earthly orphan. I can no longer pick up the phone and call. I cannot ask her about that little detail in one of her stories. And yet, I know she is exactly where she needs to be, in the presence of Jesus and reunited with all those who have gone before.

Glory in that, Mother Dearest. Sing and shout and praise to your heart's content. You no longer need any "stuff" other than that. I love you.

Today's Truth: For we know that if the tent that is our earthly home is destroyed, we have a building from God, a house not made with hands, eternal in the heavens. 2 Corinthians 5:1

August 9

It didn't just happen

My mother's life was full of "It Didn't Just Happen" moments. In fact, she wrote an entire book entitled just that. Nothing is coincidence. Everything is sovereignly ordained. Every. Last. Detail.

In these last few days, our family has experienced God's careful planning, even if only recognized in the rearview mirror. It all began when we got the call that Mother had been taken to the hospital. Should I get in the car and start driving, or wait until the next morning to begin the journey? I chose the latter but talked to Mother on the phone that evening. Then I set about to find a place to stay. The intention was to visit for a few days before returning home. I was not planning on her passing so quickly.

But everything changed when the phone rang as I was driving along. It was Brooke, my niece. Mother had taken a turn for the worse. I turned around and headed home to get Gary. I really needed him to be with me if Mother was going to meet Jesus. The trip that normally takes 6.5 hours extended to eleven hours due to multiple accidents and delays. In the meantime, we got the call that Mom had passed. We missed it. But because we were not there, Mother was ushered into eternity as Brooke sang, "Turn your eyes upon Jesus." Mother deserved that. Mother needed that.

Yesterday we went through Mother's apartment, separating the "keepers" from the donations. Later, Gary began to research the intricacies of dealing with wills in the state of Pennsylvania. It was depressing, especially when our host told us her own horror stories as an executrix. We began to pray that we could find a non-greedy lawyer to help us navigate the process.

Then our host scribbled the number of an estate lawyer she finally found to help her. It was Sunday, but I called and left a message anyway. To my surprise, the office assistant called—on a Sunday—within a few hours. "Yes. We understand and can help. We offer our services at a flat fee, not a percentage."

Had I chosen a hotel instead of the private home, had we not started talking about wills, had the host not given us the phone number of a lawyer, had I not left a message on a Sunday. . .we may have missed the graciousness of God to work out the details way beyond our imagination. God is good.

Today's Truth: The heart of man plans his way, but the Lord establishes his steps. Proverbs 16:9

AUGUST 10

REMEMBER?

Do you recall the story of Josiah, king of Judah (circa 620's BC)? He was the kid who became king at eight years old. About eight years into his reign and at the ripe ol' age of 16, his heart was drawn to God, creating a desire to restore the temple that had fallen into ruin. It must have been exciting to find the plans and charge the craftsmen to bring the center of worship back to its original glory. Then came the day that Hilkiah, the priest, found the long-lost Book of the Law that was given to Moses. Imagine! The very law that God had given to Moses centuries ago. It is no wonder the people had been acting so poorly. That generation did not know the Law.

Hilkiah gave the Book to Shaphan, the king's righthand guy, who then read it to Josiah. Josiah set out from there to bring the Law to the people, reading to them for hours on end. The people embraced the words and turned their attention back to their God.

It is always exciting to find unexpected treasures. We found some of those when we finished moving everything out from Mother's room. Pictures from long ago. Hand-written letters between Mother and her parents that reveal deep family love. Hundreds of index cards, neatly alphabetized and stored in plastic boxes, filled with names of missionaries for whom she prayed. We discovered an equal number of greeting cards sent to her from friends around the world, and the trinkets she held dear bore Scripture verses. We found (and kept) her well-worn Bible, filled with notes and underlined passages.

You can tell a lot about a person by what they treasure. Mother loved people, and it showed. She engaged with them, sharing Jesus in normal conversation. She was generous in every way. "Why sure, you can take this book and read it." She looked for opportunities to share her resources, never an ounce of stinginess surfacing. She drew her caretakers into conversation, asking them questions and getting involved with their lives. "May I pray with you?" she often asked. So many of the nurses and aides spoke to us today, and with tears in their eyes, told us of the love Mom showed them.

I am honored to be Mother's daughter. What a legacy! Tomorrow we bury a vacated body. "She" is not there. Mother graduated to heaven and will live on for eternity. Her treasures we hold onto serve only as reminders of what is profoundly important.

Today's Truth: And the king stood in his place and made a covenant before the LORD, *to walk after the* LORD *and to keep his commandments and his testimonies and his statutes, with all his heart and all his soul, to perform the words of the covenant that were written in this book. 2 Chronicles 34:31*

AUGUST 11

THE INTERNMENT

My mind swirled as I laid my head on the pillow last night. It was hard to believe that the events of the last three or four days were going to come to an abrupt halt come morning. In the darkness of the hotel room, I began to cry silent tears, Gary, and my brother John already asleep. Had it not been for a self-reprimand to maintain control, the cries could easily have become resounding sobs.

It had been a whirlwind to get Mother's room cleaned out, but working together, we turned in the keys and closed the door on that chapter of life. Mother had been the matriarch of the family for over 30 years, Dad passing away in 1986. Now it was up to my brothers and me to continue the DeLancey legacy so well established. What a challenge. So much so that when I woke up at 3 a.m., I was still thinking about the earthly finality of Mother's life and the new roled placed upon me.

It was with nervous trepidation that I dressed and waited for the time to head to the cemetery. Praying for control to keep from turning into an ugly, blubbering mourner, I greeted my family as they arrived. Little Addyson was her bubbly self, fascinated with the variety of tombstones in this centuries-old burial place. But finally, it was time to gather under the tent, Mother's simple, bronze-colored coffin poised to be lowered into the earth.

With young and old standing respectfully, we listened to stories of Mother's faithfulness to her Lord, her family, and to service. Pam, who had never met Mother, could certainly get a sense of how her grandmother-in-law lived out her faith. There were moments of laughter when niece Brooke shared her memories. Pastor Doug offered reflections on her willing heart and vivacious prayer life. Aaron's blessing from Numbers 6 was offered in Hebrew by brother John. From a family full of singers and musicians, we harmonized when singing "Amazing Grace." I almost did not want the service to come to an end, but it did with brother Dan's rendition of "Turn Your Eyes Upon Jesus," the song that ushered Mother into eternity.

Rejoice now, Mother. You are home where you belong.

Today's Truth: The Lord bless you and keep you; the Lord make his face to shine upon you and be gracious to you; the Lord lift up his countenance upon you and give you peace. Numbers 6: 24-26

August 12

The common denominator

I'm not sure how math works nowadays, but back when I was learning arithmetic, we learned to add, subtract, multiply and divide. We arranged numbers in tidy columns to make the process a little easier. We also learned about fractions. Early on, a picture of a pie cut into four pieces might be used to show that four pieces together make a whole. As the math became a bit more complicated, we learned to manipulate fractions, having to find the common denominator before performing the function. Doing so allowed for the fractions to be joined together in a way that made sense.

Over the last couple days, I have witnessed the personification of a common denominator. He is called the Holy Spirit. The Spirit tied together very different people, allowing us to be unified in function.

My Mother told me that when her mother died and the time to clean out the house came along, the siblings and spouses gathered to pray for wisdom and unity. She made me promise to do the same. First thing. So, we did. Very different people came together to work together in love and with purpose.

David, the first born, led the way as a professional tennis player, Navy fighter pilot, and tech guru. He has more "If I told you, I would have to kill you" stories than should be humanly allowed. Dan and John, my younger twin brothers are as different as night and day—and have always been that way. John was a long-time pastor, has an earned doctorate, and now leads tours and teaches seminars on biblical archaeology. Dan is a creative, talented, and hardworking guy with his site-work company, daily playing with life-sized Tonka trucks and heavy equipment. Then there is me; the only girl who has tried her hand in medicine, teaching, and writing.

We are like different fractions that first must be converted to a common denominator. We are different parts of a whole. But just as the well-known analogy of the Body of Christ having many parts, so do we as family. Each does his own job. Each is equally important to the whole. The whole is not complete if someone goes missing. We need each other now more than ever, united by our common denominator of the one sent from God, His Holy Spirit.

Today's Truth: There is one body and one Spirit—just as you were called to the one hope that belongs to your call— one Lord, one faith, one baptism, one God and Father of all, who is over all and through all and in all. Ephesians 4:4-6

August 13

You Call This an Anniversary?

I will spare you the suspense. Skip, my brother-in-law, walked out of the hospital earlier today. This evening, he and Joy (Gary's sister), went out to dinner to celebrate 43 years of wedded bliss. But it almost did not happen.

Through an odd set of circumstances, Skip was finally told that his worrisome symptoms over the last year or two probably resulted from a stroke. It was true he had stroke-like symptoms that included nausea, extreme vertigo, and wacky vision. The first time it happened he was in California at Joy's sister's husband's funeral. Doctors there could not put their finger on a specific malady. Over the last year and a half, these unfortunate episodes reared up at the most inopportune times, like in front of a bunch of engineers attending one of his lectures. But eventually, the symptoms cleared but a problem with his mitral valve was identified. Off to the #1 ranked hospital he went, though far from home. The surgery was to be yesterday.

They arrived at the hospital on cue, getting all the pre-op shenanigans out of the way before Skip was wheeled back to the operating arena. Joy headed to the apartment they called home for the duration of this away-from-home medical care. Then she got the call no one wants to get. "The surgeon needs to speak with you right away." That is never good.

Two surgeons and one anesthesiologist sat across from Joy explaining that Skip had an allergic reaction of epic proportions to a yet-to-be identified drug given in the OR. He turned bright red, his lips, tongue, and throat grossly swelling. "His blood pressure was extremely low. We had to work for an hour to get him back. We could not do the surgery. He is intubated and in ICU. We are keeping him sedated."

Could it be? Would we lose another family member? I prayed hard when Joy told me the gripping details of the ordeal. Was his brain intact? How long had he been without oxygen? Only time would tell.

Skip was extubated last evening. When the sedatives wore off, he started telling jokes, completely amnesic to all that had transpired. He was going to be fine! Today, he walked out of the hospital, more testing scheduled before another go at the surgery next week. Basking in a celebratory meal is way better than planning a funeral.

Today's Truth: The prayer of a righteous person has great power as it is working.
James 5:16b

AUGUST 14

SUFFERING TOGETHER

I really needed some inspiration after hard days. It was exactly one week ago today that Mother passed away, but I was trying my best to get back to normal life. It was normal alright. After another horrible run this morning, I was ready to lay back and exhale this evening.

Fortunately, Netflix offers the entire series of Eco Challenge Fiji 2019. Touted as the toughest race in the world, this multi-disciplinary team race covering at least 300 miles was inaugurated in 1995. The race became a reality TV show, inspiring millions—including me—to dream about accomplishing something incredibly hard and almost unimaginable. The race continued through 2002. But last fall, the challenge that requires four teammates (one of whom must be female) was resurrected. My binge on these shows began tonight.

The contestants ranged from professional adventure racers to regular people who dared to dream big. But the race is not for the faint of heart. Each team is given eleven days to complete the adventure: trekking, mountain biking, ocean paddles in flimsy boats, stand-up paddling, climbing, conquering water-filled canyons—upstream. A handful of teams compete for a position on the podium. Some teams race to accomplish something cool. But the back-of-the-packers race to survive through the finish. Not all do.

All who enter the fray never question whether they will suffer. The question becomes how bad will the suffering be? Even the most experienced teams deal with accidents and illness. There are equipment malfunctions that add to the misery. The heat and humidity take their toll. A tropical storm dumps torrential rain. Skin breaks down, gaping blisters forming on hands and feet. Calories are at a deficit and sleep is rare. So why do teams put up tens of thousands of dollars if they know they will suffer like never before, accepting the possibility of serious injury and even death?

They do it for the challenge. They know that what does not kill them makes them stronger. They know that if they function as a true team, they are better together than on their own.

We are wise to embrace suffering. We are wise to join arms to avoid being swept away in flood waters. We are wise to live unselfishly, leaving no teammate behind. No man is an island. There is power in striving together.

Today's Truth: If one member suffers, all suffer together; if one member is honored, all rejoice together. 1 Corinthians 12:26

August 15

Trash to Treasure

It is a rainy, cool Saturday, reminiscent of an early fall day. What started off as a leisurely morning quickly picked up speed. I was fired up to have the day to clean, organize, suck up corner cobwebs, and tend to other neglected chores. But even more importantly, it was Project Day.

Now, promise to not laugh at me. The reason I headed to the workshop all started off several weeks ago. I was off on a run. It was hot, humid, and miserable. But adding to the weather status, my innards started rumbling. Shoot. I hate it when that happens. I did what I could to prevent an accident as I ran against traffic on the wide 460 highway shoulder. Dropping my drawers in plain sight of oncoming traffic was probably not the best move. Hence, I waited until I made the turn onto a county road, progressing another half mile before arriving at a secluded spot right off the road.

I will admit that I have used this spot before when nature sounded the call. Someone along the road long ago used it as a graveyard for an old boat, odd bits of machinery, and random hard-to-dispose of stuff. That mess was simply strewn between trees and left to rot. But now, the place is overgrown, providing just the right amount of cover to a runner in distress.

As I squatted behind a tree to take care of business, I looked around. A first glance, a discarded item looked like a porcelain bowl. But flipping it over, it turned out to be an industrial light fixture painted green on the exterior. Wow. Those things are popular to repurpose nowadays. Could there be another one laying around? Sure enough. Another lay five feet away, complete with an unbroken bulb. I gathered both metal light shades and hid them at the base of a tree. Hiding them was probably over-kill given their abandoned nature, but I was taking no chances. I ran home with mounting enthusiasm at my find. Since it was nearly dark, I hopped in the car and sped down the road on the retrieval mission.

Today those treasured finds took on new life, now hanging over my dining room table. I am delighted that I was able to take dirty, discarded "trash" and turn it into a usable, functioning fixture to shed light on those gathered at the table.

I am also delighted that God is in the habit of remaking, reforming, and repurposing all who have been separated from God and feel like discarded trash.

Today's Truth: And when Jesus heard it, he said to them, "Those who are well have no need of a physician, but those who are sick. I came not to call the righteous, but sinners." Mark 2:17

AUGUST 16

LOUD AND UGLY SOBS

I hate it when I cry because I cry ugly. My nose wrinkles, my mouth contorts, and within a minute or two, my eyes become red and swollen, somewhat akin to a rabid racoon. (Not that I have seen a rabid racoon, but that's how I imagine it to be.) Growing up, if our family was watching a TV show that pulled at the heart strings, all three of my brothers simultaneously turned to look at Mother and me. "Your nose is twitching. Haha. You're going to cry" they chided. They were usually right.

I have certainly cried these last nine days since Mother met her Maker in person. But surprisingly, I had not all-out sobbed. Until today. For some reason, much of the day has been hard.

Being Sunday, we headed off to church as we always do. One of the elders asked how I was doing. I got a little teary but maintained control. Everyone else, all of whom I consider family, seemed to avoid me. Perhaps they did not know what to say.

Then came the singing. "Really? You had to pick "It is Well with my Soul," I mused to myself. "Of all hymns to pick in a time of grief." I managed to sing the first few phrases before the tears rolled. I stopped harmonizing and simply listened. That did not really help, nor did the second hymn. Memories of Mother, church music, and her wonderful alto voice flooded my brain. "Great. I'm leaving," slipping out ninja-like to the restroom to wipe away the smeared mascara and assess the damage.

I hid in the vacant locker room until I took a deep breath and tried again. I had hope that everything was under control. Nope. A second set of hymns was next in the line-up. It was useless. Good-bye. Back to the stalls for me. We headed home quickly at the final amen.

Standing at the sink, alone in the house, the floodgates opened. I sobbed ugly. I was in the bathroom when Gary came in. I was sobbing again. "What's wrong?" he inquired.

"I think it's called grief." That was not the last time I sobbed today and likely will not be the last. It is part of the process. It is my new normal. But I will be okay. The Father understands.

Today's Truth: You have kept count of my tossings; put my tears in your bottle. Are they not in your book? Psalm 56:8

August 17

Smart Watch Sync

For months I have been contemplating getting a smart watch. That demands, however, a smart someone to use the smart watch. And therein lies the problem.

I have an ancient GPS watch that sort of works—assuming I could remember the series of buttons to push and places on the bezel to touch. It is not intuitive now, nor was it ever. The watch itself is so big it could be mistaken for a sundial. It hangs over my scrawny wrist and bruises the protruding boney structure. Granted, the watch will tell me how far and how long I am on my feet, but if it goes over four or five hours, it's lights out. Dead. Useless. No good.

An Apple watch with its recent ability to record an EKG is appealing given my cardiac issue. However, what is not appealing is the price tag for converting to an iPhone in addition to the purchase of the watch. I certainly do not have an extra $1100 to do all that. So, when a friend asked if I wanted to buy his FitBit Versa Lite for $30, I could not resist.

The watch is on my wrist at this very moment. I successfully downloaded the app on my phone so this fangled, gently used watch could talk to it. While I am certain they have exchanged a few words, it seems like there is much more that could be said in that conversation. When I come across a choice on the watch such as "weather," it tells me I need to ask my phone to sync that info to the watch. Hum. Not sure how to do that. And when I see Strava capabilities on the watch, it too indicated that the phone must advise the watch what to report. I believe a Google search for an instructional video will be necessary to optimize this watch/phone connection.

Sometimes I feel disconnected when I pray or when I plan. It feels like I am not syncing properly with the source of truth. Why is that? Has the source of truth, God himself, changed or moved? I doubt it. I suspect the problem is on my end and not His. Perhaps one of my settings to receive the needed information needs adjusting. Or maybe I have not assimilated the truth in the proper order for the whole thing to work the way it should. My heart and His spirit need to be aligned so I can fully understand his perfect ways.

Lord, connect me with your Spirit through prayer, the smart way to sync.

Today's Truth: What am I to do? I will pray with my spirit, but I will pray with my mind also; I will sing praise with my spirit, but I will sing with my mind also. 1 Corinthians 14:15

AUGUST 18

A NEW ROLE

I have been a lot of things in my lifetime. Daughter. Wife. Mom. Athlete. Student. Radioimmunoassay tech. Coach. Teacher. Cardiovascular perfusionist. Online instructor. Writer. Grandma, and probably a few other things along the way. But today I became an executrix for my Mother's estate. My mom had named all four siblings to hold those responsibilities, but for practicality purposes, my three brothers reneged their appointed roles so coordination efforts would not have to be difficult. It made sense.

The word executrix hits me in an odd way. Does that make me the executioner or the one fixing to be executed? I sure hope this new role does not mean I'll get the axe during the settlement process. But because probate court has moved to an online affair, our attorney assures me I can get all the necessary paperwork completed in one more trip to Pennsylvania. Let's hope so.

Mother was always concerned about being fair. She must have thought it equitable for her four children to be involved in the estate settling process. But this fairness thing was always in her blood. She kept precise records of what every Christmas gift cost, right down to the penny. If one of my brother's gifts totaled $25.00 and my gift was $23.75, I would get a check for $1.25. No joke. She wanted no hard feelings or sense of partiality. What was good for one was good for the other. She did not have to be that way. She could have given one person a gift and not the other and been perfectly within her rights to do so. She could have decided not to give any gifts at all. But she extended grace and mercy by giving us gifts we likely did not deserve.

God is like that. He is more than fair when He did not have to be. We are sinful, separated from a holy God who cannot tolerate disobedience. And yet, before the foundations of the earth were laid down, He designed a way to extend grace, mercy, and redemption through the blood sacrifice of His son, Jesus. There is not one of us who deserves anything but eternal punishment. *But thanks be to God, who gives us the victory through our Lord Jesus Christ* (1 Corinthians 15:57).

Today's Truth: Thanks be to God for his inexpressible gift! 2 Corinthians 9:17

AUGUST 19

GET FIT

How many times have you (and me) made a commitment to get fit? Okay, let's be honest. The commitment was more like a good intention gone wrong. But I digress. We are not going to talk about abandoned New Year's Eves resolutions in August. Rather, my granddaughter provided an interesting perspective on fitness a little earlier this evening.

Displaying energy worthy of a feral squirrel, both Addy and a beagle named Rasta were driving Seth and Pam crazy. They were trying hard to make decisions about their tiny house project. When they saw I was ready for a run, Pam offered, "Addy, maybe you can go running with Grandma." Addy jumped up and down with joy as Pam sheepishly looked my way and inquired, "Is that okay?" In the meantime, Addy dashed away to put on shorts and shoes. Off we went into the unknown.

I really had no idea how far I could take her. But before I knew it, we were chatting about the rules of running on a road, talked to the cows in the pasture, laughed at a donkey that came running toward us, and waved at the handful of cars and pickups that passed by. We picked out a mailbox to run to before making the turnaround toward home. I glanced at my watch. It reported we had gone 1.3 miles.

Switching to the other side of the road on the return trip, Addy kept pace talking and running. When she said her legs were tired, we picked a landmark to walk to before resuming running. I thoroughly enjoyed the time together. It was even a joy to teach her how to pee in the woods when necessary. (And it was necessary.) She thanked me for teaching her because in her words, "You can't expect a toilet to magically appear in the forest." True that.

After gaining the top of the last hill, the rest was predominately downhill. "Grandma. Let's do this. We are so close. I'm glad I am now fit." With that, she began sprinting to complete the journey.

I was curious. "Addy, can you get fit in one night?"

"Nah. It probably takes a couple times to get fit." I laughed but wished it to be true.

We all know that fitness is a process that takes time and energy. Fitness happens when we do what we should even when we do not feel like it. Fitness does not happen on its own. Likewise, spiritual fitness is the same way. It takes effort and energy and time.

Keep at it. Keep moving down the road toward fitness, physically, mentally, and spiritually.

Today's Truth: Do your best to present yourself to God as one approved, a worker who has no need to be ashamed, rightly handling the word of truth. 2 Timothy 2:15

AUGUST 20

IT TAKES TIME

After Addy's premier run last night, she called me at work, informing me that she told her daddy she wanted to run again. "Can we?" she inquired. How could a running grandma possibly say no?

During an after-work stop at the store for necessary dinner ingredients, my eyes landed on a pair of sparkly pink running shoes in Addy's size. They were marked down by 60%. Even better. Of course, it was my pleasure to add them to my cart.

The questions of "When are we going to run?" began as she met me halfway down the long driveway. She climbed into the car to "help" me navigate the rest of the way, talking the whole time about our run. To say she was excited with her new shoes is an understatement. She tested them out by running around the house. Her analysis? Yep. They made her run fast!

Once supper was over and the time drew near, Baby Girl, as I sometimes call her, was insistent we go further than last night. "OK. Which way?" She pointed to the left and off we went. About a mile in, she put into practice what she learned last night. Pick a spot and run to it. When you get there, take a little walk break, pick another spot, and begin running when you arrive. We walked more than last night, there were a few more "my legs are tired," but she led the two of us in rousing rounds of "I spy with my little eye," the rhythming game, and even the creation of a few lines of poetry. Occasionally she took off running, breaking into a huge smile and self-proclaiming, "There's your energetic girl!"

She was still chatting about this and that when we turned down the long, gravel driveway. We arrived back at the house none the worse for wear having clocked 2.99 miles. Not bad for a little kid! A bowl of chocolate ice cream before immersion into a bubble-filled tub was met with delight.

Addy's assumption last night was that fitness is gained in a single outing. But tonight, I think she came to grips that getting fit may not be quite so easy-peasy. Sure, she was more tired tonight than the first night. But despite the difficulty, she adapted to the circumstances, kept a smile on her face, and continued to take one step at a time. She did not rue what she could not yet do. She embraced what she could do and was satisfied.

Therein is a lesson we all could learn: Be in the moment. Be thankful for what you can do. Do not be discouraged by what you cannot yet do. Keep moving. Do not be shaken.

Today's Truth: I have set the Lord always before me; because he is at my right hand, I shall not be shaken. Psalm 16:8

August 21

To Monitor or Not to Monitor

The activity watch I bought from a colleague has been on my wrist all week long. I wrote previously about suspected miscommunication between the watch and my phone. That has been confirmed. My phone is so old that it refuses to talk with the FitBit watch. It is frustrating because the details of each run are locked inside the watch and refuse to come out until it has a newer model phone with which to chat. Nevertheless, there is still a massive amount of info I could monitor on the watch itself. But do I really want to do that?

I spent time thinking about that as I waddled along the trails this morning. It was nice for the phone to vibrate each time another mile was traversed. And there were some observations I found curious about heart rate and the correlation of how I felt. At the run's conclusion, the watch informed me of total mileage, time, average pace, average heart rate, maximum heart rate, and calories spent. To me, that information is valuable. At the end of the day, it tells me how many steps I took overall, and the total miles traversed. Those are fun facts.

But if I wanted to, I could track every ounce of water I sip and log each bite of food. It can also track my sleep and the quality thereof. I have no idea how it figures that, but I already know my sleep is poor. I am sure there are other things the "too smart for its own good" watch can do, but do I care?

I would like it to track elevation gained and lost, wishing it were a true GPS watch. But for the $30 I paid for it, it covers the basics of mileage, pace, and heart rate. I must admit, however, I am fighting a neurotic pull to constantly check the watch for data. I can only imagine how easy it would be to be consumed by the numbers. Small changes at first, but given time, lifestyle could transform dramatically due to the constant monitoring.

I wonder what would happen if we constantly monitored the work of the Spirit in our lives? "Would Jesus act this way? What would His response be in this situation? Did I offend with those harsh words? What can I do to encourage today? Am I representing Christ well? Spirit, what truth are you trying to teach me?" In this case, constant monitoring is a great idea.

Today's Truth: Be sober-minded; be watchful. Your adversary the devil prowls around like a roaring lion, seeking someone to devour. 1 Peter 5:8

AUGUST 22

BEFORE, BEHIND, BESIDE

It is Saturday and other than a checking out yard sales for a couple of hours, it was uneventful. Of course, I should put a qualification on that because if Addyson is involved, rarely can the time be deemed as uneventful. She was extraordinarily cute as she looked through potential treasures, scoring an Elsa brimmed hat with attached long, blonde braid. "I am going to prank people. I bet they won't be able to tell that I am Addyson. I don't even recognize myself!"

Deciding to give my body a break, I never ran today. Instead, I floated in the pool while Addy role-played mermaid, pulled weeds afterwards, and promptly fell asleep on the couch mid-afternoon. Supper was a non-descript piece of pizza followed by a drive with Gary to view some country property. But when we got home Addy was ready for adventure, the fourth day in a row. She clipped on a waist light to her shorts, I grabbed my light, and off we went for a woodland excursion.

With waning light, we came upon several deer, staring them down until they spooked and ran off. When we came across one of Gary's trail cameras, Addy had fun making funny faces in front of the lens. But soon enough, we left the open pasture and found a trailhead leading us into the deep, dark woods. "Come on Grandma. Follow me!" Like a tiny forest fairy, she scampered down the muddy trail, hopping over downed limbs cluttering the path. She talked non-stop, her pink-clad feet moving as swiftly as her mouth. When the trail became difficult to follow, she used her light to figure out the proper direction. Without fail, she was right. "I know the way. Let's go."

Sure enough, we made it back without incident, save bits of spiderwebs clinging to our skin. But as we walked through the front door into the air conditioning, I compared our interactions over the last several days. At times, she wanted to run behind me. Sometimes, like tonight, she wanted to lead, but more than a few times, her little hand grabbed mine as we journeyed side by side.

My Mother always prayed the same prayer before we pulled away after visiting her. She petitioned, "May the angels go before, behind, and beside you." We need protection from all sides and the angels do their job well. But what is the lesson to be learned? Sometimes we lead. Sometimes we follow. And sometimes we share the journey together.

Today's Truth: Then the angel of God who was going before the host of Israel moved and went behind them, and the pillar of cloud moved from before them and stood behind them, Exodus 14:19

August 23

Why My Foot Slips

I have been sitting here in my living room watching Addyson act like a cat, hissing, rubbing up against my shoulder for me to pet her, and jumping around on all fours. Please do not ask me why. Maybe it just goes along with a five-year old and her vivid imagination. But simultaneously, while keeping one eye on the unpredictable "cat" lest she strike, my other eye was tuned into a program showing random wild, crazy stunts.

There was Go-Pro footage of mountain adventurers traversing a knife edge. And when I say knife edge, I mean it. The ridge of the mountain was nothing but rough, jagged rock not even a foot's width wide in some places. On either side were precipitous sheer drops into oblivion. One misstep and the athletes would surely be a-goners. It gave me the shivers just to watch. But when one of them began to run across the rocks, I closed my eyes. There is not a single cell in my being that would ever want to risk life and limb for that "thrill."

I wonder if the writer of Psalm 94 was up on some rocky precipice when he penned the words of verse 18. *When I thought, 'My foot slips,' your steadfast love, O Lord, held me up.* Surely, he would be speaking from personal experience, right? I know I would be screaming for help if my foot slipped high on a mountain. But then again, would he necessarily need to be on a mountain to have his foot slip?

Last night when Addy and I made our way through the woods, much of the trail was muddy and slippery, particularly in the bottom near the creek. The mud made it difficult going downhill, but equally as hard to go up. Without great traction from our shoes, one step up meant slipping back two. It was tough, but if the Psalmist had experienced the slimy mud (like I did when racing through the jungles of Brazil), I can see why he would be crying out for the Lord to steady him!

Slipping is part of the human experience. It is okay to cry out to God for help when our foot slips and we are in danger of falling. And when our cares and concerns seem overwhelming, it is also okay to be consoled by the sovereign God who orchestrates all things for our good and His glory.

Today's Truth: When I thought, "My foot slips," your steadfast love, O Lord, held me up. When the cares of my heart are many, your consolations cheer my soul. Psalm 94:18-19

AUGUST 24

EXCUSES

It is 8:30 p.m., darkness has arrived, and I am sitting here on the couch having a conversation with myself. I did not run today, nor did I yesterday or the day before. I had been doing so well with consistency; six to seven runs each week. What is happening? Yes, my morning routine was messed up because I was Addyson's taxi back to her mom. Then it was pressing work on a writing project, a phone call, volleyball practice, and prep for a meeting tomorrow. Then home, clean up the kitchen, unload the dishwasher, prepare supper, clean up, and head to Wal-Mart for needed items. And oh, yes, it is thundering and promising to downpour outside. How could I possibly squeeze in a run?

Sounds like lame excuses to me. I should know. I excuse-make a lot! Then after I come up with the excuse, I rationalize away my decision to appease the inevitable guilt I feel. What a sorry mess I am!

Recently, I read a story about Lou Gerhig. Though many associate his name with the disease, back in the day he was well-known as a New York Yankee. It is reported that his initial role on the team was as a back-up first baseman to a guy named Wally Pipp. When ol' Wally got sick, Gehrig covered the base. He played so well that Pipp never regained the starting position. But get this, despite seventeen hand fractures during his career, Gehrig never missed playing in a game for thirteen straight years. That comes down to 2,130 games! Who does that? Well, not many, that's for sure. What an amazing ability to find a way despite the challenges. No excuse—valid or not—kept him from the mission.

Reading that fun fact confirms I am a wimp. It is so easy to make an excuse of why I did or did not do something. I may even give great lip service to its importance, but when it comes down to it, I back out.

I read in Proverbs an interesting verse describing someone so lazy that he claims a lion waits outside to devour him. Hence, he has no recourse but to stay inside the walls of his home. Lest I scoff at that fella, I am challenged to examine my own lame reasons for not running, not taking time to read, ignoring prayer, or neglecting relationships. Shame on me.

I best finish this story and get in a workout before it gets any later than it is.

Today's Truth: The sluggard says, "There is a lion outside! I shall be killed in the streets." Proverbs 22:13

August 25

Navigating the Unknown

"Okay, I hate to sound ignorant, but what in the world is a medallion stamp?" I listened to the company representative try to explain. "Huh?" When she explained it for the third time, it began to make sense, and yet, I could not keep my mind from picturing a four-inch diameter golden coin. Why it is called a medallion, I will never know. I was still thinking about a hunk of metal when she moved on to instructions about filling out the various forms. "Geez," I mused while involuntarily letting out an exasperated sigh. "Will I ever keep all these steps straight? I sure hope I don't screw up my attempt to settle Mother's estate."

Being the executrix of the estate is proving to be a challenge. Simply gathering (and I use "simply" not as a descriptive of how "easy" it is) all the information to figure out what gets probated and what does not has taken hours of investigation. Some folks I have talked to have been generous in helping me find answers. But a few, bound by organizational regulations, bulked at confirming even the most basic details.

I have never served as an executrix of an estate. When my father died, everything conveyed to my mother. Though Gary was the executor of his father's will, he and his siblings had the foresight to set everything to be paid out at the time of death. No probate necessary. Therefore, these are uncharted waters for me. I think I might be sinking fast.

I wonder if Peter felt like that when, amid a raging storm, he squinted through the rain from his fishing boat vantage point to see a ghostly form walking to him. Whoa! That had to be terrifying! But when he realized it was Jesus, over the side he went without thinking. His feet skimmed the surface as he raced to meet the Lord. Oops. A giant wave must have distracted him enough to notice the big-bad trouble surrounding him. Peter got a good soaking as he went down, down, down. But not for long. When he refocused on the Savior, he came bobbing up to follow Jesus back into the safety of the boat. From there, Peter's bearings were set straight in the presence of the Lord.

"Lord, help me not lose sight of you."

Today's Truth: So Peter got out of the boat and walked on the water and came to Jesus. But when he saw the wind, he was afraid, and beginning to sink he cried out, "Lord, save me." Jesus immediately reached out his hand and took hold of him. . . Matthew 14: 29b–31a

AUGUST 26

WISE WORDS

Ever feel inadequate? Do you get the feeling you are at the bottom of the totem pole? Do you compare yourself to everybody else, creating a mental score card on who is winning? If so, I am right there with you.

Over the last several weeks, I have been spending massive blocks of time writing a Bible study on the book of Proverbs. The intention is to guide coaches through all thirty-one chapters over a fifteen-week period, pulling over at particularly poignant vistas to fully appreciate the view. I am excited to see how the study is received.

Chapter 27 was part of my study today and verse four stopped me in my tracks. *Wrath is cruel, anger is overwhelming, but who can stand before jealousy?* Throughout the entire collection of wise and pithy sayings, there are almost too many warnings to count against angry outbursts and vengeance. But if I am not mistaken, this may be the first time the concept of jealousy is introduced. And the way the verse is written, we get the idea that jealousy is more egregious than fury.

But why is jealousy so dangerous? So what if I wish I were as thin and pretty as So and So? What's the big deal if I read an incredibly compelling blog post of a friend and become embarrassed at the thought of anyone reading my work? What is wrong with looking at race results and almost being happy when a competitor who I used to top has a lousy race? Friends, I'm being honest here. Jealousy is ugly.

When I am jealous, I am essentially telling God that he screwed up. He did not equip me optimally. His design was faulty because I am not who or what I wish to be. But this is false thinking. He had purpose in making me the way he did. But He also gave me the ability to control certain things. I can study harder. I can train smarter. I can practice my craft with greater focus. And at that point, I need to stop looking at other people, comparing myself to what they can do. I need to be thankful for how God made me, embracing the opportunities to develop and be the best He intended me to be.

Today's Truth: Wrath is cruel, anger is overwhelming, but who can stand before jealousy. Proverbs 27:4

August 27

Patience, please

Some years ago—ok, twenty years ago—I was working as a perfusionist at the local hospital. It was a busy morning with several heart cases on the schedule, and an operating room busting at the seams with other procedures. Orderlies ran ragged trying to fetch and deliver the patients in a timely manner. It was chaos. Suddenly, the voice of the Operating Room director rang out over the intercom, set at the highest volume. "I want patients, and I want it now!" We all knew what she meant, but the fact she asked for patients without exhibiting any patience was ridiculously funny. We probably should not have laughed.

My own patience was tested today as I dealt with estate-related issues. Given, I am no investment guru and have no interest in becoming one. My mother was not one either, but she had help in making her money work for her. Hence, as a beneficiary of a portion of said investments, I am responsible for filing the appropriate papers.

The language on those forms makes absolutely no sense to me, but I did my best. They were scanned and emailed back to the representative. She called not long after that. "You left a few things blank. You can add that info, initial and send it all back again." OK. I can do that. She called again. It looks like you used white out on an item. We can't accept that." So, I reprinted all eight pages and with the greatest of care, filled them out—again. Back they went for the third time. I received an email shortly thereafter. "Looks good." Whew. Glad that's over!

I was on the brink of losing patience. She obviously knew I was an idiot when it came to investment lingo, but she just kept rolling with it, leaving me to hit and hope that I did it right. It took the greatest effort to thank her for her patience with this new client of hers—and I tried *really* hard to be sincere.

It is no wonder that King Solomon talked a lot about the benefits of displaying patience, keeping temper and rage at bay. And should we be surprised that one of the fruits of the Spirit is also patience? God knows none of us do patience naturally.

Today's Truth: But the fruit of the Spirit is love, joy, peace, patience, kindness, goodness, faithfulness, gentleness, self-control; against such things there is no law. Galatians 5:22, 23

AUGUST 28

IT'S FRIDAY

Arriving home, I plopped down on the couch, take-out pizza in hand. I was exhausted, fighting the urge to snooze mid-bite. This first week of the new semester had done me in. Am I getting too old for this job?

I guess it does not help that I am still not sleeping well. Interrupted sleep makes me crazy! But today, Friday, serves as the period at the end of a sentence. Thank. The. Lord.

On the courts with the tennis team at the start of the day, I chased hundreds of balls to make practice go a little smoother. After several hours back in the office, I checked off a few pressing tasks before taking a hike up the mountain to the natatorium. To meet the new dive coach and touch base with the swimming coaches meant at least four miles of hoofing it on foot. The humidity covered me like a wet blanket by the time I returned to the office.

Within the hour, my next call of duty was volleyball practice. Another trek across campus, an hour of shagging balls, and a final return to my desk came next. Whew. I loved the interaction with the athletes and coaches, but there is a huge energy draw to do it.

But tomorrow is Saturday. The remnants of Hurricane Laura should produce morning wind and rain. With no compulsion to train, I anticipate a slow, lazy start to the day. I have no concrete plans. None for Sunday either, other than go to church in the morning. Maybe I will get out to the mountains in the afternoon, but who knows? I will figure it out when the time comes.

Life has a fair share of ups and downs. It ebbs and flows. Some days are hard. Some days are easy. And that gives us hope. Because if a day is hard, sooner or later it will be easy. And if a day is easy, take a deep breath because something hard is coming our way.

We need rest. We need a change of pace. Why do you think God patterned a sabbath for us? Why was it promised that renewal comes on the wings of an eagle or with the rising of the sun? Because that's just the way it is.

It's Friday, but Saturday and Sunday will come before Monday. Yeah.

Today's Truth: but they who wait for the Lord shall renew their strength; they shall mount up with wings like eagles; they shall run and not be weary; they shall walk and not faint. Isaiah 40:31

August 29

Dwell or Visit?

The sun is out again after an overcast morning. Skies are bright blue with wispy white clouds dancing upon the atmospheric breezes. Gone are the remnants of Hurricane Laura that never amounted to much of anything in our part of the world.

It has been a quiet day for me. I had a slow start, never accomplishing much until I vacuumed and ran a couple loads through the wash. But the reason for the slow start was my fascination with a show called "Alone." I wrote about it earlier in the year when an acquaintance of ours was the last man standing, winning a half million dollars in the process. Last night and again this morning I found myself binge-watching the season seven episodes before a trial channel subscription runs out.

Here is the premise. Ten people are dropped off somewhere in the arctic with little other than what is on their back. No food. Just ten items they pick to be used in their survival efforts. The prize this year is one million dollars. But the price you pay for it? Enduring 100 days of arctic winter. In past years, the contest continued until nine of the ten tapped out. Never had anyone gone more than 80-some days.

The strategy this time seemed different in terms of dwellings. Knowing there was no money unless they went the distance meant the survivalists would be there in the dead of winter. Temps can reach -40 to -60F. Snow flies and the lake freezes over several feet deep. The shelters could neither be flimsy nor temporary, which might suffice if you were camping for a few days. But 100 days in that hostile winter season? They needed a place where they could be warmed by the fire, stay dry, and keep food supplies they gathered safe. They required a place where they could dwell well. They were in it for the long haul. There had to be a distinct difference between shelters that previously sufficed and full-on, secure shelters needed for this go-around.

Feeling safe and secure comes from having a place to dwell. That place is in the presence of the Lord and in the power of His Word. Those who visit for a spell may benefit, but those who stay to dwell well will thrive.

Today's Truth: Let the word of Christ dwell in you richly, teaching and admonishing one another in all wisdom, singing psalms and hymns and spiritual songs, with thankfulness in your hearts to God. Colossians 3:16

August 30

Rattles in the Woods

Crossing the creek and heading uphill on the rocky trail, I was deep in thought. But when I heard a very distinct rattle, my mind snapped back to reality. There were three possibilities, I quickly surmised. 1) A small child was playing with her rattle in the depths of the forest. 2) A mariachi band's maraca player was having a practice session in private, or 3) A rattlesnake was making itself known.

Sure enough, the first two possibilities were quickly eliminated when I glanced behind me. I had run within two feet of the fattest reptile I had ever seen. With his little forked tongue flickering and his rattles a shak'n, I positioned myself at what I considered a safe distance. He was stretched out straight and not curled up in the strike position. I think he must have just eaten a very hearty meal. He was grossly bulging. "Perhaps he can't move all that fast if I annoy him," I mused. Still, I took no chances when I used the zoom function on my phone to snap a picture before continuing up the trail. So much for deep thinking. I stayed alert to my surroundings from then on out.

Most people do not list snakes as favorite creatures. Although today's encounter was with a poisonous snake, most are not dangerous. Still, there is something about those long, slithering reptiles that is unsettling. But then I got to thinking. When Adam and Eve had their close encounter, did they fear? Did they have a preconceived notion of danger? I don't think they did because up to this point, everything was peachy-keen perfect in the Garden.

The question then becomes, should their radar antennas have given off a signal when the talking serpent told them things opposite of what God said? God had only given them one rule: Do not eat from THAT tree. The serpent questions them. *Did God actually say, 'You shall not eat of any tree in the garden'?* And that was enough to reconsider their action. He continued, *You will not surely die. For God knows that when you eat of it your eyes will be opened, and you will be like God, knowing good and evil.*

All it took to reel in Adam and Eve was for that sneaky, crafty, cunning snake to twist God's words away from the original intent. They gave in, and sin was ushered onto the planet.

Lest we think harshly of the original humans, let's remember it does not take a lot for us to rationalize away our errant, sinful thoughts and action. Stay alert, people. Stay alert.

Today's Truth: Be sober-minded; be watchful. Your adversary the devil [that snake!] prowls around like a roaring lion, seeking someone to devour. 1 Peter 5:8

August 31

Tell-tale numbers

"One, two, three, four. . .nine, ten, eleven. What? That can't be." I counted again, this time muttering the numbers under my breath as I pointed to each of the players spread out across the gym.

"Where is everyone?" I asked Brett, an assistant coach. At 6'5", he deliberately turned his head and looked down at me. He said nothing, but his eyes, seen above his mask, suggested a story. "Did something happen?" I quarried. I hoped not, but I was compelled to ask.

"Yep. Several of the girls opted out. They won't be playing." I viewed the roster in my head and looking around, put a name to the MIA athletes. But besides those who walked away from their college volleyball careers, that still left two unaccounted for. "They might have been around someone who had Covid. Both are fine. No symptoms. But they are quarantined for fourteen days."

Wow. We went from a roster of nineteen to eleven. When the potential virus girls return, we will have thirteen. No one who remains is a libero/defensive specialist, a very necessary position on any team. That could prove interesting.

It felt like a giant elephant had lumbered into our circle at the beginning of practice. Everyone was trying to process what this meant for the team. With the season postponed until spring (but with no promise of that happening), some of the upcoming December graduates decided to forgo the strain of training. Others just decided to move on with their lives given so much uncertainty. How would the players who remained respond?

Practice seemed "off" at first, but by the end the talented athletes competed hard. Bodies flew around the court, sets were made with precision, and balls got pounded in front of the ten-foot line. They seemed united in purpose and re-focused to the task.

I suspect the turn-around happened because they came to grips with several ideas. 1) It is what it is 2) This is an opportunity disguised as a disappointment and 3) It is a chance to play with unbridled joy and enthusiasm, rising to new heights of accomplishment.

Sure, there will be adjustments, everyone needing to step up big time. But what a chance to burn the ships and venture into a new and exciting land.

Today's Truth: They said, "Arise, and let us go up against them, for we have seen the land, and behold, it is very good. And will you do nothing? Do not be slow to go, to enter in and possess the land. Judges 18:9

September 1

Train 'em Up

There are a lot of different ways to train a dog, a kid, an athlete, and even a grouse. Oops. I meant to type spouse. But anyway, there are remarkably stunning similarities among all the trainees.

Consider this. Using examples is an effective training method. "Watch this and do it just like me. Start with your right foot forward. . ." Or how about using rewards? With treat in hand, "Here puppy. Sit. No Sit. Sit, girl." Girl sits. "Good doggy. Here's your treat." Repetition can also work. If you do something correctly enough times, sooner or later it will become habit. Of course, using words and good 'ol reasoning can be an effective tool to teach and train.

Addyson, my little whippersnapper of a five-year old granddaughter, happens to be sitting with me on the couch. Although, come to think about it, sitting is an inadequate description of what she is doing. She slouches, then she shifts to laying on her back, then one leg goes over the back of the sofa before positioning herself into a headstand against the cushions. She is in constant motion, all the while playing a game called "Tag w/ Ryan" on my phone. It is a cute little game where one character chases the other through a series of scenes riddled with obstacles, the chased character trying to duck under, jump over, and make sudden turns picking up rewards.

The funny thing about the way Addyson plays is that she becomes wholly involved, especially when she makes her character jump. On the screen she sweeps her finger up to make him bound. Simultaneously, her right leg kicks out quickly—every time—as if to help the little cartoon dude take a flying leap. Has she been trained? Yep. How did that happen so quickly and efficiently? I certainly had nothing to do with it.

Some things come naturally. We do not have to train a child to be selfish. But can we be intentional to train him to display the important character skill of unselfishness? You bet! You see, we must embrace the fact that children—regardless of age—have a natural disposition to sin. If we want them to think and act righteously, we must be intentional and consistent in that training. It takes great effort, but it will be worth it.

Today's Truth: Train up a child in the way he should go; even when he is old he will not depart from it. Proverbs 22:6

September 2

Decisions, decisions

Every day and in every way, there are decisions to make. Each decision is based on fact, opinion, or a combination of both. And there is always a consequence of each decision.

Some decisions are easy. The last two days I have had appointments with the cardiologist and ophthalmologist. At the cardiology appointment, discussions about my lack-luster running and troublesome medication side effects led to two solid decisions: schedule a nuclear stress test and stop the drug for two weeks before restarting at half the original dose. At that point, we reassess.

At the eye doctor, the exam revealed low-grade cataracts (which are of no consequence at this point) in addition to a change requiring a step-up in the power of my bi-focal contacts. And yes, bi-focal contacts are a thing. Nevertheless, after considering the facts, I walked out having purchased a year's supply of the new prescription.

Other decisions, however, can be incredibly tough. To be authentic, I will admit that for months I have been conflicted about my work. I love "my" girls and their coaches. I cherish the relationships formed with them. But I feel unsettled with some of the strategies embraced by the organization. Besides, I have writing projects going on, future book ideas in the "on deck" circle, and potential job opportunities that would be incredibly fantastic. I guess at 63 years of age, I simply cannot decide what I want to be when I grow up. Should I stay the course or jump ship?

My boss and I had a lengthy discussion today. He listened carefully and offered thoughtful responses. He did not convince me one way or the other—nor did he try. But what he suggested is that I take an earned 30-day sabbatical. "Just step away and use that time to seek God's face on what your future holds. Add on your vacation to extend the time if you like. I heartily recommend you do this."

Could I walk away from what I love? What about my girls? Would they think I abandoned them? And my coaches? Will they assume I stopped caring? Lost interest? But in the end, spending focused time to have deep conversations with God is just what the doctor ordered. I think I will do it. I am getting excited at the prospect.

Today's Truth: Hear, O Lord, when I cry aloud; be gracious to me and answer me! You have said, "Seek my face." My heart says to you, "Your face, Lord, do I seek." Psalm 27:7, 8

SEPTEMBER 3

EVERYDAY.

I was nervous coming to work this morning. Not because of anything on my to-do list, but because of one little—no, big detail. Parking. Yes, parking.

I have the type of parking permit that is about as good as it gets. However, the lot by my office building is shared with commuter students, faculty, campus staff, athletic staff, and athletes. I have discovered that if you arrive before 10 a.m. or after 2 p.m., it is likely there will be open spots. But arrive somewhere in the middle and you end up circling the lot lying in wait to stalk some poor soul walking to their car.

I had Addy with me this morning for an impromptu "bring your grandkid to work" day. Not leaving the house until 9:35, our ETA was around 10 a.m., the exact time one should avoid arriving. Turning onto campus and heading down the hill to the parking lot, I prayed out loud, "Lord, please give us a parking spot."

"Grandma, did you just ask God for a parking spot?" she asked incredulously. Answering in the affirmative, I explained that God cares about the little things as well as the big things. Just then, we turned in and found an empty place as close as you can get to the front door.

"Thank you, Lord!"

Addyson followed suit. "Yes, thank you, God. We appreciate it."

Later in the day we ventured out to deliver lunch to Seth and his brother who were working hard on a flooring project. Addy had my phone and was deeply involved with a catch me if you can video game of tag. She was happily jumping over and ducking under obstacles as she gathered up crowns. As her score continued to grow toward her personal best record, I heard her whisper, "God, can you please help me get really high points?" After a little while longer, I heard her continue the conversation with God. "God, thank you for helping me do my best!"

I smiled, letting her know how happy I was that she was talking to God about normal, ordinary stuff. "Don't ever forget that we can talk to God about anything, my dear Addy."

Out of the mouth of babes.

Today's Truth: Rejoice always, pray without ceasing, give thanks in all circumstances; for this is the will of God in Christ Jesus for you. 1 Thessalonians 5:16-18

September 4

If You Can Hear Me

Gary headed out to the back field. He was doing the final preparations for the annual dove hunt. Not that you slither through the woods in search of the little birds. Rather, you position yourself around a field that has been carefully cultivated to produce "seedy" plants, such as millet and sunflowers. At the proper time, the field is mowed to disperse the seeds, hopefully drawing in birds hungry for an easy-pick'ns meal. At that point, you blast away for as long as the birds fly into and across the field.

Addy and I were in the house when she asked if we could go look for PopPop. "Well sure. Go put on your socks and running shoes. We'll have to go down the trail and up the big hill to the field." Quick as a bunny, she came back ready to go. Off we went, stopping only briefly when her feet slipped out from under her, Addyson momentarily crying at the shock of landing hard on her backside and scraping her palm. Recovering quickly from the mishap, we arrived at the edge of the field. PopPop was no where to be seen.

Addyson led the way but put her hand out to stop me in my tracks. "Listen," she adamantly commanded, "I think I hear him! He's down there. I know he is. Come on!" Down there was very thick forest, hardly a place for him to be in these circumstances. When I finally convinced her that he was not in the woods, she took another approach: "PopPop. Come out, come out, wherever you are! If you can hear me, yell twice," she screamed. Continuing, "If you don't hear me, yell once."

Yes. I laughed. Hard.

We never found Gary in the field. He must have returned on one path as we went out on another. But aren't we as illogical as pint-sized Addyson? If we can hear, we can respond. If we cannot hear, we have no chance of responding. We are incapable of "yelling once."

I am so glad that when Jesus called my name, he gifted me the ability to hear and respond.

Today's Truth: And Peter said to them, "Repent and be baptized every one of you in the name of Jesus Christ for the forgiveness of your sins, and you will receive the gift of the Holy Spirit. For the promise is for you and for your children and for all who are far off, everyone whom the Lord our God calls to himself." Acts 2:38, 39

SEPTEMBER 5

TO NEW HEIGHTS

If there was ever picture-perfect weather, it might have been this morning. The oppressive plague of humidity that has afflicted our area did a disappearing act overnight. We woke to dry air and temps in the high 50's. The open windows ushered in a slight breeze and sounds of nature as the birds sang their morning songs. What a great start to a Saturday morning.

After a cup of joe was sleepily finished, I dressed for a run around our country block. It was slow and not completely steady. Still, it felt good not to suffer under a blanket of heavy air. Pool cleaning came next but not before I texted a friend of mine, "You wanna go on a cool hike?" Soon thereafter, Andy, an assistant college basketball coach responded. "Hum, sure?" I smiled.

As we drove to the starting point, chatter was non-stop. Windows open, hair flying, we could have easily been listening to a typical Beach Boys carefree summer kind of song. With the trailhead parking areas crowded with cars, I drove to a lesser-known spot, hid my keys, and handed Andy the pack I prepared. Off we went. Up, up, up. Our conversation was as constant as the incline.

After our feet covered about two and a half miles of steady hiking, we arrived at the first of my favorite vantage points. Huge boulders serve as a natural backrest to stop and survey the view. Off in the distance, mountain peaks bearing the typical blue tinge so common in these Blue Ridge Mountains could be appreciated. Far below our vantage point, the James River looked like a golden ribbon winding its way through the verdant valley. I pointed out where our journey had begun. We sat, unhurried, on the slab of rock, feet dangling as we took in the majestic scene.

Andy, despite the length and difficulty of the climb was game to carry on further up the mountain, across the ridge, and to the top of the next peak. It was far from easy, but my friend was thrilled to see the vistas she never knew existed. Now that she knows what a mountaintop experience can be, she wants more. I, for one, will always volunteer to be her guide.

Today's Truth: Exalt the Lord our God, and worship at his holy mountain; for the Lord our God is holy! Psalm 99:9

SEPTEMBER 6

AN HONEST COUNT

If you learn one thing around our house, it is that everything, year-round, points to a hunting season of one sort of another. Yesterday was just the beginning. It was the first day of dove season.

Yep. I am talking about the medium-sized grey birds that fly high and low in search of a supper of seeds. Planning for the the birds' arrival began weeks—even months—ago when Gary set his sites on the annual dove shoot. That meant killing weeds, plowing, planting, and mowing down the plants to disperse the seeds. Every night for the last week or two, Gary headed to the field to survey the number of birds that sat on the wire strung between posts or flew down to have a snack. Sometimes he was happy with what he saw. Sometimes not.

Yesterday was the day. His select buddies came and positioned themselves around the field, shotguns loaded and piles of ammo at the ready. At times, during the hours of noon and 6:00 p.m., it sounded like World War III. Some of the guys were great shots, killing their limit of fifteen birds apiece. A few left without ruffling many feathers (if any), but happy to have spent the day trying.

Not far from our farm is the property of a good friend. He, too, hosted a dove hunt. With a much larger field, he hosted thirty guys to shoot at the feathered fowl darting across the countryside. From the reports, they had a magnificent time enjoying the great outdoors on a perfectly fine September day.

Earlier today Gary was scrolling through Facebook, commenting on various videos, news events, and postings from friends near and far. And then he started laughing. "What now? I inquired. He continued to laugh, looking over at me with the same grin that I found so endearing forty-five years ago when we met in college.

"I doubt this was a smart thing to post on social media," he said, still laughing. His friend's post about the dove shoot bragged about three guys shooting twenty birds each. That is impressive but there is one tiny, little problem. The daily limit is fifteen. Oops. Nothing like admitting in public that the law was broken. Now it was my turn to laugh. Silly boys.

Today's Truth: But if you will not do so, behold, you have sinned against the Lord, and be sure your sin will find you out. Numbers 32:23

SEPTEMBER 7

GOOGLE IT

It was a wonderful day to get away. Moderate temps and sunny skies greeted us as we made the two- hour trip to Joy and Skip's house. Joy is Gary's younger sister and Skip is her husband. Just two weeks after cardiac surgery to repair a misbehaving heart valve, we were anxious to spend time with them. Skip looked great, we enjoyed al fresco dining on the patio overlooking the lake, losing ourselves in conversation. All too soon as the sun set over the water, it was time to head home.

Off we went, jackets now on to ward off the chilly breezes in the '94 Corvette convertible. We were on high alert as we rode along curvy country roads, eyes watchful for any deer with a hankering to commit suicide. When we got to one confusing intersection where I-64 crossed, Gary commented, "I have never seen so many signs in my life!" Uh-oh. My stream of consciousness kicked in and ran rampant.

"Who sang that song, 'Signs, signs everywhere signs. Do this. Don't do that. . .'" I inquired. Gary had no idea but thought it was from the late 60s or early 70's. Well, there was one way to find out. Google. Turns out it was first released by the Canadian group, "The Five Man Electrical Band." Now we knew.

Soon after, we passed through the town of Palmyra, VA. Gary asked, "Was there a mention of Palmyra in the Bible." I did not know. Guess what? Google knew. Palmyra was an ancient city in present day Syria, an oasis in the desert. There is mention of this city in 2 Chronicles, although it was called by another name. In 2015, ISIS destroyed most of the walls and temple. It is now considered a war zone and is unsafe for travel.

Soon after that, I contemplated the abundance of okra in our garden. We have harvested mountains of these finger-like, vitamin-A laden vegetables. However, some have been fibrous and inedible. I have had a hard time figuring out when to harvest. Ah. Google probably knows. Yep. Harvest when the pods are three to five inches long.

Isn't it funny how our go-to nowadays is Google? It has almost become an unquestionable knowledge source. But what if we looked at Scripture like that? I may not be able to find out how to harvest okra in between the Bible's covers, but it is certainly THE source for knowledge and wisdom.

Today's Truth: The fear of the Lord is the beginning of wisdom, and the knowledge of the Holy One is insight. Proverbs 9:10

September 8

Level ground

Anyone who is a runner knows that level ground is much easier to traverse than hilly terrain. Mountain climbs are exponentially harder than hilly climbs. Therefore, in the spirit of the mathematical transitive law, then mountain climbs are way, way, way harder than running on level ground.

This little fun fact is not a new revelation. I have known it for decades. I think the first time it impacted me was during those two-a-day high school field hockey practices. The 1950's era building was situated on several plateaus, each one a little higher than the previous. Thus, to get from the upper hallway to the bottom-most, a series of ramps connected each level. Not a single staircase existed. I suppose it was ADA-compliant before it was cool.

The grounds, however, gave even more evidence of the uneven ground. The field hockey field was at street level. However, the track and tennis courts sat on the next level up. The third plateau was a soccer practice field, and far above that and along the tree line ran the cross-country course. As in the building, no steps connected each level, but our coaches never let that stop them from making us run repeat sprints up those very steep grassy hills. We groaned each time we heard "To the hill with your sticks." It was incredibly difficult, but I suppose racing up and down the hillsides put us in the kind of shape by which our team was known. It made us tough and gritty.

There is not a day I run that I do not encounter hills and mountains. Not surprisingly, it still takes toughness and grit to climb those hills. Of course, I do not feel very tough and gritty nowadays, but I continue to try my best. Sometimes, however, I make a choice between an uphill gravel road and a rocky, rooty single track trail that rises to the top of the mountain. The uphill seems less intimidating on gravel than it does on a trail requiring much more concentration.

There are plenty of hills and mountains to face in our daily living. It can be tough. Super tough. Nevertheless, the difficulties teach us how to persevere. They make us stronger and more capable. But to be honest, sometimes it is nice to run, at least for a distance, on level ground. It is a time to breath again and enjoy the blessings in that part of the journey.

Today's Truth: Teach me to do your will, for you are my God! Let your good Spirit lead me on level ground! Psalm 143:10

SEPTEMBER 9

IT'S OFFICIAL

I got the official email today. My 30-day earned sabbatical has been approved. Oh, and the fifteen days of vacation I have coming to me also got the green light. (Use it or lose it.) That is a lot of time off. I am not used to that. In the last six years, I have probably only taken off two or three weeks—total—for vacation. Can I really do this? Can I essentially walk away? It may be hard to believe, but I am more than a little nervous about this.

The company I work for graciously allows each employee a time of respite (with pay) after every six years of service. Ministry can be exhausting and the pressure of fundraising overwhelming. With the encouragement of my boss, I chose to take my 30-consecutive days beginning October 12. The time will be used to seek God's face about sports ministry in the future, will serve as a time to read and write, and give me the opportunity to help Gary and Seth as they begin a new business venture. Being the executrix of my mother's estate, I will also have the flexibility of making trips to Pennsylvania to deal with the logistics of fulfilling the will.

But what about the girls I mentor? And the coaches I try to encourage? Can I simply walk away and not care about the relationships that have been established? No. I care deeply. Those weeks away are in no way indicative of a loss of interest. I simply need to clear my head and assess the future.

I told the coaches today, talking to one of them in person. "I'm glad you are doing this. We want you to be involved with our girls regularly, but we understand the need to catch your breath. Since the girls will all head home a week after you come back, we will start up again once the girls return in January. I wish all of us could take a break!"

A senior administrator and I chatted today as well. He voiced the same sentiments. Both his and the coach's comments left me more settled about leaving campus for a period in order to gain perspective.

I look forward to the sabbatical that was patterned in the Old Testament for the Jewish people. Even now, I pray for a time of restoration and clarity.

Today's Truth: For six years you shall sow your land and gather in its yield, but the seventh year you shall let it rest and lie fallow, that the poor of your people may eat; and what they leave the beasts of the field may eat. You shall do likewise with your vineyard, and with your olive orchard. Exodus 23:10

SEPTEMBER 10

DON'T WASTE YOUR LIFE

"Want to meet me for lunch? My treat." This text went out to Hannah, a recent college grad whom I coached when she was in high school. She just happens to be one of the Shindiggler Jrs. who followed me to the mountains and beyond in pursuit of ultrarunning dreams. She is talented and driven, passionate and committed. That is probably why she earned several impressive internships at the State Department in Washington D.C., securing a permanent position with the agency after graduation. She was scheduled to begin in late August.

Was scheduled. Yes, you read that correctly. A day or two before I texted her, Hannah texted me. "Hey Coach T, would you be willing to be a reference for me? I've made some big life changes. I am pursuing missions. We should really get together to run and chat!"

Whoa! I could not wait to hear about this 180-degree turn. But then again, once I thought about it, I should not have been surprised. Hannah was the youngest member of a mission trip to Costa Rica. Traveling with a group of female athletes, Hannah was the boldest of them all, sharing Christ with whoever would listen. We panicked for a slim minute when we lost her momentarily as she boarded a local bus to find someone who needed a Gospel tract.

Over chips and salsa, tacos, and fajitas, I listened intently as Hannah described the working of God in her life. For months, she felt the pull to missions upon reading John Piper's book, "Don't Waste Your Life." Those words and the conviction of the Holy Spirit reduced her to an emotional basket-case. Still, she told no one.

After grappling with the conflict, she finally gave in. She let the State Department know she would not become a government employee. When she gathered her family to share the news, her Grandpa confirmed Hannah's call to service. He revealed his specific prayer over the years for her to commit to missions. The missions pastor at her church is now providing support and guidance as she takes the first steps.

Praise God for young people who listen intently, obey, and refuse to waste their lives.

Today's Truth: And he said to them, "Go into all the world and proclaim the gospel to the whole creation." Mark 16:15

SEPTEMBER 11

FAILURE

Sweat dripped from the player as she battled on the court. Humid conditions had returned, the air thick with moisture. The talented tennis player who we will call Lisa was across the net from a teammate with an entirely different game. Lisa is a power player, every stroke capable of crushing her opponent. When she is "on" nothing can stop her.

But she was not "on" today. In fact, it has been quite a while since I have seen "on" level of play. I can always tell how she is playing by looking at her face and body language. She can be effervescent, exuding joy and delight when hitting that punishing backhand or watching an overhead grab the line and bounce into the stands. She roams the court with the fierceness of a lioness, yet she never loses sight of her prey. It is pure magic to watch her play so well. She makes it look effortless. It should almost be unfair to be that strong of a player.

But lately, she gets inside her own head if she surrenders a series of points. In her Southeast Asian culture, she was shamed if she lost. Her worth was deemed high if she cinched a match and low when she did not. Failure, even in the context of a practice set or drills, was reason enough to be chastised. When you are handed a steady diet of that mentality from childhood to young womanhood, it becomes difficult to push those emotions aside.

But Lisa understands the dilemma and is improving her mental game. She is beginning to view failure, even small ones like a forehand into the net, as a necessary part of the process. Failure must be viewed as an opportunity to learn and grow.

I reminded her today to smile—especially when she is not playing well. There is brain chemistry that changes when the corners of the mouth uplift. And just that little gesture can serve to put things into perspective, prompting a turn-a-round that leads to playing with freedom. But without the difficulty in the first place, the freedom to play well and with joy could never be appreciated.

Weakness and failure truly are part of the process. Embrace it for the opportunity it is.

Today's Truth: For the sake of Christ, then, I am content with weaknesses, insults, hardships, persecutions, and calamities. For when I am weak, then I am strong. 2 Corinthians 12:10

September 12

The molder

I got the idea months ago but finally managed to pull it off today. To say I feel accomplished is a mild understatement.

At the home improvement store I took a seat on the flatbed cart parked conveniently in front of the array of concrete products. Staring at the available packaging, I knew what I did not want. The heavy bags of QuickCrete™ lined the shelves behind me. They were fine for securing posts into the ground, but the gravel in those mixes would not do for my project. I needed smooth concrete.

I finally decided on a twenty-pound bucket of quick-setting concrete intended for repairs. Carrying the twenty pounds was far easier than had I chosen the 40-or-80-pound bags of the QuickCrete! Then, a stop at the Dollar Store completed the shopping trip. There I purchased several round and square plastic food containers of various sizes before heading home. I was excited.

Discovering the bucket contained two ten-pound bags of the concrete mix, I eagerly dumped one bag into a bucket, added water, and stirred until it was a heavy-batter consistency. The plastic containers were paired one inside the other after surfaces were slathered in cooking spray. The smooth concrete was transferred to the larger containers before the smaller ones were inserted into the middle to create a void in the concrete bowl. Then it was time to wait.

With anxious anticipation, I gave the smaller container a wiggle. It popped out with ease. So far so good. Then it was time to turn over the bigger containers. Each one slid gently into my waiting hand. Ah, each of the three concrete masterpeices were perfect! Artificial succulents and dollar store white rocks filled each of cavities. They looked so good. So expensive—but in reality, so inexpensive and easy to make.

I played the role of molder today. Now I have so many other ideas for concrete-fun projects. My imagination and vision will, I hope, help me create all kinds of things. It is wonderful to create, but it is equally as grand to be the one created. I am very thankful that God is continuing to mold and refine me into the creation He intends me to be.

Today's Truth: But who are you, O man, to answer back to God? Will what is molded say to its molder, "Why have you made me like this?" Has the potter no right over the clay, to make out of the same lump one vessel for honorable use and another for dishonorable use? Romans 9: 20, 21

SEPTEMBER 13

INTEGRITY

Wow. Looking at the photo, it was just what I was looking for. A real wood dresser with three drawers and attached mirror. None of our bedrooms needed more furniture, but my plan was to repurpose it for my dining room. For several decades, a white metal bakers rack held the set of dishes I got from my mother when she downsized to apartment living. It stands guard by the front door and with its four shelves, tends to accumulate "stuff" as the dishes simultaneously accumulate layers of dust. That latter problem could be solved by storing away the china in drawers.

Seth and Pam texted me from a tag sale this morning. "Want it? $25.00 dollars. It's over 100 years old."

I called back rather than texting. "Yes! Grab it but make sure we can pick it up this afternoon or tomorrow. I heard him ask the owner who confirmed that the pick-up plan was perfectly fine. Yeah! Seth paid the man the agreed upon price and my mind began planning for the rearrangement of furniture.

Seth and I chatted as we drove the twenty-five miles back into town. Seth greeted the older gentleman with a hearty howdy and big smile. The man responded, looking Seth right in the eye. "It's $125. Right?" He was not smiling but Seth, completely startled, looked at the man in bewilderment.

"What do you mean? You're pulling my leg, aren't you? You said $25. Pam heard it and so did your wife. She even agreed."

"No. I can't let it go for $25. I know that's what I said but my wife says that's too cheap."

Seth, still not sure if he was kidding or not, reminded him again that all four were in on the discussion. He got nowhere. "Well then, I need my $25 back." The man reached for his wallet and pulled out the cash.

As we prepared to leave, the man changed his mind. "I feel really bad. You can have it for that price." I could not get a good read on him, but if he let me have it for $25, his wife would be angry. I did not want that to happen. Then again, maybe he reneged because someone came along and offered him more money. Who knows? I left without the dresser.

If we promise something, we need to follow through. Let your yay be yay, and your nay be nay.

Today's Truth: But above all things, my brethren, swear not, neither by heaven, neither by the earth, neither by any other oath: but let your yea be yea; and your nay, nay; lest ye fall into condemnation. James 5:12 (KJV)

September 14

Connections

An emailed newsletter hit my inbox a few minutes ago. Lesley is a sports ministry chaplain at a large secular university. Under normal circumstances, she would be reporting about their vibrant weekly "huddles" for student athletes, specific opportunities to serve teams by shagging balls, and in-depth huddle discussions for coaches. But not this time.

She reported that she is not yet permitted to step foot on campus and has not been since March. That really changes the normal approach! Fortunately, she can text the girls and conduct Zoom sessions that are Gospel-laden. The same thing goes for the coaches' huddles; all virtual, nothing in person. As beneficial as virtual meetings are, however, there is something to be said for being able to look a person in the eye who is in the same physical room.

I fired back an email asking her additional details about ministry on that campus. In the middle of our responses bouncing back and forth, she reported that her cousin, a student where I serve, was having a hard time finding community outside his dorm. I hope my offer to pick him up on Sundays and take him to church is taken.

It is not surprising that when the opportunity to meet in person is taken away, there is a sense of loss. Consider Paul. Whenever he was imprisoned, he wrote how he missed the fellowship of being with his brothers and sisters. He asked that various Believers be sent to him, even requesting such practical things as a coat to shield him from the cold. In Acts, we see incredible things happen when people of faith gather. In Chapter 4, verse 31, *the place was shaken where they were assembled together; and they were all filled with the Holy Ghost, and they spake the word of God with boldness.*

There is no doubt that God can move in big ways whether or not we are seated next to someone. But if nothing else, these days of quarantine remind us to never take up close and personal encounters for granted.

Today's Truth: When you are assembled in the name of the Lord Jesus and my spirit is present, with the power of our Lord Jesus, 1 Corinthians 5:4

SEPTEMBER 15

STOP ENCOURAGING ME?

Just when I thought it was the right time to cry "uncle" and leave ministry, I get encouraged. What's with that?

It has been a tough couple of months. I suppose the two months sitting at home followed by coming to a campus with posted signs that only students and employees could enter may have messed with my mind. Add to it the rage over social issues bullishly offered up on Facebook and Instagram, and the pervasive paranoia over the Covid-19 monster, and you have a recipe for mental meandering.

I love the work I have been doing in sports ministry for the last six years. I love the campus I serve. I love the coaches with whom I have established relationship, along with the athletes I am privileged to encourage and mentor. But I do not love raising money to support my efforts (which, I suppose, is why I am not very good at it.) The requirement seems like a constant millstone around my neck. And now that Covid's impact has resulted in disappearing donors, this year's budget beginning on the first of this month has been whittled down by over 25%.

Pressure from having to report certain metrics to my superiors every two weeks is not helping. Some of the measures are not applicable to me in my role on this campus. What I do is nothing like what happens on a secular campus. I feel like I am an outlier to my organization. I feel like I do not fit. Therefore, the conclusion I came to a few weeks ago was that I needed to consider shifting gears.

Wouldn't you know it? Just when I was feeling down and out, eight coaches climb aboard and commit to a weekly walk through Proverbs, a study I had written over the summer. Opportunities to speak into the life of some athletes came to me on a silver platter. Several unexpected checks came in the mail that will help bridge the financial gap.

Right when I am trying to feel sorry for myself, God keeps providing encouragement that I am not sure I want. It might be easier to leave than to stay. But now, do I take the encouragements as "signs" pointing to continued ministry efforts for the foreseeable future?

I am not sure what my future holds, but as the old quip goes, I know who holds the future.

Today's Truth: For I know the plans I have for you, declares the LORD, *plans for welfare and not for evil, to give you a future and a hope. Then you will call upon me and come and pray to me, and I will hear you. Jeremiah 29:11, 12*

SEPTEMBER 16

SQUARE PEG. ROUND HOLE.

I am unsure if I am the square peg or the round hole. But regardless, sometimes I just do not fit.

Being an outlier is not a new experience for me. For most of my life I have been different. In junior high and high school, I was one of few athletes who did not smoke, drink, or date. In college, I was the one who married while still juggling school and athletics and whose best friends were guys. After college, I took on a little-known medical profession that was dominated by males. In my 40's I began running long distances, not wanting to fit the "fat, frumpy and 40" expectation. And even now, I feel like I put the "ab" in abnormal. There are simply not a lot of mid-60's gals who "get" me. I am weird (compared to most) in my interests and ambitions.

Over the summer I took on a project to write a fifteen-week study for coaches based on the book of wise sayings, otherwise known as Proverbs. It is now being trialed by a group of eight college coaches. It was written to lead the coaches through the 31 chapters with pregnant pauses at verses with particular application to coaching. The coaches are enjoying the sessions if easy banter and vigorous discussion are valid indicators.

Several weeks ago, it was suggested I share the project with a particular publisher. I was happy to present the material considering this publisher produced my last project. The return message was, "Yes, we are interested." Ah. Music to my ears, particularly since this project, like me, is not what anyone would call "typical."

Today the publisher wrote asking if I would entertain a conversation with another author. "Perhaps this could be a joint project." Though I assured him I was happy to have that conversation, something inside of me stirred. I did not want anyone messing with this project. I had zero interest in a re-write just to fit another's format.

The author and I spoke, both of us concluding that my material was far different. It was trying to pound that square peg into a round hole. We quickly let the publisher know the formats could not be blended. I figured it was the end of the road. Imagine my surprise when he replied, "I have published plenty of other materials that don't fit that format."

Different is not necessarily bad. It's just, well, different.

Today's Truth: **But my servant Caleb, because he has a different spirit and has followed me fully, I will bring into the land into which he went, and his descendants shall possess it. Numbers 14:24**

September 17

The bracelet

There is an addition to my wrist tonight. It's a hospital bracelet. Do not be too concerned. I am not currently in the hospital but spent a good majority of the day inside those walls.

If you have been reading along in this year-long saga, you know I have been whiney about not being able to run very well. It just seems like it is way harder than it should be. So today I had a nuclear stress test to see if there was an obvious problem. Turns out, it looked like the status of my heart was acceptable. But when the cardiologist called to discuss results, there was one more detail to factor in: several syncopal episodes. In plain language, I have passed out several times for no good reason and without warning, the latest incident while reading a magazine two nights ago.

It looks like another cardiac cath is in my near future. But that is perfectly fine by me. I would much rather have a telling picture—literally—of my coronary arteries than have to guess. Seeing the dye flow through (or not flow through) the coronary arteries will provide valuable information. Knowing the truth will make my daily assessment of how I feel much easier. I should have a better idea of how much I can ask my body to do in training.

Perhaps it would be easier to live an effective life if we had a picture of how it really is. It is so easy to form opinions based on culture and popular opinion. But is that truth? Just because most people think in a certain way, does it make it right? Can we make appropriate decisions if we have no confidence that those are based on a sound foundation? I suspect the answer is no.

So where do we get a clear picture of truth? As glib as it sounds, we must go to the Scriptures, the source of absolute truth. It is only when we see the condition of our hearts set against the purity of a holy God that we know what is wrong and what must be done to correct the problem. It is called the Gospel.

God loves us but our sin separates us. So, God sent his Son to die, bearing all our sins past and present so that we can be reconciled and brought into relationship with the Father. See it for yourself.

See yourself in the picture of God's salvation.

Today's Truth: For God so loved the world, that he gave his only Son, that whoever believes in him should not perish but have eternal life. John 3:16

September 18

A changed heart

Fog sunk into the low places, creating an opaque carpet of white. After torrential rain yesterday, the earth was doing its best to absorb the excess moisture. It made the world seems quiet and serene. That feeling continued upon arriving at the trailhead for a morning run on the campus mountain. Mine was the only car in the parking lot, meaning the mountain was mine alone.

After yesterday's stress test, I mentally set a goal to run free, not worrying about my heart. With a sensitivity of 81% for the nuclear stress test, that meant statistically, there was only a 19% chance that a major blockage was missed. The results certainly do not rule out a problem, but somehow, it made me feel more willing to suffer.

As the gravel crunched under my feet, I drew in the scents of wet leaves and noticed the drip-drip of moisture giving up its grip on the branches. Water ran in rivulets down the trail and into the swiftly flowing creek. The predominantly downhill nature of the first two or three miles presented an opportunity to find my long-forgotten rhythm.

Before long, however, I turned off the gravel road onto single track trail, following it to the next gravel road. That road would lead me back up the mountain, the operative word being "up." It was a predominantly two-mile ascent. Last fall, I was able to run every step of it. In the last several months, it was torture to cover the distance, needing to stop and walk every 50 yards. I tried every mental trick in the book to be tough and gritty. I simply could not find a way.

Today, however, something was different. I was tired of being a wus. My goal became to make it a no-walk-run. I was not sure if I could do it but decided to try. "Small steps. Be slow and steady. Make it to that big tree. Come on. I don't care how bad you feel or how hard you are breathing, just do it!" My brain carried on this conversation with my inner self. Despite the suffering—and I did suffer—I accomplished what had been impossible for months. I was not fast, but I did not walk.

What changed? My belief about the condition of my heart changed. And in that, my heart ruled the body. Likewise, when God changes the disposition of our heart, it changes the way we think and the way we behave. A changed heart is a powerful thing.

Today's Truth: But thanks be to God, that you who were once slaves of sin have become obedient from the heart to the standard of teaching to which you were committed, Romans 6:17

SEPTEMBER 19

CLEAN THE INSIDE AND OUT

There is nothing like anticipating dinner guests that motivates me to clean. From the moment I got up until shortly before our guests arrived, it was non-top action.

A bumper crop of garden vegetables—bags of peppers, okra, and tomatoes—claimed prime territory inside the upright freezer. There was no more room. Something had to be done. But the kitchen's freezer was a grand mess as well. Out came all the contents before I began the thawing and chipping away at the built-up ice. After a long and messy process, all the food was returned to the shelves in an orderly fashion. OK, then. Check off one box on the to-do list.

Then it was time to prepare food for the meal and clean up the resulting mayhem. That meant vacuuming and giving all the surfaces a good wipe down. But I was not done. Living in the country, I think we must have more than our fair share of spiders given the vast number of cobwebs in the corners and wrapped around every chair leg in the house. Drives me crazy! Of course, it was impossible to leave them there. Out came the damp rag to dispose of those annoying, ever-present webs.

When the bathrooms got cleaned and the table was set, it was time to turn my attention to the details. Lamps on and lighting bright. The scented wax melting pot began to simmer. Glasses were checked for spots and dried-on dishwasher gunk. The furniture and counters got a dose of lemon-scented polish, and the mish-mosh of accumulated "stuff" on the dormant wood stove was either relocated or thrown out. Then it was time to sit, breath, and wait for our company.

Isn't it amazing how inclined we are to do a great job of cleaning up those things visible to other people? Yes, the place looked decent when Ken and Liz walked in. But they did not see the room that served as the "dump" for all that relocated "stuff."

I think we tend to clean up our own selves, hoping that people see only the squeaky-clean, presentable exterior. It might be a better idea to focus first on our insides, those thoughts and actions that we try to hide. If the inside is cleaned up, the outside will follow.

Today's Truth: Woe to you, scribes and Pharisees, hypocrites! For you clean the outside of the cup and the plate, but inside they are full of greed and self-indulgence. You blind Pharisee! First clean the inside of the cup and the plate, that the outside also may be clean. Matthew 23:25, 26

September 20

As if?

The sign on the church read: "Pray as if everything depended on God." As if? Seriously?

Maybe it was intended as a tongue-in-cheek quip. Maybe the intent was to shock people into praying more fervently and with more frequency. But the theology is flawed.

The arguments regarding the free will of man and the sovereignty of God probably started right after Adam and Eve decided to take a giant chomp out of the forbidden fruit. Shortly thereafter, I suppose, were heated discussions questioning if God changed his mind because of the way they prayed. Tough questions to answer, but at least they had something to talk about once they got the boot from the Garden.

I have no intention of answering these mind-blowing queries. But I am compelled to stand by the proposition that everything does depend on God. His will is his and his alone. He does not make his decisions based on knowing what we will do or not do. But what does that truth mean to me right now?

It means that though I am confident God has already orchestrated my future, I will pray hard that he gives me insight into what I am supposed to do with my life in the next six months. It means that in the process I will seek wise counsel. I will investigate various opportunities. I will write out lists of pros and cons. And in the end, I will make my decision and be confident that God ordained it because I asked him to lead.

It means I will pray that God grants me a healthy body despite some of my current physical challenges. It means that while I pray, I will seek competent medical advice and follow it. It means that I will not intentionally obsess or worry about the what ifs.

It is our duty to pray because God commanded it. I do not have to understand how it may or may not influence the Father. But it is God's duty to have His way because He is, well, God. That's what He does.

So yes, I will pray because I know that it all depends on God.

Today's Truth: First of all, then, I urge that supplications, prayers, intercessions, and thanksgivings be made for all people, 1 Timothy 2:1

September 21

Laugh out loud

My gut still hurts. I could not stop laughing. Neither could Gary, our two grown sons, and their better halfs. The house echoed with raucous howling that came and went in waves. And of the six sets of eyes in the room, not one was without tears of sheer merriment. It was A.W.E.S.O.M.E.

McKinley's birthday, Caleb's partner in crime, was earlier in the month. However, despite valiant efforts to schedule a family dinner, it had to be rescheduled twice. This evening was finally a go. After dinner we lingered around the table, catching up on life. Soon we moved to the kitchen where we shared in what has become a tradition for McKinley's birthday: sugar cookie decorating. Out from the freezer came the batch of cut-out cookies in the fall shapes of leaves that I had made several weeks prior. Then came the icing and the sprinkles in neon pink and electric blue. (I thought I had gold and silver and yellow sprinkles in the cupboard, but I thought wrong.) We worked together and gobbled down the sweet treats.

With the sugar coursing through our veins, the pump was primed for a good time. Seth pulled out the old DVD player and popped in a tape from the first four years of his life. Of course, Caleb, being the older brother, was also prominently featured in the videos. It was nothing short of hysterical. From the early 90's fashion choices to the antics of the kids, we rolled with laughter, tears streaming down our faces.

In one Christmas recording, we had a few "Ahhhhh" moments when my mother and Gary's mom and dad showed up on the footage. Such sweet memories hearing their voices and watching them open gifts, delighted to have family all together.

But the laughter was the best. Tonight was good for me, really, really good. I have not laughed that hard and long for a very long time. To have our grown sons and their wives together in the living room, enjoying the time together did my heart a world of good. I am so very thankful God equipped us with the ability to show emotion; to laugh and express joy.

Today's Truth: A joyful heart is good medicine, but a crushed spirit dries up the bones. Proverbs 17:22

September 22

Grand fails

I am hesitant to admit that I sometimes flick on the TV "just because." Tonight was one such night. A late arrival home from work, cleaning out the refrigerator and giving the leftovers a make-over was par for the course. Once all the bits and pieces of dinner united into a presentable form, we took our plates and sat on the couch. The channel, one of the few pulled in with an antenna, is a 24/7 channel of great feats and great fails. Just think Funniest Home Videos without narration.

My favorite thing to watch are the mind-boggling exploits of enormously talented people. The demonstration of strength, balance, coordination, and kinesthetic sense amazes. Little kids to grown men and women. Such incredible acts.

But then there are the miserable fails. I cannot tell you how many people are shown to walk out their front door and wipe out on icy steps. Or the parkour runners who over-rotate a jump only to faceplant into a concrete wall. There are skateboarders who crash and mountain bikers that launch themselves, much like the Roadrunner, into rocks. No one can watch without shouting "oohs and ahhs," wondering how many bones broke or how much blood was lost because of the great misfortunes.

My fails may not be as spectacular, but there have been many. Yes, there have been physical fails, especially when I was a gymnast about a million years ago. A grand leap on (and then off) the balance beam resulting in broken ribs immediately comes to mind. That sure hurt. But there were plenty of other types of fails.

I fail when I have an unrepentant, bad attitude toward another. I fail when my words are harsh. I fail when I am lazy and unproductive. I fail when fear rules instead of trust. I fail when I refuse to obey God. I fail when I think my way is better than God's way. I fail when I do not listen intently and learn. I fail when I do not pursue wisdom. But in all my failure, there is grace and mercy and a boatload of second (and third, and fourth. . .) chances.

Today's Truth: My flesh and my heart may fail, but God is the strength of my heart and my portion forever. Psalm 73:26

September 23

Personal Advertising

The predominantly black t-shirt with cut off sleeves pictured Taylor Swift. Her face was front and center. It was apparently a souvenir from the RED concert tour. The young woman who bore this shirt was a college student, likely eighteen or nineteen years old. She must be impressed with the superstar performer.

Then there were kids sporting shirts bearing the colors and emblems of soccer clubs, football teams and high school clubs. I think it is safe to assume they hold their teams as favorites. They must be fans.

In the building where I work, which is strictly for NCAA Division 1 athletes, administrators, and athletic support staff, there is a constant reminder that everyone represents something higher than themselves. These athletes, male and female, have gear that covers from the top of their heads to the bottoms of their feet. In addition to the university logo, hats, coats, shorts, leggings, warm-ups, shoes, and even socks all bear the well-known Nike™ symbol. In fact, no gear from a Nike-competitor is permissible for these athletes. They stride the hallways in our school colors, clothing and backpacks displaying prominently the school's logo and team name. There is little doubt who they represent.

You can tell a lot about who or what someone values by looking at what they advertise. Some shirts, for example are vile and vulgar. It is a pretty good guess that the person wearing the shirt is likely not a conservative, churchgoing, on fire-for-God Christian. But I could be wrong.

Just because someone wears a "John 3:16" or "God is Awesome" t-shirt does not necessarily mean they have a steadfast relationship with the Savior. It could be that their "I am Christian" shirt is worn to make everyone think they have it all together. But here again, I could be wrong.

The moral of the story is that regardless of our intentions, we are walking advertisements for what and who we represent. People around us will make judgments, fair or not, about what we wear. Even more so, however, is that people will make judgments if what we do is *not* consistent with what we say. We should be careful to advertise our faith by our actions and attitudes because that is the best marketing plan possible to advance the Kingdom of God.

Today's Truth: For the Lord sees not as man sees: man looks on the outward appearance, but the Lord looks on the heart. 1 Samuel 16:7

September 24

The ring

"That's odd," I thought to myself. I was on the tennis courts with the team when I stuck my hand deep inside my pocket. There was something hard and round. About the only thing that makes it into my pockets are tissues, candy, and lip balm. This was different.

I pulled out a silver "True love waits" ring. How in the world? Am I that senile? There was absolutely nothing in the memory banks about putting a ring into that pocket. It was obviously not mine, but how did it get there? None of the tennis players knew anything about it.

This afternoon at volleyball practice, I asked the question as the girls huddled around to hear Coach's instruction. "May I make a PSA announcement?" I inquired. With permission granted, I posed the question. "Does this ring look familiar to anyone? I found it in my pocket but have no earthly idea how it got there."

Aspen, who happened to be standing beside me responded, "It's mine," and slipped it on her finger. I volunteered to hold onto it (along with her bracelet), but Coach stepped in.

"Why don't you all put your earrings and jewelry in your bags. We don't want anyone to get a finger or earlobe yanked off." The girls scattered to do as instructed.

When Aspen returned, I asked her when she gave me the ring. Her answer? Yesterday. Seriously? I have no recollection. None. "Oh, I didn't really give it to you. I saw you had a pocket that was open and just slipped it in there. I forgot to ask for it back after practice."

"You have a future as a pick-pocket," I quipped. I had no knowledge of how or when she transferred that ring to my jacket. I suppose if I had paid better attention, been more alert, I might have picked up on the move.

God has a habit of sneaking things into our lives when we least expect it. We call those things blessings. Blessings are gifts from God, so undeserved and unanticipated, but such a demonstration of his goodness and generosity.

Today's Truth: Blessed be the God and Father of our Lord Jesus Christ, who has blessed us in Christ with every spiritual blessing in the heavenly places, Ephesians 1:3

SEPTEMBER 25

WHAT A PAIN

I dread writing on this subject because I feel like a whiner-heimer. I am not sure that whiner-heimer is a real term, but to me it has always meant "one who whines way too much." I have written so many times of my slug-like running, continuing cardiac story, and the number the evil statins have done to my muscles and joints. I fear that if I bring up another body part, I will lose all credibility.

But here goes. Something happened to my knee a few weeks ago when I took a friend on a hike in the mountains. We were casually walking—not running—down the trail when I stepped on a rock making my left ankle give way. I caught myself on a tree but felt something pull in my right knee. There was no swelling at all. But the pain at the top of my knee and the bottom of my quad was unlenting once we got back to the car. Since then, I can walk okay, but going up and down stairs is a challenge. Running down hill is hugely problematic, and even pushing my foot into my shoe causes a great deal of pain. An undeniable ache develops when I drive, to the point of making me nauseous.

This frustrates me to no end. It is not like I have terminal cancer or need to have a leg amputated. But why now? Why do I have to contend with what I suspect is a significant injury on top of everything else? It's not fair, right?

Waa, Waa, Waa. What a baby I am. My grown-up self knows that despite the unfortunate knee issue, I have several options in dealing with the pain. 1) Be mad about it, which accomplishes nothing 2) Ignore the pain as much as possible and carry on, which could cause additional injury 3) Give it a good rest and pray it heals 4) Wrap and support the knee, finding alternative activity to build fitness and avoid impact.

Some of these options are better than the others. I have decided to give #4 a try for a few days. But I wonder if there is a broader principle in dealing with pain; the pain of loss, the pain of injured relationships, the pain of significant suffering.

We need to see pain as a convex lens to focus our attention, to embrace the challenge and find smart solutions. To use the pain as a door to growth and maturity. Though easier said than done, it is worth the effort.

Today's Truth: But I am afflicted and in pain; let your salvation, O God, set me on high! Psalm 69:29

September 26

Treasures in the Junk

"What have we gotten ourselves into?" I thought to myself, looking at the mounds of "stuff." Back in August, we cleaned out my mother's room. It was challenging but was confined to only one room. This time is different.

We are dipping our toes in the waters of offering a service to clean out people's attics, basements, and entire houses. We landed our first job, were given the keys to the house, and hit it hard early this morning. Where to start? The owner of the home is a 92-year-old woman who has outlived her three children and her husband. She is in poor health and was recently moved into a facility. Now her power of attorney needs everything gone. Quickly. In a week to ten days.

Every dish was in the cabinets. The bed covers were thrown back as if someone had just gotten out of bed. Food was in the cupboards and meat in the freezer. Household items lined shelves in the basement. Furniture, appliances, towels, knick-knacks, cleaning supplies. Everything needs to be sold, given away, or discarded.

We jumped in with two feet, each of us tackling a different area. Some of what we found was junk, destined only for big, black trash bags. But among the piles and stacks, we found quite a few things that have value. After researching an interesting piece of furniture tucked away in basement corner, we found it is worth about $1500. Imagine that! The dirt and grime covering the surfaces led us to believe the piece was of marginal value. We assumed wrong.

I wonder how often we miss seeing the value in people around us. Maybe we only see the messy exterior and assume that person has little value. Perhaps the other person does not think like us or talk like us. We make assumptions which may not be true.

If we need an example of seeing value, consider the Father. Despite our ugliness, He sees us as redeemable. He offers grace and mercy regardless of what we look like inside and out. He takes the ugly and makes it beautiful.

Today's Truth: Do not let your adorning be external—the braiding of hair and the putting on of gold jewelry, or the clothing you wear— but let your adorning be the hidden person of the heart with the imperishable beauty of a gentle and quiet spirit, which in God's sight is very precious. 1 Peter 3: 3, 4

SEPTEMBER 27

THE GRAND GIVE-AWAY

It was not the way we normally spend our Sundays. In fact, I do not recall any Sunday in my entire life even close to this one. But sometimes, ya gotta do what ya gotta do.

Assuming your short-term memory is intact, you will recall that I wrote yesterday of our major rummage through a house to clear it of all the contents. We called in some help, my sister-in-law and her husband. Joy has expertise in all things glassware and dishes, familiar with prices since she wheels and deals in that arena. She proved invaluable in pricing the old Pyrex and Fire King bowls and cookware. There were several odd, and quite frankly, ugly ceramics that turned out to be worth $80 - $100 each. Those will be sold on-line. But perhaps the most surprising discovery was an old 1952 book, "The Coon Hunters Handbook." We found one online that sold for $800! It went directly into the protective custody of my car to be sold later.

In the meantime, we sold a whole bunch of stuff in the "everything has to go" yard sale. The more someone bought, the better the prices we offered. There are still piles of things, but we are quite pleased with the progress.

While we were packing up for the day, three teenage boys came along on their bikes, slowing down by the driveway to look. Engaging with them, I found out they were moving to a bigger house and needed to furnish it. I suggested they go get their Mom, which they did. Soon, she drove up and thus began the process. "So, you have three boys?" I asked with a smile.

"Actually, I have five boys and four girls." I was floored! She shared her story of six natural- born kids and three they were fostering. They had been in a three-bedroom, one bathroom house for ten years. They needed more room, bought a much larger house, and will close in November. The more she talked, the more I was convinced she was a Believer. We went from room to room, finding things she could use. I cleaned out the food pantry and gave it all to her. She took kitchenware to stock the second kitchen that is in the new house's basement. By the time we finished, she and her husband, who had joined her, made three or four trips to their house and back again. "First the Lord gave us a perfect house when we weren't even looking. Now today, you are an answer to prayer and a huge blessing! Thank you so much for your kindness!"

Giving stuff away is way more fun than keeping it for myself.

Today's Truth: In all things I have shown you that by working hard in this way we must help the weak and remember the words of the Lord Jesus, how he himself said, 'It is more blessed to give than to receive.' Acts 20:25

September 28

What to Say

Do you ever think about all the words you say during a day—and HOW you say them? Honestly, I am not always analyzing my speech word for word. I simply have conversation as it comes along. But today? Today I am desperately trying to speak well while refraining from being overly obsessed with how I might be perceived.

This is the situation. The university I serve has a fantastic video production group for athletics. Dubbed "Game On," they purpose to show interesting sports-related human-interest stories that ultimately become God-focused narratives. In a bizarre series of events, one of the voices of "Game On," Matt Warner, had his Mother ask "Do you know Rebekah Trittipoe? She works there at Liberty." She apparently had run across a story about me. Hence, Matt started to investigate.

We got together last week to discuss what a story on sports ministry might look like. The video package will include one-on-one interviews as well as clips from various practices I attend. Additionally, footage from a coaches Bible study is also slated for coverage.

It all began this morning at that Proverbs Bible study. With a live mic clipped to my jacket and the camera guy shooting from various angles, I was aware that everything—and I mean everything—I said was being recorded. Then it was on to volleyball practice. Still, I was self-conscious of my words, endlessly shifting my body positions when listening to Coach speak and waiting for court action to resume. Tomorrow they film while I am on the courts with the tennis team.

This experience demonstrates the need to intentionally choose my words whether or not the mic is on and cameras are rolling. Today, because I did not want to come across as a blubbering fool, I was more thoughtful in my speech. That is probably a good daily habit to develop. I will be less likely to offend and more likely to encourage by allowing my speech to *always be gracious, seasoned with salt, so that you may know how you ought to answer each person* (Colossians 4:6).

Today's Truth: Let the words of my mouth and the meditation of my heart be acceptable in your sight, O Lord, my rock and my redeemer. Psalm 19:14

SEPTEMBER 29

FADED PHOTOGRAPHS

The experiment continued tonight. Our family's foray into the world of clearing out houses took another turn. Sunday was the big day for selling. Tonight, Monday, was advertised as a huge price reduction on the furniture still up for grabs. What we did not advertise was that all the small stuff, the housewares, trinkets, dishes, and about anything else you could pick up and carry off, was free! People left with armfuls at our encouragement. Everything they took from the house meant less for us to deal with.

But amid the mayhem, Gary received a message from a woman claiming it was extremely important to speak with him. He called back to find the woman desperate, almost beside herself. It turned out she was a niece of the woman whose belonging we were selling or giving away. "There was a box of pictures. That was our family heritage. Have you found them?" she inquired. "The lawyer was supposed to notify us when the house was going to be cleaned out. He did not."

I had found them this past weekend, but they ended up in a trash bag that was now getting rained upon. I felt bad when I threw those recorded memories out. But with the owner on her death bed and not being aware there were any family members who cared, there was no other recourse.

With this new-found information, I rummaged through the mountain of accumulated trash bags. I was hopeful but kept coming up empty. However, deep inside one bag filled with old bits of fabric, there they were: several framed pictures and a bag of faded photographs of days gone by. It was a relief to know this woman's legacy was not destined for the landfill.

The niece and her husband were delighted. "You are so kind. Thank you very much. I am so glad to have these pictures!" We wondered around the house, chatting about this and that. There were several things she decided to take including the china, some art that had been on the walls, and a book or two. They left knowing they preserved a little piece of family history.

Digging through trash in the rain was inconvenient and messy. But I am glad I did. Perhaps it is those little acts of kindness that can be the most effective demonstration of our love for Christ and service to others.

Today's Truth: Whoever pursues righteousness and kindness will find life, righteousness, and honor. Proverbs 21:21

September 30

Rights and responsibilities

Driving onto or walking across campus, the scene is the same. Students everywhere, most peering into their phones as if nothing else mattered. The rest of them? They have earbuds wedged into their ears, oblivious to their surroundings. They mosey along the sidewalks, backpacks strapped on for the journey. When they approach an intersection or crosswalk across a traffic circle, few pause to look up and around. Without breaking their slow, deliberate pace, they enter the zone for cars and busses, meandering to the other side. They do not seem worried for their safety. Afterall, it is a state law that cars must yield to pedestrians. The walker has the right of way.

But does the walker also have a responsibility? Sure, if Pete the Pedestrian gets hit while in the crosswalk, the driver of the vehicle will undoubtedly be charged even if the pedestrian was careless. But should the pedestrian bear some responsibility for their actions? I think so.

Just because we have a right to do something, in this case, cross the street with the law on our side, does not mean we should not be thoughtful. Perhaps we would be better citizens if we became more aware of our surroundings. When we see a car approaching, wait to make sure they are slowing. Venture into the roadway only when we make eye contact with the driver to confirm his intention to let us pass. And when we do take that first step, walk briskly out of respect for the person in the vehicle that was required to stop. It is simply a matter of courtesy.

I suggest that many of our societal problems stem from a lack of courtesy, a lack of cooperation, and a self-centeredness that influences our actions. Too often, it becomes all about "me" rather than "you." As Believers, we have certain rights, but we have far more responsibilities. These are the "ought to's." We have the right to be called the Sons of God, but we ought to—we have the responsibility to—live like a son or daughter of the Most High.

Today's Truth: Finally, then, brothers, we ask and urge you in the Lord Jesus, that as you received from us how you ought to walk and to please God, just as you are doing, that you do so more and more. 1 Thessalonians 4:1

OCTOBER 1

THE VALUE OF A PICTURE

"A picture is worth a thousand words." It is a common quip and is especially important if you are a visual learner. Hand a visual learner pages of instructions and you might cause them to pull out a sword and promptly fall on it. But provide a clear diagram to those same people and you will have them leaping for joy. That picture registers in the brain, providing clear guidance for next steps.

Today I was able to visualize a condition that should provide great direction for the future. I had my second left heart catheterization and implantation of a loop recorder (used to monitor my heart rhythm for the next three years). My inability to run and train well prompted this procedure. The angina I felt before last year's stent had returned. On top of that, several syncopal events over the last couple years, and as recent as two weeks ago, led to the decision about the loop recorder. Despite the invasiveness of both procedures, I eagerly consented. I needed to see the dye coursing through the heart's arteries for myself. If the stent was open and no other blockages existed, there was no reason for me to fear an imminent heart attack.

The sedation was light in the cath lab, allowing me to watch much of the procedure on the monitors. Sure enough, the stent was wide open and though there were four other areas of blockages, they were insignificant at 10 − 30%. This knowledge should help me navigate my training plans, knowing that when it feels tough, it is not because of any big, bad stenosis.

The cath accomplished, the electrophysiologist came to surgically implant the loop recorder in my left chest. This tiny piece of incredible technology, about the size of a slim thumb drive, will look for abnormalities in my heart rhythm. It then transmits that data via cellular signal to the cardiologist who can make the proper judgment and form treatment options.

I now know there is nothing to worry about in terms of dangerous blockages. I am also confident that should I have rhythm issues, those can be identified and treated for the next three years, which is the life of the battery.

The fact is, when we have confidence in the truth, we live differently. Know the truth. Be confident. Live boldly.

Today's Truth: And most of the brothers, having become confident in the Lord by my imprisonment, are much more bold to speak the word without fear. Philippians 1:41

October 2

The hidden things

It is a dangerous writing strategy to begin with "I." "I" is so egocentric. "I" is so self-serving. But in this case, the story is hard to tell without using "I." Humblest apologies in advance if these stories seem to be all about me. They are not intended to be that way.

The events taking place yesterday at the hospital occurred because the medical team taking care of me was in search of the reasons behind my symptoms, a mystery hidden at this point. The heart cath successfully revealed the stent is open and the rest of the coronaries are in pretty good shape. Check that off the list. Whether or not the loop recorder will provide telling insight is yet to be determined. But among the myriad of lab tests that were run, several indices in the complete blood count prompted another battery of tests.

Hidden among the results was a clue that could prove helpful. Sparing you the hematologic details, it appears I have developed a hypochromic microcytic condition. My ferritin levels are also very low. Could it be that addressing this problem with an intake of iron will solve my sluggish running? A college runner, Noel, experienced the same thing a few years ago. Iron supplementation made a world of difference, taking her from a lethargic twenty-minute 5K to a 16:28! If I could walk up the steps without getting winded, I think I would be happy.

Answers we search for are often hidden deep, requiring serious digging. Digging requires time, effort, and hard work. It takes a commitment to carry on and persevere even when the going gets tough. But when you find the answer, that wonderful hidden treasure, it sure is worth it

Keep searching. Keep digging. In Christ *are hidden all the treasures of wisdom and knowledge* (Colossians 2:3).

Today's Truth: yes, if you call out for insight and raise your voice for understanding, if you seek it like silver and search for it as for hidden treasures, then you will understand the fear of the LORD *and find the knowledge of God. Proverbs 2:3-5*

OCTOBER 3

NESTING 101

Memories of being very pregnant came flooding back. I'm pretty sure what I experienced decades ago is like the feelings of millions of women about to pop out a kid from their loins. That nesting syndrome kicks into high gear to prepare the house for the child's homecoming. The fur flies as floors are swept, blinds cleaned, loads of wash run through, and organizational skills exhibited that would put HGTVer's to shame. Rooms are purged of items past their state of usefulness to make room for everything baby. This process usually begins in the last couple months of waiting.

To be sure, I am not pregnant (!) but acted the part today. From the time of waking until well past dark, bags of trash expanded nearly beyond their capacity limits. The washer and dryer ran constantly with bedding, curtains, and mounds of towels we confiscated from the house we emptied. The sweeper sucked up so much dirt, hair, and random grime it had to be emptied twice. I spritzed cleaning products, dragged mops across the floors, and scrubbed the tub. Every drawer in the bathroom was dumped out, purged, and re-organized, so much so that there was empty space. As I now type, our bedroom and the bathroom are gloriously spotless.

The obvious question is, "Why?" I admit that I occasionally enter a cleaning frenzy for no good reason. But this time, there is a reason. I am at the cusp of a very different period in my ministry. This next week I will be at a ministry conference the entire week. But the four weeks after that I will be taking a thirty-day sabbatical. This is an offering by my organization that after six years of service, a period of rest (with pay) is available. Based on the Old Testament practice of a sabbatical year every six years, the purpose is renewal and restoration.

To say I am looking forward to this time is an understatement. I have a lot of thinking and praying to do about God's plans for my future. I cannot do my best work amid a mess. Hence, today was the day to get my physical house in order so that my heart can be prepared for purging the accumulated junk and scrubbed clean.

Today's Truth: Create in me a clean heart, O God, and renew a right spirit within me. Psalm 51:10

October 4

Just sing

A song spontaneously erupted. The small child snuggled next to me began an original tune: "It is hunting season. It is hunting season…" The little ditty mimicked a phone conversation she was overhearing between her grandpa and his hunting buddy. It was not the first time the child composer came up with an original tune and lyric. There always seems to be a song in her heart.

Yesterday Addyson, her daddy and his wife went exploring at the drive-through Safari Park. I was not there but saw the pictures and videos, of which there were many. Giraffes, llamas, and zebras made the drive exciting, especially the llamas with their aggressive quest for food. Running after cars to find the open window, they eagerly stuck their heads into the interior to munch a bunch of animal treats. It looked like a lot of fun for my three humans and even more so for the creatures.

After supper tonight, Pam shared a video of driving slowly through the wooded park, Addyson was hanging out the window, arms stretched wide. As the warm autumn breeze ruffled her hair, you could tell Addy was basking in the moment. Her contentment and joy could not be contained. Singing to no one in particular, the song lifted to the sky: "The first day of fall is looking to be just like fall. The first day of fall the leaves turn colors. The first day of fall is looking to be just like fall…" Her smile told the story. Her simple song revealed her delight.

Addy is never without a song. Music wells up inside of her until she has no recourse but to let it out. The lyrics are never complicated, but they reveal the nature of the moment. Without fear or hesitation, Addyson spontaneously offers her gift of song to anyone within range, even if that happens to be a playhouse full of dolls.

This five-year old's passion for music should serve as an example to us. Sing to the Lord a new song. Sing with joy. Sing praises. Sing of his strength. Sing of his steadfastness. Sing of the glory of his name. Sing of justice. Just sing.

Today's Truth: My heart is steadfast, O God, my heart is steadfast! I will sing and make melody! Psalm 57:7

OCTOBER 5

SWEET SMELL OF MANURE

Arriving at the conference right on cue, I donned my mask and went into the hotel complex to start the check-in process. The event is a yearly regional ministry conference that takes place each October. I look forward to interacting with colleagues I have little chance of seeing otherwise. But this year I find myself ambivalent and confused. The university I serve is pleased with the job I am doing, but the decision-makers have taken the initial steps to shift all sports ministry in-house. Hence, my position as an outside ministry is vulnerable.

With thoughts running rampant, I needed to get out and go. Conveniently, a "rails-to trails" path runs behind the hotel. It extends for about two and a half miles in one direction, is flat as a pancake, and lined with crushed gravel. With footing so ideal, running becomes mindless, giving room for ideas, thoughts, and prayers to swirl.

The easy path also gives ample opportunity to experience the sights and sounds of country living. Surrounding the sports complex and hotel are beautiful farms. An Amish plow was turning up the soil, drawn by five rugged horses bridled together. It was a sight for the senses—as was a powerful smell about halfway down the path. Manure; a stinky, nose-hair curling scent.

In my odd stream of consciousness, I wondered about the smells Noah had to contend with on the ark. With two of every kind of animal and the excrement of eight humans, what did they do with the pile of poo? I guess they could have thrown it overboard, but there were no windows save the one to let the bird come and go as it looked for land. Did God give them instructions to build a ventilation system into the impressive monster of a ship or did they simply get used to the stench? I doubt we will ever know, and realistically, it would not change anything to gain that piece of trivia.

What does matter is to clearly understand what God considers as a stench in His own nostrils. It is sin. It is unrighteousness. But what is the other side of the coin? What is pleasing to God and His people? The answer is unselfishness and obedience. Paul experiences that reality when he received from the Philippians a care package while in prison. That simple act was anything but the stench of manure. It was a fragrant offering.

Today's Truth: I have received full payment, and more. I am well supplied, having received from Epaphroditus the gifts you sent, a fragrant offering, a sacrifice acceptable and pleasing to God. Philippians 4:18

October 6

Clarity

Out the door, down the hallway, into the stairwell, and along the corridor to the food court. The alluring smell of bacon was impossible to deny. My salivary glands kicked into overdrive. I gathered the rest of my breakfast onto the tray and carried it to the balcony area. Sitting down, I waited for my friends to arrive.

Glancing around, my eyes fell on the two-story wall of windows. At first, I thought they were treated with a privacy coating. But not so. The fog outside was so dense there was nothing to see. It was a thick wall of whiteness.

At that point, I wished I had gotten up early enough to run. Thick fog gives me the sense of being alone. I feel embraced and safe in that surreal state of being surrounded by the lowest of clouds. I'm not sure why I like it so much. Maybe its because I am an introvert, comfortable going it alone. But alas, it was only mine to speculate how wonderful it would have been because within a few hours, the sun came out and the fog disappeared.

Nevertheless, after the conclusion of dinner and the evening meeting, I knew I had to escape for my solo time. Strapping on a waist light, I headed for the trail behind the hotel. I had the whole thing to myself. Being a rails-to-trail pathway, the footing was easy; fine cinder with very few divots on which to stumble. I ran with the light on the lowest setting, heading for the terminus several miles away.

After touching the sign at the far end, I retraced my steps and paused on the only bench along the way. Turning off my light, the babbling of the nearby creek and cacophony of creature noises seemed amplified. I sat for a spell, thinking, and praying for clarity. Amazingly, the longer I tarried, the more acutely I could see despite the dark sky. My eyes adjusted enough to make out the trail's edges and surface. So much so, I was able to run with a level of security without the light. Still, it was easier going with the beam turned on.

I have been for praying for clarity in my professional future. To predict what God has assigned me to do in six months is not possible. But little by little, as my eyes adjust to the uncertain darkness, I am confident God will continue to guide, at some point providing a bright light to make the way obvious. But until then, I must walk by faith and not by sight.

Today's Truth: Your word is a lamp to my feet and a light to my path. Psalm 119:105

OCTOBER 7

EVEN THE STRONG LION

Picture this. You are in the wide-open African savannah. Mountains rise across the plains, tall, wispy grass swaying as the breezes blow across the hot, dry landscape between here and there. A herd of elephants gather to the right, gazelles bound across the open land with antelope and barbary stags grazing nearby. Down by the watering hole, hippos wallow in the mud to fend off the heat, and crocodiles maintain their submarined pose in hopes of capturing unsuspecting prey.

But across the way is that pride of lions laying in the shade of a particularly large baobab tree. The old wise males seem oblivious to the antics of the juvenile lion cubs, while the lionesses maintain constant vigil. The lions are near the top of the predator ladder, few other animals being much of a threat. The young lions have learned their hunting skills from the older lions. Speed and agility play in their favor. More times than not, a prowling cat brings home supper.

But there are times when the pride goes hungry. The chased gazelle leaps out of harms' way at the last minute, the antelopes escape across the river, or the lion simply gets weary in the chase. There is no meal. Even the strong and swift fail from time to time.

Psalm 34 was read aloud today in a session with my like-minded ministry partners. The Psalm begins: *I will praise the* LORD *at all times. I will constantly speak his praises. I will boast only in the* LORD*; let all who are helpless take heart. Come, let us tell of the* LORD*'s greatness; let us exalt his name together.* The writer goes on to brag of the Lord's providence and protection; how He calms our fears, extends joy, protects, and provides.

And then comes a comparison. *Even strong young lions go hungry. . .* I guess the lion is not perfect all the time. The lion runs into hard times. But, and this is very important, *those who trust in the Lord will lack no good thing.* That means always. Every time. No misses—unless God deems the miss to be a good thing. This should give us confidence that no matter our strength or outcome, we can fully trust God to not withhold what is best for us in the moment.

Today's Truth: Even strong young lions sometimes go hungry, but those who trust in the LORD *will lack no good thing. Psalm 34:10*

OCTOBER 8

HIDDEN TREASURES

Don't you just love it when you find a treasure? Sure, sometimes the item is hidden away, which makes it fun to experience the joy of random finds. But other times, the treasure is hidden in plain sight. Such was the case of my newly acquired Hoosier cabinet.

Remember when I referenced cleaning out a house a week or two ago? We were able to sell or give away everything but a few items, deciding to keep them for ourselves. The Hoosier cabinet did not look like anything special at first glance. It was in the workshop area of the basement, piled high with buckets of bolts, light fixtures, and miscellaneous junk. It was so non-descript that we failed to realize it had intrinsic value the first few times we went into the house. But once we cleared away the mess, we saw a hint of its past beauty and future potential.

This wooden piece came into the house tonight. I scrubbed it down with oil soap before rubbing in a light coating of furniture polish. Rather than make the cabinet shiny and new, it brought out the beautiful patina of the early 1800's wood. I transferred the dishes brought from my Mother's house to the cabinet, tucking them away behind closed doors. The baker's rack on which they had been stored was transferred outside to begin a new role as a garden potting bench. Everything else in the dining room and sitting area was deep cleaned and organized. A vintage metal potato chip is now a perfect place for potted flowers, and an old-fashioned red step stool is home for another potted plant. I get to appreciate how old becomes new.

Matthew records many parables of Jesus. In chapter 1, he tells of the excitement a man feels when he unexpectedly finds a hidden treasure in a field. Later, he likens a scribe writing Scripture to a homeowner who puts to use both old and new possessions. In both cases, there is value in the old and the new. But how much better is it to discover the beauty of truth hidden in the Holy Scriptures?

Today's Truth: And he said to them, "Therefore every scribe who has been trained for the kingdom of heaven is like a master of a house, who brings out of his treasure what is new and what is old." Matthew 13:52

OCTOBER 9

CHOOSING TO TRUST

With the ministry conference over and last night spent in my own bed, I looked forward to getting back to my normal routine. That meant rising early and driving to the trail head near campus to run before diving into the activities of the day. So that is exactly what happened--except for the fact that absolutely nothing beyond the run went as predicted.

I wanted to use this day to catch up on tasks and visit with the tennis, volleyball, and basketball teams. My freshly showered self ran into one of the volleyballers who informed me there was no practice. It was their off day. Bummer. I really wanted to spend time with them. Regardless, my next move was to walk down the hill to the tennis courts to joyfully serve as the ball-pickerupper for the girls with the racquets. Much to my surprise, the courts were empty save for a few college students who demonstrated no talent for tennis. Where could the entire tennis team be? I was 0 for 2.

Circling campus from the vacant courts I ended up back in the office to chip away at my work. I will admit, I had a hard time finding my groove. I suppose the thought of an earned 30-day sabbatical beginning on Monday, a slim three days from now, was a distraction. But soon enough, it was time to head to the arena for basketball practice. And it was there, after a discussion with the head coach, that my suspicions were confirmed.

The university where I serve is making moves to handle sports ministry in-house. I knew this was a possibility, but now all the head coaches had been informed. A director was hired to guide the effort, and people are being put in place to serve the various teams. I am not part of the discussion. In fact, my organization is likely going to be un-invited to serve on campus. The timing, however, is up for grabs.

My heart is broken. My relationships with the teams run deep after years of investing time, energy, and love. But I remind myself that our God is sovereign. It may be that this season of ministry is coming to an end. Perhaps I am to serve in a different capacity. I must choose to trust God along this uncertain course. I must.

Today's Truth: As for God, His way is perfect; The word of the Lord is proven; He is a shield to all who trust in Him. 2 Samuel 22:31

OCTOBER 10

RESOLVED

In the aftermath of the ministry conference, the rainy Saturday meant only one thing: catching up. There was laundry to do, food to prepare for coming visitors, shopping to replace a rug in the guest room, and standard vacuuming and scrubbing. Now sitting down before calling it a day, I find myself still contemplating the conference theme: Resolved: Purposeful, Determined, Unwavering. I like that.

Allow your mind to go back to Daniel and his friends. These captured Jewish young men had been brought into the king's household to receive the best education and training possible. They had available the best food and drink and were expected to eat it. But Daniel did not. He stuck with his fruits and veggies. Old King Nebuchadnezzar mandated no one was permitted to pray to the God of the Jews. Daniel did. The egomaniacal King said everyone had to bow down to the humongous statue made in his own likeness. Daniel did not. The subsequent king said anyone who disobeyed would be thrown into a den of ferocious lions. Daniel did not care. He resolved to do right no matter what.

Daniel had three buddies, Shadrach, Meshach, and Abed-Nego. With the edict to worship the golden statue of the king, they did as Daniel. They would not and did not bow despite the reality of a trip to the fiery furnace. The King was furious. The furnace was cranked up and they were shoved in. That must have taken great resolve because death by fire would be an excruciating way to go. But if they were worried, they held onto the truth. They said, *If that is the case, our God whom we serve is able to deliver us from the burning fiery furnace, and He will deliver us from your hand, O king. But if not, let it be known to you, O king, that we do not serve your gods, nor will we worship the gold image which you have set up* (Daniel 3: 17, 18).

To have resolve, real resolve, requires unwavering confidence. Resolve is not resolve if what you intend to do (or not do) changes over time. Resolve requires an "I will" of epic proportion. Resolve means that even when threats abound and the situation is grim, we trust the foundation of our faith.

And what is it that I resolve tonight? I'm working on it. This is nothing to take lightly.

Today's Truth: But Daniel purposed in his heart that he would not defile himself with the portion of the king's delicacies, nor with the wine which he drank; therefore he requested of the chief of the eunuchs that he might not defile himself. Daniel 1: 8

OCTOBER 11

FAITHFULNESS

There are some teachers I could listen to all day. Voddie Baucham is one such expositor. Fighting off a head cold (not Covid) and not wanting church members to freak thinking they have been exposed, I elected to stay home. With computer in hand and YouTube cued up, I simply typed in "Voddie Baucham sermons." "Faithfulness that Honors God" began to play. It was audio only, allowing my full attention to be given to the words.

The sermon came out of Daniel 6, a curious choice given yesterday's thoughts about Daniel and his resolve. But Voddie brought to light things I either never knew or did not remember. Daniel was among many young men carried off to Babylon after Jerusalem had been captured. The King was Nebuchadnezzar, who did his best to turn the captives into good Babylonians. But as much as the king tried, Daniel lived by principle. A principle that led him to give his all to the duties assigned him—except in the case that the directives opposed God's law. By the time King Nebby loses his kingship to his son at the end of chapter four, it is the King who praises the God of the Jews.

Then in chapter five, the son, Belshazzar, takes the throne. Daniel continues giving his best service to which he was providentially called. He serves the king, even interpreting dreams and the infamous handwriting on the wall. Daniel was promoted to be the third ruler over the country. That very night, however, Daniel was called to change course when the Mede, Darius, killed Belshazzar and took over the throne. How in the word did Daniel handle yet another change of power in a foreign land?

Those who opposed Daniel knew the only way to upend him was to get him to disobey the king. And the only way he would disobey the king was for the law to disobey the law of Daniel's God. Hence, the king was coerced to declare no one could pray to any god for thirty days. And what does Daniel do? He heads to his house and prays in an open window facing his beloved Jerusalem, just as he had done three times a day for the last 70 years of his captivity. His civil disobedience led to his visit with and miraculous protection from the hungry lions.

That is the kind of faithfulness that God honors.

Today's Truth: When Daniel knew that the document had been signed, he went to his house where he had windows in his upper chamber open toward Jerusalem. He got down on his knees three times a day and prayed and gave thanks before his God, as he had done previously. Daniel 6:10

October 12

Real life is grand. Not.

I must be honest. I am having a rough day; physically, emotionally, and perhaps spiritually.

The events of last evening would not have predicted how I feel now, twenty-four hours later. Our older son, Caleb, along with his better half, McKinley, visited for dinner in celebration of his birthday. It made my heart happy to linger at the table, catching up on life with both our sons and their spouses. It felt so "grown-up." I loved every second.

At 9:30 p.m., the second wave of visitors made their way down the muddy, country driveway. Kirby, a chaplain at the Naval Academy drove down from Annapolis, MD so his three sons could see Liberty University for themselves. Come morning, Kirby accompanied me to a coaches' Bible study I lead every Monday morning. The boys took their Dad's credit card to the Starbucks and had a great time ordering fancy drinks that are described in no less than four words.

On this first official day of my earned sabbatical, we wandered the campus, up and down hills, inside buildings, and across the wide expanse of campus. It was a delight to show off this school that I cherish, hugging the necks of athletes and coaches that we ran into along the way.

But now I am home. I feel exhausted and achy for no good reason. Not even a short, slow run interspersed with walk breaks could snap me out of this dismal feeling. I have no earthly idea why I feel so low and physically spent. However, I suspect it has something to do with the uncertainty of my future.

The University has created a new position to spearhead all sports ministry efforts. There is no discussion that I am being considered in that plan. My heart feels empty at the thought of losing the relationships built with athletes and coaches over the last six years. Maybe even depressed and nauseous.

Let's get real, people. Life is not always predictable. Life is not always the way we wish it to be. I already miss the teams I serve. The thought of not being able to watch these young women be-bop down the hallway to my office rips at my very core. But is God sovereign? Yes. I know he is. But the path that provides the next steps for me is going to be an adventure-filled with conversation between God and me.

Today's Truth: Give ear to my words, O Lord; consider my groaning. Give attention to the sound of my cry, my King and my God, for to you do I pray. Psalm 5:1, 2

OCTOBER 13

A PLAN?

If I were assigned a grade for this second day of my sabbatical, I think I would get an F. Okay, maybe not an F, but a D-. My experience thus far is not very positive, and for that, I am disappointed.

Maybe it is because I have no energy. Everything seems to take a tremendous amount of effort; more than it should. Forcing myself to get outside and begin the myriad of landscaping tasks, it was all I could do to stay upright. Still, the words of my father—and my mother, come to think of it—bounced around in my head. "If you get up and get moving, you'll feel better. Laying around does no good." I had no choice. I kept moving until I couldn't.

Maybe I am coming down with something. Maybe I cannot stop thinking about my coaches and athletes and the possibility that ministry could come to an end. I feel sullen and short-tempered, something that normally does not define me. I hate feeling this discombobulated. It is deeply disconcerting. I just want to take a nap and then go to bed early. Weird. This is very weird.

When I opened a Bible app a little while ago, Jeremiah 29:11 was the verse of the day. I know this verse is taken out of context more times than not, but it is true, nonetheless. So, what is the context? The prophet Jeremiah, who is in Jerusalem at the time, writes to the exiled Jews in Babylon. To these captives of King Nebuchadnezzar, he begins: *Thus says the* LORD *of hosts, the God of Israel, to all the exiles whom I have sent into exile from Jerusalem to Babylon:* (29:4). Wait. Hold the phone. *Whom I sent into exile?* You mean God planned it that way? Jeremiah proceeds to tell them to make the best of it. *Build houses and live in them; plant gardens and eat their produce. Take wives and have sons and daughters; take wives for your sons, and give your daughters in marriage, that they may bear sons and daughters; multiply there, and do not decrease. But seek the welfare of the city where I have sent you into exile, and pray to the* LORD *on its behalf, for in its welfare you will find your welfare* (29: 5-7).

It almost sounds like despite the uncertainty those captured Jews must have felt, God called them to have focus, faith, and trust their future to the Sovereign God. That is a lesson I need to learn.

Today's Truth: For I know the plans I have for you, declares the LORD, *plans for welfare and not for evil, to give you a future and a hope. Then you will call upon me and come and pray to me, and I will hear you. You will seek me and find me, when you seek me with all your heart. Jeremiah 29: 11-13*

October 14

Heart search/Job search

Starting the day early (because I could not sleep anyway), a puffy black blanket not only covered my still-pajamaed body, but it also seemed to cover the disposition of my heart. Snuggled into the love seat that has become my reading spot, the floor lamp illuminated the pages as the sun seemed hesitant to rise above the horizon. The book? *"Blessed are the Misfits: Great news for Believers who are introverts, spiritual strugglers, or just feel like they're missing something"* by Brant Hansen. He writes the way I think; somewhat scattered with a hint of lunacy.

Hansen is an author, obviously, but also the voice of a syndicated Christian radio show. He is highly entertaining yet profoundly, if not oddly, wise. Diagnosed in adulthood as a high functioning Autism Spectrum Disorder fella, his perspective is peculiar and not based on rampaging emotions. Rather, he focuses on obedience and faithfulness, justice, mercy, and unity. On loving people and trusting God. The reality of becoming depressed yet joyful at the same time, with biblical examples to prove the point. I find his perspective refreshing, especially since I am in a rather ambiguous time in my career.

Today I spent nearly two hours traipsing through the forest. Alone with my thoughts, I had plenty of time to pray, confessing my darting thoughts, fears, and dreams. It was a good conversation with God because, thank goodness, He is totally capable of making sense of my nonsense. By the time I got back to the car, I made the mental decision to trust the process, investigate possibilities, and see how it all plays out in the long run.

Hence, I followed a lead. Seeing a post about a long-time nurse friend who was just awarded a promotion at a local hospital, I messaged her. The gist? Can you think of any positions appropriate for an old perfusionist like me? Her response? "Actually, yes, come to think of it. I spoke with Dr. So and So. We have a meeting to discuss next week."

I have no idea if anything will come of it, but I am thankful I followed through on the random idea that popped into my head earlier today. Maybe it is part of this process called "God's leading."

Today's Truth: For you are my rock and my fortress; and for your name's sake you lead me and guide me; Psalm 31:3

OCTOBER 15

UNBRIDLED JOY

BabyGirl, otherwise known as Addyson, our granddaughter, burst through the door with unbridled energy. "Grandma!" she shouted. "You're home!" With that, she ran across the room, dove onto the couch where I was recovering from a day of hard work, lunging at me with a bear hug.

"Addy, did you really climb that mountain all by yourself?" To more than fulfill her virtual kindergarten physical education requirement, she, her dad, and Pam had gone across the valley to the well-known Peaks in the Blue Ridge Mountains. Taking my suggestion to heart, they decided to complete the four-and-a-half-mile hike of Harkening Hill with a side expedition to the preserved pioneer farm belonging at one time to country doctor, Dr. Johnson, and his large family.

"And Grandma, I hiked the whole thing. No one had to carry me one little step!" As she gushed with further details, I learned that she and Rasta, the beagle, ran ahead, leaving Seth and Pam in the dust. She then delivered an accurate description of the huge boulders on which they climbed, the view from the top of the 3353-foot mountain, and their detour to see the centuries-old cabin and restored barns.

When Addy finally took a breath in her story telling, we shared the news that she would have private gymnastics lessons every other Friday. If she was excited before, ecstatic more aptly described her emotion. At the news, Addyson dropped into a split and then popped up into a back bend. She screamed, ran in circles, and gained new heights jumping on the sofa. I smiled, maybe even joined her in laughter, because her attitude was totally contagious. It was impossible for me to feel depleted when surrounded with such exuberance.

I guess this is a good reminder that we can—and do—effect people around us with our own disposition. I am often guilty of being sullen and detached. I wonder how many people I put off by doing that? How much better would it be to intentionally project the good and not the bad? The blessings instead of the difficulties? The joy rather than the heartache?

Yes, we need to be honest, but we honestly need to embrace the goodness and faithfulness of God—and show that to others.

Today's Truth: Then our mouth was filled with laughter, and our tongue with shouts of joy; then they said among the nations, "The Lord has done great things for them." Psalm 126:2

October 16

Just not feeling it

Fair warning. This may be the shortest story in this book. At this point, I got nutt'n for you. I have had no epiphany. Nothing significant comes to mind. In fact, neither is nothing insignificant. My lack of physical energy and mental fog has completely taken over. I do not understand it. I am simply being honest that the only thing I really want to do is drop off into a deep sleep.

I think I may be getting sick. Hence, no energy to even walk across a room. My attempt at yard work this morning was slow and pitiful. I am aware that "this too shall pass," but the sooner the better. I do not even like me in this state.

I read some of the Psalm's written by King David. Talk about a guy who had everything. But he also struggled. He felt depressed, crushed in spirit. Enemies came after him right and left. And yet, even at his lowest, he kept perspective. He might have talked about how down and out he felt, but he always balanced that with confidence in God.

I feel weak when my disposition bottoms out. I should be tougher. I should be able to shake it off. But I cannot. Maybe it will be better in the morning, but not now. So, I leave you with a Psalm.

Today's Truth: For God alone my soul waits in silence; from him comes my salvation. He alone is my rock and my salvation, my fortress; I shall not be greatly shaken. How long will all of you attack a man to batter him, like a leaning wall, a tottering fence? They only plan to thrust him down from his high position. They take pleasure in falsehood. They bless with their mouths, but inwardly they curse. SelahFor God alone, O my soul, wait in silence, for my hope is from him. He only is my rock and my salvation, my fortress; I shall not be shaken. On God rests my salvation and my glory; my mighty rock, my refuge is God. Trust in him at all times, O people; pour out your heart before him; God is a refuge for us. Selah Psalm 62: 1-8

OCTOBER 17

TRAPPING AN EXAMPLE

Yesterday was a total waste. It's not like I was dying. Yet, that was what real life felt like; nearly impossible to navigate. So, when I woke up this morning, it was with nervous trepidation. Would today be more of the same?

I decided not to make any big moves. Coffee in hand, I watched Addyson rearrange the rooms of her dollhouse. But once she scampered off to the next activity on her agenda, it was time to test the waters. Several neglected flower beds needed utmost attention. I might as well give it a try, I reasoned.

I cut, pulled, and chopped away at the weeds, wild strawberries and morning glories that seemed to be overtaking the world. Addyson found much too big gloves and helped with the work. She took pleasure in snipping off random bits of thorny vine. The pile of horticultural waste rose on the tarp used to capture the plunder. Finished there, we pulled it around the corner to the other side of the house. That is where it got interesting.

This azalea-laden bed had not gotten any attention as of late since it runs along the driveway for the new garage. An old bike brought from Pam's house somehow landed in this bed. It was ensnared with vines winding through the wheels and along the frame. With great effort, I yanked and pulled to free it from its captors. But then I saw the animal trap. No amount of yanking could free it.

"Addy," look at this. "Several trees have grown right through the cage! What do you think we should do?" With that, she ran inside, as if an idea had suddenly come to her. She emerged moments later with her new backpack strapped on. Plunking herself down in a sunny spot, Addy pulled out a notebook and pencil, and began "writing." With great intention, she meticulously scribed a series of letters to fill three lines on her paper. "What are you writing, Addy?"

Without hesitation she responded, "I'm writing a story about the trap being trapped, just like you write every day."

Kids have a way of picking up a lot more than we think they do. Addy sees me writing every day. I suppose it is not that odd she wants to capture a good story as well. What a great reminder to watch our Ps and Qs because little ones are watching—and learning. We set the example.

Today's Truth: For I have given you an example, that you also should do just as I have done to you. John 13:15

OCTOBER 18

COUNTING THE YEARS

"Grandma, I want to go!" Addyson politely knocked on the bathroom door, entered, and saw that I was changing into running clothes. After rough days from a physical standpoint, today was the first time in the last week that I had even the slightest desire to run. And though I felt willing and ready, the idea of making the outing a bit more pedestrian was appealing.

Addy dashed away to get her running shoes. We headed up the driveway, rehearsed the rules for road running, and headed to the right. Her little hand reached up to mine, content to walk rather than run. Down the hill then up the big hill on the curve. At the top I asked, "Straight or turn right? You've never gone to the right before." That settled it. We turned right. But not for long. Passing by a tiny clapboard church, she took note of the cemetery. Before long, we strolled and cartwheeled our way up and down the rows of tombstones. (To be clear, Addyson cartwheeled. I did not.) She was eager to learn how long-ago people were born and how old they were when they died. When we found one gentleman who had lived for an entire century, she was in awe.

Later in the evening, Gary and I drove to a friend's house. Several couples gathered at the invitation of Darren's wife. Trying to surprise her husband whose 50th birthday is later this month, she arranged for us to get there before he arrived home from helping a friend. "Surprise!" we shouted. He was, and that fact surprised the rest of us. His wife had pulled off the impossible dream.

One hundred years. Fifty years. Both are finite chunks of time. I wonder if the man who lived to be 100 was fulfilled. I wonder if he made the most of the time God gave him. I wonder if our 50-year-old birthday boy is being all that God desires him to be. (And knowing him well, I suspect he is.) I also wonder if my 63-year-old self is pleasing to God every day He continues to give me breath. If my first thought each morning was to make the most of the day because of the Lord's steadfast love, my answer might be a little more confident.

Today's Truth: The steadfast love of the LORD *never ceases; his mercies never come to an end; they are new every morning; great is your faithfulness. Lamentations 3:22, 23*

OCTOBER 19

SUNNY SKIES

What a difference a day can make! Lovely fall temperatures and bright, sunny skies certainly contributed to my carefree, easy feeling. I have not stopped smiling all day.

I have written before about the uncertainty of continuing my ministry to coaches and athletes. There has been a massive amount of prayer for wisdom, direction, and discernment. I have poked around on various websites in their "career" sections, but have yet to fill out an application, mainly because I have not come across anything that excites me. And yet, in the past 48 hours, two unrelated positions that had not yet been created, are now being developed for—get this—me! How does this even happen?

Just so you have an idea of how strangely wonderful this is, a director in the Career Coaching department of the university saw my resume. Her mind began to whirl with possibilities as she read further down the pages. Unbeknownst to me, she wrote a proposal for a brand-new position. Her boss is now in the process of moving it along the approval train, all the way to the provost's office. There is even money available to fund the position. It is almost too good to be true.

But then came along my "chance" sighting of a long-ago hospital friend who was awarded a promotion. A congratulatory note prompted "There wouldn't be a position for an old perfusionist, would there?", which migrated into a discussion with a surgeon and the director of the entire cardiac umbrella (invasive and non-invasive cardiology and surgery). Needing someone to help in the development of an LVAD (left ventricular assist program) and working conjointly with ECMO efforts (Extracorporeal membrane oxygenation), I got the text to stay tuned. They want me!

I must admit. It is nice—really nice—to be wanted and appreciated. I have no crystal ball to know how all this will pan out, but I sure am thankful for a God who cares in life's big (and little) details. I want nothing more but to trust and obey.

Today's Truth: Delight yourself in the Lord, and he will give you the desires of your heart. Psalm 37:4

October 20

Does relaxing mean lazy?

For the last two and a half hours, my coffee cup has gone from full to empty, books surround me, and my laptop has been, not surprisingly, on my lap. I am seated comfortably on a loveseat with a clear view of the front yard and fishpond. The house is quiet save the churning of the old, worn-out dishwasher. I have the house to myself. I love it.

My mind is churning in concert with the dishwasher, but it is not a frantic churning. It is more like a slow, steady meandering of thoughts and prayers and spiritual pondering. Surely, there is potential for huge changes in my near future. But in this quiet moment, I appreciate the absence of "have to's." I do not have to go to campus, being in the second week of my earned sabbatical. I do not have to get started on building a much-needed deck off the back door. I do not have to scrub the house from floor to ceiling. I do not have to outline a new book. I do not have to do anything. So, is this okay or am I simply being lazy and lethargic?

There are certainly lots of things I could be doing right now. And honestly, I'm pretty sure I will be productive later today. But from where I sit, perhaps doing "nothing" is actually doing "something." I know I am enjoying a quiet moment that is rare in my everyday hustle. I suspect there will not be countless times in the future when I have the luxury to sit and think and write. But for now, it is a privilege to bask in the beauty of silence, listening intently for the still, small voice of the Spirit.

I am not waiting for an exceptional, extraordinary voice from heaven to speak aloud. Nor am I anticipating handwriting on the wall. I am simply soaking in the time to contemplate biblical truth, have an honest conversation with God, and practice trusting my future to an all-sovereign Father who knows what is best for me.

So, is simply sitting on the loveseat looking out at the fishpond a waste of time? I don't think so. It is a time to truly rest, relax, and realize that sometimes we are most productive when we stop moving so fast.

Today's Truth: He restores my soul. He leads me in paths of righteousness for his name's sake. Psalm 23:3

OCTOBER 21

STAINS BE GONE

This sabbatical thing has its perks: no need to set an alarm, slow start to the day with piping-hot coffee, and a chance to do whatever I want. Unfortunately, there is also a downside. I tend to be more productive when I have a full-on schedule. A packed day forces me to value every minute, plan well, and get stuff done. Yes, it can be a little frenetic, but on most occasions, it works well for me.

Maybe my sabbatical would work better if I made distinct plans for each day. I had a general idea of what I wanted to do today, but somewhere along the line, I got distracted. The six browning bananas sitting on the counter met their fate as the key ingredient in chocolate, chocolate chip banana bread. I have a sneaking suspicion that when Seth and Pam get a hankering for banana bread, they buy the fruit and purposely leave it on the counter to ripen. Just like all the other times, it worked. They got their bread.

As the loaves baked, the loveseat shouted out to me for more attention. That piece of furniture has become my reading spot, but the dog seems to have adopted it as well. The white slipcover has not fared well, muddy paw prints and bits of snack crumbs speckling the surface. Into the washer it went, along with the quilt and blanket that share the space. But what about the rug? Oh my.

The five by eight area rug has seen better days. Occupying the space between the loveseat and the cedar chest that serves as home to Addy's large wooden doll house, the rug gets abused. Spilled coffee, ground-in play dough, and mushed crumbs made it look sad and forlorn. After wrangling it out from under the furniture, it ended up on the brick sidewalk under sunny skies. Looking even dirtier in the bright light, the only option was to get a bucket of soapy water and start scrubbing. Then it was rinse, rinse, rinse. Though it is still drying, it is amazing how much better the rug looks now that the stains have been scrubbed away. It is now worthy to come back in the house.

Jesus used his own blood to give us a good cleaning. His sacrifice works like that scrub brush—only better. He takes the stain of guilt and sin and disobedience and scrubs away until we are whiter than snow. Does it mean we will be perfect from here to eternity? No. But does it make us positionally acceptable to come into the house as a cleaned-up child of God? Yes.

Today's Truth: Purge me with hyssop, and I shall be clean; wash me, and I shall be whiter than snow. Psalm 51: 7

October 22

Straight Paths

It was just too beautiful to stay indoors. With temps headed to the low 80s and nary a cloud in the sky, I headed into town. The destination? A series of paths called Blackwater Creek Trails. If you presume there to be a creek running through the area, you are correct. The paths on the banks of the creek are dirt but they connect with a lengthy six-foot wide blacktopped trail. This trail, which meanders off in several directions, covers about nine and a half miles.

The blacktopped portion of the trail runs along old railroad grade. This means only one thing: it is relatively flat. In a city dubbed "The City of Seven Hills," a flattish ribbon of smooth blacktop is almost too good to be true. When I worked at the hospital, this trail system became my stomping grounds, being just a hop, skip, and jump away from the hospital's front door. But in recent years, running those pedestrian pathways has been infrequent, maybe even rare.

I had forgotten what it was like to run on flat, smooth ground. Even the country roads around my house are a series of rolling hills. Although it was a bit of a slow start, I ran from mileage post to mileage post and watched the miles click off. I would have preferred to have complete solitude along the way, but those whose paths I crossed were pleasant enough: moms with strollers, seniors on beach-cruiser bicycles, and plenty of joggers of various shapes and sizes. My route took me to downtown, back through a reclaimed train tunnel, and along a forest-lined path. I purposely avoided the single-track trail, my usual preference. The seven continuous miles I ran brought satisfaction.

I know Scripture must be taken in context, but I came across a passage from Hebrews. The writer has laid the foundation to be steadfast and not grow weary despite the inevitable discipline that accompanies the Christian walk. And then comes what seems to be a pep talk. Not to be sacrilegious, but it made me laugh out loud. I needed this kind of run today to allow my weary knees to heal and decrease the risk of body parts coming out of joint.

Today's Truth: Therefore lift your drooping hands and strengthen your weak knees, and make straight paths for your feet, so that what is lame may not be put out of joint but rather be healed. Hebrews 12: 12, 13

OCTOBER 23

READY TO FOCUS

I heard the pitter-patter before I saw the pitter-patterer. It was Addyson, descending the staircase in all her glory. "Grandma, may I please have some strawberry yogurt?" Handing her the tiny kid-sized container which could easily be consumed with four reasonably sized spoonfuls, she took her place beside me on the couch. With spoon in hand, she dipped into the creamy substance and covered only the front quarter of the spoon. Then into her mouth it went, careful to lick the concave portion of the spoon, the back of the spoon, and the sides of the spoon before going in for another tiny rat-sized bite. Intermingled with morning-time chatter, it took about fifteen minutes to consume the container's contents.

Addyson rarely shows interest in ravenous eating. In fact, I am pretty sure she has set a few world records for the longest time to finish a meal. Maybe it has to do with focusing on a single task. To her, there are plenty of things that are far more compelling than chewing and swallowing.

As she nibbled away at her yogurt, I questioned her about her on-line schooling. "Are you going to be focused and attentive today?" I queried. Addy's blond head nodded, her disheveled bed-head hair creating the illusion of a crazy mad scientist. Then off she dashed to "do school."

At this very moment, I hear a song blasting from her laptop. It must be for the purpose of learning numbers and counting, because she intermittently calls out various numbers in response. She seems quite pleased with herself if her enthusiasm is any indication.

Learning is a whole lot easier when focus and full attention is given to the task. I can struggle with focus just like Addy. I get busy with one thing, notice something else that requires attention, hustle to get that thing done before realizing that I never completed the initial task. With all the pride we take in multi-tasking, maybe we are missing something important: the ability to focus on one thing alone.

When we are captured by a single thought, everything else is put in perspective.

Today's Truth: O God, you are my God; earnestly I seek you; my soul thirsts for you; my flesh faints for you, as in a dry and weary land where there is no water. So I have looked upon you in the sanctuary, beholding your power and glory. Because your steadfast love is better than life, my lips will praise you. Psalm 63:1–3

October 24

Living scared

I had to do it. I had to steal away to the mountains by myself. I desperately needed solitude, lured by the beauty of the falling leaves and gorgeous shades of yellow, red, orange and gold. I refrained from informing Gary of my plans until moments before I walked to the car. I was confident he would never demand I not go, but I could tell from the way he said "Okay" that he was nervous for me to run alone. Afterall, I had a recent heart cath, a loop recorder inserted, and Gary was only a few weeks out from me telling him about my syncopal episodes—twice when running. To ease his mind, I communicated where I was going to park and the route I planned. Promising to text my progress along the way, I left the house to begin the long journey on foot.

I got the solitude I desired for the first three miles. The trail led me up and around one mountain to a gap between two larger mountains. Crossing the Blue Ridge Parkway, I turned to continue the uphill assault, traveling south on the Appalachian Trail. Though there were five or six cars parked at Petite's Gap, I was pleased that I still had the trail to myself, at least for a mile or so. But all too soon, hikers began to stream by. Several overlooks where I had intended to sit and think were occupied by other visitors young and old. The closer I got to parking areas along the Parkway, affording leaf gazers easy access to the trail, family groups and screaming kids became the norm. All I wanted was peace and quiet. What I was getting was not that. My plan changed to get off the AT and descend back to the car on a rarely used blue blaze trail.

Shortly before I made that turn, I looked up to see two day-hikers coming toward me, a man and woman likely in their 60's. Much to my surprise, when they spotted me, they both gasped in a panic. Grabbing their masks, which they obviously had at the ready, they quickly placed them over their mouth and nose before stepping off the trail. Their glare was piercing. I wondered if perhaps I had a scarlet letter written on my forehead. How could they be so fearful of contracting the virus while in the middle of nowhere? I offered pleasantries as I passed them, though they had moved even further into the woods by that time. They muttered something I could not discern. Once passed, I shook my maskless head and pitied them for the unreasonable fear they exhibited. I have no interest in living scared.

Today's Truth: In God, whose word I praise, in God I trust; I shall not be afraid. What can flesh do to me? Psalm 56:4

OCTOBER 25

A SUNDAY AFTERNOON NAP

The night was way too short. As hard as I tried, I could not fall asleep. My legs were as restless as my mind. I tried reading. I tried taking melatonin and a sleep aid, which made me a bit woozy-headed but failed to produce much-needed sleep. I tried a hot bubble bath. I tried flipping channels but few of the choices via old-fashioned antenna were clear due to the storm outside. Even the usually hypnotizing tick-tock of the living room clock failed to induce sleep. By four o'clock in the morning, I left the couch and crawled back into bed next to Gary. Sleep eventually came.

It was no surprise that the sermon at church seemed long. Very long. My eyelids had a problem staying open, and the content never found its mark. I sunk into the car seat on the way home, anticipating a glorious nap after a not-so glorious grilled-cheese lunch.

There was the couch, large and gushy. It was calling my name. With head on a pillow and the blue fuzzy throw covering my body, I snuggled in. There was no problem falling asleep. Though I surfaced to consciousness on occasion before sinking back into slumber, I stayed put for the better part of three hours. Three hours! Wow, I had not done that for a very long time. It was glorious. It was refreshing. It felt good to have rest on this cold and rainy Sunday afternoon.

Sure, I know all the warnings about sleeping too much and being lazy. But I also know that God himself modeled the need for rest. He created for six days before taking a day off. I do not believe He was physically tired because, for one thing, He is a spirit and spirits do not have bodies to get tired. But still, the day of rest was intended to be a day of respite and reflection. In fact, God must have thought it so important that one of the Big Ten is to observe the Sabbath and keep it holy. Even the Israelites who wandered around in a giant sandbox for 40 years gathered extra food on Fridays so they could rest the next day.

Resting is not one of my strengths. I have this underlying need to be doing, to be moving lest I feel lazy and unproductive. But a day like today is a wonderful reminder that rest is not such a bad thing.

Today's Truth: In peace I will both lie down and sleep; for you alone, O LORD, *make me dwell in safety. Psalms 4:8*

October 26

The good samaritan?

There is a first time for everything. I called 911 when I was out on a run. Yep. Sure did.

It is fortunate that I carried my phone. When I run within a couple miles of the house, I seldom cart along the device. But it had been in the pocket of my tights all day and ended up heading down the familiar country road with me. Being mid-afternoon, a big yellow school bus passed me going my direction, apparently turned around at the end of the road, and came back toward me to drop off a student. The girl, maybe a nineth of tenth grader, began the walk down her long driveway before turning to me. "There is a man walking down the road. His name is Randall. Just be careful."

Okay. Let's process that info. These are my safe, beloved country roads. What evil could possibly be lurking? She was hesitant to say more, but I thanked her and continued running. Soon enough, a nice-looking guy in his late teens came walking toward me. He was well groomed and pleasant. There was nothing about him that made me nervous. Did she really mean THIS guy?

Without a second thought, I turned right onto a dirt road and ran another half mile. This time, I was startled to see a shirtless guy, heavily tattooed, bent over clutching his belly. Maybe THIS was Randall. He was likely late 20s and obviously not a runner. I had never seen him before. "I think I'm having a heart attack," he stated, wild-eyed. I crossed to his side of the road and questioned him. "Move to the other side of me," he screamed. I reached for my phone. "What's in your pocket?!?" He threw up his arms yelling "I don't have any weapons!" The conversation went downhill from there. He refused to answer any questions and could not describe what was wrong. He snarled, "I'm on a monitor," when I was brave enough to ask if he was on something. A plethora of "F" words streamed from his mouth demanding I go home. He was paranoid, made no sense, becoming increasingly more aggressive toward me by the minute. The next time he screamed for me to leave, I did. Quickly.

When out of his sight, I called 911. They promised to check out the situation. My desire was to be a good Samaritan. I am not sure calling 911 qualifies but then again, it was clear he was not in his right mind. He needed help I could not give. I pray that his tormented soul be visited by the Spirit, who can turn lives upside down and right-side up.

Today's Truth: Which of these three, do you think, proved to be a neighbor to the man who fell among the robbers," He said, "The one who showed him mercy." And Jesus said to him, "You go, and do likewise." Luke 10: 36, 37

OCTOBER 27

DIGGING IN THE DIRT

The trip to the home improvement store was to fetch lumber for a display box I want to craft for the kitchen. It was a bit of a puzzle getting the lumber to fit into the little Suzuki I drive, but once accomplished I navigated to the other end of the parking lot which is close to the garden center. Can you say, "clearance plants"?

I hit the jackpot! Hundreds of perennial shrubs were marked down by fifty percent. Tall ones, short ones, some flowering, some not. There were so many to choose from. My cart filled with three of one kind, two of another that had purplish leaves, with two healthy blueberry bushes to round out the grouping. The first five would line the driveway to the new garage, while the fruit bushes were destined to find a perfect home in one of the new beds.

Though I positioned the potted plants where I wanted them, I had no intention of digging holes. After all, it was six o'clock and dinner was behind me. But when Seth said, "Want me to start bringing up mulch for the new bed with the tractor," I traded my after-dinner tea for a shovel.

Five holes needed to be dug. I found out quickly that not all holes are created equally. On the first hole, I bounced right off the shovel when I jumped on it. Whoa. The ground was hard and nothing but red clay. Not a wonderful environment for a transplant. But I eventually got the hole big enough and deep enough, threw in some mulch, and tucked that sucker in for safe keeping. But when I moved ten feet away to start the next hole, my shovel found little resistance when plunged into the ground. That soil was rich and brown. I am no horticulturalist, but my money is on the plant in this hole.

Now that the mulch is spread, it is impossible for an onlooker to tell which plant has the best soil. They look equally happy in their new environments. But only time will tell if one thrives while another barely survives.

The Gospel can be like that. We sow the seed, obediently, and wait to see what the Spirit will do. Are we wise if we amend the soil to be as fertile as possible? Sure. Are we wise if we water and fertilize? Absolutely. But ultimately, we have no control over what will grow and what will not. We just need to be good farmers and plant the seeds (or in this case, the shrubs).

Today's Truth: As for that in the good soil, they are those who, hearing the word, hold it fast in an honest and good heart, and bear fruit with patience. Luke 8:15

OCTOBER 28

KEEP CHOPPING WOOD

There is nothing like stacking firewood to reveal what a weakling I am.

Dealing with firewood was not on the original agenda. It was supposed to be a crafty day with a little gardening thrown in for good measure. I manicured the mulch we put down last night, dug the holes and got the new blueberry plants in the ground, pulling weeds in the process. Then it was on to spray paint the okra I had dehydrated in the quest for unique but shiny silver, gold, and copper Christmas ornaments. Feeling rather accomplished, it was time to heed the rumblings of my tum-tum.

Wouldn't you know it? I glanced out to the field and heard the chain saw running. Seth was cutting up fallen trees, hauling them over to the woodshed, and reducing them to reasonable sizes with the ancient gas-powered splitter. Wanting to make it easier for him with this labor-intensive task, I asked, "Need some help?" I should have known he would say yes.

My task was to stack the logs after he split them. I soon found out there is an art to stacking logs to prevent them from falling off the ends of the rows. But after a while, I got the hang of it, picking up log after log to add to the stack growing upward toward the shed's tin roof. It was tedious to say the least. I normally handled but one log at a time given the weakness of my arthritic hands. Nevertheless, by the time we broke for a late lunch, we had managed to see our wood pile grow substantially.

It has been said that you do not chop wood to use now. You chop wood to be prepared for the next season. I guess that sounds about right. The green wood we split would prove difficult to burn. But by next year, the wood we chopped today will be dried out and ready to give us that warm, cozy feeling in the dead of winter.

I suspect that if I patiently lived my life knowing that what I did today was preparing me for the future, I might be less inclined to whine about the work. Share the truth of the Gospel today. See the Spirit bring it to life in ten years. Spend time learning the Scriptures. Be amazed when God brings to mind exactly what you need two weeks from now. So yes. Chop wood today. Reap the benefits later.

Today's Truth: Prepare your work outside; get everything ready for yourself in the field, and after that build your house. Proverbs 24:27

OCTOBER 29

BAD TEETH

Did you know that the profession with the highest suicide rate is dentistry? At least that is what my dad told me decades ago.

Dad was an old-time kind of dentist. He worked solo. No hygienist. No receptionist or appointment maker. No one to answer the phone. No x-ray tech to take the images and develop them in the dark room, unless you count me when as a high school student, I dipped the x-ray film and sterilized instruments on Saturdays. Dad was an excellent, hard-working dentist, cared for his patients, and never had the heart to charge people the going rate. His schedule was full of satisfied patients. Nevertheless, my father internalized the fact that practically no one liked to go to the dentist. He took it personally at times. Though he died of heart disease, a good number of dentists self-inflict their deaths each year.

That said, I hope my dentist never has such a thought. She is a wonderful and talented dentist, caring for her patients with kindness and consideration. Still, today's appointment to fill two cavities was not necessarily embraced with joy.

These are not my first cavities. I have a mouthful of repaired teeth. I try my best to take care of my teeth, but I suspect genetics are working against me. But think about it. Cavities do not form overnight. It takes months, even years, to break down the enamel and eat away at the tooth. Bacteria, sugary foods, poor hygiene, lack of the right stuff in the slimy saliva, and a host of other things contribute to the decay process. The potential for decay is always there but being alert to address the controllable factors is paramount in keeping those choppers healthy.

Like tooth decay, sin and disobedience come naturally, producing a stain and ugly cavity in our lives. But it is our responsibility, with the help of the Holy Spirit, to direct our thoughts and actions to eliminate the causes of the decay. Do we know the Scriptures? Do we put them into practice? Do we pray and seek wisdom? Are we careful to build relationships and heed all the "one anothers" described in the Bible? If we are not proactive, decay may sneak up on us, creating a bigger problem that needs filled in.

Today's Truth: Those who live only to satisfy their own sinful nature will harvest decay and death from that sinful nature. But those who live to please the Spirit will harvest everlasting life from the Spirit. Galatians 6:8 (NLT)

OCTOBER 30

GYMNASTICS 101

Our granddaughter has boundless energy. Every time she took a break from her virtual kindergarten school, there she was, flipping and jumping on the trampoline out in the front yard. We drew a chalk line across the surface so she could practice doing her cartwheels in a straight line. What joy she displayed as she flipped and flopped her lithe, tiny body inside the protective perimeter nets of the trampoline.

Addyson is very coordinated. Two weeks ago, we had the opportunity to provide her first private gymnastics lesson. Her coach, Jessie, now 25, was one of my track athletes when she was in high school. As a level ten gymnast herself, she took to pole vaulting, becoming a record setter as a Division 1 athlete in college. Now, with years of experience as a coach, we are delighted she has taken on Addy for Friday night instruction.

Since that first lesson two weeks ago, Addy has been relentlessly practicing. All that practice is paying off. "I can't believe how much better she is than the first week!" Jessie commented after tonight's session. Addy was focused, attentive, and looked to have made more progress tonight. But one thing struck me about Jessie's coaching.

"Addy, you need to finish each move properly. Once your body and brain memorize the movement, it will become natural." With that, Addy did another cartwheel, concentrating on the hand-hand-foot-foot-finish sequence, hands above her head in a "crown" position, left foot in front of the right. Again and again, she repeated the skill, ending even the botched landings with the appropriate finishing stance.

Isn't it interesting that success dictates a commitment to repeating skills with precision and discipline? It certainly does not come naturally at first, but with time, those skills become second nature. There are life skills that we need to commit to practice with precision and discipline so that we live effective and productive lives.

Today's Truth: For this very reason, make every effort to add to your faith goodness; and to goodness, knowledge; and to knowledge, self-control; and to self-control, perseverance; and to perseverance, godliness, and to godliness, mutual affection; and to mutual affection, love. For if you possess these qualities in increasing measure, they will keep you from being ineffective and unproductive in your knowledge of our Lord Jesus Christ. 2 Peter 1:5-8

OCTOBER 31

LET THE DEAD SPEAK

Ghosts, goblins, and freakishly gruesome characters are common sights on Halloween. Personally, the frightening death and sadistic mayhem of the "holiday" does not sit right with me. Playing dress up with creative non-threatening costumes is amusing. Princesses, cute little animals, cardboard cars with a kid plunked in the middle, and walking robots are fun and fanciful. But the blood and guts and evil characters? I doubt those fall into the category of *whatever is true, whatever is honorable, whatever is just, whatever is pure, whatever is lovely, whatever is commendable, if there is any excellence, if there is anything worthy of praise, think about these things* (Philippians 4:8).

With that said, I ended up resting on my bed, the TV on. Without cable or satellite, the channel choices are never great. But after a few clicks I landed on "Dr. G, Medical Examiner." Yeah, I know, *whatever is lovely.* Hardly fits, right? So, I rationalize. These are true stories of mysterious deaths. The cause of death is never obvious, if for no other reason that the boring cases would make a terrible television series. But good 'ol Dr. G uses her best super-sleuth medical knowledge and skills to eventually conclude why the deceased ended up dead.

Forensic medicine is fascinating—if you can get past cutting into a corpse. But if you look hard and long enough, there is telling information about how the person lived and died. Sometimes the clue is hidden inside an organ. Sometimes it is in the brain or the heart or the blood. But just think. If you understand what caused the death, it might be prevented in someone else.

What about Christians who look like they are descending into a bad place? I do not mean hell, because we are secure in Christ if we truly believe. I refer to behavior that kills the testimony. Actions and attitudes that make the person who is supposed to be alive in Christ look like a dead man walking. Perhaps we need a good forensic study to determine the cause. Is it a loss of focus? A lack of knowledge and application of the Word? Selfishness? Bitterness? Corrupt language? Impure thoughts? There could be a million reasons.

I remind myself. Take heed. Investigate at the first sign of trouble. By the time I make it onto the autopsy table, it will be too late.

Today's Truth: Therefore let anyone who thinks that he stands take heed lest he fall. No temptation has overtaken you that is not common to man. God is faithful, and he will not let you be tempted beyond your ability, but with the temptation he will also provide the way of escape, that you may be able to endure it. 1 Corinthians 10: 12, 13

November 1

New hope rising

The news reported it. There was to have been a full moon last night, one that is called a blue moon. The last time a blue moon occurred on Halloween was 76 years ago. The next time it occurs will be in August of 2023. In general, a blue moon rises every two and a half years.

But what is a blue moon? It has nothing to do with the color, although at times, the moon can take on a hint of blue due to particles in the atmosphere. However, the term Blue Moon was first described in the Farmers' Almanac in 1930. It was designated as the third full moon in a season (winter, spring, summer, or fall) that sports four full moons instead of the usual three. Since then, the term has come to erroneously mean the second full moon in any given month.

Last night the moon was on full display. Bright and shiny, it cast a brilliant light across the landscape. From the minute the moon rose above the horizon, it was as if someone had flipped on a light switch. I regret not running under that bright glow. It was a lost opportunity.

I love running at night. But I love running at night lit by a full moon even better. There is something about running through the forest at nighttime that is thrilling. Not thrilling like a death-defying roller coaster ride might be. But thrilling in that all the cares of the world evident in the daylight seem to vanish. Poof. They are gone. The darkness embraces me. I feel caressed and secure. I am focused on what really matters. The inconsequential disappears into the shadows. It is ethereal to make my way along paths lit only by the moon's light filtering through the limbs laid bare by autumn.

I find hope running in the light of the moon. I am content. I am blessed. I gain perspective because the darkness of night is not as dark as it could be. The sun's light is reflected off the moon, lighting the way and instilling confidence as I continue to make progress, one step at a time. Hope is hung from every moonbeam sent from above.

Today's Truth: having the eyes of your hearts enlightened, that you may know what is the hope to which he has called you, what are the riches of his glorious inheritance in the saints, Ephesians 1:18

NOVEMBER 2

A RAY OF HOPE

Do you like rays of sunshine? I do, and suspect most people feel the same way, (unless, of course, you are a total grump-head). On this gloriously brisk, windy, but sun-filled day, a jaunt through the woods was exactly what I needed.

Happy to be running alone, the trails I chose are seldom busy. Come to think of it, I have never seen another runner, although several people out walking their dogs have been spotted. True, I do not frequent these trails, but they are conveniently located between town and home. An industrial park, in conjunction with the county, had the wisdom to build an undulating series of single track in the woods behind the warehouses and through yet-to-be sold vacant wooded lots. The longest of these looped trails is roughly five and a half miles in length. While it has some roly-poly short hills, it is tame compared to a mountain trail.

The last time I targeted the "orange" loop for my run, it was terrible. It was like beating a dead horse. I just could not go. I was short of breath, legs felt like they might fall off, and I had to convince myself that it was a day to walk when a hill challenged my forward progress. Back at the car, I felt wiped out. Spent. Done in.

But today? Today was as different as night and day. Though I was not particularly speedy, my self-talk encouraged me to be steady and joyful at running along leaf-strewn trails. My breathing was appropriate. Had someone been with me, I think I could have carried on a healthy conversation. When the short hills came into view, there was no hesitation, no desire to walk. In contrast, I enjoyed running up the hills, thrilled that I was perfectly fine upon cresting the incline. Arriving back at the car, it felt like—for the first time in a very long time—a walk (or in this case, a run) in the park.

The moral of this story? Don't ever lose hope. These past months have been depressing considering my heart issues, iron deficiency, and painful knees. But today hope glimmered through the remaining golden leaves clinging to the branches.

Today's Truth: Not only that, but we rejoice in our sufferings, knowing that suffering produces endurance, and endurance produces character, and character produces hope, and hope does not put us to shame, because God's love has been poured into our hearts through the Holy Spirit who has been given to us. Romans 5:3-5

November 3

Voting day

I want to turn on the television. But then again, that is the last thing on earth I want to do. My desire for social media runs hot and cold as well, especially on this national election day. I risked a glance earlier this morning and came away with a sick feeling. So much hatred. So much yelling and screaming and "fact checking." Those leaning right decry the coming socialism, disregard for life with the abortion of millions of unborn babies, and loss of constitutional liberties. Those counterbalancing with a left lean rale against the current leader and his brash and brazen approach. The liberal lot demands tolerance from the right, meaning that disagreeing with their own position is paramount to hatred. And yet, few on the left exhibit any tolerance for viewpoints other than their own. It so frustrating.

But for the few moments I spent online, I was also reminded by fellow Christians, regardless of political affiliation, that the outcome will be God-ordained. Of course, I intellectually know this to be true, but it is a hard pill to swallow when the ramifications are considered. How could God allow the further degradation of the family unit? How could He sit back and see babies murdered in the womb and even in the birth process itself? How could He see religious liberties be swept from the table and disgarded? How?

So, let's start with this. God is sovereign in all things. Look at how often his own people were held captive. Did that prevent the coming of the Christ? Look at the torment the early Christians endured at the hand of Nero and others? Did that destroy the church? Consider the millions who have died at the hands of communism, radical Buddhism, Islam, and Hindi—and continue to be tortured for the name of Christ. Has it destroyed the Christianity? No.

Each time, though shoved underground, the church rises to the surface stronger, firmly rooted, and holding onto the promises of God. Does anyone wish to endure, suffer, even die for the cause? Of course not. But in the end, God's purposes are accomplished, whether we like it or not.

God help us all understand this truth more fully, continuing to love our neighbors as ourselves, being patient and kind, and yet faithful to the truth.

Today's Truth: Let every person be subject to the governing authorities. For there is no authority except from God, and those that exist have been instituted by God. Romans 13:1

NOVEMBER 4

UNCERTAINTY

Yesterday was national election day. Do we know who will serve as the next president of the United States of America? Nope. The lawsuits have already been filed claiming significant cheating. It makes you wonder how many dead people "voted" or how many folks voted multiple times using contrived identities. Could it happen? Sure. It has been evident in previous elections. But will it be enough to keep the Democrats from reaching the magic 270 electoral college votes. Who knows?

So, what now? It all seems to be up in the air. There is uncertainly on Wall Street. Uncertainty on the streets. Mental health professionals tell us that anxiety is at an all-time high given the political and social unrest. And that is on top of the messy Covid-19 situation. How do we deal with all of this and not lose our marbles, an expression my Mother liked to use?

My thoughts turn toward Joseph. He was the youngest of twelve, all boys. (Think about what a saint the two Mamas must have been to deal with all that testosterone!) Jospeh really was his Father's favorite, a fact known by the brothers. Remember the story? The bros dump him in a pit and sell him off to a band of Egyptian traveling salesmen. He ends up in Egypt and does well until he finds himself in jail. But Joseph is exceptionally good at interpreting dreams and does so while in the slammer. However, no one remembers to tell the powers to be when they get out about Joseph's talent. Several years pass. Think about the uncertainty this misplaced Jew must have felt.

When Joseph is finally sprung from the dungeon, the Pharaoh is impressed, granting him a very powerful position. A famine drives his brothers to travel to Egypt to ask for food. With the tables turned, Joseph messes with his brothers, none of whom recognize him. After several encounters, the family is reconciled by Joseph's forgiveness, his family is provided for, and the ultimate purpose of God is finally realized.

It is safe to assume there was consternation and doubt along the way. "What in the world are you doing, God? I don't get it." I am not unlike Joseph. I don't get it either. But I am compelled to trust God's timing and plan even when I do not understand.

Today's Truth: So Joseph remained in Egypt, he and his father's house. Joseph lived 110 years. Genesis 50:22

November 5

Home is where the heart is

I missed it yesterday. Sometime while I was sauntering along a Blue Ridge mountain ridgeline, a "house" was delivered to our property. The driveway had been expanded weeks ago in preparation, but an emergency tree removal transpired two nights ago when the wind toppled a huge tree. The "house" now rests at its targeted location, the opening to the cedars, or as Addyson calls it, "The Enchanted Forest."

The house is technically a play shed. It measures 16 x 40 feet. It has the cutest angled front porch with three windows, allowing light and fresh air to stream inside. Two lofted areas provide bonus space at both ends of the building. If you possess a robust imagination, a kitchen, bathroom, bedroom, and living room can be visualized.

But now, the interior is a blank canvas. This building is going to become a home for Seth, Pam, and Addyson. Thanks to Seth's electrical prowess, the humble shed already has power to a newly installed outlet. By tomorrow, I have no doubt the entire space will be wired. They bought a trailer-load of new materials late this afternoon with a couple large windows for the bedroom and lumber to frame out the bathroom and laundry.

Gary and I are excited for them to be forging a future together. A future that does not include living on the second floor of our house, to be exact. Not that it has been a problem. In fact, it has been nothing less than delightful. But as a newly married couple, they need their own space. And honestly, as an old married couple of 43 years, we could use a space of our own as well.

Isn't it interesting, however, that the size and level of impressiveness does nothing to establish a home? A house is simply a highly organized amalgamation of building materials. A home, on the other hand, is an amalgamation of highly organized relationships. Husband. Wife. Kid. And yes, even puppy. A home is a haven filled with love and truth and honesty. It is not perfect, but it is a safe place; a sanctuary. It is where imperfect people humble themselves to be patient, unselfish, and generous, always regarding the others higher than themselves.

God bless this little family as they take that shed and turn it into their home.

Today's Truth: Therefore a man shall leave his father and mother and be joined to his wife, and they shall become one flesh. Genesis 2:24

NOVEMBER 6

MORE THAN EXPECTED

I think we have a budding gymnast on our hands. Addyson, our five-year old granddaughter, began her quest several weeks ago and shows promise. Yes, I know. I am her Grandma and may have an over-inflated idea of her athletic ability. But even with a thirty-minute lesson per week with a private coach, she takes to the skills like a fish to water. Tonight, she worked on bars, beam, floor, and even started vaulting progressions onto a big, fat mat. She was in her element.

It's not like she goes for her lesson and then forgets about it. She practices. All the time. Everywhere. Today we were in Walmart. In a bit of a rush, I was walking a few steps ahead. When I glanced around to have her catch up, there she was, poised for action. In the middle of the women's clothing isle and with front foot pointed and her arms in the "crown" position overhead, she executed a cartwheel, ending in that glorious "I stuck it" stance.

At the playground earlier in the day she cartwheeled on the grass, on her way to the swings, and back to the behemoth of a play area where she climbed up backwards and underneath a runged set of stairs. She hung and swung from the bars like a lithe little monkey. I doubt I could have hung on for more than a few seconds. Those bars became her go-to. She is one strong kiddo.

Addy showed no sign of fatigue later at the gym. In fact, she seemed to be even more energetic than normal, jumping up and down like a pogo stick between each skill. At the conclusion of the lesson, Coach Jessie inquired of Addy, "What would you like to do?"

"I want to show you how I can flip on the trampoline."

Off they went. We could tell Jessie was telling her that this trampoline was not like our backyard tramp. Nope. It was way bouncier. Addy climbed aboard. Up in the air she went, spinning quicker than anticipated. She landed with such great force that her knees slammed up into her cute little nose. She tried very hard not to cry but a few tears escaped. Still, she is anxious to flip again.

That trampoline proved to be exceedingly more than she expected it to be. Thank God that He, too, does more than we could ever think or ask.

Today's Truth: Now to him who is able to do immeasurably more than all we ask or imagine, according to his power that is at work within us, to him be glory in the church and in Christ Jesus throughout all generations, for ever and ever! Amen. Ephesians 3:20, 21 (NIV)

November 7

Obscured View

It is almost over. My sabbatical, that is. And it is Saturday. So much to do and so little time to do it.

Technically, I do not have to go back to work until Wednesday, but I will hit the ground running come Monday. Woodworking projects were completed yesterday, checking that item off the list. Tools tidied and the shop organized, it can now rest in peace until the next project. The garden has been tended to in preparation for winter, and new landscaping is looking good. So much has been accomplished. But then again, there is so much more that could be done.

The window blinds in our bedroom snapped their cords, the slats falling willy-nilly all over the floor. The replacement blinds are over $40, which is too rich for my cheap blood. But alas, there are blinds in the bathroom that fit the bedroom window. And, wanting more light in the bathroom, adding a window film that provides privacy, is decorative, and allows light to penetrate is just the ticket. I decided to accomplish these tasks before heading to the mountains for one last run before having to contend with "normal" once again.

Here's the story. Due to the construction of the new garage near that bedroom window, I figured the glass was dirty on the outside. Still, a quick wipe on the inside would not hurt, right? Wow. Spray. Spray. Spray. Wipe. Wipe. Wipe. I have never in my entire life seen such filth on an indoor window! The gobs of paper towels I used turned black, outlining my handprint from the pressure against the glass. It was downright embarrassing. I cannot recall when I last cleaned that window, but still, how could I have been so blind to the accumulating film of dirt?

Maybe I grew comfortable in not looking. With window blinds and curtains hung in place, I suppose I became numb to what was happening behind the scenes. Afterall, some light managed to get through. It could not be that bad, could it?

Oh, yes it could. When we become lax in paying attention to the details, of not keeping our personal lives in order, the grime accumulates without us even noticing. It is only when we "clean house," so to speak, that we realize our wretched state. Let's be attentive, folks, and daily take action to keep our lives clean.

Today's Truth: Therefore we must pay much closer attention to what we have heard, lest we drift away from it. Hebrews 2:1

NOVEMBER 8

CHOOSE TODAY

We all have choices to make each day. Will I focus on being productive and efficient throughout the day? Will I exercise? Will I eat a salad or a hamburger and fries for dinner? Will I spend my evening reading, writing, or vegging on Netflix? The choices are endless. In fact, it is estimated we make no less than 35,000 "remotely conscious decisions." That is not a typo. Thirty-five THOUSAND! Whoa.

There were some heavy decisions to be made back in Joshua's day. Israel was a hot mess when Joshua decided it was time for a big 'ol family meeting. They were gathered at Shechem. He sent invites to the elders, judges, and officers. You know, the big-wigs. The conversation began, *Long ago, your fathers lived beyond the Euphrates. . .* (Joshua 24: 2). We have probably all been on the receiving end of that kind of discussion. In fact, when we get in that mode, our kids roll their eyes as if to say, "Here we go again. Back in my day when we walked five miles each way to school, uphill, in the snow. . ."

And what a thorough history lesson Joshua gave. He recounted the lives of Terah, Abraham and Nahor's father. Without exception, all of them followed other gods at some point. Then came Isaac, Jacob and Esau, Moses, and Aaron. Jacob, Aaron, and Moses ended up in Egypt. Then came the plagues and God's provision for escape. But the narrative continued.

"You cried like baby girls [my paraphrase] when the Egyptians chased you down. Yet your God protected you. God then helped you defeat the Amorites, delivering you from Balak. And remember Jericho? That was God, too."

What was the point he was trying to make? *Now therefore fear the* LORD *and serve him in sincerity and in faithfulness. Put away the gods that your fathers served beyond the River and in Egypt, and serve the* LORD. (Joshua 24:14) Why? *He is a jealous God* (24: 19).

There was a choice that had to be made. Joshua said, *choose this day whom you will serve* (24:15). And like any great leader, his choice was an example to all.

Choose wisely. Today.

Today's Truth: But as for me and my house, we will serve the LORD. *Joshua 24; 15b*

November 9

The Perfect Athlete

If you remember the 1970's Karen Carpenter song, *Rainy Days and Mondays*, you might recall the sad fact that rainy days and Mondays "always get me down." I could not disagree more. I love Mondays—at least in the last month or two.

Monday mornings are highly anticipated. The staffs of women's volleyball and women's soccer join me for an hour of discussion. We are working our way through the book of Proverbs, two chapters at a time and specifically applied to how we coach. The discussions have been nothing short of incredible, each coach learning from another, finding new ideas to consider and implement.

We were in chapters 17 and 18 today. We broached subjects like letting love cover an offense without blabbing about it to anyone else. Of course, you cannot go very far in Proverbs—in any chapter—without reading descriptions about fools, their attitudes and behavior. We read about how it would be better to be ripped to shreds by a protective mama bear than to have to deal with a fool doing his stupid stuff. Should coaches be in the business of rehabbing fools who end up on the team, or should fools not be given a first look? These are tough decisions.

I asked, "Of the twenty-six identified character skills that seem to mark any great team, which might a fool be lacking? Do you think that an intentional effort to teach and model character development could take care of the fool problem?" Each coach offered his or her opinion before one told us about "The Perfect Athlete" initiative. With the team divided into groups, they are given either a real-life scenario or athletic situation, asked to create a skit, and then act it out to show how the "perfect athlete" would respond. Most skits are humorous but make the point. The coaches offered that the "perfect athlete" has been used to hold the girls accountable when they have responded in a less than perfect way. What a practical way to teach character skills!

It is true. Sometimes we know how we should act or think, but when it comes down to it, we lack the resolve to follow through. We are human. We are not perfect. We act foolishly. But we should continue to strive.

Today's Truth: For I do not understand my own actions. For I do not do what I want, but I do the very thing I hate. For I have the desire to do what is right, but not the ability to carry it out. For I do not do the good I want, but the evil I do not want is what I keep on doing. Romans 7:15, 18b, 19

November 10

BACK TO THE FUTURE

It is hard to believe that as of tomorrow, this wonderful, magnificent, relaxed yet focused sabbatical comes to an end. Back to work I go.

It is not as though I despise work. To the contrary, I love my time on campus. I relish the time spent with coaches in bible study or more informally, chatting it up before or after practices. Chasing volleyballs and tennis balls has become a developed skill in my repertoire. Seeing the athletes in action allows me to see the "real" heart behind her jersey, allowing us to connect deeply and substantively. So yes, I love what I do. It is just that tomorrow is shaping up to be the beginning of a new season for me.

There is a nine O'clock meeting with one of the senior athletic administrators. In that meeting, I will be sharing the news that I intend to leave my role with the ministry in which I serve. This has been a very hard decision. But it appears that the University is going in a different direction in their desire to serve athletes. They are planning on handling all sports ministry with university employees, of which I am not. A director has been hired, introduced to all the head coaches, and will hit the ground running on December 15. It appears that my organization is not part of the plan, nor am I. Heavy sigh.

Am I upset? Not really. But it is a little scary. I do not have another job signed, sealed, and delivered. There are two organizations that tell me they are creating positions for me. One is back in the medical arena, which is exciting. The other is within a university department, using my experience in the medical field to serve as career counselor and coach for kids headed into healthcare-related occupations. I do not, however, know the time frame for these things to happen. That makes this decision to leave ministry a bit dicey.

But am I really leaving "ministry?" It is true that I will not have the same relationship with the coaches and athletes as in the past. But if God is orchestrating a career move in my twilight years, I must believe he has another mission for me to accomplish.

Time to turn up the trust dial.

Today's Truth: The Lord is my strength and my shield; in him my heart trusts, and I am helped; my heart exults, and with my song I give thanks to him. Psalm 28:7

November 11

Fading spots

When the phone rang at seven p.m., I knew who was on the other end. It was Suzan. Suzan lives in Ohio, which is not surprising since she was born and raised in the Buckeye State. Our paths first crossed when she was in high school and I was one of her teachers. A slim five or six years was all that separated us age-wise. To have an adult relationship today is special, although she sometimes still calls me "Mrs. T." Old habits die hard.

Suzan is a successful MaryKay gal. Her marketing efforts appear on a regular basis on social media platforms. A few weeks ago, a post about a particular product caught my attention. It was purported that said product could reduce the appearance of dark spots. Yeah. I have been looking for an answer to my problem.

You see, I come by these age spots honestly. As my mom and her mother aged, both developed darkened pigment on their hands and arms. I followed suit with the added distinction of having a large dark spot on my left cheek. A few people have even tried to wipe it off, thinking it to be a dirt smudge. I tried various potions and even had a laser procedure to lighten the spot. Nothing worked. But with a 100% money back guarantee, what did I have to lose? "Send me the miracle in a bottle," I requested of Suzan.

She called tonight wanting to check up on the progress. Reporting my consistent use but nominal improvement, she assured me it takes time and patience. "Just stick with it. The change will not happen overnight. These things take time, maybe as long as three months." I am more than willing to persist if the spot will lighten.

Most things in life take effort and patience. Results are seldom immediate, that's for certain. We need to be faithful and steady. Persistent and unwavering. Obedient and hopeful. Looking forward to what will be.

Today's Truth: For now, we see in a mirror dimly, but then face to face. Now I know in part; then I shall know fully, even as I have been fully known. So now faith, hope, and love abide, these three; but the greatest of these is love. 1 Corinthians 13:12, 13

NOVEMBER 12

RAIN, RAIN, HERE TO STAY

The fishpond outside our front door tells the story. And so does the yard, the garden, and our sad, long, dirt and gravel driveway.

It has been raining hard over the last several days. It started in the wee hours yesterday morning and is still a wet, soggy mess tonight. The news reported that we got four inches of wetness. Down the road twenty minutes saw five inches, and another twenty minutes away from there received seven inches. That is a lot of rain! Obviously, creeks and rivers are overflowing their banks. Additional flooding is expected tomorrow as the overflowing mountain streams run downhill.

In our immediate vicinity—specifically our driveway—each heavy rain points out the obvious. You see, our driveway used to be Triggs Road about a 125 years ago. Over the ensuing decades of travel, the road seemed to sink into the earth, creating a ditch-like corridor. We recently addressed the issue. The driveway comes off the main road and is relatively flat for a hundred yards or so. Then comes a steep hill for another hundred yards, flattening out through a low spot before rising gently to the house. When it rains, water creates rivulets down the hill, carrying with it precious gravel. Our task is now to create functional ditches to divert the water where we want it to go. Once we do that, the next step will be to spend thousands of dollars on more rock and gravel.

Swiftly flowing water is powerful. It can carve new riverbeds, knock buildings off foundations, and sweep away cars and trucks that stand in its way. Entire canyons have been chiseled out quickly by the tremendous power of a moving wall of water.

I wonder what Noah and his clan thought as the rains came down and the floods came up? How terrifying to see water rushing from high points to low. And as the water level rose to cover all of humanity and every living creature, how they must have trembled in awe of God's provision to seal them into the Ark they obediently built.

Today's rains might produce local floods, but if they remind us of the power behind those waters, then perhaps it is well worth the trouble caused by the rain.

Today's Truth: And I will remember my covenant, which is between me and you and every living creature of all flesh; and the waters shall no more become a flood to destroy all flesh. Genesis 9:15

NOVEMBER 13

THAT BELL—AGAIN

Humor me. Turn back to the story for June 22. Now scan it with your most observant eyes. Recall my brief encounter with a runner gal who was carrying, of all things, a bear bell. Also remember we were on trails no less than a half mile from a campground and houses. Though bear sightings occur on the rarest of occasions, it is not like anyone needs to run in fear.

But guess what? On the same trail as that day in June, I looked up to see "her" coming toward me. And sure enough, that crazy bear bell was still clattering away. "What?!?! You gotta be kidding. I can't believe she really thinks that running with a bell is providing protection from a marauding beast." But rather than voice my thoughts out loud, I suppressed a giggle before rendering a cheery greeting as we passed.

I presume that since this woman continues to make her way along wooded trails, she believes her bear bell to be effective. Afterall, there are no signs of a prior bear attack on her arms and legs, coupled with the fact that she is still very much alive and kicking. Have bell. No bear. But is this a logical conclusion?

Obviously, there is not a direct cause-effect relationship. Many other factors contribute to the fact that the woman with the bell has not become bear bait. But we can all be guilty of faulty logic. I remember climbing an excruciatingly steep series of switchbacks with a friend. Being silly and wanting to make the time pass quicker, I offered: "I have on a purple shirt. I see no elephants. Therefore, purple shirts keep away elephants."

Crazy, right? But how many times do we rationalize our behavior with bad thinking. "I'm not committing murder or adultery, and I'm not that bad of a person. Therefore, watching a dicey movie, sleeping in on Sundays, or saying a few bad words isn't a big deal." Hum. No.

Or what about this? "God loves everyone. That means I need to accept everyone and their lifestyle choices. I have no right to oppose what they do." Not quite.

Let's be sure that we understand God's truth and apply it accurately. There is no room for interjecting our own faulty thinking.

Today's Truth: Brothers, do not be children in your thinking. Be infants in evil, but in your thinking be mature. 1 Corinthians 14:20

NOVEMBER 14

A HOUSE FULL OF STUFF

I intended to get there earlier to help. It did not work out that way.

Josh and Megan, wonderful friends of ours, had a big day today. Their family of five have lived all their kid-filled life in a tiny three-bedroom, one bath house. It has been a good house, filled with love and memories. They made the most of the space they had, keeping everything neat and tidy. It was cute and homey. The backyard was good-sized and lovely, a creek running along the boundary. With no garage, the sole family car sat by its lonesome in the driveway winter, spring, summer and fall. Not ideal.

But no more. This family found the perfect house. After selling their house quickly and without complication, this four-bedroom, three bath house spreads out over four levels. It has a large garage and a humongous deck off the wide-open kitchen, dining, and living room area. The flat backyard, partly shaded by a giant tree, is plenty big enough for the kids' trampoline and energetic soccer play, in addition to a large shed tucked away in the back corner.

I knew I would be late in helping load the truck. So late, in fact, that all the happy helpers had already loaded up, navigated to the new house, and had everything unloaded by the time I got there. Big help I turned out to be.

I was surprised by one thing, however. There were boxes everywhere. I never anticipated so many! They were piled high in every room and every corner. The garage was full, and I heard the storage building was already filling its role as protectant of "stuff." So, the question became, "Where was all this stuff at the other house that had no garage and half the space as this one?" Some things will remain a mystery.

Megan commiserated about the mountains of things. "I can't believe how much stuff we have. I'm going to go through everything and get rid of as much as possible!" Her situation is not unique. I hate to think if we ever had to move. It is so easy to accumulate. Even more so, it is easy to accumulate less than useful things in our everyday living: too much TV, too much music. Too many things that distract us from being the best moms and dads possible. Too much self-love and attention.

Let's not be be crowded out by non-essentials. Purge. Clean out. Be careful not to take in more than is necessary.

Today's Truth: And he said to them, "Take care, and be on your guard against all covetousness, for one's life does not consist in the abundance of his possessions." Luke 12:15

NOVEMBER 15

PECULIAR PEOPLE

It is Sunday afternoon. Outside the winds are howling as a coldfront moves into the area. The skies are gray, and the air is misty. It is not a day that begs venturing out. So, I will not.

Our lunch after church centered around warmed up venison stew, doctored with homemade biscuits layered on top and baked to a golden brown. "This is a homey, hot lunch for a cold dreary day," offered Seth. But once our bowls were licked clean by Rasta the Beagle, everyone went their merry ways, leaving the huge, comfy couch to me and me alone. Ah, bliss.

An ESPN series of documentaries called *30 for 30* caught my attention. I am not a professional basketball fan, but this episode highlighted the ups and downs of the Detroit Pistons' "Bad Boys." There was John Salley, captain Isiah Thomas, Rick Mahorn, Dennis Rodman, and Bill Laimbeer. Together they ended up winning the NBA championship in both the 1988-89 and 1989-90. But it was not pretty.

Laimbeer was known as a man of war. He was a huge center who put the ball in the hoop. But he was antagonistic, even vicious. His goal was to rule opponents by force. Dirty play and purposeful altercations became his trademark. His sidekick was Isiah Thomas. At 6'2", his all-out, no fear play belied his stature. His constant infectious smile only confused the issue when he threw the first punch. Rick Mahorn was an uncontrolled defensive genius, perhaps the most physically ruthless of them all.

But what about Rodman? He played with reckless abandon. His effort was said to be the same relentless style no matter the game, no matter the score. And Salley? At 6'11" he still leads the franchise in shots blocked. But his role was of great importance. He was a thinker, a social architect responsible for reigning in the peculiar mix of personalities.

The take-away? Though the ruthless, unsportsman-like behaviors are certainly suspect, those men—and we are talking the whole team, not just the five—came to love each other. For Rodman, fatherless and with a mother who never voiced, "I love you," those Pistons became his family. An inseparable band of brothers. They created a culture of 100% effort on and off the court.

Were they peculiar? Sure. But aren't we? God takes us, a peculiar people, and binds us together by common purpose and Spirit. Then He weaves together a plan no one could ever see coming.

Today's Truth: For thou art an holy people unto the Lord thy God, and the Lord hath chosen thee to be a peculiar people unto himself, above all the nations that are upon the earth. Deuteronomy 14:2 (KJV)

NOVEMBER 16

LOSING FOCUS

The day dawned crisp and bright. The cold front that moved in last night left clear skies and diminishing winds. The tennis team received instructions to be on the courts at 8:00 a.m. to warm up. Their intrasquad tournament play would commence at precisely 8:30 a.m.

When I arrived at the athletic center, up the hill and a half mile away from the courts, the ladies were in the lobby at the nutrition counter, each lining up to claim their duly allotted pile of snacks. I glanced at my watch. Hum. It was about ten minutes after the hour. Were they not supposed to already be on the courts?

"Hey girls," I queried. "Are you still playing matches at 8:30?" Almost in unison, they nodded and affirmed that fact. I wondered if they had eaten breakfast or if the snacks twenty minutes before the first serve were intended to count as the first meal of the day. "Okay, see you there," not at all confident any of them were taking the match play seriously.

Sure enough, they were not prepared to begin their matches at the bottom of the hour. Coach was not happy about extending the warm-up time but did so to avoid potential injury. With few exceptions, the play was technically sloppy. One of the players gave up quickly, showing zero enthusiasm or grit to overcome. Another pouted and had extended talks with the fence when things began to go south. Overall, it was ugly. When it was over, Coach told them so.

So, what was the problem? I suspect part of it was loss of perspective. Caught in the crosshairs of the Covid conundrum, there has been no competitive fall season. Yes, they have been training. However, they are in the last week before heading home for Thanksgiving and Christmas. They are not scheduled (or even allowed) to return until sometime in January. They will then train for an abbreviated spring season, assuming restrictions due to the virus do not cancel that as well.

It is hard to maintain fervor and hard work in a situation where the future is unsure. I empathize. Only the most mature athletes can prepare now for what might come later. It is like chopping wood. You do not chop wood for this season. You chop it now so it will be ready to burn next season. It is all about being faithful and obedient in the present for the sake of the future.

Today's Truth: looking to Jesus, the founder and perfecter of our faith, who for the joy that was set before him endured the cross, despising the shame, and is seated at the right hand of the throne of God. Hebrews 12:2

November 17

Windy Conditions

I am seldom excited to go out and run when there is a good chance I will get picked up by the wind and be carried off to Oz. It is even worse when it is frigid. The wind cuts through to my very core despite best attempts to dress accordingly.

Guess what? It is cold and windy today. I suppose it explains why I am still at my desk despite a rather light schedule. The sound of the howling wind that comes through my office walls is not encouraging me to leave the building anytime soon. I wish there was a way to provide a recording. You would be impressed by how ferocious it sounds. There is something about the architecture of this building that suggests the big, bad wolf is outside doing some serious huffing and puffing.

I have never experienced a tornado up close and personal, but I have been knocked over by the wind. It is not a pleasant feeling because there is little you can do to escape its strength. The only viable recourse is to put your head down and fight your way forward. It is hard. It takes a lot of work.

When I think wind, I think of the passage from Ephesians 4. Paul is writing to the church, trying to explain the role of apostles, prophets, evangelists, shepherds, and teachers. They were (and still are) given the responsibility *to equip the saints for the work of the ministry, for building up the body of Christ until we all attain the unity of the faith and of the knowledge of the Son of God, to mature manhood, to the measure of the stature of the fullness of Christ. . .* (Eph. 4:12-13). But why? *It's so that we may no longer be children, tossed to and fro by the waves and carried about by every wind of doctrine, by human cunning, by craftiness in deceitful scheme* (Eph. 4:14).

See, Paul knew that we tend to go with the flow, or in this case, with the wind. We hear one thing, and it sounds pretty good. Then we come across another idea and plug into that. We become fickle and anything but discerning. Nevertheless, there is a way to keep from being buffeted by those false "winds of doctrine." We must lean into our leaders who value and take seriously the truth of the Scriptures. They are God's instruments for growing us up into Christ.

Today's Truth: Rather, speaking the truth in love, we are to grow up in every way into him who is the head, into Christ, from whom the whole body, joined and held together by every joint with which it is equipped, when each part is working properly, makes the body grow so that it builds itself up in love. Ephesians 4: 15-16

NOVEMBER 18

CRAZY

I have no explanation for why I feel so jittery. I feel nervous. My legs are thumping more than usual. I cannot seem to keep them still. My mind is racing as I ferociously eat peanut M&Ms. That is a tell-tale sign that something big is about to happen.

That big thing? It concerns my mother's estate. For months we have been waiting for the Pennsylvania probate court to do what they are supposed to do. To sum up their efficiency: they do not seem to have any. But finally, a call from our lawyer confirmed they had received from the court the appropriate papers needed for me to transact her estate. And the court's timing could not have been worse. The Pennsylvania governor is shutting the place down again due to Covid concerns. Yippee. Just what I needed.

A new mandate demands that all who enter the state must have either a negative Covid test within the previous 72 hours, or alternatively, choose to hunker down alone for fourteen days. The second option is simply not possible. Hence, Gary and I will be Covid tested tomorrow, about 76 hours before our anticipated arrival. That is the best we can do. And what if the results, that take between three and six days to report, do not get reported back to us soon enough? Will we be stopped by the police? Will the banks refuse to allow us passage through their lobby doors? This kind of stuff makes me crazy.

Multiple phone calls resulted in obtaining appointments at the banks, necessary because all Pennsylvania banks closed their lobbies today. My niece cannot have dinner with us because if she does, she is not permitted to go to work for two weeks. Seriously?

I need to settle my stirred-up innards. Does worrying change anything? No. Do I understand it might even be sinful to be anxious? Yes. But how can I convince my head to accept the truth my heart already knows? Perhaps the answer is in knowing and internalizing God's promises to listen to our prayers and answer them.

"Father, God, have mercy and be gracious to us. Please allow us to accomplish what we need to get done next week. Amen."

Today's Truth: To you, O Lord, I cry, and to the Lord I plead for mercy. Psalm 30:8

November 19

Am i a quitter?

As I gathered my things, I glanced down at the corner of my desk. There was a small piece of paper taped to the desk with clear packing tape. The tape preserved the words written on the card: "I promise. I will not quit."

I wrote those words years ago. Honestly, I am uncertain where I heard those phrases, but I do know it was at the race briefing of an ultramarathon. The race director had everyone repeat the pledge aloud. It was meant to be inspirational. It was to be the mantra remembered at 3 a.m., in the darkness, suffering while crawling up a big mountain after the fun meter bottomed out. I have been there. I know how the negative thoughts can turn even the most resolute competitor into a blubbering mess who decides to call it quits at the soonest possible moment.

As I venture through my days at work, I wonder if I am a quitter. Today was the last day of fall practice for the volleyball girls. They will all be leaving for home and not returning until January. I will likely have moved to a different job by then. Am I a quitter because I am moving on? Am I quitter because I no longer want to raise support? Am I a quitter because I feel unappreciated?

It is impossible for me to adequately describe how much I cherish being a part of something larger than myself. I love feeling at home on campus. I love walking into the gym or onto the courts to be greeted with hugs and high fives. I love the athletes I mentor. I love chasing down a bazillion tennis balls at practice. I don't even mind getting pelted by a hard-hit volleyball when I assist at their training sessions. I am beyond crazy about how great the coaches' bible studies have been. So, am I wrong to leave all that behind? But do I really have any other choice?

These are hard days full of conflict between my own two ears. I desperately want to make a difference in the lives of young woman. But maybe this is an opportunity to be creative in maintaining relationships. It makes no difference if I am in "fulltime ministry" or not. It is my responsibility to minister somehow, someway, no matter what.

Today's Truth: Older women likewise are to be reverent in behavior, not slanderers or slaves to much wine. They are to teach what is good, and so train the young women to love their husbands and children, to be self-controlled, pure, working at home, kind, and submissive to their own husbands, that the word of God may not be reviled. Titus 2, 3-5

NOVEMBER 20

BE KIND. MEET NEEDS

It was impressive. The ladies had been told their meal was being catered from the Olive Garden. Not that the Olive Garden does not have good food, mind you. But when everyone arrived, standard fare they did not find.

It was the women's tennis team Christmas party. Held at Coach's house, everyone arrived in anxious anticipation. Though Thanksgiving had not even passed, except for the men's and women basketballers and football team, the university was closing until mid-January. Everyone was scheduled to leave campus in the next few days. Hence, a Friday night party seemed in order.

Unbeknownst to all of us, assistant Coach Lemmi (AKA Chef Lemmi) and Coach Maren's wife, Julie, spent the entire day cooking, but not the easy stuff. Rather, they cooked a dish native to each country or state represented by each player. There were California Sushi rolls, Texas pulled pork, Vietnamese spring rolls, Brazilian cheese bread, Swedish meatballs, and dishes from Peru and England that shall remain nameless because I cannot remember what they were called. It was quite the feast. In fact, a labor of love. The coaching staff went out of their way to be kind and thoughtful. Their efforts were not lost on the girls.

The only downside was a kitchen that looked as if a hurricane blew in from the south. The sink was filled to overflowing, dirty pots rested on the stove, and leftover ingredients littered the counters. As the girls howled their way through their riotous gift exchange, I began to take on the task of cleaning up. I scrubbed each of the twenty plus serving dishes and plates, dessert dishes, pots and pans, utensils, and the miscellaneous carnage from the day-long cooking marathon. The players all left, along with the other staff members. I remained elbow-deep in soap suds—and loved every minute.

I enjoy bringing order to chaos. But more so, I enjoy meeting the needs of another out of kindness. When the last dish was put to rest in the cupboard and the sink was scoured to a shine, Julie offered, "This was the best gift you could have ever given me. Thank you." My heart was glad to have helped.

Today's Truth: Put on then, as God's chosen ones, holy and beloved, compassionate hearts, kindness, humility, meekness, and patience, Colossians 3:12

November 21

When the Kids Grow Up

If you are a parent, can you recall a time when something your kid did stopped you in your tracks? Not in a bad way, mind you. But they did something, and in doing so suddenly made you realize that this child, who once fit snuggly in the crook of your arm, was all grown up? I had two such experiences today, but neither centered around my own flesh and blood.

One of the volleyball players, Aspen, invited me to breakfast and a bible study today. We have become close over the last couple years. This tall, powerful athlete is a thinker. She takes in data, examines it, considers carefully all the possibilities, and comes to a reasonable conclusion. On and off the court, this is her normal. With several college woman gathered in her living room, she expertly took us through a discussion of Psalm 77, tied in Hebrews 4, and ended up in Exodus. She was eloquent and thoughtful, drawing out the need to be transparent in our prayers to God. She reminded us that even though our emotions can be all over the place, understanding the character of God helps us keep perspective.

From her efforts in the kitchen preparing breakfast, to the depth of her preparation for the bible study, and her desire to know Christ more intimately, I was impressed to see such growth. Ten months ago, she was struggling. Now, she was showing signs of down-deep understanding and maturity. Instead of me leading her, Aspen led me.

Leaving Aspen's house, the next stop was at an open house for a young friend of mine, Emily. I began coaching and mentoring Emily when she was a middle school kid. Today, she is a senior in college. Two of her friends are joining her in their very first independent living situation. They acquired a three bedroom, three and a half bath town home. They are doing all the necessary things homeowners do; set up accounts, make utility deposits, furnish the place, create budgets, stock the frig, and a whole lot of other things. To see her effortlessly move about in this new situation turned my heart to mush.

Kids grow up, whether they are your own flesh and blood, or not. Relationships evolve, sometimes even reverse. It is a privilege to be a part of the process.

Today's Truth: Train up a child in the way he should go; even when he is old he will not depart from it. Proverbs 22:6

NOVEMBER 22

IT IS WELL

Tears roll every time I hear the tune and listen to the opening verse: "When peace like a river attendeth my way, when sorrows like sea billows roll. What ever my lot, thou hast taught me to say, it is well, it is well, with my soul."

My moment was in the car today as Gary and I headed north. Months after my Mother's passing, I had finally received from the court the proper documentation allowing me to execute her will. With bank appointments scheduled, we were praying that all the logistics could be completed in the next several days. There was much to contemplate as we rolled along, but when that old hymn filled the car, it put things in perspective. While we have certainly sorrowed, how much more the author of those words.

Horatio Spafford was a successful attorney and real estate guru. Living in Chicago, however, he lost nearly everything in the 1871 Chicago fire, and at about the same time, buried his four-year old son who succumbed to scarlet fever. Thinking that the family could use a vacation, he put his wife and four other children on a ship to England. Tragically, their ship collided with another and sank. The four children perished. His wife survived and sent a telegram. "Saved alone. What shall I do?"

Spafford carried his grief onboard the next ship and set sail to unite with the only remaining member of his family. The captain of his ship alerted Spafford as they passed near the place where the ship went down. His profound reflections resulted in the penning of the familiar words. Consider the following stanzas, however, as he articulates the bigger picture beyond his pain:

Though Satan should buffet, though trials should come, Let this blest assurance control, That Christ has regarded my helpless estate, And hath shed His own blood for my soul.
My sin, oh, the bliss of this glorious thought. My sin, not in part but the whole, Is nailed to the cross, and I bear it no more, Praise the Lord, praise the Lord, o my soul.

Spafford carried on because he understood that his "helpless estate" was resolved in Christ. What an amazing perspective.

Today's Truth: And the peace of God, which surpasses all understanding, will guard your hearts and your minds in Christ Jesus. Philippians 4:7

November 23

A jumbled mess of emotions

Mother died over three months ago. It was difficult to drive "home" to plan a funeral, bury her body, and dispense of all her earthly goods and wares. I certainly felt sorrow and shed tears, but for the most part, I was surprised at how well I held it together. Well, if you discount the first Sunday once we got back to Virginia and went to church. That was a rough day.

Time has passed and life has returned to, well, "normal." Mom lived seven hours from us. It's not like we lived next door and visited often. I talked with her on the phone to stay in touch, but toward the end, it was hard to get her to answer anyone's phone calls. I have not spent weeks on end mourning. She was miserable in her worn-out body and ready to meet her Lord. Does this lack of deep-seated hurt and pain mean something is wrong with me?

Gary and I arrived in Perkasie yesterday, my hometown. Being the executrix for Mother's estate, we are here to deal with financial matters. Appointments with banks were made and checked off the to-do list. We ate at Mother's favorite restaurant for old-time's sake. I pointed out to Gary the houses of long-ago friends, the schools I attended, and other points of interest. And then we drove past the cemetery. I felt my eyes fill with tears the closer we got. That surprised me. I really had not intended to stop by. Realistically, however, when would I ever return? Gary turned the car and slowly made our way to the now-empty grave site.

It was so different. On this cold and windy day, the place was desolate and barren. Leaves blowing, graves unadorned. I opened the door and walked to the tombstone. Instead of a tent over the copper-colored casket and lovely flowers, only a pile of dirt remained. Two holes had formed as the dirt settled. For some inexplicable reason, I began to use my feet to fill in the hollowed places. A hole within a hole seemed to be deep. My tears blurring my vision, I felt compelled to fill the void that seemed to reach all the way to the vault six feet under. "I'll make sure you're tucked in good and tight, Mother," half laughing, half crying. Mom would have chuckled at that. Once satisfied that the mound looked satisfactory, I snapped a picture and got back in the car. We drove away. Parting is sorrowful but not devoid of hope.

Today's Truth: But we do not want you to be uninformed, brothers, about those who are asleep, that you may not grieve as others do who have no hope. For since we believe that Jesus died and rose again, even so, through Jesus, God will bring with him those who have fallen asleep. 1 Thessalonians 4:13, 14

NOVEMBER 24

IN ITS TIME

Our hotel that we had been staying in is about eight miles north of my childhood town. This is fortunate because it meant we were eight miles closer to our life in the shadow of the Blue Ridge Mountains. Our trip home took us north before turning west and then south in route from Pennsylvania to Virginia. That meant there was no final glimpse at the house where I grew up, no thoughts of my high school days, no last passage through the famous covered bridge, no last drive down memory lane. It was better that way.

With all my mother's estate-related documents tucked safely away in the car, Gary and I made the seven-hour trip back home. Yesterday was productive. We were able to access Mother's bank accounts, closing those before opening an estate account. Now comes the necessity to sell stock, pay bills, and make appropriate dispursements to my brothers and a few others per the will. Honestly, it is nerve-wracking. I do not want to make any mistakes or fail to dot all the i's and cross all those t's. I do not need the state coming after me for screwing something up!

It was my intention to begin the check-writing process tonight once we arrived home. But I reconsidered. Sitting in my own living room provides balance and perspective. Postponing that task until tomorrow will not hurt a thing. In fact, I will be less inclined to make a mistake. If I take things one step at a time, the settling of the estate will be accomplished in its time.

It became clear a long time ago that I tend to rush ahead willy-nilly. I can make rash decisions that may not be in anyone's best interest. I work at break-neck speed, hurrying frantically to cross yet another task off the to-do list. "Get out of my way. Here I come!" That is a tough way to live 24/7/365.

My goal is to work on being efficient but not hurried. To take things as they come. To trust the process. To not jump ahead and miss a step in the process. To relax knowing the sun will come up tomorrow whether I check everything off my list or not.

"Lord, help me accomplish what I must in its own time, and let the rest go."

Today's Truth: The Lord will keep your going out and your coming in from this time forth and forevermore. Psalm 121:8

November 25

Light 'em up

'Tis the season for lights, red and green, and all things festive. Well, at least most folks would agree that tomorrow, Thanksgiving Day, marks the beginning of colored verses white lights, steady verses blinking, and artificial tree verses real tree debates. For the first time in years, our family will enter the fray.

When the kids were little, I invested in a huge blue spruce artificial tree. It was so realistic that it faked people out for the twenty plus years it brightened our living room. However, when this tree was purchased, it was several decades before trees came pre-lit. It was time-consuming to weave the lights in and out of the branches, patience being the premier prerequisite. But once it was done, it was beautiful. I loved to turn off all the other lights and bask in the glow of the white lights.

But the boys? Every year they contended for colored lights. I may have conceded once or twice, but for the most part, it was my opinion that the white lights were more sophisticated. They did not care about sophistication. They just wanted bright and colorful. This year, everyone can have their way.

After many Christmases with a puny four-foot white tree, I took the plunge and bought a beautifully flocked tree tonight. The best thing about it is that there are eight different settings. White, colored, blinking, steady, and combinations thereof. I am looking forward to making our house look like Christmas tomorrow after dinner. Then I plan on sitting in the dark and staring at the magnificent glow of the tree just as I did long ago.

There is something about the dark that makes the lights seem so much brighter. The light above my sink does not need to be on during the day because the sunlight streaming in from the window renders it nearly imperceptible. But come sunset, the light from the pendant lamp becomes vitally important. The light dispels the darkness. The light allows me to see more clearly. The light shows me what is dirty and what needs to be cleaned. The light is in stark contrast to the dark.

Do I make a difference in a dark world? Is my light bright enough to give others hope and show the way? It should be.

Today's Truth: that you may be blameless and innocent, children of God without blemish in the midst of a crooked and twisted generation, among whom you shine as lights in the world, Philippians 2:16

NOVEMBER 26

THANKSGIVING

Thanksgiving dinner is in the oven and the house is quiet. The day is not what it used to be. In fact, it is not even what it was supposed to be.

When I was growing up, the day always began with a decades-old tradition: a football game of epic proportions. It was the conclusion of the Bux-Mont League football season. Pennridge High School verses Quakertown High School. School activities in the days preceding centered around the game. A pancake breakfast was held the day before followed by a pep rally and bonfire that night. Boys bought their mothers and girlfriends green mums to wear on their coats. 10,000 fans routinely showed up for the game no matter the weather. One year deep snow was necessarily shoveled off the field and piled high along the sidelines.

Mother always stayed home to prepare the special meal, having it ready to consume when dad, my brothers, and I returned. We always had extra guests, the house filled with wonderful aromas and lively conversation. It was invigorating and spectacular. Not quite like today.

Seth, Pam, and Addyson are on their way back home having visited family in West Virgina. Caleb, our other son, bowed out with a migraine. McKinley, Caleb's better half, was with her family. Gary's sister, Joy, her husband, one daughter, son-in-law, and a granddaughter also opted out after Gary reported he was in the same room with one of our elders who found out his daughter had tested positive for Covid. The table was set for 11. Now there are but five place settings.

But lest you think I am complaining, I am not. There is so much for which to be thankful. We have each other, we are healthy, we have provisions to make our lives comfortable. Our church family is awesome. It is 70-degrees and the sun is shining. I just came in from a good run. And these things do not even touch the surface.

We celebrate simply and quietly this year. (Although, it will inevitably get a little louder once Addyson gets here later today.) Mother is celebrating her first Thanksgiving in heaven, and all is well.

Today's Truth: Enter his gates with thanksgiving, and his courts with praise! Give thanks to him; bless his name! For the Lord is good; his steadfast love endures forever, and his faithfulness to all generations. Psalm 100: 4, 5

NOVEMBER 27

THE LAST TESTAMENT

The large table, cleared of place settings and random items that seem to be drawn to it by magnetic force, was ready for another insult. Out came multiple folders, envelopes, and two heavy metal boxes with dulled keys sticking out from the locks. Soon, the table was covered with piles of papers. Item by item, I sorted, organized, and discarded. These things all came from Mother's place. As the executrix of her estate, I was tasked to bring order to her affairs, pay bills, and disperse funds to those she willed.

After some time, the disheveled mounds became ordered piles of various categories: pay these bills, keep this account info, and take future action. However, the floor morphed into the dump zone. Deeds for my 1950's childhood home that had twice been sold since Mother moved out a decade ago. Correspondence that had no current relevance. Duplicates of old legal files. But amidst the mayhem, a faded letter revealed itself. It was written in Feb 1958, dictated by my father's father, and scribed in her flowing penmanship by my grandma. He dictated it less than two months before his passing. It stopped me dead in my tracks.

To Donald, Margaret, David and Rebekah, I commit my soul into the hands of my Savior in full confidence that having redeemed it and washed it in His most precious blood, He will present it faultless before the throne of my Heavenly Father, and entrust you, my children, to maintain and defend at all hazards and at any cost of personal sacrifice, the blessed doctrine of the complete atonement for sin through the blood of Jesus Christ once offered and through that alone. In love, Mother and Dad

I read it multiple times to let the words sink in through that beautifully composed and profound run-on sentence. What must have Grandma and Grandpap's discussion been like as they prepared for the last weeks of his life? Were they sad? Did they cry together? Was Grandma prepared to be a widow? Did they discuss logistics?

I guess I will never know. But one thing is evident. Grandpap was ready. Death held no power over him. He was confident that by grace alone through Christ alone, his eternity in heaven with His Father was assured.

*Today's Truth: **In him we have redemption through his blood, the forgiveness of our trespasses, according to the riches of his grace, which he lavished upon us, in all wisdom and insight Ephesians 1:7, 8***

NOVEMBER 28

IS IT WORTH IT?

Have you ever questioned if "it" was worth it? I sure have.

Consider being in the middle of a long race. It is blustery, 33-degrees and cold, penetrating rain soaking in from head to toe. The needle is no longer visible on the fun meter. There are hours and hours of racing before the finish line is in sight. Everything hurts. Your hands are numb. Fingers refuse to work the zipper on your pack. You cannot feel the tootsies inside your shoes. You are nauseous and running on fumes. Is it worth it to persist just so you can say you finished? If you do continue, it will be nothing but pain, suffering, and misery. Few would fault you for throwing in the towel.

Sound familiar? Well, it does if you are an ultrarunner, but it may not if you have never entered the fray. But even so, you do not have to be an ultrarunner to know that the question, "Is it worth it?" must be answered daily. The answer to that question, no matter the situation, is seldom easy.

Pam, my daughter-in-law, is a smart, hardworking, talented young lady. She spent years as a paralegal, has managed restaurants, waitressed, and been a food and beverage manager for the Academy of Arts here in town. While waiting for a final offer as a manager for a new restaurant, she has been biding her time waitressing at another restaurant. She is not impressed with the establishment despite rave reviews of the food. There seems to be an absence of teamwork among the workers. Some of the wait staff are constantly busy while others are left twiddling their thumbs. The latter leave their shifts with near-empty pockets.

After working a long shift last night, Pam left again this morning. Working from 9 a.m. until a break at 2:30 p.m., she made a mere $4 in tips. Assigned but one table while others were awarded more desirable tables, she was rightfully discouraged. "Is it worth it?" was on her mind before leaving again for the 4 p.m. to 11:00 p.m. shift. Would the tables again be unfairly assigned? Admirably, she decided her reputation was more important than any financial gain. She did not want to quit abruptly out of anger, risking being labeled a sourpuss. That takes a great deal of self-restraint and humility. Good for her.

Do we do well in protecting our reputation even when we ask, "Is it worth it?" We should.

Today's Truth: A good name is to be chosen rather than great riches, and favor is better than silver or gold. Proverbs 22:1

November 29

Faith, love, and hope

"Devotions for the team Monday or Tuesday?" I hurriedly texted back. "Of course. Tell me when and where!"

I get excited when Coach Green (or any other coach) asks me to do something special for the team. In this case, it was his D1 women's basketball team. Under non-Covid circumstances, I would know his girls well by this time in the season. For the past three years, Coach has allowed me to plan and lead an off-campus retreat for several pre-season days. This gives me great opportunity to deepen relationships with the returning players and get to know the new. But that did not happen this year. I simply do not feel the depth of connection this year.

So now that I know I will have some front time with the team, what will I teach? These sessions are not long and drawn out. It is neither the venue to teach expositionally nor pound away at difficult doctrinal questions. Rather, it needs to be Bible-based, easy to understand, and practically applied to their lives as women, athletes, and students. I think the first chapter of 1 Thessalonians will be just right!

Here is the situation: The trio of Paul, Silas, and Timothy together compose a letter to the church established in Thessalonica. They had all spent time there prior to this letter. Hence, the letter feels like a very personal conversation. They write about how thankful they are for these believers and for their steadfastness. Apparently, when they first learned of the Gospel, they accepted it despite *severe suffering*. There was no faking it! The power of the Gospel was evident to all.

The reputation of these Greek believers was founded on three components, each one springing into action because of the others: *work produced by faith, labor prompted by love, and endurance inspired by hope.*

What kind of impact would this basketball team have if they could become known for their work, labor, and endurance that had been produced by the outworking of their faith, love, and hope? What kind of impact might I have by demonstrating these three things in my own life?

Quite the challenge.

Today's Truth: We remember before our God and Father your work produced by faith, your labor prompted by love, and your endurance inspired by hope in our Lord Jesus Christ. 1 Thessalonians 1:3 (NIV)

NOVEMBER 30

OUTSIDE THE CAMP

Covid has hit close to home. Well, actually, Covid has hit *in* our home. I am already beginning to feel the pinch that quarantine puts on a soul.

Seth, Pam, and Addy traveled to West Virginia last Tuesday to visit with Pam's family. Like millions of Americans, visiting parents and siblings was a long-time coming. And who could blame them? Everyone was healthy and there seemed to be no immediate threat to the safety and well-being of anyone. So, off they went, returning home Thursday afternoon for our own Thanksgiving dinner.

Last night while Pam was at work, Seth was doing a construction project for his brother, and Gary and I were riding herd on our full-speed ahead granddaughter. Soon, the familiar beep of an incoming text sounded from my phone. "We all need to be tested for the 'rona. Pam's on her way home." The origin of the message was from Seth's phone. Pam's mom let them know she developed symptoms and tested positive. Shoot. I knew what was coming. Fourteen days at home.

Addy has developed a mild case of the sniffles along with a come-and-go headache. After a virtual doctor appointment, Seth and Pam took her to be Covid tested. Though her never-say-die energy level is off the charts, we await the results. Regardless of the result, by CDC standards, Seth and his little family had direct contact with a positive case, demanding fourteen days of hunkering down. Because they live with us, Gary and I become guilty by association.

The thought of being home bound for ten more days does nothing to fill me with joy. But it does cause me to think back to the Levitical laws. Those guys must have had a pretty good understanding of disease control. The leftovers from burnt offerings and dead animals had to be dragged outside the camp to prevent any potential for contamination. And people? Skin diseases, illnesses, and a variety of other conditions forced the afflicted to live for an established period in quarantine outside the camp walls. The priests played the role of doctor, deciding when they could rejoin the group. For the most part, they knew how to limit exposure and stop the spread of disease. Is there relevance to our current precautions surrounding Covid? Maybe. They got put out of the camp. We stay inside our house. But I had to giggle when I realized those guys wore masks as well! Read *Today's Truth*.

Today's Truth: Anyone with such a defiling disease must wear torn clothes, let their hair be unkempt, cover the lower part of their face and cry out, 'Unclean! Unclean!' As long as they have the disease they remain unclean. They must live alone; they must live outside the camp. Leviticus 13:44-46

DECEMBER 1

WALKING BLIND

Being quarantined has a funny way of directing behavior. For me, sitting at the dining room table with my computer open offered the opportunity to "surf." Stumbling upon a Mark Lowry video, a Christian singer, song writer (think "Mary did you know?"), and comedian, I listened as he recounted the story of Jesus healing the blind man. It comes from John 9. I revisited the passage to make sure what he said was true. It was.

Let's review. There is a guy who has been blind since birth. Jesus and his disciples walk by this fella who spends his days begging on the street. The followers ask accusingly, *Who sinned to make this happen?* Jesus must have been exasperated by the ignorance of the question. But he answers them anyway. This happened *that the works of God might be displayed in him.* Jesus proceeds to rub mud in the man's eyes before directing him to waltz over to the pool of Siloam to wash.

Wait. Understand what Jesus just asked a blind guy to do. The normal thing would be to lead a blind person to where he needed to go. But Jesus asks the man to do something risky. He essentially says: "Go ahead. Take a step of faith and find your way to the pool if you want healed." I can envision him making his way through the crowd, feeling his way, bumping into people, perhaps stumbling a bit, but eventually making it to the water. He washed off the mud as instructed before making his way back to Jesus, this time seeing every single detail along the way.

Of course, the Pharisees were not happy that Jesus did something so cool—on a Sabbath at that! The miracles were interfering with their power to control the masses. Nevertheless, no matter how much they bullied the man, the now-seeing man's testimony did not budge. When the frustrated religious leaders threw him out of the temple, Jesus got wind of this, again seeking out the sighted man. *Do you believe?* he asked.

Who is he, sir, that I might believe? asked the man. Jesus told him he was looking at him. The result? *Lord, I believe.*

Jesus used blindness to bring glory to himself. But in the process, Jesus asked the blind man to step out on faith even when he did not fully understand. We should be so bold.

Today's Truth: Jesus said, "For judgment I came into this world, that those who do not see may see, and those who see may become blind." John 9:39

DECEMBER 2

7, 10, OR 14?

Have I mentioned that sweet Addyson tested positive for Covid-19? She, her dad, and Pam (his wife) went to West Virginia last week for Thanksgiving. They left on Tuesday and returned to our house on Thursday, Thanksgiving Day. Somewhere in between, everyone was exposed to the virus. How do I know? Because Pam's mom began to have a few symptoms, got tested after everyone left Thursday morning, and got her positive results on Sunday night. Since it normally takes four to five days to feel any symptoms, we can assume Pam's mom was infected at the beginning of the week.

When Addyson said she had a headache and a few sniffles, Seth called the doctor and arranged for a virtual visit. They recommended a test. That was Monday of this week. (Today is Thursday.) The positive result came back Tuesday. She is doing great, barely affected. The physician gave instructions for fourteen days of quarantine, also saying we would need to quarantine for another fourteen days after that, for a total of 28 days. Turns out, that may or may not be the case.

The CDC came out with new guidelines. They said fourteen days may be too long. It should be ten days from the time of exposure, or seven days if you have a negative test in the last 48 hours of the week-long period. A covid-infected person is most contagious just prior to and during the first few days of illness. After day nine, there is a slim 1% chance of being contagious. That changes a lot!

So why fourteen days in the first place? One official is reported to have said, "Fourteen is a pretend number." It was picked because two weeks was an easy number to remember. However, fourteen is what everyone has come to know as gospel truth.

It is easy to make up rules that suit our purposes. And sometimes, those "rules" become the gospel. The Pharisees did it. So did the Sadducees. But we do it too. It is called legalism. We think because we do or do not do something, we earn brownie points. We think ourselves to be better than everyone else, shaming all who do not agree.

Let's be careful to stand by only what we know is absolute truth.

Today's Truth: And a man was there with a withered hand. And they asked him, "Is it lawful to heal on the Sabbath?"—so that they might accuse him. . . And the man stretched it out, and it was restored, healthy like the other. But the Pharisees went out and conspired against him, how to destroy him. Matthew 12:10

DECEMBER 3

JUST SHUT IT

If you have spent any time at all in the book of Proverbs, you will recall that nearly every other verse addresses less talk and a lot more listening—or at least it seems that way. For the last several months, a group of coaches join me for a systematic journey through those 31 chapters. The need to control what comes out of our mouths is blatantly obvious to all. So why is it that I put my foot in my mouth today? It certainly does not belong there.

It began as a normal text conversation with someone concerning our family's Covid situation. My true intention was simply to discuss the newest CDC statements concerning quarantine. I was very careful to not sound demanding or authoritative. I merely wanted to communicate recently published information from reliable scientific sources. So why was I accused of spouting "misinformation" and endangering the entire universe when suggesting a shorter period of isolation might be appropriate?

Honestly, I was a little perturbed. It was insulting that my counterpart would not even consider my perspective. But I also wanted to kick myself in the butt for having started the conversation in the first place. What did it matter in the big picture? I knew the propensity of my friend to be naturally argumentative. Did I really think I would change his mind? (And no, the person was not Gary or anyone in my family in case you are trying to guess.) Now I feel like this relationship is off kilter. That puts a knot in my stomach.

This situation begs the question. Do we avoid all discussions if there is a possibility of differing opinions? Do we keep our mouths shut to eliminate potential conflict, even though conflict is not always a bad thing? Sometimes conflict is necessary because it can clarify positions, be thought-provoking, and cause both parties to reflect and resolve.

From my understanding of Proverbs, I suspect it depends on the other person. If their character has been established as foolish, impetuous, or quick-tempered, we might be wise to avoid such interactions. If they are open to discuss the possibilities, then more power to ya. But in this case, I wish I had kept the trap door shut.

Today's Truth: Do not speak in the hearing of a fool, for he will despise the good sense of your words. Proverbs 23:9

DECEMBER 4

MOVING ON

Today seems odd. Other than my plan to use the contactless pickup feature at the local Wal-Mart, my plans are fluid. I have no must-do tasks to accomplish. Pam and Addyson are upstairs doing online schoolwork, Seth and Gary are outside tackling manly things, and I am left to sit in front of my computer contemplating life. My job prospects are up in the air, so much so that I just signed up for job alerts from Lowes. I have contemplated purging my closets and drawers, but since I have no idea if my next job will be scrubs, jeans, or business attire, it may not be wise to start chucking clothes.

In the meantime, I began to read in John 8, pondering why spending time in Scripture often becomes a last resort rather than the first. What caught my attention was the story about Jesus and the adulterous woman. Jesus came down from the Mt. of Olives to teach in the temple. He drew quite a diverse crowd; folks from all walks of life, curiosity seekers, and of course, the self-righteous scribes and Pharisees. The Scripture tells us they brought the sinful woman before Jesus, asking if they should stone her. It was a trap. But I imagine that the woman did not come willingly. I wonder what was going through her head. What if Jesus said "yes"? Was she going to die after being pummled by rocks?

Then Jesus did a curious thing. He started writing in the dirt. What did he write? Were they words or doodles? We do not know. It must have been frustrating to the religious dudes not to be answered directly. But then Jesus looks at them after what must have been a very pregnant pause and said, *Let him who is without sin among you be the first to throw a stone at her.* Then he started writing again, ignoring everyone. One by one, the leaders sheepishly walked away, presumably convicted that stone throwing was not appropriate.

All the while, Jesus and the woman remained. Once the nay-sayers were gone, Jesus stood up and asked the woman, *Woman, where are they? Has no one condemned you?* She responded in the negative. And what did Jesus do? Simple. He did not shame or rehash her sin. He simply gave a directive: *Go, and from now on sin no more.*

When I am guilted by my own sin, perhaps I need to do likewise. Just stop it and move on.

Today's Truth: Jesus stood up and said to her, "Woman, where are they? Has no one condemned you?" She said, "No one, Lord." And Jesus said, "Neither do I condemn you; go, and from now on sin no more." John 8: 10, 11

December 5

The great tidy

Our family's Covid quarantine is not all that bad. To be completely and transparently honest, it is rather nice to "have to" stay home. It makes it easy to say "Sorry, I can't." And with most of the athletes gone until January, no necessary ministry fundraising to worry about, and coaches scattered to soak in family time, I feel little guilt for not being my typical worker-bee self.

Lest you think, however, that my days are filled with idleness and naps, think again. Yes, Gary I might have binge watched a new Netflix series the last few late nights, but I have been as busy as the proverbial beaver during the days.

A handful of days ago I came across a new show to watch while sweating away on my old-fashioned Nordic track. It is called "Tidying Up with Marie Kondo." Marie is a very petite woman. She is Japanese, knows a little English but uses a translator to interact with her clients. She has wonderful ideas for keeping things in order, rarely touting the need for fancy organizers. She often recommends reusing little boxes or shoebox lids to group items together. Perhaps the best tip, however, is her folding technique. It was enough to inspire me to go through every article of clothing in our closets and drawers. I am delighted with the tidiness. Multiple bags of donatable items are ready to be carried off to Goodwill.

Beyond the organizing, Marie performs a ritual in every show. She finds a place in the house to kneel, explaining to her clients that she must introduce herself to the house; to commune with it. Eyes closed, she sits quietly for a period of time. Sometimes the owners join her in this quasi-spiritual endeavor. The organization begins in the aftermath of the bleassing, keeping only those items that "spark joy."

I get the idea that her process of blessing the house is rooted in Buddhism, though I do not know for sure. Nevertheless, it reminds me of a plaque that hung in my childhood home, asking God to bless the home. As I folded clothes and discarded items, I asked the Lord to bless our home, to help me loosen my grip on material things, and cling to only that which is eternal. I do not need more stuff that requires organization, but I do need to organize my life to best serve the Savior's purpose.

Today's Truth: Now therefore may it please you to bless the house of your servant, so that it may continue forever before you. 2 Samuel 7:29a

DECEMBER 6

CAR SHEEP

It was a relaxed moment, chilling on the couch with my laptop in hand. Because the Covid-crud prevents us from heading off to church, the morning was agenda-less. Scrolling through Facebook posts (because sexagenarians like me like to keep up with other sexagenarians), a few posts peaked a modicum of interest. But I laughed out loud when I saw a "friend's" picture post. I do not know this girl, hence the use of quotes on the friend title, but she lives in Colorado. The picture was a selfie taken in her car. The description was something like "When you take your sheep to Starbucks." Guess who was in the back seat? Yes. A very large sheep, starring into the camera as if to say, "You look'n at me?" with a thick New Yorker accent.

There was no further explanation. The vehicle looked to be a decent SUV. Did she make it a habit of loading up her favorite Baaaa Babe into the back seat for a Sunday morning drive? Was she a sheep farmer? Did she own but one pet sheep? Was the sheep going to the butcher shop to become a pile of lambchops? So many questions. So few answers.

I wonder if it was a difficult task to get said sheep into the vehicle. But then again, sheep are known to hear and heed their owner's voice. From what I have read about shepherding, the reason the shepherd is often surrounded by little ones is because once they learn the master's voice, they become very loyal. Even in a moment of rebellious scampering away, the little one is drawn back when called by the familiar voice.

I love it that Jesus often used the analogy of the shepherd and the sheep. It paints a wonderful picture of an attentive, caring shepherd leading his flock to the greenest of pastures and under his watchful eye. But ever wonder why we are likened to sheep? Why not chickens or cows? A goat? How about an elephant or tiger or lion? I presume it is due to the special relationship a good shepherd has with the flock. He cares for them, protects them, leads them to where they need to go, and he disciplines out of kindness when the sheep run off. The shepherd has such a tight relationship that he searches for the lost sheep and brings it to the place of safety.

I am thankful to be a sheep in Jesus flock.

Today's Truth: My sheep hear my voice, and I know them, and they follow me. I give them eternal life, and they will never perish, and no one will snatch them out of my hand. John 10: 27, 28

December 7

Words are important

There she was. Sweet Emily was front and center in her Zoom box. As her mentor and supervisor for an internship program this semester, we needed to finalize a few things.

I met Emily years ago when she was in late middle school. Emily's interest in running led her to me, the cross-country coach. She was a coach's dream athlete. She was all in, listening to instructions with rapt attention. Emily did exactly what was asked of her. My plan was her plan. Because of her dedication, she continued to improve. She sought excellence as an athlete, student, and leader. Emily was incredibly perceptive. Her radar lit up when a teammate was down and struggling. She was not my top runner, but year after year she was one of the most important athletes to the tenor of the team.

Emily is now a college senior, graduating a whole year early because of her hard, consistent work. One of the course requirements this semester was to complete a 250-hour internship. She chose to work with me, her end goal being full-time sports ministry. It was a perfect fit. Emily was able to shadow me to college team practices, led middle school and high school huddles, and assisted the area ministry office with logistics. But she also wrote.

One of Emily's goals was to become a more skilled writer. We decided that she could write and submit her work to be used in the daily devotional emails that National sends out. After tedious editing, Emily submitted the first two pieces eight weeks ago. Our efforts paid off. Both of those stories have already been used in an online format.

Our Zoom call today included a harsh edit of several more devotionals Emily had penned. Before we even got started Emily confessed. "Coach T, I don't like the sound of this one. I know what I want to say, but it sounds confusing and unclear. And it is too long." Together we wrestled with every line, chopping filler words and paying particular attention to clarity of message. Within a short time, the final edit was complete. Emily now has a strong, publishable piece of writing.

Words matter. As believers, we should be the first to communicate effectively and admirably.

Today's Truth: Let the words of my mouth and the meditation of my heart be acceptable in your sight, O Lord, my rock and my redeemer. Psalm 19:14

DECEMBER 8

ACTIVELY WAITING

Is there anyone who loves a waiting room? Not me. Waiting seems to be a waste of time. There are so many things I could be doing other than sitting still. And yet, I was reminded this morning that waiting can serve a powerful purpose.

I recently discovered a guy by the name of Coach Jay Mills. He was a college football coach turned pastor, author, and speaker. After signing up to keep track of his book in progress, notices of short video clips labeled "Chalk Talks" began to hit my inbox. This morning's two-minute talk was just what I needed.

I had a hard time getting to sleep last night. Most of the evening was spent updating my resume and sorting through a myriad of potential jobs. I felt a strong compulsion to do something, anything, to give my future substance. I found out yesterday that the job supposedly waiting for me at the hospital had fallen under the nursing banner. I am not a nurse. Hence, no matter my background as a perfusionist, the message "You are not being considered for this position" made my heart sink. Feelings of inadequacy overwhelmed me. I had to make something happen.

I told Gary I was concerned that I may be rushing ahead of God looking for jobs—even at home improvement centers. Was it not possible God expected me to be proactive in securing a job with benefits? Then I watched Coach Mill's video. He spoke of having heart surgery, spending fourteen days post-op in the hospital rather than the estimated four or five days. He concluded that just because he was waiting, it did not give him license to do nothing. When he embraced the possibility that God had work for him to do within those hospital walls while he waited, everything changed. His roommate came to faith, and many opportunities to serve and encourage staff and patients alike came to fruition.

Yes, I am in a waiting period. But I must see this time frame as an opportunity to serve those around me. I must believe that God, in His perfect timing, will make a way for me. Is doing my due diligence required? Yes. I think so. But I dare not attempt to manipulate circumstances.

I do not like waiting but I am looking forward.

Today's Truth: Therefore do not throw away your confidence, which has a great reward. For you have need of endurance, so that when you have done the will of God you may receive what is promised. Hebrews 10:35, 26

December 9

A trip gone bad

It started out nice enough. Gary and I got in my new-to-me eighteen-year-old car and headed to Richmond, a two and a half-hour trip. Being in the car together hardly broke our quarantine, and at our destination, Gary would interact from a distance with just one man. We looked forward to some time away from our property.

For the past few months, Gary has been driven, no pun intended, to find a big truck. Towing capacity and an extended cab were the two main considerations. When my wheeler-dealer husband found this truck a day ago, he did his due diligence, researched it, and decided it was the one. Off we went like a herd of turtles.

Sure enough, the truck was exactly as advertised. The transaction complete, the plan was for me to follow him on a different route back home. His GPS normally worked well, which is more than can be said for mine. Mine is a finicky thing, normally calling out "GPS signal lost" about 45 seconds after I tell it to "go."

Gary's first several turns were puzzling. Still, I figured he knew what he was doing. We ended up in downtown Richmond. To make matters worse, the stoplights seemed to turn red just as I reached the intersection. In rush hour traffic, I lost him on several occasions. We could not stay on the phone because his power level was 20% and falling fast. Could it get much worse?

Yes. Gary rarely gets upset. But he was tonight. He was frustrated because he failed to realize he had chosen the wrong route out of the three choices his phone presented. I was frustrated because I kept losing him. After 45 minutes of unproductive travel, I risked calling. He answered. My suggestion was to turn left at the next light, fill our vehicles with gas to appease the descending gauges, and regroup.

Regroup we did. Finally finding our way, we both regained hope that the day would eventually come to an end in our own bed. Our minds settled and perspective returned. We had both been on the brink of a major meltdown simply because we lost patience with our situation. Lack of patience is not uncommon, but it is a character skill we can work to improve.

Today's Truth: I therefore, a prisoner for the Lord, urge you to walk in a manner worthy of the calling to which you have been called, with all humility and gentleness, with patience, bearing with one another in love, eager to maintain the unity of the Spirit in the bond of peace. Ephesians 4:1-3

DECEMBER 10

PLEASE SIGN AND RETURN

With Gary in full-on EBay mode and Seth ordering massive amounts of supplies for his new house, there is no telling what we will find in the mailbox. It is not uncommon for the mail carrier to make her way down our third of a mile, bumpy driveway to the house to deliver whatever fails to fit in the oversized mailbox.

Today there was a mound of mail, much of it worthy of nothing more than the burn barrel. But I smiled at a sweet thank-you letter sent by a college student whom I mentor. A DMV notice ended up by Gary's computer for him to deal with, and an ornament sent by a non-profit in appreciation of a donation was carried straightway to the Christmas tree. And then I saw it. A letter from the IRS addressed to "Mr. Jack Trittipoe, Deceased." That got my attention.

There were several pages of gobblety-goop inside the envelope that I promptly opened, figuring there was slim to no chance that my dead father-in-law was going to care. It was something about a missing tax form. But I found the instructions curious. The papers required they be signed by Jack Trittipoe. Wait. Jack Trittipoe has been dead for nearly three years. How is that going to happen? There was absolutely no referral to an executor or living family member. Good luck on getting Jack Trittipoe to sign and return the documents.

The absurdity of the IRS expectation is laughable. Still, I might be guilty of having similar expectations. I expect to run a long race with good results despite not putting in tough training. I expect my husband to read my mind when I am unwilling to clearly express myself. I expect to grow spiritually without spending time in the study of the Scriptures. I expect an unbelieving friend to understand and accept my stand on certain social issues based on biblical truths.

In each instance, I need to be careful when it comes to expectations. Baseless expectations will only lead to frustration. Reasonable expectations based on that which is true, however, will keep things in perspective.

Today's Truth: Jesus answered, "Truly, truly, I say to you, unless one is born of water and the Spirit, he cannot enter the kingdom of God." That which is born of the flesh is flesh, and that which is born of the Spirit is spirit. John 3:5, 6

December 11

The mountains call

The weather guy predicted that today's temperature would be fifteen degrees higher than normal. That meant sunny skies and 60's. This is the kind of news that excites me, especially when I am officially using up vacation time. The lack of work expectations offered the freedom to run. The mountains called my name, and I had to go.

Later tonight, the Hellgate 100K+ trail race will begin. At 12:01 a.m. the race director will send out waves of brave souls into the night. Those who succeed will cross the finish line sometime tomorrow, 66.6 miles later. They will need to navigate rocky trails, climb mountains, descend the same, and fight off sleep demons in the middle of the night. I have completed this race ten times and failed twice. I love to hate this race. It is so hard. But I can not be involved this year. No running the race. No crewing for another who will run. No spectating. Covid has plagued our house since Thanksgiving, preventing me from risking exposing others to the virus.

But that could not stop me from going alone to the mountains. I left a note for Gary this morning, who was picking up more motorcycles to flip. The notecard made him aware of where I would park and the route I planned. I purposely picked my course to overlap the Hellgate course. I could check the course markings to make sure the runners would not be left wondering where to go.

Of course, running the course in daylight is much different than in the dark. Water cascading over the rocks in the stream will not be appreciated by the runners. The grandiose views from the side of the mountain will be lost on them. The beautiful black bear standing off in the distance will be camouflaged by the inky night. But, on the flip side, the dark disguises the difficulties ahead. The night caresses you, shutting out distractions and helping you focus in the moment.

Which is better? Running in the light or the dark? The light may be easier in some respects, but the dark offers lessons and opportunities not possible in the light of day. Perhaps the take home message is this: sometimes God calls us to *walk in the light as He is in the light.* Other times, our task is to walk by faith in the dark. Wherever I find myself, I have no choice but to be content to run on.

Today's Truth: The people who walked in darkness have seen a great light; those who dwelt in a land of deep darkness, on them has light shone. Isaiah 9:2

DECEMBER 12

I AM JEALOUS

One would think that after running 23 miles up and down mountains sleep would come easy. Not tonight. Not for me. That is why I am typing away at 3:30 in the morning.

Insomnia has been my nemesis for months, although it seems to be getting better in the past few weeks. In fact, tonight is the first night in recent days that sleep has completely alluded me. True, Gary and I did not turn off the TV until nearly midnight when a movie's credits rolled, which would be even more reason to find sleep quickly. But maybe it is the fact that 150 crazies began their Hellgate quest at about the same time. Maybe the problem is my jealousy.

With head on pillow and inviting slumber to come, I felt guilty being cozy between the new flannel sheets. Many of my friends had elected to forgo sleep, choosing instead hours upon hours of running and hiking and making forward progress. It was depressing that I was not able to be part of this race. Not only was I unable and ready to run the miles, but I was also not able to observe the race first-hand given the unlikely risk of becoming "that" person to unwittingly pass along the virus.

I specifically thought of Bethany and Sophie. Bethany was the first person to make me feel old and slow. Taking on the ultrarunning challenge as a college student, she has earned incredible numbers of podium stands in the last twenty years. Even in my younger days, I was never as good as her.

Then there is Sophie, a friend who is closer in age. Sophie has also made me feel like an inadequate has-been, breaking many of the age group records I once held. She, too, has ten Hellgate finishes. After achieving that milestone, she unequivocally stated that ten was enough. Yesterday I found out she had changed her mind. She answered my "What gives?" question by saying, "Life is too short. I didn't want to stay on the sidelines."

It comes down to this reality. I am envious of their ninja-like running along the trails at this very moment. I am jealous of the congratulations they will receive upon their finishes. I am green-eyed over the sense of accomplishment and fulfilment they are sure to experience given the race's difficulty and demand for perseverance. I am jealous, and that is ugly. Lord, forgive me.

Today's Truth: A tranquil heart gives life to the flesh, but envy makes the bones rot.
Proverbs 14:30

DECEMBER 13

GET COMFORTABLE

Six years ago yesterday, little Addyson graced the world with her presence. This one and only grandkid of ours has been a bright spot in our lives ever since. She has unbounded energy, sharp wit, an incredible vocabulary, and an imagination and creative streak that knows no end. She is obedient and kind, helpful and delightful, thoughtful and unselfish. I love her with all that I am.

After being home-bound at our house with Covid, she was finally able to re-unite with her mom a few days ago. Since then, her schedule has been befitting a social butterfly. Not one, not two, but three birthday parties with that side of the family. But in addition, that little pip-squeak was promised pierced ears. Addy was very excited and looking forward to that. "Grandma," she told me before returning to her mom, "I'll get sparkly stud earrings first, but then I may get some hoop earrings."

Pictures popped up on social media. Addy was all smiles, those new earrings twinkling in the bright lights of the jewelry store. But I also noticed she clutched to her chest, "Lamby." Lamby is a now-bedraggled stuffed animal given to her when a baby. "Lamby means so much to me," she has told me. "I love her so much. I've had her since I was born." It was obvious she took that "stuffie" to comfort her as small holes were punched into her ear lobes.

It got me thinking. What do I use to comfort myself when I am fearful or apprehensive? My first impulse is not to drown myself in gallons of ice cream, although a nice bowl of mint-chocolate chip can be soul-soothing. Alcohol is not a temptation since I have never had a drink. Slices of toasted home-made bread might have a chance to slow down raging thoughts. But more than food, my tendency is to isolate from everyone to be alone with my thoughts. This, however, can be counter-productive. Being alone has the potential to send my thoughts into a wild, spiraling, catastrophic cyclone.

Where should I go when comfort and reassurance is needed? I need to run "to the Rock that is higher than I." I need to hide in the *Shadow of his wings. I need to bless the God of all comfort.*

Today's Truth: Blessed be the God and Father of our Lord Jesus Christ, the Father of mercies and God of all comfort, who comforts us in all our affliction, so that we may be able to comfort those who are in any affliction, with the comfort with which we ourselves are comforted by God. 2 Corinthians 1: 3, 4

December 14

What to Do?

It is a dank and dreary morning. 39 degrees with rain. Earlier, Gary stoked the wood stove after it sat dormant over the last three 60-degree days. The house is now quiet. Gary left to take care of DMV matters, and Seth and Pam are cleaning out the office where Pam used to work. I am on the sofa trying to figure out what the day holds for me. It is wonderfully peaceful but lonely.

I am in a holding pattern. There are three job applications floating out there. I know they have been received and supposedly forwarded onto a decision-maker. But the timing? Who knows? Maybe nothing will happen until after the new year. Maybe the employers have gotten more qualified applicants and never intend to contact me. Maybe I am simply not good enough. Maybe they think I am too old, my resume extending back into the 1970's, an era just after dinosaurs roamed the earth.

It is humbling to think I may not have much to offer an employer. Should I start collecting social security early and retire, allowing plenty of time for my creative outlets? But what about insurance? Surely, I cannot afford to not have insurance given my medical issues and pharmacy bills. I am so conflicted.

Waiting is not my strong-suit. Plus, I do not like it. But that is exactly what I seem to be doing. With each notification I get of ministry donors stopping payments upon news of my resignation, I feel the walls of the waiting room closing in. There is no going back. No changing my mind. My current assignment is to stay in that sterile room until a door opens wide enough for me to go through. But now, I don't even see a closed door, let alone an open one. With no communication from potential employers, it seems like I am in a room with no escape.

In the restaurant biz, a waiter must rely on those at the table for instructions. It is only then that she knows what to fetch and bring to the customers. But until that happens, her only choice is to be ready to serve.

Lord, help me wait well and be ready to serve when the time comes.

Today's Truth: Wait for the Lord; *be strong, and let your heart take courage; wait for the* Lord! *Psalm 27:14*

December 15

Just Another Day

Vacation days punctuated by a Covid quarantine is making for an interesting time around here. Not that I mind, however.

Every closet and dresser drawer has been purged, organized and re-folded, giving me glorious moments of joy when I gaze upon the tidiness. The house is now decorated and glowing in the spirit of Christmas sparkle. The kitchen bears witness to batches of decadent biscotti. And on the unseasonably warm days, the planting beds outside have been readied for winter. But with each passing morning, it is getting harder to plan out a productive day.

This morning was a case in point. Having gone to bed without a plan, I lingered between our cozy flannel sheets until reaching an undeniable level of awakeness. A hot cup of tea and quick check of any email and messages came next. A virtual coaches' "huddle" took up another hour. After tidying the kitchen and running the vacuum for the second time today, the decision was made to go to a local park and run trails. There was nothing I absolutely had to do on this bright but chilly day.

I ran the technical, winding single track over the river and through the woods. The trails were mine alone to enjoy. My motion was smooth and efficient, my heart steady and uncomplaining. Over the course of eight and a half miles, no hill proved too steep. It was a no-hike day.

Was it just another day in my mostly house-bound life? Am I getting used to the freedom of being relaxed and under-planned? Was I aware and thankful that God allowed me a run that cleansed my spirit as well as my lungs? Did my hot soak in our clawfoot bathtub, book in hand, sooth my soul and my muscles in the aftermath? And with the dishwasher providing background noise at this very moment, did I enjoy preparing a tasty dinner for my family? You bet!

I am, by nature, a hard-driven worker. It is hard for me to swallow the proverbial "chill pill." And yet, I am learning to cherish these "go with the flow" days, for each day God gives me is an opportunity to rejoice and be glad.

Today's Truth: This is the day that the Lord *has made; let us rejoice and be glad in it. Psalm 118:24*

DECEMBER 16

NO SNOW. . . AND OTHER DISAPPOINTMENTS

At one point, the weather forecast was fantastic. Snow! Parts north of here, Maryland and Pennsylvania, were bracing for anywhere between twelve and twenty inches of snow. Even if the weather warmed after that, it almost assured them of a white Christmas. The weather maps showed some hope for us in Central Virginia as well. Our location was predicted to get one to three inches of snow before turning to sleet and freezing rain. The way I figure it, some snow is better than no snow.

I was up at 3 and again at 5 a.m. this morning. When I checked both times to see if anything was happening, I was not overly surprised that nothing fell from the sky. Afterall, the forecaster said it would all begin somewhere around 6 a.m. All the area schools closed last night in anticipation. I crawled back in bed, still hopeful that a winter wonderland would reveal itself come daybreak.

Ugh. Not a flake. Just a very wet, cold-to-the-bone rain. In my mind, there is no reason for it to be cold if the white fluffy stuff fails to pile up. But I guess God felt no compulsion to consult with me on this weather situation. He chose nasty rain instead of super snow. It is disappointing.

Likely, this disappointment will not be my ruin. But other disappointments can be harder to accept. There are the disappointments of less than stellar performances, whether it be my own, my family's, or my team. Or maybe someone disappointed me by their behavior or attitude. I know I will feel hugely disappointed if all the job applications I submitted come back rejected.

Is feeling disappointment wrong? Is it an emotion that has no place in our lives? If God is truly sovereign and controls all things, is being disappointment paramount to rejecting God's good pleasure and purpose?

I do not think so. In the hours leading up to the crucifixion, Jesus spent time in the garden, had to endure watching his disciples choose to sleep rather than pray, and then bear Judas' betrayal. Jesus had to feel disappointment regardless of knowing what was going to happen and understanding why.

And Peter? Jesus tells him he would end up denying Christ three times. Peter protests, and yet does exactly that. His display of disappointment? He weeps bitterly.

Disappointment is an emotion that serves to point us back to God.

Today's Truth: And Peter remembered the saying of Jesus, "Before the rooster crows, you will deny me three times." And he went out and wept bitterly. Matthew 25:75

December 17

One cent

There it was. A tiny copper-colored coin amongst the dirt and cinders. It was just a penny. Nevertheless, I felt compelled to pick it up and carry it home. I always pick up the one-cent pieces when I see them tossed aside. At least, I do ever since I was taught an object lesson about a penny years ago.

I was traveling with a bunch of my high school athletes in Costa Rica. It was my privilege to lead this group of young women on a sports-oriented trip in conjunction with a local short-term missions organization. We served in schools, played with the kids, took part in a camp, and served in a local church. It was fun staying in the home of a missionary family, enjoying meals and bible study in close fellowship. The time spent together made life-long memories.

When it was finally time to return home, we grouped together at the airport. LaMar, our host, went around our circle and handed each of us a penny. "What do have in your hand?" he asked. "Look at the side that describes the value. What does it say?" None of us had thought about that as we squinted to read the fine print.

"One cent," someone yelled out. With that, LaMar made another trip around the circle and collected everyone's coin. "Indian giver," I moaned.

With our seventeen pennies now held in his cupped hands, he gave them a little shake. They jingled together in a soft clatter. "I gave each of you a penny; one lonely cent. But what do you get if we put all the one cents together?" The girls were puzzled, calling out funny answers to his question. We laughed and waited for LaMar to let us in on the secret. "Look, girls. Each one of you has been given a mission. You each are one who is sent. But when all those who are sent get together," he paused to again rattle the coins together, "you get change." The message was clear.

"Ah, we get it! While we each have a job to do, we are better together. God can use each of us little pennies, us 'one sents,' to bring change to the world." With that, our pennies were returned to us for safe keeping.

Every time I see a penny, I have no choice but to pick it up. I remind myself that I am "one sent" on mission. Lord, help me be a part of change.

Today's Truth: There was a man sent from God, whose name was John. John 1:6

DECEMBER 18

TRAVELING MERCY

Gary just pulled back into the driveway in his big 'ol truck, trailer obediently following behind. He was returning from a quick trip to South Carolina to pick up three vintage motorcycles and a truck bed full of parts. He has become quite the wheeler-dealer since he officially retired earlier this year. It was a relief to have him home in one piece.

I take driving for granted. Most of the time, that is. I walk out to the car, buckle up, put the key in the ignition and off I go. I normally do not think much about it. That is a far cry from childhood memories of my mother's approach to driving.

There was never a time, not even once—and I do not exaggerate—when Mother got behind the wheel without asking God for protection. The prayer was not complicated. It went something like this: "Dear God, please give us a safe trip. Amen." She did not move the car an inch until that prayer, or the prayer of one of us kids, was voiced heavenward. After prayer, it was go-time.

Mother never took even the most benign daily functions for granted. She understood that interesting intersection between the command to pray about everything and God's sovereign control over those same things. Praying for safety in the car became second nature. For that matter, praying before meals was second nature. Praying over her daily activities was second nature. Praying for us to have a good day at school was second nature. Praying before she led the church choir practice was second nature. Praying before bedtime was second nature. Get the idea?

I was a little uneasy when Gary left on the long trip yesterday. I prayed for his safety. Maybe it was because I assumed the traffic might be heavy, the trailer adding another layer of potential problems. But why don't I pray when he heads to the auto parts store? Why do I not pray when I leave to pick up groceries? Why do I not ask for protection when I have an extra-special occupant (granddaughter, Addyson) as a passenger?

Lord, help my simple prayers become second nature.

Today's Truth: Rejoice always, pray without ceasing, give thanks in all circumstances; for this is the will of God in Christ Jesus for you. 1 Thessalonians 5: 16-18

DECEMBER 19

CRAFTY

My head is screaming at me as I sit down to write. The jack-hammering comes in the aftermath of two and a half hours of crafting with sweet Addyson. I hope recovery comes soon.

Time with Addy is precious. We adventured along wooded trails earlier in the day, bundled up to ward off the freezing air. Once we knocked off the caked-on mud from the soles of our shoes, off we went to the grocery store, but not before a stop at our favorite dollar store. Addy, being a big girl now that she turned six, pushed the cart straightway to the isle with the craft materials. With a well-trained eye, she quickly and without hesitation picked elastic and colored beads to make a necklace and bracelet for her mom. A tiny wooden birdhouse was selected for her step-dad, a heart-shaped box just screaming for paint for Pam (her step-mom), and alphabet beads to make a bracelet for her dad, planning to spell out both their names along the aqua-colored elastic.

It was hard for me not to interfere in the crafting process. Nevertheless, I did nothing but gather the paints and brushes and paper towels. She insisted on shaking each paint bottle. She selected the colors and wielded the brush across the surfaces. The elastic cords soon filled with lovely patterns of beads, handing it off to me only to knot the ends together. Addyson insisted on choosing the wrapping paper, cutting it, and tucking the gifts inside the decorative paper with copious amounts of tape. I know the recipients will be delighted that this little girl took such care and pride in following through, declaring more than once, "I don't need help. I got this."

I love the way God equips certain people to create and paint and make. I suspect Addy is one of those people—at least on some rudimentary level—and am delighted with the joy she displays in the process. I find it interesting that even in ancient writings, the work on the Jewish temple was done by incredible craftsman. In fact, we find that the Lord intentionally equipped certain guys with both skill and intelligence to perform the intricate work. It is obvious that God sees value in the beautiful.

Today's Truth: "Bezalel and Oholiab and every craftsman in whom the Lord *has put skill and intelligence to know how to do any work in the construction of the sanctuary shall work in accordance with all that the* Lord *has commanded." Exodus 36:1*

DECEMBER 20

A BRIGHT CONTRAST

PopPop, aka Gary, dutifully ascended the stairs at Addyson's request. "PopPop, can you come up here and turn off the light in my room? We are going to have a light show and I need it to be dark." After what seemed like a longer-than-necessary unit of time, Gary came back down with a fluorescent green index card. On it was written an invitation penned by our sweet grandkid, inviting me to the light party. "And we're gonna dance, too!" she exclaimed in person. Oh boy.

I followed her up the steep farmhouse steps to her darkened bedroom. Gary, Seth, and Pam came in as well. There were three blown-up balloons with tiny lights placed inside. The glow of her Christmas tree lights added to the ambience. "Daddy, will you please put on music so we can dance?" With the very first note she began to traverse the room with cartwheels and rounds offs, a bit of juvenile break dancing thrown in for good measure. It was quite entertaining, especially when she asked her Daddy to join in the fun. My heart smiled.

After the display of lights, I returned to the living room but was soon joined by Addy. "Addy, I loved the light show and your dancing. Thank you so much for such a special treat. The light in the balloons was such a contrast to the darkness. The dark room made the lights seem bright!"

"What's contrast, Grandma?"

"Well, contrast is when there is a big difference between two things. If it would be daytime, those little lights in the balloons would be hard to see. But at nighttime, those same lights are visible because there is such a big difference between light and dark." Addyson seemed content with the explanation, bounding back up the stairs to move on to the next activity.

What a wonderful time of year to be reminded of the brilliant contrast the Savior brought to a world in darkness. Jesus was the light that dispelled darkness. And we, as His followers, are privileged to continue providing a contrasting light in a dark and lost world.

Today's Truth: The people who walked in darkness have seen a great light; those who dwelt in a land of deep darkness, on them has light shone. Isaiah 9:2

December 21

A tough day

Talk about a roller coaster of emotion. Today that roller coaster did funny things to my stomach, slammed me sideways in my seat, and whip-lashed me into a day-long headache.

It did not help that last night was one of those times when sleep failed to arrive until somewhere around 4:30 a.m. Waking up before eight does not come close to a legit night's rest. My head was already throbbing and my tum-tum was tied up in knots. Though I was going to play taxi to get Addy to a friend's house for a play day, I knew the biggest challenge of the day was to clear out my campus office occupied for several years. The accumulation of supplies for team building exercises and games, folders filled with every interaction I had with the athletic teams, bible study materials, and a bookcase full of heavy volumes taunted me. I did not fancy the physical work it was going to take to clear out the office, but the emotional turmoil was going to be worse.

I am not being asked to leave my post. No bridges went up in smoke in the process. I resigned on my own volition once it was clear that the university was moving in a different direction. The potential jobs presented to me will not wait, leaving me little choice but to cut the cord at year's end. Armed with boxes and bags, the process of deconstructing my office began. Multiple trips to the car were made until the car was packed to the max. I drove that load home, unpacked, and headed back to town to complete the task.

Tears welled up when I reflected on the great times I had with coaches and athletes alike. But I could not help but wonder why I had not gotten as much as a "Thank you" or "We'll miss you" from the athletic administrators. Was my service so undervalued that any discussion about a transition to become part of the university family was non-existent? I felt like a failure.

Have I missed the mark? Have I ventured off course? Are my days of influence over? Does God have another plan, or did I mess up by walking away?

I am conflicted. The door behind has closed but the path ahead is tangled. How long must I wait for joy in service to be restored?

Today's Truth: For his anger is but for a moment, and his favor is for a lifetime. Weeping may tarry for the night, but joy comes with the morning. Psalm 30:5

DECEMBER 22

A MESSY ROUTE

I was a dog today. Or at least, I played the role of a dog.

Gary and his hunting buddies planned a late season hunt in quest of a shooter buck. The rut is over and the big boy bucks become predominantly nocturnal. But if they get disturbed or spooked, they can be coaxed to get up and run around. For the hunters, having a "dog," human or otherwise, thrash around in the woods can be useful.

Since no one has a trained dog, I was recruited. Gary spent a lot of time printing off a map, writing directions, and giving me verbal instruction. In addition to this walk in the woods, I was to leave scented dryer sheets in particular areas, and smear baby fresh stick deodorant on trees. The hypothesis was that the non-natural smells would be enough to make the nervous deer get up on their feet, flee the scent, and run right in front of the waiting hunters.

It sounded like a great plan. I am certainly comfortable in the forest. But there was one little problem. Well, maybe more than one. First, Gary has hunted this property for twenty years. He knows the landmarks. But when offering directions such as "At the end of a field, turn left up a hill into the woods," something gets lost in the translation. Do I go to the top of the ridge and follow that? What about these mountain bike trails? I eventually see the houses to the right, like he said, but the woods are nearly impenetrable with blow downs and thick briars. I get nowhere fast, drawing blood in the process.

I texted him my confusion about where I was supposed to go. I was not happy. Gary tried to calm me down. Over creeks, up steep hills, 300 yards turned into what seemed like half a mile, one deep ravine turned into two, and the end was nowhere in sight. My phone died. Asking for clarification was no longer an option. With dusk impending I face-planted hard. I nearly cried. But crying would serve no purpose. I took note of road noises and formulated a plan I hoped would work. It did. I finally got back to the car.

What can I learn from this "not fun" experience? Is there a life lesson hidden among the briars? If anything, my take-away is this: life can be messy. But even though there appears to be no defined path, there is a way. The journey may draw blood but is seldom life-threatening. Just keep walking.

Today's Truth: And I will lead the blind in a way that they do not know, in paths that they have not known I will guide them. I will turn the darkness before them into light, the rough places into level ground. These are the things I do, and I do not forsake them. Isaiah 42:16

December 23

Solitude

On this day before Christmas Eve, the house smells of fresh baked banana bread, chocolate pies, peanut butter cookies, and a boatload of Chex Mix. The baking journey began earlier this morning, interrupted only by an emergency run to the store for more milk and flour. I feel content and happy, preparing for time spent with our children and their mates.

While I was working in the kitchen, I propped open my laptop to watch the last installment of a Netflix series entitled, *Win the Wilderness*. This show chronicles six English couples who compete for a magnificent property in the Alaskan wilderness.

The current owners made their way into the wild 30 years ago, carving out life in the forest. Their property is over 100 miles from the nearest road. There are no power lines. The water supply comes from collected rainwater and a harnessed spring. Together they constructed a log home, an almost inconceivable task without heavy equipment. The threat from bears and moose is very real. The only way in or out is either a trek on foot or an airplane ride. They are completely isolated in the winter months. Now in their 70's, the couple want to pass on the legacy of living in the wilderness. They end up giving their property to the younger couple of their choosing. The last scene shows the older couple closing the front door for the last time, the new owners watching from the living room.

It is hard to imagine being given such a property. The Ose's, the long-time owners, did their best to assess if the couples had what it takes to live in solitude. Filmed in the summer of 2019, the task of maintaining the property was significant. But imagine the reality of long winter months, no way in or out, and understanding that your job is reduced to simple survival. The only human contact would be relegated to your mate.

I love being alone. I enjoy solitude. But I wonder if I could ever be sequestered away for say, one year, let alone 30. There is certainly a place for solitude; Jesus went off by himself on occasion. But in the long-term, I think we were made for community. I doubt Gary and I will ever be contestants for the opportunity to become hermits.

Today's Truth: And let us consider how to stir up one another to love and good works, not neglecting to meet together, as is the habit of some, but encouraging one another, and all the more as you see the Day drawing near. Hebrews 10:24, 25

December 24

Christmas Eve

Can it be? Is it really Christmas Eve? Seth and Pam went to the store today and brought home a wonderful Christmas bouquet of flowers that now have a prominent place on the coffee table. The mantle lights are on and both the large and small Christmas trees are shining brightly. The manger scene, where Addyson arranged for one of the shepherds to chat with a wiseman, is perfectly perched on the mantle. Presents are arranged by the tree and massive amounts of food have been prepared for the festivities, as understated as they may be. So yes, I guess Christmas is upon us.

Our sons and their better halves will be with us tonight and again tomorrow. Because Addyson is with her mother for the holiday, it is sure to be much quieter than if she were here. With both Gary's and my parents gone from this earth, it seems strange to be the oldest generation. There is no need for us to travel to faraway places. And while we normally enjoy celebrating with Gary's sister's family, that is on hold until after the holidays.

I think of Christmases past. The mayhem with my cousins when we visited them in Pittsburgh. The Christmas bread my grandmother made. The reading of the Luke 2 passage by my father before the first gift was opened on Christmas morning. Our organized approach to gift opening based on chronologic age. Family meals with a few extra guests seated with us at the table. Such great memories.

But we dare not forget that the baby whose birth we celebrate was born with purpose. Jesus, as he was called eight days after his birth, came by the express will of the Father. He was the only way to reconcile us sinners to a righteous and holy God. Christ was born to die. As the old hymn proclaims,

Good Christian men, rejoice
With heart, and soul, and voice;
Now ye need not fear the grave:
Peace! Peace!
Jesus Christ was born to save!
Calls you one, and calls you all,
To gain His everlasting hall:
Christ was born to save! Christ was born to save!

Today's Truth: For unto you is born this day in the city of David a Savior, who is Christ the Lord. Luke 2:11

December 25

A day of thanks

It is quiet. Seth and Pam are upstairs wrapping gifts. Gary is in the other room planning his next E-Bay campaign, and I am sitting alone in front of the wood stove. Our meal of non-traditional lasagna is in the oven as we await the arrival of Caleb and McKinley. The wood has been stock-piled to keep the deep chill out of the house, and the cinnamon rolls, fresh from the oven are long gone. The stillness makes it a great time to reflect on life, love, and the goodness of our Lord.

It comes as a surprise to no one that 2020 was a tough year. Covid hit hard, shutting down normalcy. Initially, we thought it would be over within a few months. Unfortunately, we are almost a year into the pandemic with threats of increasing fatalities in the coming weeks. Life slowed down, almost halted completely at times. People lost jobs and livelihoods. Some lost all hope. Suicide rates and child abuse skyrocketed. Domestic violence escalated. Smiles disappeared behind the masks.

It was an ugly year politically, no matter what side of the fence you live on. Violence. Riots. Destruction. Injustice in the name of justice. Lines were drawn. Shame and blame rampant. Hatred and social posturing could not be escaped. It all felt dark and sinister. So, what is there to be thankful for?

Jesus. Grace. Mercy. Forgiveness. Long-suffering. Hope beyond the grave. Sovereignty. All of which should renew our desire *to act justly, and love mercy, and to walk humbly with your God* (Micah 6:8).

It is mind-boggling to think that somewhere in eternity past, God initiated a redemptive plan for people who would sin against his holiness. Mankind's disobedience required a solution to restore fellowship. A substitutionary sacrifice was necessary. The Father sent his perfect son, born miraculously of a virgin, to cover the sins of the world—past, present, and future. The Lamb of God walked this earth over 2000 years ago, wholly human, and wholly God. He was sinless, blameless, and yet despised and rejected. He went to the cross, bearing the unimaginable pain of a Father who turned his face away for the sake of redeeming those who believed. But death had no dominion. Though Jesus went into the grave, he did not remain. He lives even now, interceding for us before the Father. He is our light and our hope. He is the only way.

So yes, even in a year like 2020, there is much to be thankful for.

Today's Truth: Again Jesus spoke to them, saying, "I am the light of the world. Whoever follows me will not walk in darkness, but will have the light of life." John 8:12

December 26

Don't you just hate it when you get two different answers to the same question?

Back in the days of high school calculus, my friends and I used our lunch periods to compare answers for the assigned homework. With calculus immediately following lunch, it gave us a chance to see if we were on the right track. When everyone got the same answers, it was a great feeling. We couldn't all be wrong, right? But when our answers turned up non-identical, that is when we knew there was a problem. At least one person was wrong, and maybe more. The disparity drove us to frantic recalculations of the problem, hoping to produce the one and only correct solution.

Sometime ago I bought a FitBit Versa watch from a friend. I was mostly interested in tracking heart rate, mileage, and pace. I heard good things about the brand and had high hopes for its accuracy. But the numbers it gave often seemed a little off. Heart rate was all over the place, especially when I was running. And those numbers did not always match with what I counted when I manually felt my pulse. Then there was the issue of mileage. After a couple runs, I suspected the watch might be overestimating distance covered. I sort of liked that because my calculated pace turned out better that way. Still, I had a sneaking suspicion that my watch lied to me.

Last week my Christmas present from Gary arrived in the mail. It is a Coros Pace 2 GPS watch. With brilliant battery life and many features of $600 watches in this $200 package, I was excited to strap it on and take it for a test drive. All the independent online reviews of the watch touted excellent accuracy. The problem is, if the watch is telling me the truth, I am running slower paces over shorter distances. Given that my running feels so much better than before, it is discouraging to find out I am not doing as well as I thought.

We must fight the urge to trust in a false truth. (Yes, I know. That is an oxymoron.) We may conclude that our thoughts and actions are right, but if we fail to measure up against the "real" truth, we are lulled into a false security. We must be willing to have discernment and be intentional in following only that which is honest and true.

Today's Truth: Finally, brothers and sisters, whatever is true, whatever is noble, whatever is right, whatever is pure, whatever is lovely, whatever is admirable—if anything is excellent or praiseworthy—think about such things. Philippians 4:8

DECEMBER 27

A MAKE-OVER

I ran out of steam today. I am not sure why. For once, I felt I slept okay, even though my fancy sleep-detecting watch says otherwise. I sat like a lump of coal left over from Christmas stockings in the passenger's seat on the way to church and slept all the way home. Lunch was nothing more than left-over warm-ups eaten from the comfort of the couch. That was convenient since it facilitated horizontal blanket snuggling that resulted in two hours of deep, glorious sleep.

There is something I must admit. I feel lost and a little bit down. Maybe that is why I readily escaped into the land of nod. The reality is that by week's end, I will no longer be employed. Sure, I have a handful of applications submitted and an interview next week, but nothing is set in stone. I feel sad that relationships cultivated with coaches and athletes cannot continue as is. The medical job that looked so promising has vanished, and I do not have the nurse credentials for another. I feel inadequate and unproductive. What will become of me?

I need an overhaul, just like the chairs I bought yesterday. Those five barstools need lots of love and attention. The legs are a rusted mess, the seat coverings faded, and the dried-out wooden slats on the backs of each chair are a tired, ugly brown. Taking a grinding wheel to those legs is the only hope for restoring them.

With drill in hand after my nap, I deconstructed each one. As a result, there is now a pile of seat backs, metal supports, rusted legs, metallic footrests, and the round seats. Though I have not firmly established the plan for those mid-century chairs, it was necessary to break them down into smaller, workable units before I could hope to turn them back into usable furniture.

I believe God has a big job in front of him. I feel like one of those chairs that needs deconstructing before becoming useable again. The process is likely to hurt, stripping away undesirable ugliness. And it might take a while. Change seldom comes overnight. So, for now, I pray I will submit myself to the creativity of the ultimate DIYer. I am anxious to see what the final product might look like.

Today's Truth: Create in me a clean heart, O God, and renew a right spirit within me. Psalm 51:10

DECEMBER 28

NO PAIN. NO GAIN.

Remember how I wrote about the data discrepancy between my two watches? Because of this revelation, my mindset needs to change. Thinking I run under eight-minute miles on roads and under ten minutes on trails is now wishful thinking. This truth, if I am serious about making true fitness gains, will force me to venture into the deepest pain cave. Ugh. The thought is not appealing.

Nevertheless, there was no better day than today to begin my pursuit of increased fitness. After my watch captured my heart rate and acquired the GPS signal, it was time to hit the start button. Off I went. But the thing I dislike about starting from my front door is that the first third of a mile is all uphill. It always feels hard. Hence, nailing down a great first mile split is difficult.

I did my best to ease into a pace that was neither too hard nor too easy. I listened in anticipation for the watch beep marking each passing mile. By the time I hit the turn-around point on this out and back run, I was working harder than normal. My heart rate was high, and my breathing was something akin to a frenzied two-year old on a rampage. I knew it would take effort to maintain my pace until arriving back at home.

When I finally hit the stop button, my tum-tum was feeling queasy. (I suspect the fajita I enjoyed for lunch was a contributing factor.) Regardless, I anxiously synched the watch with my phone. There it was. The truth. My average pace/mile was 9:06 with the best mile at 9:03. Forgetting my best running days when seven-minute miles felt easy, I now have an honest baseline. A nine-minute plus mile makes me work hard. But it also motivates me to endure the discomfort so that I can run faster longer.

Improvement never occurs without concerted effort. The effort takes energy, intentionally subjecting oneself to some level of pain. Though it hurts and is not pleasant in the moment, it is necessary if progress is to be made.

The same principle applies to spiritual growth. God never, ever promised a bed full of roses. He did promise hardship, ridicule, suffering, persecution, and even death. But the result? Endurance, hope, and character. That makes it all worthwhile.

Today's Truth: Through him we have also obtained access by faith into this grace in which we stand, and we rejoice in hope of the glory of God. Not only that, but we rejoice in our sufferings, knowing that suffering produces endurance, and endurance produces character, and character produces hope, Romans 5:2–4

December 29

A HIDING PLACE

On the couch next to me is a jumbled puffy black blanket. If you did not know better, the assumption would be that it is left-over from another one of my "too restless to fall asleep in bed" nights. But alas, there is a deep, muffled snore coming from under the blanket. What—or who—could it be?

When Pam married Seth, we not only got a daughter-in-law, but we also added a dog to the household. We have never, ever had a pup. It has been cats all the way. But as far as dogs go, this little beagle is a nice dog. After never being off a leash living on a busy road, she has adapted very well to farm life. She explores the forest, sniffs out scraps of food we chuck into the woods, and ducks under the fence to have conversations with the cows in the field next door. This new lifestyle is helping the pooch shed the extra pounds gained from too many table drops.

Rasta Dog is cute, following you with those big brown eyes as you pass by. She sits at the door, wagging her tail when she hears a car pull up. She even tolerates wearing doggie sweaters when the temperatures plummet. And that dog can sleep!

So, getting back to the blanket beside me. The dog burrows like a groundhog. She gets her head under the blanket and tosses it into the air, quickly ducking underneath as it descends. She will stay there for hours, her snoring the only clue that something living is under cover. She has narrowly missed being sat upon when she naps silently. Rasta is obviously content and secure whenever she is tucked away in her hiding spot.

There is great wisdom in knowing where and when to hide. Ask any kid who loves to play hide-and-seek. But us grown-ups? We need to have that safe place, a shelter, to seek solace and refuge. We need to be confident that when we hide, we are safe from the outside. Does it mean that scary stuff is not raging beyond our hiding spot? Obviously not. But sheltering away helps us re-focus and gain perspective.

With all the uncertainty in my personal life, I am very thankful to have a place to hide.

Today's Truth: You are a hiding place for me; you preserve me from trouble; you surround me with shouts of deliverance. Selah Psalms 32:14

DECEMBER 30

REJECTION

"You are not being considered for this position, but we encourage you to apply for other positions that interest you."

It was not a good morning to have this message slap me upside the head. Since 4:30 a.m., I had been awake contemplating my job possibilities, which seemed to be growing slimmer by the day. Promising positions at the hospital have vanished into thin air. For some, I do not have the nursing credentials they desire. But even the job that prompted the latest message required only a college degree and educational experience, which I have.

Thoughts swirl. Am I not good enough? Is someone adding up my job experience going back 40 years and figuring I am too ancient to be worthwhile? Has my usefulness come to an end? Does my resume portray a jack of all trades but master of none? Should I resort to a part-time job in the gardening department at Lowes, which could be fun?

On my second last writing installment of 2020, this may be coming across as a "Debbie-Downer" day. But here's the thing. While I am desperately trying to talk myself out of it, there is no one who is immune to discouragement. Discouragement is part of the human experience. But how, pray tell, do we get past the emotion, moving on to productive attitude and action?

I must remind myself of the truth of who I am regardless of where my paycheck comes from. I am a child of God. I am a personal friend of Jesus Christ. I am justified (made right) in God's sight. I am bought with a price. I am free and forgiven. I am complete in Christ. I am no longer condemned. I am free from the power of sin. Everything works together for my good. I was chosen specifically by God in eternity past. I am on God's team. I am given a spirit of power, love, and self-discipline (NOT fear!). I am held securely by Christ, to keep me from sinning (Shielded from Satan). I am empowered by the Holy Spirit. I am God's temple, the residence of the Holy Spirit. I am God's masterpiece who was made to do good things. I can approach God boldly and without fear. I am equipped to do all things by Christ's strength.

Understanding who I am requires me to know who God is.

Today's Truth: For I am the Lord your God. Consecrate yourselves therefore, and be holy, for I am holy. Leviticus 11:44a

December 31

We made it!

The day did not seem much different from others when I woke up this morning. Coffee got things kickstarted as the Christmas tree was de-ornamented, folded up and packed away in the box. With some difficulty, it was hoisted up the pull-down stairs and stashed in the attic. The closet under the stairs that serves as home to the boxes of decorations was tidied up before storing everything away for another year. Regardless of how beautiful the tree and mantel, it was gratifying to appreciate an uncluttered space once again. I gave little thought to what day it was. It was simply the day after Addyson belatedly opened her presents. It was time.

It was nice to work on a few other projects before sauntering off for an easy run around the country block. It was then I realized that tomorrow was the first day of 2021. Wow. 2020 was a rough one that will go down in the record books. But it looks like we made it.

There have been extreme mountain top highs balanced with below sea level lows. The joy of athletic ministry verses job hunting. Miserable attempts at jogging verses the elation of being able to run up a mountain. The intense grief that came from my Mother's passing verses the joy of knowing she is singing her lungs out in heaven. The nights I felt empty and blank when I sat down to write verses those days when the Lord offered fresh insight into His truth. Answered prayers in the form of drastically changed lives verses spending time in the waiting room for other yet unanswered requests.

I am grateful that my family and I are healthy and able to walk into 2021 in a few scant hours. We must remember, however, those three-hundred thousand plus folks in the United States (and many more abroad) who died of Covid or its complications. Families grieve tonight for those losses, and others are buried under the stress of joblessness and lack of funds. We also reflect on the unrest, riots, and political fighting. Not even George Orwell could have predicted a year such as the one we are finishing.

Has God made himself scarce? Does He not care? Or can we be confident that all these things—the good and the bad—were ordained from eternity past. All serve to bring glory and honor to the Father. Praise be to God.

May God bless you in the coming year.

Today's Truth: Now to him who is able to do far more abundantly than all that we ask or think, according to the power at work within us, to him be glory in the church and in Christ Jesus throughout all generations, forever and ever. Amen. Ephesians 3:20

Postscript

Sometimes a good mystery remains unsolved. That can be frustrating. So, to avoid any guilt from keeping you in the dark, allow me to resolve the question: Did Rebekah ever find a job?

Yes. Providentially, I was offered the job as a career coach at Liberty University, serving the students in the College of Health Sciences. I began February 1, 2021. It is a privilege to coach these students in building career tools (such as resumes and CVs) and helping them discern how their God-ordained interests and talents can be used in service to others.

God proved himself faithful to create this avenue of service for me. I still have relationship with some of the athletes and coaches I previously served. However, I embrace the deep relationships that are developing with students, faculty, and staff in the realm of academics and careers. It delights me that I am still called to coach, despite the absence of the athletic arena.

Once a coach, always a coach. Praise God.

ABOUT THE AUTHOR

Rebekah Tritipoe is a wife, mother, and grandmother. She loves God and family. She writes from the heart, honest and transparent. But her perspective and observations did not come easily. They were born out of a lifetime of experiences.

Growing up in small-town USA, she enjoyed an active childhood. She was forced to be tough, holding her own as the only girl among three brothers. As soon as organized sport became an option as a 9th grader, it was non-stop action. Field hockey, gymnastics, softball, and track became the mainstays during high school. Adapting quickly, she had successful collegiate careers in field hockey, volleyball, and tennis. But it did not stop there.

After college it was USTA Tennis and USVBA volleyball, with her first foray into ultrarunning coming in her mid-30s. Much has been learned over the years on the fields, courts, and along mountain trails. Injuries, pain, and suffering abounded. But those things were critical in learning the lessons necessary to appreciate the victories as well as the defeats.

No doubt, athletics shaped the mind and heart of Rebekah. She used those transferable skills across the last four decades to find fulfillment as a teacher, coach, medical professional (cardiovascular perfusion), speaker, writer, athletic chaplain, and career coach. She continues her pursuit of excellence and quest for adventure.

The EveryDay is the sixth title penned by Rebekah. Please visit her website, **http://rebekahtrittipoe.com** to learn more about her writing and speaking.

Quest for Adventure, David Horton's Conquest of the Appalachian Trail and the Trans-America Footrace (1997)Under an Equatorial Sky (2006)
Pace Yourself: 366 Devotions from the Daily Grind (2010)
Best Season Yet: 12 Weeks to Train, Coaches' and Athletes' Editions (2013)
Creative Coaching Across 3 Dimensions, 57 Practical Strategies to Unlock Your Athlete's Potential (2019)

Final Thoughts

What did you think as you worked your way through *The EveryDay?* We truly appreciate it when someone leaves a kind review on Amazon.

Do not forget to visit **http://rebekahtrittipoe.com** and sign up for notifications of new blog posts.

Should you need a speaker for your event, please drop your request to Rebekah at **rtrittipoe@aol.com**. We would love to hear from you! It is always a privilege to engage with audiences, large, small, and inbetween.

Made in the USA
Monee, IL
07 July 2026

56553293R00221